WOMEN AND GENDERED VIOLENCE IN CANADA

To the generations of women who have championed women's right to live violence-free lives, and in honour of two women who inspire us: Gundi Barbour and Anne-Marie Zilliacus.

ILLUSTRATIONS

ACKNOWLEDGMENTS

We would like to express our gratitude for the amazing colleagues in the Department of Criminology at the University of Ottawa who, in many cases repeatedly, assisted with ideas, clarifications, and references. Special thanks go to Steven Bittle, Kathryn Campbell, "Martian" Dufresne, Maritza Felices-Luna, Jenn Kilty, Justin Piché, Dominique Robert, and Valerie Steeves. A particular note of gratitude to Holly Johnson, who not only provided advice and resources, but also generously produced the sexual assault attrition pyramid (Figure 5.1) found on page 119. We are also grateful for Brittany Mario's excellent and timely assistance.

Thanks as well to those who helped keep up our morale over the intense writing process: Emily Symons and Brent (Chico) Ward; Kate Fletcher and Paul Robertson.

We extend our gratitude to the anonymous reviewers of both the original proposal and the completed manuscript; we have endeavoured to do justice to the ideas, suggestions, and insights you generously shared.

Leanne Rancourt deserves special mention for her meticulous copyediting (and unending patience); it was a pleasure to work with such a gracious professional.

The staff at University of Toronto Press have been amazing. Particular thanks go to Anne Brackenbury for guiding us through the process from proposal to publishing; Julia Cadney for, among other things, chasing down permissions; and Anna Del Col for sharing her considerable marketing and design skills. A shout out to Megan Pickard; although she is no longer at University of Toronto Press, her enthusiasm and contribution to the project in its early stages is much appreciated.

EXPANDING THE LENS ON GENDERED VIOLENCE

On December 6, 1989, Marc Lépine entered the École Polytechnique at the Université de Montréal and massacred 14 women; it was, undeniably, an act of horrific gendered violence committed by one man. It was also an act informed by gender scripts and the visceral enactment of everyday misogyny—a punishment of women who did not "know their place." In this regard his selection of an engineering class as opposed to, for example, a teachers' college, where there would have been more women, is telling. In Lépine's words, "You're women, you're going to be engineers. You're all a bunch of feminists. I hate feminists" (Elgin and Hester 2003, 52). The Montréal Massacre helps us understand that gendered violence washes through society to the detriment of us all. Further, the impact of the violence does not end when the assault ceases; rather, it ripples through the lives of not only those who are victimized first hand but also the many others who are touched by it. In the aftermath of the Montréal Massacre, the lives of the victims' families and friends were forever changed; Sarto Blais—a male student in the classroom who could not live with the guilt—completed suicide eight months later, and his parents followed within the year (CBC 1998). And another generation of women confronted the reality of gendered violence.

The Montréal Massacre shattered not so much Canadians' collective innocence as our collective denial. The aftermath, however, speaks to resilience, resistance, and further repression as those with political capital endeavoured to undermine women's gains. On the one hand the tragedy that unfolded that wintery day in 1989 was the impetus for a societal awakening that gendered violence is not a women's issue but a much larger social justice imperative. It led to a National Day of Remembrance and Action on Violence Against Women, the federal Canadian Panel on Violence Against Women (Abraham and Tastsoglou 2016), and the 1995 *Firearms Act*. On the other hand, many of the gains, including the long gun registry, were subsequently dismantled, and recognition of the underlying misogyny continues to be persistently denied by those who attribute individual rather than societal responsibility—for them Lépine was not the ultimate manifestation of deeply entrenched misogyny but a "madman." Of course individual men must be held responsible, but when we fail to appreciate context we squander the possibility of making meaningful change.

This book endeavours to develop a more holistic understanding of gendered violence by elaborating on the connections between the violence women experience and the historical, social, discursive, and legal contexts in which it unfolds. To that end, an intersectional and interdisciplinary approach employing concepts from diverse theoretical traditions and drawing on a range of disciplines, including criminology, history, sociology, political science, legal studies, economics, critical race studies, and, of course, gender studies, is used. In order to provide a point of departure for subsequent chapters, this Introduction begins with a historical overview of feminist resistance to violence and inequality, which, as we will see, has been characterized by vigorous debates about the project(s) of feminism and what it means to be radical. From there, we move on to present the conceptual point of departure for this book; we conclude with an overview of the volume's four sections.

Feminism: A history of conflict, contestation, and resistance

Western history is littered with examples of gendered violence: from the burning of women outside of patriarchal control—wise women, midwives, healers— as "witches," to the gossip's or scold's bridle where "chattering" or otherwise troublesome women were physically punished by having their (wagging) tongues pinned in place (see Figure I.1), to the preachers who exhorted men from the pulpit to discipline their wives not out of malice but for the good of their souls. Indeed one could argue that gendered violence has not only been normalized, it is a cornerstone of our society. Of course things have gotten better. Today it would be unthinkable for legislators to laugh, as they did in 1982, when Member of Parliament Margaret Mitchell raised the issue of intimate partner violence in the House of Commons. We are also seeing an expansion of naming (or at least renaming): gaslighting, bullying, and everyday intrusions are new in the sense that they are widely recognized as issues that warrant our attention.

There is no denying that we are witnessing increased sensitivity to and public engagement with the violence women experience. Young women are standing up, speaking out, and institutions are taking note, introducing, for example, measures to address sexual harassment at universities. Similarly the

FIGURE I.1: Gossip's or scold's bridle

media have gone from implicit reinforcement of the idea that intimate partner violence is a rarity to be explained in relation to the psychological shortcomings of the victim to recognizing that this is a widespread problem worthy of serious consideration. In short—the existence of "men's rights" movements and persistent pushback notwithstanding—it would appear that gendered violence has successfully been transformed from a private trouble into a social problem (Spector and Kitsuse 1977). Today, gendered violence is the site of much public debate, innumerable local and nationwide initiatives, and social justice actions; it has a strong narrative presence in our institutions.

It has taken a while to get here, and credit is deservedly given to the generations of women activists who persistently and doggedly problematized the intertwined issues of women's inequality and violence. This history is, generally speaking, presented in relation to three waves of feminist thought. Women of the nineteenth and early twentieth century fought for the right to divorce on the basis of physical cruelty and, firmly believing that alcohol led to family violence, supported temperance. The explicit focus on violence lessened as women's lack of political and property rights took centre stage at the turn of the twentieth century, and suffragettes, the first wave of feminists, focused their energy on securing basic civil rights—most notably the right to vote and to own property. Many of these reformers, valorizing women's unique characteristics and virtues, espoused a narrative of moral superiority. Some mainstream suffragettes, Emily Murphy notable among them, used explicitly racist arguments and tropes to further their causes (see Figure 9.1 on page 211). Early second wave feminists located women's oppression within social institutions and practices that render woman object/other and man agent/normative. While this analysis continued, the focus of what was then called the women's liberation movement was overshadowed by a more intense engagement with the question of violence against women. By the 1970s the issue of rape, and relatedly sexuality, became narratively centred within mainstream feminism; Susan Brownmiller's 1975 classic tome *Against Our Will* and Catharine MacKinnon's 1987 *Feminism Unmodified* came to represent the orthodoxy of this movement. Throughout the 1990s the fragility of white middle class feminist claims of sisterhood was increasingly being exposed. Since the turn of the twenty-first century, a third wave of feminism has dramatically changed the activist, institutional, and discursive landscape. Partly in response to the canons of the second wave and informed by a range of social justice movements, this third wave rejects the essentialism of earlier feminists and broadens the focus by recognizing the need to integrate analysis of oppression on the basis of, for example, race, class, and sexuality.

Historical context is important; to that end, many of the chapters include a brief section that discusses socio-historic considerations. However, it is also important to question narratives that impose homogeneity and appear to be principally about identifying "revolutionary ancestresses or petty bourgeois leaders whose errors we can blame for our current oppression" (DuBois 1979, 137). The sweeping oft-told story of the women's movement in three waves presented above, while providing a useful temporal framing device used throughout this text, glosses over conflict, vibrant debate, and diversity; it writes the activism and analysis of countless working class, racialized, and socialist women out of history; and it denies us the ability to interrogate power relations by considering what version of feminism gained legitimacy. In short, it reproduces the historic invisibilization of "others."

If we are "to understand the history of which we are part, and the changes we may be able to bring to it" (DuBois 1979, 137), then we need to acknowledge that colonization and slavery conditioned women's social and political engagement "from the onset" (Forestell 2016, 145). We need to recognize, for example, the "critical gender consciousness" (ibid., 145) and fierce resistance of Indigenous women against the denial of mobility and property rights that started well before Confederation and continues today (Carter 1993), and the role of Black women leaders in Nova Scotia who, recognizing that restrictions on the education of Black students entrenched racial oppressions, fought for equal access (Moreau 1997). It is also vital to acknowledge that Canada's second wave included working class women who pushed their union brothers to address "women's issues," giving rise to the important voice of organized labour for gender equality we see throughout this book (Maroney 1987); and women of colour like Rosemary Brown, whose "commitment to civil rights, socialism and feminism" (St. Amand 2010, 34) informed her activism and long political career, which included campaigning (using the slogan "Brown Is Beautiful") for the leadership of the federal New Democratic Party in 1975; and Indigenous women, like the women of Tobique First Nation in New Brunswick who, in the mid-1970s, determined to address sexual discrimination in the *Indian Act*, took on first their band council and then the Canadian state (Silman et al. 1987). It necessitates that we meaningfully engage with the scholarship of women such as Angela Davis (1983), who documented the ceaseless resistance and activism of Black feminists in the first wave and critiqued the white middle class and essentialist bias of mainstream second wave feminists. And we recognize that since the late 1960s Canadian socialist feminists (e.g., Benston 1969; Morton 1971) have brought a robust critique of capitalism into conversation with gender inequity to trouble "the costs of privatized social reproduction" (Rosenberg 1987, 181). Finally, we need to acknowledge the feminists trained in criminology who put forth a critical analysis of the criminal justice system and questioned the law's potential to be a revolutionary instrument (e.g., Currie 1990; Smart 1984, 1989; Valverde 1985).

That this history and the critical knowledge produced has been sidelined is telling, though perhaps not surprising; over 30 years ago Heather Jon Maroney (1987) noted that "state-sponsored feminism, or radical feminist ideology, wedded to reformist tactics, have succeeded in presenting themselves as feminism *tout court*" (99). We refer to this white middle class feminism, which dominated the narrative from the 1970s to the millennium, as **mainstream second wave feminism**. These reformists—well intentioned and pragmatic, albeit unreflexive regarding their own privilege—explicitly proposed solutions that fit neatly into state discourses and established institutions; as such, their reforms worked seamlessly with, indeed offered justification and legitimation to, state initiatives and repressive regulatory apparatuses. For example, MacKinnon, along with her colleague Andrea Dworkin, famously established anti-pornography ordinances in a number of US jurisdictions (Halley 2006), causing indignation among sex-positive feminists who argued the "exclusive focus on danger … makes women's actual experiences with [sexual] pleasure invisible, overstates danger until it monopolizes the entire frame, [and] positions women solely as victims" (Vance 1992, xvii). Unsurprisingly, the solutions of reformist feminists that leave underlying ideology and relations of power untouched find their way into the talking points of (even conservative) parliamentarians; absorbed into regulatory state practices these "feminist justice projects have moved off the street and into the state" (Halley 2006, 20).

Today we see echoes of this mainstream second wave narrative in **governance feminism**—feminists who, positioning themselves as experts, work with state and powerful non-governmental organizations to develop and advocate for legal and institutional governance-based solutions (ibid.). Similarly **carceral feminists** (Bernstein 2010) call for more laws, greater use of imprisonment, longer sentences, and sometimes lessening the rights and protections of accused persons, thus championing criminalization policies that are "aligned with neo-liberal government[s] to incarcerate ever-increasing numbers of (primarily) poor, young Aboriginal and Black men" (Snider 2014, 268). These profoundly white and middle class solutions to deep-seated problems, as we see throughout this book, offer remedies that can have disastrous effects on "othered" women, including those who are working class, racialized, and im/migrant.

Recognizing the contribution of earlier generations of feminist scholars and activists does not, of course, negate the important critiques and analysis put forward by those of the third wave. In particular, the foundational concept of intersectionality, which recognizes the simultaneous effects of and mutually constitutive relationship between identity categories including race, class, sexual orientation, citizenship, ability, and gender, is central to this book (Crenshaw 1989; Hill Collins 2015). Intersectionality allows for nuanced analyses and sheds light on the complex interplay between social and structural factors that condition women's individual and collective experience of, and vulnerability to, violence. In this regard we consciously refer to *gendered* rather than *gender-based* violence to foreground intersectionality—while gender is the unifying thread throughout this book, the diverse instances and forms of violence examined are based on a multiplicity of factors intersecting with gender. Moreover, by implying that the violence is grounded in or a direct result of gender, the concept of gender-based violence excludes violence to which women are vulnerable that does not originate in gender but is a more indirect outcome of gender inequity (e.g., nurses' experience of violence from patients and their families).

While acknowledging constraints, it is also important to recognize and highlight women's agency. Starting with Michel Foucault's (1982) insight that power and **resistance** are mutually constitutive and that we can use resistance "as a chemical catalyst so as to bring to light power relations" (780), some of the many tactics and strategies employed to subvert, contest, or counter oppressive social or structural factors (Scott 1990) are highlighted. Accordingly, we can trouble the victim trope by acknowledging resilience and recognizing the ways that women both collectively and individually use the tools at their disposal (in turn conditioned by an individual's or group's socio-economic location(s) and access to resources) to challenge oppressive individuals, institutions, policies, practices, and discourses. As we see throughout this book, these tactics and strategies of resistance—which must always, to a greater or lesser extent, employ existing framings (e.g., gendered) and mechanisms (e.g., institutional)—give rise to the potential for backlash and/or unintended consequences. As such they risk, for example, exacerbating the issue, opening up new spaces of oppression, and (further) legitimating repression. This does not mean resistance is futile; it is, however, as the outcomes of some of the mainstream second wave initiatives clearly demonstrate, fraught.

Its necessarily incomplete, partial, and situated nature and inevitable messiness notwithstanding, resistance also informs the language throughout this book: We refer to gendered *violence* rather than gendered *victimization* as an acknowledgment that women can, and do, fight back. That said, while recognizing that women make sense of their experiences in ways that reflect their personal beliefs, politics, and the resources to which they have access—for example, some women may identify as a victim, others prefer survivor, some consider themselves thrivers, still others do not relate their identity to experiences of violence at all—the terms *victim* and *victimization* are employed to indicate and discuss the targeting of particular women by violent acts or policies.

Positionality: Who is the we narrating this book?

Following our critical engagement with feminism, it seems appropriate to position ourselves within feminist movements and the conversation on gendered violence. We are two feminist academics separated by a generation but united in a commitment to social change. We bring to this project our disciplinary training in criminology, gender studies, and legal studies as well as fine arts (Tuulia) and sociology (Chris). We also bring life experiences that have shaped our thinking about the subject areas we touch on in this book, including sexism and exploitative labour conditions in various jobs (e.g., bars, restaurants, academia); being catcalled, groped, or followed in public spaces; managing tension-filled intimate relationships; negotiating shifting class locations; and as privileged subjects (white, cis women) navigating the politics of our (not always middle class or heterosexual) gendered presentation of self. These experiences have informed our teaching and research activities and our involvement in activism.

Like women everywhere we have navigated and (individually) resisted gendered violence—in relationships, at work, and from the state. In our capacity as social justice activists we have also participated in collective resistance: writing letters, signing petitions, peaceful sit-ins, walks and vigils as well as more chaotic protests, and, of course, because we are Canadian, attending (and sometimes speaking at) innumerable outdoor rallies on bitterly cold winter days. Inasmuch as we continue to participate in these actions we recognize that, rather than revolutionary overhauls, they are at best momentary ruptures in (and discomfiting reminders of) relations of power (Foucault 1982), after which we return to the comfort and banality of our daily lives.

As such we are mindful of our multiple and intersecting privileges as we struggle to create space at the same time as we take up space (both as writers enjoying the privilege of access to a scholarly press and as settlers living and teaching on the territories of the Algonquin, the Haudenosaunee, the Huron-Wendat, and the Anishinabek). As will become evident throughout the book we are motivated by past, present, and emerging critical scholars—women like Elaine Craig, Dawn Currie, Liz Elliott, Karlene Faith, Sarah Hunt, Robyn Maynard, Trish Monture, Melissa Munn, Viviane Namaste, Fran Shaver, Loreen Snider, Dorothy Smith—brave Canadian women who mobilize(d) their privileged positions to speak truth to power by carefully crafting texts that shed light on hidden processes and practices, challenge(d) normative tropes and "common" knowledge, and ensure(d) counterhegemonic discourses are on the record. We are inspired not only by these activist-writers but also by the multitude of social justice activists working tirelessly in diverse movements (e.g., prison justice; Indigenous rights; Civil Rights and racial equality; trans, gay/lesbian, and queer rights; the labour movement; sex worker rights; anti-war activists; environmentalists; the list goes on) to expose injustices and inequities in the structures governing our daily lives. Evidently, we also build on the work of generations of scholars who theorized and researched gendered violence in its many incarnations; that we are critical of essentialism, and the governance and carceral feminist tendencies, in some of this literature does not diminish its contribution.

Women and gendered violence: Power, vulnerability, and resistance

Today we see the enduring dominance of governance feminism in the pitiful image to which we are so frequently exposed—on textbook covers, in stock news photographs, and in awareness campaigns. The vibrant counter-narratives and robust literature examined in this book disappear in the oft-repeated images of the (almost inevitably) white victimized woman: She is bruised, dejected, and either looking away/down or staring forward with terror-filled eyes; sometimes a hand covers her mouth; or perhaps she is raising her arm, as a show of protest or more likely in anticipation of an impending blow. She is a victim—an ascribed master status that erases all else (Hughes 1945). Almost invariably, *she is alone.* The accompanying text reinforces the personal scale at which this violence, or its solution, is imagined to occur: She is your sister/

mother/daughter; speak out, fight it, stop it! Even the grammar isolates the problem: A certain number of women will experience violence in their lifetime; a certain number are murdered every week. Like the woman in the image, the language is passive; she has been victimized. Certainly these images are effective at raising awareness about gendered violence, but what is conspicuously absent is the back story, the humanity, the context.

Imagery is powerful. As Susan Sontag (2003) argues, photographs of suffering victims "are themselves a species of rhetoric. They reiterate. They simplify. They agitate. They create the illusion of consensus" (6). Moreover, to read into such images only that which confirms one's opinion—a general abhorrence of violence—is to ignore and abdicate responsibility for engaging with questions of culture, nation, politics, history; it is to render violence generic (ibid.). By expanding beyond the frame of this pitiful image, or better, finally putting it aside, we can move away from a "bemused awareness ... that terrible things happen" (ibid., 13). In this way, we can make space for agency and resistance and venture toward a more complex understanding of the interplay of systems, institutions, and structures, which are not only sites of and create the conditions of possibility for gendered violence, but also shape social–structural responses. To this end we need to expand, by first dismantling, the continuum of violence.

The concept of a continuum of violence, as it has conventionally been used in feminist theory, was elaborated by Liz Kelly (1987). Using the dictionary definition of a continuum—a continuous series of events that seep into one another and share a basic underlying character—as her starting point, Kelly applied it to violence against women. For Kelly, a continuum of *sexual* violence means a continuum of heterosexual interactions between men and women. The concept of a continuum, then, allowed her to conclude that "[t]here is no clear distinction ... between consensual sex and rape, but a continuum of pressure, threat, coercion and force" (ibid., 58). This in turn positioned her to characterize all women as victims and imply that all men are offenders, which simultaneously renders women's positive sexual experiences invisible, negates differences among women, demonizes men, and validates punitive carceral solutions; it also blinds us to much of the violence women experience and the social structures that create the conditions for that violence.

To avoid reproducing such homogenization of the causes of gendered violence or women's experiences thereof, we must start by recognizing that violence inflicted on women is not only rooted in patriarchy but in a host of interlocking social, political, and economic systems that work through and with patriarchy, including colonialism, neoliberalism, capitalism, and national and global economies. This also relates to third wave feminists' assertion that women experience violence and discrimination in particular ways according to intersecting aspects of their identities, social location, and negotiation (or rejection) of gender norms. Thus, in addition to denying the possibility of women's sexual agency and pleasure, the mainstream second wave feminist conceptualization of sexual violence as a continuum overlooked the ways in which the violence women experience is not simply an interpersonal or sexual issue but an intersectional and structural one. In other words, rather than occurring exclusively between men and women, gendered violence can also be perpetrated by agents of the state (e.g., the neglect and abuse experienced by Indigenous women at the hands of police), by women (e.g., domestic workers at the hands of their employers), by co-workers and customers in the workplace, and indirectly as the result of policies (e.g., austerity measures that culminate in ill health). In short, turning away from a continuum that homogenizes sexual relationships and overlooks institutional and structural ones positions us to make distinctions.

To do this we draw on the work of Bandana Purkayastha (2009), who adapted the continuum of violence to conflict studies in order to expand the notion of violence and to recognize not only the multiplicity of ongoing, institutionalized, and episodic violence occurring at numerous levels, but also the efforts by individuals, groups, and institutions to respond. To this end we recognize a continuum not only as a coherent collection, but one in which the degrees of variation between its constitutive elements are essential to unpack and understand. An intersectional perspective on the continuum of gendered violence, then, allows us to move beyond an understanding of sexual violence as perpetrated by men against women. It positions us to recognize the complex interplay of social–structural factors that condition women's vulnerability to violence, the nature of that violence, and women's resilience and resistance. This book contextualizes and interrogates underlying structures, discourses, and narratives—the myths and stereotypes constructing women and the normative expectations constraining them. These narratives exist in tension, portraying women as, for example, self-sacrificing mothers; moral and frigid; irresponsible sluts who "deserve it"; unrealistically beautiful, appropriately sexy, and well "put together"; hysterical, irrational, or intellectually inferior; untrustworthy, vengeful, devious, or liars. They also include stereotypes that are racialized, for example, constructing Indigenous women as lascivious or lazy, Black women as Jezebels or Mammies, Asian women as docile or devious, and Muslim women as oppressed or terror threats. This contextualization is necessary to move beyond merely documenting—continuing to succumb to the allure of that pitiful imagery. It necessitates we expand our understanding of what violence is beyond the normative framing (i.e., a physical altercation occurring between two people) to appreciate that violence is not always interpersonal but can be mundane, bureaucratic, institutional; violence can occur even when there is neither an identifiable perpetrator nor an intended victim. In short, we need to broaden our lens. Consequently, this book cannot address all the myriad factors conditioning women's experiences of violence; acknowledging diversity inevitably means that it is impossible to do justice to all the complex intersections women navigate.

Defining gendered violence

Consistent with this expansive framing, this book defines gendered violence as harm rooted in, emanating from, and/or based on an individual's gender expression or identity:

- It can take different forms, including (but not limited to) sexual, physical, psychological, economic, emotional, verbal, and environmental, and can encompass neglect, abuse, harassment, microaggressions, erasure, and exploitation.
- It can be categorized as interpersonal, symbolic, state, slow, or structural.
- It may simultaneously target or pivot on perceptions of other facets of identity, including (but not limited to) race, ethnicity, class, dis/ability, religion, sexual orientation, culture, or age.
- It is potentially exerted through a range of mechanisms, including (but not limited to) discourses, ideologies, social and economic structures, as well as formal (e.g., laws) and informal (e.g., social norms) regulation.
- It may occur in diverse locations and contexts, including institutions, workplaces, community or public places, online spaces, and private homes.

Scope and outline of the book

Although an intersectional perspective on the continuum of gendered violence takes into account global systems shaping women's lives and experiences (see, for example, Hill Collins 2015; Mohanty 2003) and recognizes the outsized cultural impact of Canada's southern neighbour, this book's focus is national. As such, the issues addressed are those that affect diverse groups of women in the geographic space we now call Canada, including colonial violence against Indigenous women, Islamophobia, racism, homophobia and transphobia, poverty, neoliberal capitalism, and violence by the state and its agents. While chapters focus on particular themes, each chapter considers the impacts and interplay of history (linking past and current framings), informal and formal regulation, and resistance. The chapters also feature textboxes, a few of which highlight key points or legal cases relevant to the discussion; most, however, showcase women's narration of their own experiences, their resistance, and how these are shaped by their social location. Each chapter ends with an exercise designed to encourage reflection, discussion, and critical analysis; these exercises are intended to be adapted to the context in which they are used and (where appropriate) pedagogic goals. The glossary, defining key concepts used in the text, can be found at the end of the book; to facilitate referencing, glossary terms are bolded the first time they are applied.

To give an idea of the scope and forms of violence and concurrent challenges that women face in Canada, some statistics are presented. We do this, however, mindful of the many "blind spots" of numerical measures and the hidden nature of women's victimization. For example, as we see in Chapter 5, numbers of sexual assaults can change drastically depending on whom they are reported to and if they are recorded by gatekeepers. We are also reticent to describe change numerically given that statistics cannot capture all the factors contributing to social shifts (Huff 1954). Of course some statistics, such as women's annual earnings, are more reliable—after all they are collected through government mechanisms to which Canadians are required to provide information (e.g., the National Household Survey census). But even here, the information is shaped by what people say, which is not necessarily a fulsome reflection of what they do (ibid.). Given these limitations, an analysis of interlocking oppressions paints a more nuanced and fulsome picture; this picture has four parts.

Part A: Contextualizing gendered violence in Canada

Situating the book in feminist thought and continuing the discussion of this chapter, Part A examines key factors that are violence in their own right at the same time that they create the context in which gendered violence occurs, and condition the personal, social, and state response to that violence. To this end Chapter 1 (intersections and diversity), Chapter 2 (socio-economic locations), and Chapter 3 (representations) analyze historical and contemporary trends and policies and introduce foundational concepts that inform the analysis in the rest of the book. Importantly, this first part sets the discussion in a Canadian context, considering interlocking systems of oppression. In exploring the exclusionary foundations and practices of the labour market, politics, the media, medicine, and the law, Part A also uncovers the normative discourses that shape women's vulnerability to violence. It lays the groundwork to understand how gendered violence unfolds amidst unequal power relations, provides context by unpacking the mutually constitutive relationship between power and knowledge, examines myths about women (and how they should and should not act, and in turn what behaviours are sanctioned and what forms of violence are excusable), and sheds light on stereotypes of particular configurations of race, class, gender, and other identities.

Part B: Interpersonal violence

Part B complexifies normative framings of interpersonal violence as men's victimization of women. Chapter 6 invokes the socio-economic, political, and discursive contexts presented in Part A to explain diverse women's experiences of intimate partner violence, examining not only violence in heterosexual relationships but also **LGBTQ** experiences. This section also considers the divergent forms and environments in which interpersonal violence plays out: cyberbullying, everyday intrusions on the street (both in Chapter 4), and harassment and sexual assault on college and university campuses (Chapters 4 and 5, respectively) and in homes (Chapter 6). Throughout we see how gendered violence is normalized through the myths and sexual scripts laid out in the previous section, how women are responsibilized through the *slut* discourse, and how they are targeted and discredited through racial and class stereotypes pivoting on otherness. This also positions us to problematize regulatory responses and the way women are treated in the criminal justice system, as (less-than-ideal) victims, and (sometimes simultaneously) as offenders. While acknowledging the hard fought legal reforms won by mainstream second wave feminists (e.g., sexual assault laws and domestic violence charging practices), these chapters also question our cultural propensity to punish. Women's resistance is showcased through examples that are normative (e.g., calling for more state and institutional regulation), that reject state intervention (e.g., women refusing to cooperate with mandatory prosecution policies), that are creative and collective (e.g., the Slut Walk), and some that are reactive and visceral (e.g., when women literally take matters into their own hands).

Part C: Workplace violence

Given that women now make up 47 per cent of the Canadian labour force (Statistics Canada 2017h), paid work is a significant part of most Canadian women's lives. To this end, Part C extends the framing of gendered violence to consider women's experiences of intersectional violence at work, including interpersonal violence, exclusionary practices that facilitate violence and inequality, and state policies that result, sometimes decades later, in violence. This allows us to appreciate that, while workplace violence is not specifically a women's issue, vulnerability to violence is gendered, classed, and raced; conditioned by an individual's social location, it can be understood in terms of relations of power. Women are more likely to experience workplace abuse, violence, and exploitation; not only are they disproportionately employed in low-paying and precarious jobs, women also migrate across the globe for work, sometimes residing with their employers (as do live-in domestic workers). Thus, gendered violence—occurring among co-workers as sexual harassment, microaggressions, or bullying (Chapter 7); when predators target vulnerable workers intentionally, when clients act aggressively, or when auster-ity measures create volatile environments (Chapter 8); or facilitated by a lack of labour protections/recognition (Chapter 9)—unfolds in workplace climates in which dominant discourses and myths about women converge with institu-tional structures and practices. Continuing to interrogate the accessibility and appropriateness of regulatory solutions, these chapters also consider some of the ways formal approaches reinforce dominant norms and at the same time exclude (and therefore fail to protect) the most vulnerable women.

Part D: Structural violence

Reflecting on the violence, for example, that Indigenous women experience at the hands of social welfare agents or that sex workers experience from police, alerts us that gendered violence is more widespread and insidious than conven-tional wisdom holds. The final section of the book focuses on three mutually reinforcing systems: capitalism, the state, and colonialism. While these systems are not generally considered violent—indeed, they are often not considered at all—they inevitably condition our lives and shape women's diverse vulner-abilities to and experiences of violence. Some of these forms of violence—for example, the symbolic violence implicit in the beauty imperative examined in Chapter 10—are subtle, delivered through cultural and corporate messag-ing and resulting in self, but also institutional, discipline. Others, such as the violence of police abuse, incarceration, and criminalization (which was under-appreciated in mainstream second wave and governance feminist framings), come into sharp focus with an intersectional lens (Chapter 11). We see too the need to further interrogate the relations of power beyond those between men and women and recognize the ways laws, policies, and practices that disadvan-tage less-empowered groups serve to advantage the dominant group. Perhaps nowhere is this more clearly evident than with colonialism, which continues to engender violence against Indigenous women directly through govern-mental regulation and indirectly through the reproduction of dehumanizing and misogynist discourses (Chapter 12).

Pulling together conceptual and substantive threads, the Conclusion offers a final reflection on the relationship between the forms, prevalence, and contexts of gendered violence in Canada. It then turns to examine the consequences of the systems explored throughout this book but highlighted in Part D (capi-talism, the state, and colonialism) on a global scale, examining how they are integral to discursive, interpersonal, institutional, and structural violence in other regions of the world that at the same time resemble and diverge from the experiences of women in Canada.

EXERCISE: IDEAL WORLD—PART 1

Envision a world where there is no gendered violence.

Write down what your ideal world would look like.

Get into groups of 4–6 individuals and share your vision; collectively identify 10 things that would need to change for your visions to become reality.

Share the list and reasoning with the larger group or the class.

Hand in or save your list and reflections.

Contextualizing Gendered Violence in Canada

Part A is the foundational section of the book that lays out the context shaping the experiences of women in Canada. This section examines deep cleavages in relation to, for example, class, race, and gender expression (Chapter 1); the impact of gender on social, economic, and political location (Chapter 2); and how women are constituted in and through medicine, law, business, the media, and politics (Chapter 3). Part A also fleshes out many of the book's key concepts (e.g., class, colonialism, deviantization, discipline, discourse, gender, neoliberalism, privilege, resistance, responsibilization), introduces the theoretical lenses deployed (e.g., intersectionality and interlocking oppressions, power/knowledge, sexual scripts), and defines slow, structural, and symbolic violence.

CHAPTER 1

AN INTERSECTIONAL LENS ON GENDERED VIOLENCE

As we saw in the opening of the Introduction, Canada is a place where misogynist attitudes can result in horrific violence such as the Montréal Massacre. At the same time, it appears possible to defend Canada's national image as a nice, safe country by arguing—as some people did—that Lépine was merely a disturbed individual. What are the consequences of such individualistic thinking? What structural oppressions—and whose experiences—are obscured? Alternatively, does the attention paid to the Montréal Massacre imply that all Canadian women are equally at risk of gendered violence, or is the significance afforded the event indicative of who is considered a worthy (or unworthy) victim? This chapter challenges various facets of Canada's national image of "niceness" (its friendliness, welcoming attitude toward immigrants, lauded multiculturalism, and tolerance of diversity) and concurrent narrative of equality (as a classless and colour-blind meritocracy) on which this image rests. It reflects on the contexts and forms of, as well as the putative solutions to, women's diverse experiences of violence. In so doing, the mutually reinforcing norms underlying Canada's façade (Christian values, entrenched gender roles, white privilege, and heteronormativity) are uncovered. We begin with a brief consideration of the imperial project and the framing of "othered" women, which are integral to colonialism, moving on to define and examine the emergence of the concept of intersectionality and its corollary, privilege. Intersectionality is then illustrated by examining how myths and stereotypes constituting specific groups of women as "other" precipitate various forms of violence, including hate crimes and exclusion from the freedoms, rights, and entitlements of citizenship. A relatively invisible yet powerfully exclusionary aspect of intersectionality is also considered: socio-economic class. The chapter concludes by reflecting on how women from divergent social locations resist violence in ways that speak powerfully to exclusion, state violence, and privilege.

The imperial project: Constructing gender, race, and nation

The narrative of Canada as a welcoming multicultural country notwithstanding, history shows something much less gracious and decidedly more oppressive. In contrast to Canada's contemporary secular self-conception, Christianity played a central role in colonization and the development of the modern capitalist nation-state. Although the goal of imperial projects was to expand national territories and exploit new sources of wealth, European rulers justified colonization through religious doctrine. Namely, they asserted that Christian nations had the (literally) God-given right, even responsibility, to colonize any lands they discovered and convert and "civilize" the Indigenous inhabitants. In this way, "it was contended that people were being colonized for their own benefit, either in this world or the next" (TRC 2015a, 46).

A second justification used by European imperialists similarly failed to recognize the validity of Indigenous cultures, or indeed the humanity of Indigenous peoples, by characterizing the lands they were claiming as no man's land—*terra nullius* (TRC 2015a, 46). Coupled with Christianity's dichotomous conception of gender roles, this understanding of Indigenous peoples as "uncivilized" continues to inform perceptions of Indigenous women. As Sarah Carter (1993) documents, in spite of knowing full well that disease and poor living conditions on reserves were consequences of repressive policies, official documents nonetheless blamed Indigenous women by characterizing them as "idle and gossipy" (149). At the same time, to deflect criticism for the liaisons of white men with First Nations women, and Indigenous women's victimization at the hands of Euro-Canadian men, Indigenous women were framed not only as "accustomed to being treated with contempt" but blamed for behaving "in an abandoned and wanton manner" (ibid., 153). In this context, the mythical "Indian princess," who "like Pocahontas violates the wishes and customs of her own 'barbarous' people to help, heal, or rescue white men" (Green 1990, 17), was supplanted by her "darker twin the Squaw" (ibid., 19). Indeed the image of Indigenous women as licentious, hypersexualized, and immoral became an unquestioned "truth" embedded in the *Indian Act*, used to justify the pass system and other restrictions. Moreover, Indigenous women were seen as prostitutes and "threats to morality and health" (Carter 1993, 155)—a characterization that was incorporated into the *Criminal Code* through specific provisions to regulate "Indian prostitution" in 1880 (Backhouse 1985, 422). In short, Indigenous women victimized by men and the state were perversely responsibilized for the spread of both disease and immorality.

Just as the colonial legacy of sexualizing and fetishizing Indigenous women's bodies is evident today (an issue examined in Chapter 12), so are the deeply entrenched stereotypes of Black women that cast them outside narratives of fragile white middle class femininity in need of protection (Maynard 2017). The Mammy and Jezebel tropes propagated during the transatlantic slave trade are another incarnation of the Madonna–whore dichotomy, one that continues to resonate in the **misogynoir** that haunts the lives of Black women (an issue we see throughout this book, but most explicitly in Chapter 11). It is important to point out that, in contrast to Canada's national narrative of saviours that celebrates our participation in the underground railroad, Black persons were enslaved in Canada until 1834 (see Figure 1.1) (Nelson 2017). As Robyn Maynard (2017) points out, while the Mammy was a construct of a Black woman who "gratefully raised the white children of her master or employer, and performed her servitude willingly," the complementary Jezebel trope constitutes Black women as hypersexual (117). The former justified and obscured Black women's economic exploitation, while the latter legitimated and negated sexual violence: "[I]t was Black women, and not the men who harmed them, who were to blame, as their nature made them immoral, wayward, and threatening" (ibid.).

Embedded in both tropes is a dehumanizing "less than" narrative. One graphic illustration is the racial characterizations made of a woman brought to "perform" in Europe by a French doctor in the early 1800s who came to be known as the "Hottentot Venus" (Stephens and Phillips 2003). Displayed like a zoo animal, the crowds non-consensually prodding her buttocks, Sarah Baartman (the name she was assigned) refused European scientists' requests to examine her genitalia (ibid.). Shamefully (but given the scientific racism of the imperial era unsurprisingly) this did not stop them from examining Ms. Baartman far more invasively after her death in 1816. Dionne Stephens and Layli Phillips (2003) argue that the scientists' examination and dissection of her sexual anatomy, and likening her to an orangutan, furnished narratives that echo today: Black women are understood as "primitive, wild, sexually uninhibited, and exotic" (7). This characterization of animal sexuality continues to legitimate the narrative of Black women (unlike middle class white women) as neither chaste nor morally virtuous, and therefore unrapable (Crenshaw 1989).

Conceptual tools: Intersectionality and interlocking oppressions

To put the above in feminist theoretical terms, colonialism, Christianity, and capitalism are fundamentally interlocking, and their mutual constitution enabled the production and reproduction of gender, racial, and class norms against which women continue to be measured and "othered" in myriad ways.

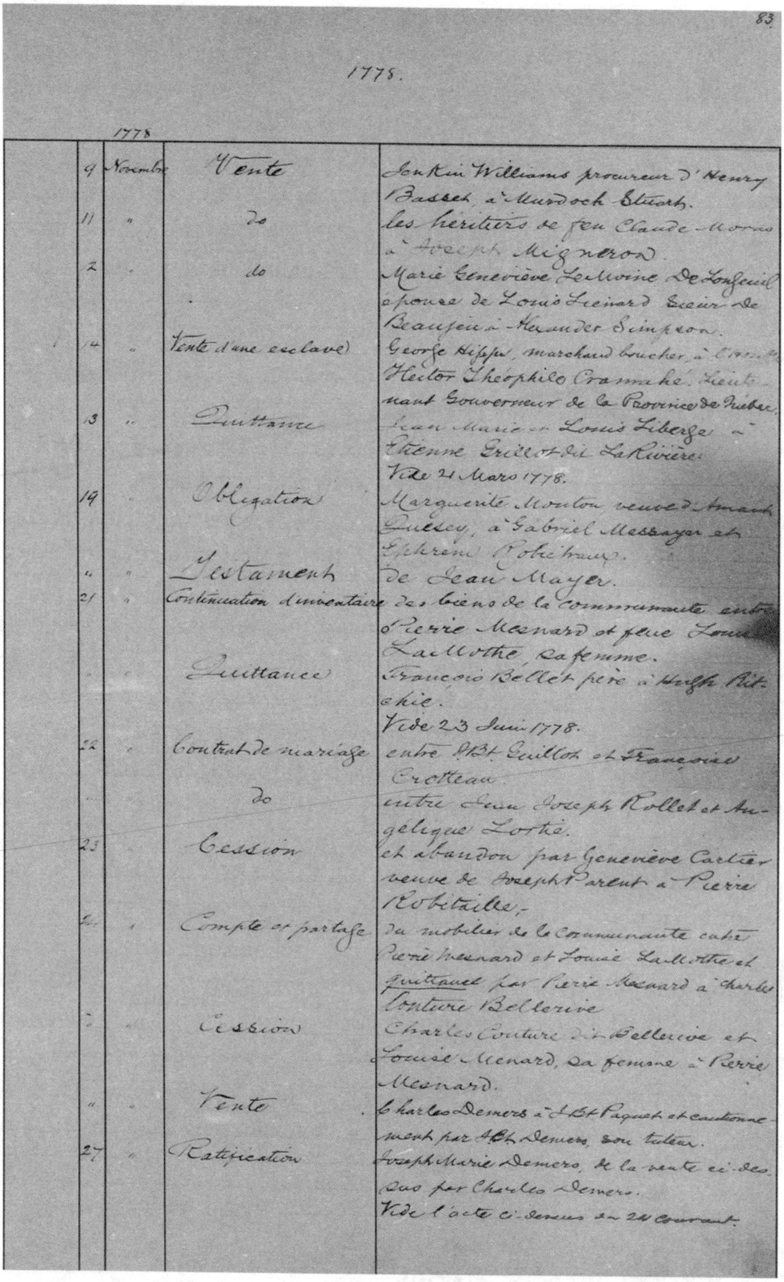

83

1778.

1778			
9	Novembre	Vente	Jenkin Williams procureur d'Henry Bassett, à Murdoch Stuart.
11	"	do	les héritiers de feu Claude Morin à Joseph Migneron.
2	"	do	Marie Geneviève LeMoine De Longueuil épouse de Louis Liénard Sieur de Beaujeu à Alexander Simpson.
14	"	Vente d'une esclave	George Hipps, marchand boucher, à l'Hon. Hector Théophile Cramahé, Lieutenant Gouverneur de la Province de Québec.
13	"	Quittance	Jean Marie et Louis Liberge à Etienne Grillot dit LaRivière. Vide 21 Mars 1778.
19	"	Obligation	Marguerite Mouton, veuve d'Amant Quesey, à Gabriel Messayer et Ephrem Robitaux.
"	"	Testament	de Jean Mayer.
21	"	Continuation d'inventaire	des biens de la communauté entre Pierre Mesnard et feue Louise LaMothe, sa femme.
"	"	Quittance	François Bellet père à Hugh Ritchie. Vide 23 Juin 1778.
22	"	Contrat de mariage	entre J.Bt. Guillot et Françoise Crotteau.
"	"	do	entre Jean Joseph Rollet et Angélique Lothé.
23	"	Cession	et abandon par Geneviève Cartier veuve de Joseph Parent à Pierre Robitaille.
24	"	Compte et partage	du mobilier de la communauté entre Pierre Mesnard et Louise LaMothe et quittance par Pierre Mesnard à Charles Couture Bellerive
"	"	Cession	Charles Couture dit Bellerive et Louise Menard, sa femme à Pierre Mesnard.
"	"	Vente	Charles Demers à J.Bt Paquet et cautionnement par J.Bt Demers, son tuteur.
27	"	Ratification	Joseph Marie Demers, de la vente ci-dessus par Charles Demers. Vide l'acte ci-dessus au 24 courant.

FIGURE 1.1: Slave bill of sale from Québec, 1778

As we saw in the Introduction, violence against women has been both a central concern of and a site of disagreement among feminist activists and scholars, prompting productive (albeit sometimes divisive) theoretical developments. **Intersectionality** (deeply rooted in the rich critical race scholarship) mobilizes Crenshaw's (1989) critique of mainstream second wave feminism. In contrast to feminists like Susan Brownmiller (1975), who asserted that rape is "a conscious process of intimidation by which all men keep all women in a state of fear" (6), Crenshaw (1989) drew on the historical record noted above and the contemporary stereotyping of Black women to argue that, for Black women, rape can be a "weapon of racial terror" (158).

Intersectionality grew out of Crenshaw's (1989; 1991) concerns about the invisibility of Black women's experiences, both in mainstream feminism and in anti-discrimination law, and a lack of recognition about how they differ from both Black men's and white women's experiences. Using a traffic intersection as an analogy, Crenshaw (1989) argued that Black women may experience discrimination from any direction of the intersection or several ways simultaneously—in other words, Black women confront discrimination on the basis of race or gender or as Black women in particular. The term has since been adopted by feminist activists as well as academics attending to questions of social location. In contemporary scholarship, intersectionality is generally understood as the mutually constitutive relationship between identity categories, such as gender, race, class, sexual orientation, ethnicity, citizenship, and ability (Hill Collins 2015).

These hierarchical categories are reproduced in social institutions and structures that, in turn, are perpetuated through their mutual inter-reliance. Intersectionality also attends to power relations and questions of structure (Cho, Crenshaw, and McCall 2013), which are referred to as **interlocking systems of oppression** (Hill Collins 1991). As Sherene Razack (2008) argues, *interlocking* connotes a deeper relationship in which systems give content to and are constitutive of each other. Mary Louise Fellows and Razack (1998) explain that systems of oppression are mutually reproducing, such that "class exploitation could not be accomplished without gender and racial hierarchies; imperialism could not function without class exploitation, sexism, heterosexism, and so on" (335). Albert Banerjee and his colleagues (2008), arguing that violence against personal support workers is overwhelmingly an issue of violence against women from racialized and/or immigrant groups, illustrate the co-occurrence of intersecting discrimination and interlocking oppressions. Structural barriers, such as a lack of recognition of foreign credentials and limited access to education and training, intersect with the under-valuation of women's skills and labour (examined in Chapter 2) to contribute to the over-representation of racialized and im/migrant women in occupations that, as we see in Chapter 8, are characterized by high rates of violence. This vulnerability is further exacerbated by understaffing and inadequate occupational health and safety measures in the healthcare sector (ibid.). In turn, women's experiences and interpretations of workplace violence are shaped by their cultural and racial identities (Welsh et al. 2006). For example, research by Sandy Welsh and her colleagues (2006) reveals that Black women find workplace racism/racial harassment a more pressing concern than sexual harassment, while **migrant** women workers—preoccupied with the limitations engendered by their lack of citizenship—interpret sexual abuse more ambiguously than their Canadian-born counterparts. Thus, an individual's experience is influenced by intersecting identities and interlocking oppressions working in and through each other. In the rest of the chapter (and indeed this book), the concept of intersectionality is employed to examine how differently situated women experience violence in specific ways and to map how interlocking systems of oppression condition these experiences. First, however, we consider an under-examined implication of inhabiting multiple, intersecting identity categories: privilege.

Unpacking privilege

Central to intersectionality is an understanding that women experience oppression in varying configurations and in divergent degrees of intensity. It means that while all women experience oppression on the basis of gender, women are nevertheless differentially subjugated by the varied intersections of other social structures. Shedding light on intersections and taking an **anti-essentialist position** that foregrounds women's diversity necessitates that we consider the natural corollary to systemic disadvantage: **privilege**. Recognizing (our) privilege is challenging precisely because privilege is rooted not in exceptionality but the inverse—the unexceptional. It is the norm, the taken-for-granted category; the group that requires neither name nor qualifier nor adjective. The assumption is that one is heterosexual, non-disabled, and cisgender—modifiers are added to describe (and differentiate) the "other." Indeed, it is not unusual for white people in Canada to think they have no race—white is simply the default. That the root of privilege lies in invisibility also means that the benefits and freedoms *feel* natural. This may explain the backlash we see when privileges are threatened: The men's rights movement, the rise of white nationalism (i.e., white supremacy), and the uproar when schools or students endeavour to be inclusive (e.g., Islamic prayer rooms, gay–straight alliance groups) are examples of responses to the perceived loss (or extension) of rights and privileges to which holders assume (only) themselves to be entitled. This also alerts us to the dialectic relationship between power and knowledge that is examined in Chapter 3; that we have Black History Month reminds us that the conventional framing of Canadian history is white. And certainly the history of the country settlers named Canada would look very different if written from the point of view of Indigenous peoples.

Peggy McIntosh (1989) describes "white privilege as an invisible package of unearned assets that I can count on cashing in each day, but about which I was 'meant' to remain oblivious. White privilege is like an invisible weightless knapsack of special provisions, maps, passports, codebooks, visas, clothes, tools and blank checks" (1). In other words, there are unearned benefits of belonging to a dominant social group that confer advantage. McIntosh rendered white privilege visible through a sensitizing checklist that has been adapted by others to highlight the invisible privilege enjoyed by, for example, Christians, heterosexuals, and those who are not disabled (see the exercise at the end of this chapter). The intent is the same: to bring to light the advantages afforded people who fit into a specific social group. McIntosh's work alerts us that ignoring privilege is to perpetuate it, or put another way, silence and complacency is complicity. Recognizing diversity also reminds us that privilege is in a dialectic relationship to oppression—oppressions do not negate privileges and the benefits conferred. In other words, privilege (and oppression) can be mediated and partial. For example, a white, working class, genderqueer woman certainly experiences systemic barriers and oppression; that does not negate the privileges she enjoys on the basis of her race. As we see below, and throughout the book, systems of oppression interlock in complex ways to condition women's experiences of violence.

Women and hate-motivated violence

While gendered violence can manifest in numerous contexts and interpersonal relationships, violent policing of gender norms often arises out of anxieties around real or perceived violations of other norms. It is here that the influence of stereotypes, myths, and layered narratives of the "other" are invoked to justify acts of violence against particular demographics of women. The examples that follow speak to the diversity of women in Canada and how their positioning at the intersections of various social locations conditions their experiences. Unlike much of the violence discussed in other chapters of this book, hate crimes are usually committed by strangers. Because it targets people based on their (negatively) perceived difference, and in particular their violation of one or a number of social norms, hate crime is illustrative of how women's experiences of violence are profoundly intersectional. Its manifestations, and even victims' perceptions of their experiences, further highlight the impacts of women's specific social locations. To illustrate this we examine the experiences of LGBTQ and Muslim women.

Women in the LGBTQ community

An intersectional perspective allows us to see how the policing of gender, sexual, and racial norms intersects in instances of verbal and physical victimization of LGBTQ people of colour by white people and by people from the same racial or ethnic community. Doug Meyer (2012) argues that racialized individuals experience homophobic hate crimes differently depending on their racial or ethnic identity and socio-economic class location, regularly interpreting their experiences of violent victimization as attempts to punish them for not appropriately representing their racial communities. For example, in Meyer's (2012) research, Black lesbians interpreted their experiences of homophobic violence as emanating from a perception that they harmed their racial community by "converting" other Black women to lesbianism. Reflecting women's greater risk of victimization through sexual violence, racialized lesbians and trans women also face higher levels of sexual violence compared to gay men of colour. However, feminine gender norms play a role in homophobic harassment and violence in both cases: While lesbians and trans women are targeted for transgressing norms of femininity, gay men are targeted because they are read as too feminine (Meyer 2012).

The application of these dichotomous gender norms in specific ways informed by race, culture, and ethnicity can be traced back to colonialism. Nicole LaViolette (2014) examines this issue intersectionally, pointing out that unlike gay men, lesbians suffer from gender norms working to repress women's political and economic participation as well as their sexual and reproductive freedom. In this context rape can be "a sexualized attack upon lesbians as a punishment for their sexual and social nonconformity" (Millbank 2003, 77). This is, of course, analogous to Crenshaw's (1989) characterization of rape as a "weapon of racial terror" (158). As LaViolette (2014) reminds us, persecution for sexual transgression is often the result of perceptions of gender non-conformity. To this end, gay men and transgender people are targeted for violating masculine gender roles in countries where homosexuality is persecuted. Colonialism continues to engender violence here as well through sexual and gender norms introduced with Christianity: That 71 per cent of Commonwealth countries continue to criminalize homosexuality (comprising almost half [49 per cent] of the places in the world where same sex relations are illegal) suggests "that the criminalisation of homosexuality may be a legacy of the British Empire" (Gerber 2016).

Muslim women: Violence at the intersections of gender, race, and religion

In looking at Western feminists' conceptions of oppression and liberation we see that Crenshaw's (1989) argument for intersectionality, which emanated in part from mainstream second wave feminism's failure to include and recognize Black women's experiences, continues to hold true. In Western countries, this is certainly the case for Muslim women, whose experiences and lives continue to be read through racist and nationalist lenses framing them as devoid of agency and oppressed by their "backwards" culture (Razack 2008). This in turn serves to reinforce perceptions of Muslim men as inherently misogynist and violent, complementing stereotypes of Muslim men as terrorists (ibid.). As Wahiba Abu-Ras and Zulema Suarez (2009) note, while both Muslim men and women report that their lives became more difficult after 9/11, Muslim women in Western countries feel especially vulnerable to and affected by hate crimes because their variously intersecting gender, cultural, and religious identity, immigration status, language barriers, and style of dress (i.e., modest and covered) can render them simultaneously more isolated from the dominant culture and more visibly "other" (see also Chan and Chunn 2014).

In turn, Muslim women's experiences are distinct from both Islamophobic violence targeting men and gendered violence targeting women of other backgrounds (Perry 2014). A common form of attack against Muslim women involves their hijabs being forcibly and violently removed—as Barbara Perry (2014) points out, such instances demonstrate how the very sign through which Muslim women are read as exploited is, paradoxically, exploited by aggressors. In Canada, there were numerous hate-motivated violent incidents targeting Muslim women following terrorist attacks in Western countries in 2015: Two men severely beat and removed the hijab of a woman in Peterborough (Ross 2015); a man physically encroached upon and then violently elbowed a Toronto woman wearing a niqab; and two teenage boys pulled the hijab of a pregnant Montréal woman, causing her to fall (Fine 2015).

Understanding this violence necessitates that we also consider the role of the state and its actors. For example, when police disproportionately target Middle Eastern women for traffic stops (Foster, Jacobs, and Siu 2016), they signal that Muslim women are "other," without entitlement to the same rights non-Muslim citizens enjoy. This suggests that stereotypes and interlocking oppressions impact the focus, content, and application of laws and other regulatory tools, and highlight the need to interrogate how the state itself can be an agent of violence and instrumental in perpetuating systems of oppression—in other words, we must attend to **structural violence**, the social structures and institutions that create and entrench inequality (Galtung 1969). Indeed, there are recent examples of legislation that may foster or even exacerbate violence against Muslim, im/migrant, and racialized women (and men). For example, in 2015 the federal *Anti-Terrorism Act* became law; the same year there was a 60 per cent increase in police-reported hate crimes against Muslims in Canada; 53 per cent of the victims were women (Statistics Canada 2017f).

Moreover, Islamophobia and anti-im/migrant sentiments are legitimated and reinforced when legislators draw on stereotypes and narratives of the "risky other" to justify discriminatory policies and laws. Here Québec's *Act to Foster Adherence to State Religious Neutrality*, which came into effect on October 18, 2017 (although on December 1 of that year Justice Babak Barin of the Québec Superior Court granted a stay pending restriction guidelines), is a case in point. The law "imposes a duty of religious neutrality" (Ch. 1) but in effect targets only Muslim women who wear the niqab or burqa. Specifically the Act does not prohibit Christian religious symbols (e.g., crosses, nun's habits) but does prevent anyone with their face covered (except if it is an occupational or task-related requirement) from receiving or providing public services in Québec. Revealingly, the ban is further justified on the basis of needing to verify identity "for security purposes" (ibid.). Security also featured prominently in the federal government's challenge to the right of a woman to take the citizenship oath wearing a niqab (by the Conservative Party of Canada during the 2015 federal election). We also find that scripts of the uncivilized, dangerous "other" underpin laws like the bluntly titled *Zero Tolerance for Barbaric Cultural Practices Act* (2015), which frames already criminalized activities (e.g., polygamy) as barbaric and implies they are more likely to occur among "other" cultures. In short, we see the interlocking nature of colonialism, Christianity, and Canadian nationalism and how (xenophobic) stigmatic assumptions pivoting on the notion of risk become embedded in state policies and practices—what Stacey Hannem (2012) calls **structural stigma**.

The Canadian nation-state: Equal protection for all?

Structural violence is not only evident in explicitly regulatory and punitive state policies and practices; it also emerges, somewhat counterintuitively, in ostensibly protectionist laws and in the de facto exclusion of some populations from seemingly broad-based rights. As we see in Chapters 5 and 6, while various forms of violence against women, including sexual assault and intimate partner violence, have been subject to significant legal reforms, there has been much debate over the extent to which these changes in law and enforcement practices are indeed helpful to women. Section 15(1) of the *Canadian Charter of Rights and Freedoms* guarantees "the right to the equal protection and equal benefit of the law without discrimination and, in particular, without discrimination based on race, national or ethnic origin, colour, religion, sex, age or mental or physical disability." However, racialized, im/migrant, and Indigenous women continue to experience hate-motivated crimes at alarming rates.

As Wendy Chan and Dorothy Chunn (2014) explain, legislation prohibiting the promotion of hate against an identifiable group has existed in Canada since 1970, but it was not until 1996 that Canada introduced measures officially recognizing hate-motivated crime. There are several sections of the *Criminal Code* pertaining to particular manifestations of hate crime. These include sections 318 and 319, which prohibit hate propaganda; section 718.2, which pertains to motivation based on bias, prejudice, or hate; and also part of section 430, which characterizes mischief to religious property as a hate-motivated offence (ibid.). However, in spite of these provisions, hate crime itself is not defined in the *Criminal Code*—instead, regional and local police administrations work with their own definitions, which can range from meagre to expansive explanations, resulting in inconsistencies in enforcement (ibid.). Moreover, the processing of hate crimes through the criminal justice system has been characterized by few successful prosecutions, as well as a high burden of proof. In addition, hate crime is thought to be significantly under-reported (ibid.). This begs the question—considered throughout this book—whether and to what extent criminal justice responses to violence are helpful to victims or, more specific to our focus, women.

Similar to the way the threat posed by the "otherness" of Muslims has been invoked in regulatory discussions, trans women's perceived deviation from Western gender norms are (albeit in a different way) also framed as dangerous. This was apparent in media coverage of Canadian and American debates over whether transgender individuals should be allowed to use the bathroom that corresponds to their gender identity. Discrediting and disregarding trans identity, opponents of the inclusion of trans women in women's washrooms invoked (cisgender) women's and girls' safety, suggesting trans women are deviant, risky, and potential predators. As activists counterargued, however, signs or rules about who is allowed to use public women's washrooms are unlikely to stop sexual aggressors from carrying out acts of violence (Schmidt 2013). Moreover, the narrative of trans women as dangerous not only fails to acknowledge (and thereby renders invisible) the disproportionately high rates of verbal, physical, and sexual violence experienced by trans women—especially those who are racialized (Bauer and Scheim 2015; Marcellin, Bauer, and Scheim 2013)—but also affirms a narrative of the "other" that underpins the violence and abuse to which trans people are disproportionately subjected, both in their families of origin and in society more generally (Davidson 2015).

In the context of these widespread, albeit baseless, anxieties about women's safety, the Alberta minister of education nonetheless allowed trans students to use the bathroom that accords with their gender identity (Alberta Education 2016). This regulatory change can be seen as part of a national debate that is moving toward the recognition of trans rights. A key part of this is the passing of Bill C-16, *An Act to Amend the Canadian Human Rights Act and the Criminal Code* (2016), which received royal assent on June 19, 2017. The Act enshrines gender identity and gender expression as prohibited grounds of discrimination in the *Canadian Human Rights Act*, and extends *Criminal Code* prohibitions against hate propaganda and hate crimes to include gender identity and expression. Of course the Act will not remedy the inconsistencies in police enforcement against hate crimes nor eliminate the violence people who are trans experience.

Intersecting marginalizations, and the use of state-enshrined protections to undermine the equality of some women, come into sharp relief when we interrogate the complicity of feminist organizations that deny services to trans women. While some Canadian women's shelters welcome trans women, this is not consistently the case. Similar to the bathroom debates above, women's safety was the issue being contested in *Vancouver Rape Relief Society v. Nixon*, in which Kimberly Nixon, a trans woman, was denied the opportunity to volunteer for the Vancouver Rape Relief Society (VRRS) on the basis that she was unacceptable in a women's only space. A significant component of VRRS's defence was that they wanted volunteers who shared their clients' *lifelong* experiences of gender oppression; the Vancouver group was ultimately allowed to deny Nixon the volunteering opportunity on the basis that organizations have the right to exclude certain populations from their staff if deemed unsuitable for the organization's goals (Chambers 2007; *Vancouver Rape Relief Society v. Nixon* 2005). Not only did this decision fail to recognize Nixon's gender identity, it also discredited her experiences of gendered violence at the hands of men both before and after sex-reassignment surgery (*Vancouver Rape Relief Society v. Nixon et al.* 2003; Chambers 2007). VRRS has not changed its position in the intervening decade; on May 10, 2017, Hilla Kerner, representing VRRS, argued against the adoption of the above-mentioned Act in front of the Legal and Constitutional Affairs committee of the Senate, carefully distinguishing between a "female-born woman" and an individual who "feel[s] like a woman." She expressed the group's concern that the law will "undermine the rights of women and the crucial work of women's groups to serve and organize with female-born women" (Senate of Canada 2017). This anti-intersectional intervention speaks to ongoing issues within mainstream feminism and fears that perceived entitlements will be lost—a conflict, as we see below, that also emerged in the context of the 2017 Women's March.

As we are starting to see, and will continue to examine in subsequent chapters, state regulation can engender, alleviate, and/or exacerbate gendered violence. Moreover, regulatory solutions are inherently limited insofar as they operate within the confines of systems like colonialism and capitalism. Canada's treatment of LGBTQ refugees exemplifies the limits and challenges of a legal approach to the problem of homophobic/transphobic violence and persecution emanating from colonial British laws. LGBTQ refugee claimants seeking protection in Canada to escape violence—which may include serious criminal sanctions (including the death penalty); violence by police, community, or family; blackmail or extortion; restrictions on freedom of expression or association; diagnoses of mental illness; or accusations of crimes against religion—must provide evidence they are being persecuted or have a well-founded fear of persecution and proof that they are unable to obtain protection from their country of origin (LaViolette 2014). However, it is difficult to acquire independent human rights documentation in regard to LGBTQ persons in many countries; as we will see with sexual assault, low official statistics may speak to a lack of reporting, signalling distrust or fear of state authorities rather than a lack of victimization (ibid.). In practice, the decision to grant refugee status may also pivot on decision makers' assessment of the claimant's credibility—as a result an applicant might be rejected because she or he does not look "gay enough," according to Western stereotypes; these readings are further rendered unreliable by the huge variation among different countries, cultures, and individuals in presentation of self (ibid.). Trans individuals face particular barriers (e.g., possessing official documents with only their birth name), which can be especially problematic given that misrepresentation of one's identity can be grounds for deportation (ibid.).

Returning to the question of whether the Canadian state offers equal protection for all, the examples elaborated above appear to suggest it does not. As various chapters of this book document, there are numerous reasons women do not turn to the state for protection or redress against gendered violence—gender norms and myths about women (e.g., as deserving or blameworthy) among them. In addition, based on experiences such as those we have seen in this chapter, racialized, Indigenous, poor, and LGBTQ women have little reason to believe they will be protected by the laws, the systems, and the people who enforce them; nor do they enjoy the same level of protection as middle class white women even when they do choose legal solutions. It appears the best safeguard from hate crime, discrimination, and exclusion does not lie in appealing to special refugee status, or seeking equality through the courts, or human rights mechanisms, or hate crime provisions, but in privilege that precludes being targeted by violence in the first place. Doubtless, some such privileged women—white, heterosexual, Canadian-born citizens who disappear into the stereotypical image of Canadianness—feel protected by the state not only by laws criminalizing violence but by legal instruments like the *Zero Tolerance for Barbaric Cultural Practices Act* and the *Vancouver Rape Relief Society v. Nixon* (2005) ruling that keep other women "othered."

Class matters: Social, economic, and cultural capital

There is another element to consider in our reflections on intersectionality: class. Class is all too often ignored—or coded as poverty and/or conflated with race (i.e., the assumption that all racialized persons are economically marginal; Emejulu and Bassel 2017). As Beverly Skeggs (1997) notes, however, "to think class does not matter is only a prerogative of those unaffected by the deprivations and exclusions it produces" (7). As such, just like assertions of a post-race society inevitably emanate from white authors and not those who are racialized, class "blindspots" speak powerfully to privilege and the social location of knowledge producers. It also speaks to the complexity of teasing out class in advanced post-industrial neoliberal societies; what we mean by class, and what class means, is considerably murkier than when Marx (1974/1859) distinguished between capitalists (the bourgeoisie) who own the means of production and those whose labour power they purchase (the proletariat). As such, class does not operate in isolation but is always conditioned by gender, ethnicity, race, im/migration status, sexual orientation, and the myriad other ways our ever-more-fractured identities are constituted—in other words it "never exists in 'pure' form" (Clement 1988, 22) and must be understood intersectionally.

But that does not mean class is not economically real (indeed, neoliberal capitalism has, as we see in Chapter 2, increased income disparity and consolidated class power), experientially significant, or culturally entrenched. We are surrounded by loaded narratives: Working class people are depicted as violent, short tempered, and aggressive and framed as unintelligent, slow witted, and short sighted—the dualism that operates in relation to gender examined in Chapter 3 is also evident in the classed mind–body divide. Certainly, cultural representations suggest people who labour in mines, stores, hair salons, and restaurants are "not too bright," perhaps possessing good hearts and street (but not real) smarts. The few television shows that feature working class families formalistically use stupidity—often brought into sharp relief by the brilliant child inexplicably in their midst—as a key comic device (*The Simpsons* is just one among many examples). The (denigrating) script about working and underclass people is not only about intellectual capacity, it is also about values, morals, and (importantly) respectability (Skeggs 1997). For example, when the prime minister of Canada, echoing the assertions of politicians across the political spectrum, declares that middle class families "believe in working hard to get ahead and hope for a better future for their children … aspire to a lifestyle that typically includes adequate housing and health care, [and] educational opportunities for their children" (quoted in Smith 2017) the inevitable corollary is that working class folks do not believe in hard work and do not aspire to better lives for their children. We also see stigmatic assumptions about the working and underclass affirmed in the widespread (but evidently inaccurate) assumption that Canada is a meritocracy—after all, if those with skills, drive, and intelligence rise to the top, then those who do not must have a poor work ethic, lack ambition, and be less intellectually competent.

In short, class distinctions—the presumed superiority of all things middle and upper class and, since class is by definition a relational categorization, the implicit or explicit devaluation of the working and underclass—surround us. As examined in Chapter 3 in relation to the concept of symbolic violence (Bourdieu 1998), the power of class lies precisely in its invisibility and the normalization of these distinctions (Bourdieu 1984); so pervasive is the discourse that it is absorbed into our common-sense framing of the world even (to an extent) by those who are the objects of disdain and recognize the fallacy of the depictions. Expanding on a point we also see in Box 1.1, Joanna Kadi (1996) explains that growing up, "I knew people in my family had brains and the bosses didn't. My extended family joked about it frequently. But just as frequently, they indicated they believed it. And at deep levels, I internalized the lie and lived with it for years" (45). Her comments also alert us to another (hierarchical) class distinction—the differential prestige, value, and status afforded to the competencies, credentials, and jobs associated with the middle as opposed to the working class (e.g., the abstract reasoning and aptitude required to theorize are assumed to speak to intelligence, while the abstract reasoning and aptitude required to measure and draft a pattern and construct a garment are seen as simply acquired skills).

What is the significance of these normalized discourses, distinctions, and class **stigma**? At one level, they justify economic inequity and high profit margins by legitimating the low wages paid to those who labour in working class jobs. But they also obscure and naturalize middle and upper class *privilege*— the rewards of class location become (perceived as) entitlements. Here Pierre Bourdieu, who insisted that "[c]lass analysis cannot be reduced to the analysis of economic relations; rather, it simultaneously entails an analysis of symbolic relations" (Weininger 2005, 122), is useful. Bourdieu (1984) envisioned social actors inhabiting different class locations depending on the form, trajectory, and configuration of their capital—"the set of actually usable resources and powers" (114) to which an individual has access. He distinguished between

BOX 1.1: NAVIGATING CLASS MATTERS

We've built every university that has ever existed, yet we're shunned and despised within academia's hallowed halls. Explicitly and implicitly we've been taught our place—and it's not the student's desk or the professors' lounge. We're needed to construct the university, maintain, clean and repair it.

Oh, we're welcome here, as long as we stay where we're supposed to. We know the monster that presents itself if we dare step out of place. *Stupid. We are too stupid to study, learn, think, analyse, critique. Because working-class people are stupid.* So much energy goes into the social lie that poor people are stupid: capitalism needs a basic rationalization to explain why things happen the way they do. So we hear, over and over, that our lousy jobs and living situations result from our lack of smarts. I internalized this lie. Rationally, I knew money and brains didn't go hand in hand. But on deep unconscious levels I believed in my own stupidity and in the stupidity of working-class people....

Levels of elitism and arrogance vary with regional difference, size, prestige, and how many misfits end up on campus, but the core system remains: privileged people belong here. If only I'd known that years ago! Then anger, instead of feeling crazy, alienated, and stupid, would have been uppermost.

Kadi 1996, 39–41

economic capital (financial resources and assets), social capital (social connections and networks), and **cultural capital** (Bourdieu 1986). The latter refers to the symbolic markers of class location, which can be embodied (e.g., taste, social competencies, mannerisms), material (e.g., clothes, property, home), or institutional (e.g., credentials or qualifications). As such, cultural capital comprises the (largely unacknowledged) resources (or privileges) that condition not only access to opportunities but also play out interactionally; those who cannot, or do not endeavour to, "pass" as middle or upper class are read according to deeply entrenched stereotypes that equate poverty with, for example, laziness, ignorance, slovenliness, immorality, and lack of ambition. As we see in subsequent chapters, cultural capital, often intersecting with racialization and other markers of social stratification, can impact a woman's access to employment; her vulnerability to violence; the extent to which she is blamed for her victimization; and whether (and how) she is protected or victimized by the state, its institutions, and its actors.

Class and higher education

The university, and indeed the very construct of "higher learning," illustrates how social stratifications are perpetuated and the ways this is obscured in and by the ethos of neoliberalism. When those who pursue post-secondary studies are lauded (by others and themselves) for making good *choices*, the assumption is that those who do otherwise are making bad choices. And while some thought may (in liberal circles) be given to the economic barriers to higher education, little consideration goes into pragmatic issues like daycare and even course scheduling (e.g., a single mother working full time simply cannot take those gender studies courses offered in the middle of the day!). Nor is there reflection on the deeply alienating experience of sitting in classes where one's life, family, and neighbourhood are transformed into "the objects of sociological inquiry" (Smith 1987, 117), perhaps even as the harbingers of criminogenic factors—the destabilizing nature of being taught that one's family, friends, or oneself were "deviant, or worse, pathological ... either to be feared and ignored or treated, managed, and corrected" (Munn 2012, 147).

Nor is much consideration given to the challenges that navigating the institutional language, bureaucratic logic, and geography of universities may pose to working and underclass students who, unlike their middle and upper class peers, have not learned about university life from parents and siblings and are therefore not conversant with "reference points and contexts, ranging from GRE's and LSAT's to Ph.D.'s and post-doc fellowships" (Kadi 1996, 45). Absent too from the conversation are the multitude of ways navigating university requires class culture and intangible, in-your-bones knowledge—or what Bourdieu (1986) called *habitus*: Students from impoverished backgrounds may not be familiar with the interactional styles and presentation of self (e.g., the "right" way to apply makeup) that appear natural to their more privileged university peers; they may lack knowledge about, let alone the confidence to, self-advocate (e.g., question a grade, challenge an administrative decision); they may be unable to participate in leisure and/or conversational pursuits of their middle class peers (e.g., international travel, shopping, cottage weekends). There are a multitude of ways that signal to working class students they do not belong; not least of which are the potential for class stigma to manifest in the subtle and not so subtle glances, flickers of distaste, and shocked looks when they (resistantly or inadvertently) "out" themselves by sharing an anecdote, employing the "wrong" words or grammar, or when their "cheap" makeup, lack of a "good" haircut, or bad teeth mark them as "low class" (see also Box 2.2 on page 50), or when their expressive style and language choices are read by peers and professors as dull and uncouth. All these factors, of course, not only operate in their own right but also intersect with, for example, race to mark a student as an outsider. The result is that working class students often "feel required to deliver 'performances' … to choose between tiresomely contouring [their] style of dress, manner of speech and even opinions lest [they] are rendered hypervisible, and perceived as unintelligent and devoid of 'culture'" (Addo 2017). Here, and as Kadi explains in Box 1.1, we see class reproduction in action: Not only are students without economic means less able to afford higher education, but even those who find ways to do so experience campuses and classrooms as deeply alienating and stressful environments in ways their middle class peers are oblivious to—the very mark of privilege. The result is less scholastic success and decreased likelihood of undertaking advanced degrees; hence they are rarely the legitimated knowledge producers, but instead "provide the raw material of bare facts and touching stories" that are transformed into theory at the hands of middle and upper class scholars (Kadi 1996, 40). That said, the knowledges of "outsiders" also hold the seeds of transformative reflection; a case in point is Pierre Bourdieu himself, whose status as a leading intellectual was at odds with his "low social origin"—his "cleft habitus" (Bourdieu 2007, 69); as a result he always "felt ill-at-ease and an imposter in the academic world" (Burawoy 2008, 1). We also see this ability of the "other" to perceive (and shed light on) that which privilege renders invisible in the work of critical race theorists, queer scholars, and feminists, whose embodied insights inform diverse resistance tactics by "othered" women.

Resistance: Centring intersectional experiences

In the face of repressive social structures and processes, problematic narratives, and inadequate or counterproductive legal solutions, women are not passive but resist. Of course just as intersecting power relations condition women's vulnerability to and experiences of victimization, so too do they shape the options, strategies, and resources through which they can challenge oppressive relations of power. For example, while a credentialled woman who is sexually harassed at a unionized workplace may start a campaign for institutional or legislative change (see Chapter 7), this is not an option for a woman with less educational and cultural capital employed in a precarious job (see Chapter 2). In this context, and in response to their continued victimization and the inadequacy of the regulatory tools and enforcement practices described above, women are invoking intersectionality as a rallying cry and a scathing critique of the invisibilization of their experiences. We see this in the vibrant social movements that challenge the dominant narratives that frame some women as "other" and thereby enable discrimination, hatred, and violence.

Sometimes women's resistance addresses both interpersonal and structural violence. One such example is Idle No More, a grassroots Indigenous rights movement in Canada that was started by women. Demanding respect for the environment; Indigenous, treaty, and sovereignty rights; democratic representation; resolutions to issues of Aboriginal title; and actions to address violence against Indigenous women (Idle No More, n.d.), Idle No More exemplifies intersectional resistance. Its genesis was a 2012 email discussion among three First Nations women in Saskatchewan, Jessica Gordon, Sylvia McAdam, and Nina Wilson, and one non-Indigenous ally, Sheelah McLean, about how to mobilize against Bill C-45 (2012), an omnibus bill by the federal Conservative government that included harmful changes to land management on reservations and weakened protection of waterways and environmental laws (Caven 2013). The movement, whose name explicitly articulates a renewed commitment to challenging oppression, attracted considerable media attention when Chief Theresa Spence of the Attawapiskat First Nation in Northern Ontario took on a hunger strike in December 2012 to urge then Prime Minister Stephen Harper to reconsider the bill (ibid.). The movement continues to draw attention to the interconnections between environmental justice, Indigenous self-determination, and human rights.

Intersectional resistance is also evident in Black Lives Matter (BLM). In contrast to the Civil Rights Movement of the 1960s, which Fredrick Harris (2015) describes as hierarchical, clergy-based, and led by men, BLM was founded by three Black women: Patrisse Cullors, Opal Tometi, and Alicia Garza. As Marcia Chatelain and Kaavya Asoka (2015) point out, Civil Rights leaders' single-issue framing of racism resulted in the allocation of funding to alleviate challenges facing Black men and boys, contributing to the marginalization of Black women by positioning their problems—and implicitly their experiences—as lower priority. As a collective intersectional response to anti-Black racism, including police violence toward both men and women, BLM challenges dominant discursive framings of Black lives as less valuable and at the same time draws attention to anti-Black racism in social justice movements (ibid.).

Kimberlé Crenshaw (1991) has argued that "ignoring difference *within* groups contributes to tension *among* groups" (1242, emphasis in original), and although in reference to feminism, this critique could certainly be applied to the LGBTQ rights movement. And this is precisely what Black Lives Matter Toronto (BLMTO) activists did in their 2016 intervention halting Toronto's Pride parade—they called out the white privilege implicit in perceiving police as protection. This interruption brought attention to the invisibilization of Black LGBTQ lives and contributions to Toronto Pride, problematizing the privilege that white people enjoy in the LGBTQ community and how this contributes to the erasure of radical politics and the increasing commercialization of Pride celebrations (Khan 2016). In so doing, BLMTO reminded Pride goers that Black queer, trans, lesbian, and sex working women have made important contributions to the movements and rights the LGBTQ community enjoys, and from which their Black comrades are, paradoxically, excluded (see Box 1.2). Pride organizers finally acceded to all of BLMTO's demands in January 2017, including perhaps the most contentious issue, the banning of uniformed police officers from the Pride parade (BlogTO 2017); at the same time, as we see in Box 1.2, BLMTO organizers paid a personal price for their righteous stand and victory.

BOX 1.2: BLMTO STATEMENT—PRIDE PROTEST

We brought the Pride parade to a full stop with a list of demands reflecting the needs of some of Toronto's most marginalized LGBTQ2SIAA community members. These demands challenged the erasure of Black infrastructure and called for the removal of police floats from the Pride parade and community fair....

Our action was in the tradition of resistance that is Pride. We didn't halt progress; we made progress.

We achieved a commitment to our demands despite intense push-back from a primarily gay white male community. The same community did not want Black Lives Matter involved in Pride at all, even going so far as to create a group on Facebook called No BLM in Pride. Gender and sexual diversity, it seems, does not preclude racism or white privilege.

The majority of the leadership within Black Lives Matter Toronto and Black Lives Matter internationally identify as queer or trans. Pride has always been for the most marginalized, and has always been for us.

Since the action, I have received hate mail and death threats, primarily from gay-identifying men. I have been screamed at on the street. I have been called a "nigger" more times than I care to count. People have told me I'm no longer part of the queer community because my Blackness has no place there.

People who are not under the LGBT2QSIAA umbrella have used our action as an excuse to attack us with racist vitriol. Their actions are revealing the racism that prompted our intervention at Pride in the first place.

We are not all on a level playing field fighting for the same equality. Any such claim is absurd.

Khan 2016

Similarly, the 2017 Women's March on Washington put intersectionality at the forefront, marking interconnections between women's rights, human rights, and racial and economic justice. In highlighting the experiences of "Black women, Native women, poor women, immigrant women, Muslim women, and queer and trans women" (Bandele et al. 2017, 2), organizers of the march wanted to provoke much-needed discussions on race and migration following the election of Donald Trump. Rather than engaging in this debate, however, some middle class white women declined to participate in the march, reading the invitation to acknowledge and unpack their privilege not as an opportunity to recognize the differences among women (and in turn their own privileges) but as hostility and anger (Stockman 2017). Of course racialized women's reactions *did* include frustration and anger—given that they have been making the same critique of feminists for over 40 years, justifiably so. The hurt feelings and defensive response of these white feminists overlooked the radical potential of anger, which as bell hooks (2000) reminds us, was the impetus of feminism in the first place.

Concluding reflections

As we have just seen, calling people out on their privilege can be a form of resistance against invisibilization; for privilege holders, such resistance can precipitate an uncomfortable moment of "seeing" what may have previously been invisible (to them)—or in Foucault's (1982) terms, render the invisible visible. Reflecting on privilege also has the potential to steer women away from carceral and governance feminist solutions toward strategies grounded in intersectionality and the recognition of interlocking systems of oppression. Notably, reflecting on privilege highlights how state protection and opportunities for redress are not available to everyone, and that people may inhabit identities that are situated along various axes of oppression and privilege. For example, Kimberly Nixon, a white trans woman who experienced physical, sexual, and emotional gendered violence from men, as well as the denial of her identity as a woman, had the financial stability necessary to volunteer at VRRS and the cultural and economic capital to pursue her discrimination case through the courts. Her example alerts us to how privilege and oppression, and violence and resistance, can coexist without cancelling each other out.

In highlighting how violence can be perpetuated by the state, this chapter has also sketched some of the ways in which systems of oppression interlock in Canada. For example, we have seen that colonialism engenders violence against Indigenous women through oppressive policies and harmful stereotypes; its dichotomous Christian conception of gender has also shaped homophobic and transphobic attitudes and laws that create the conditions for violence against LGBTQ people both here and internationally. We have also seen Western conceptions of citizenship and gendered freedom colonizing the bodies of Muslim women in acts of violence targeting their symbolic "otherness." In the next chapter, we examine how neoliberalism and capitalism (deeply enmeshed with colonialism) operate dialectically with intersecting forms of discrimination to maintain class, gender, racial, and economic inequality.

EXERCISE: EXAMINING PRIVILEGE*

This is a sensitizing exercise that is not intended to be exhaustive of the multiplicities of systemic privileges and disadvantages circling through Canadian society.

Identify the statements in the checklist below that apply to you. Reflect on the implications of the privileges and disadvantages in your life.

- ❏ You see the group of people you identify with widely represented in the media.
- ❏ Your native language is English or French.
- ❏ You were never called names because of your background, race, or ethnicity.
- ❏ Your parents are (or were) professionals (e.g., doctors, lawyers, teachers).
- ❏ The history of your ancestors is part of the mainstream school curriculum.
- ❏ You are not fearful of calling the police to report a crime.
- ❏ You never missed a meal or went hungry because there was not enough money to buy food.
- ❏ You were never singled out in school or not hired at a job because of your background, name, race, or ethnicity.
- ❏ You were encouraged by your parents to attend university or college; additional checkmark if your attendance was assumed.
- ❏ Your family owns/owned the house in which you grew up; additional checkmark if they own(ed) a second home.
- ❏ You can show affection for your romantic partner in public without fear of ridicule or violence.

❑ You have never been concerned that you were hired only to fulfil an equity requirement.

❑ You have never been misgendered and no one has suggested you are not a "real" woman or man.

❑ You never worry about disclosing health struggles for fear of being stigmatized.

❑ You know the appropriate clothes and mannerisms to adopt in elite environments (e.g., university).

❑ You have never been stopped by the police or followed by private security because you are Black, brown, or Indigenous, or look poor.

❑ You and your parents are Canadian citizens or permanent residents.

❑ You have never been harassed in public because of your gender, your gender presentation, or your perceived religion or race.

❑ You never worry whether a building will be accessible or that accommodations to ensure your participation in an event will not be made.

*Adapted from the University of British Columbia
Privilege Walk Worksheet

CHAPTER 2

SITUATING CANADIAN WOMEN: SOCIO-ECONOMIC LOCATIONS

On November 4, 2015, responding to a query about why a gender-balanced cabinet was important, Prime Minister Justin Trudeau famously quipped "because it's 2015." His celebrated comment implies a great deal: that gender equality is (or at least should be) a non-issue, a taken-for-granted reality. But what is actually going on? Prime Minister Trudeau's 2015 cabinet notwithstanding, how are Canadian women positioned in the public sphere? How do class, racialization, xenophobia, transphobia, and ableism intersect with gender to restrict and/or facilitate individual women's opportunities and ultimately condition their socio-economic location? How do interlocking structures function to disadvantage all women at the same time as some woman are (relatively speaking) privileged? And how can we understand the prime minister's lofty narrative in the face of women's poverty and a persistent gender pay gap? In this chapter, as we continue to both sketch the contours of structural violence and contextualize gendered violence, we are guided by these questions. In order to situate women as a group, and at the same time attend to intra-gender difference, this chapter considers two interconnected areas: economic positioning and labour site location. We conclude by returning to the running theme of this book by reflecting on the ways women's social, economic, and labour location is entangled with gendered violence.

Women, class, race, and poverty

Canadian women are not only poorer than men, but are also at greater risk of poverty (Sharma 2012). Indeed, women workers in Canada earn an average of 66.7 cents to the male dollar, and even when only the annual wages of full-time workers are considered the rate is 74 cents (CWF 2017b). In 2014 Canada's gender income gap was the seventh highest out of the 34 OECD member countries (ibid.). The social and personal costs of women's poverty are profound and enduring, affecting everything from an individual woman's ability to leave her abusive partner, to the capacity of children to realize their potential, to the well-being of the Canadian economy.

When we look a bit closer, we see that poverty (and relatedly class) intersects with racialization in the combined effects of discrimination, racial segmentation of the labour market, and the segregation of low-income neighbourhoods to exacerbate the economic marginalization and, as we see in Chapter 3, political exclusion of racialized and immigrant women in Canada (Galabuzi 2005). In other words women, as a group, are poorer than men, but this inequity is not evenly distributed—some women experience the impact particularly profoundly. The UN Human Rights Committee (2015) has raised concerns regarding the high "pay gap, which is more pronounced in some provinces such as Alberta and Nova Scotia, and disproportionately affects low-income women, in particular minority and indigenous women" (para. 7). Thirty-six per cent of Indigenous women living off reserve live below the poverty line. For "visible minority" women, the rate is also alarmingly high (28 per cent), and almost one in three women with disabilities are poor (33 per cent). Similarly, the income of one in five single mothers (21 per cent) falls below the low-income cut-off established by the Government of Canada (CWF 2017b). According to the 2016 census, 18.6 per cent of immigrant women live below the poverty line, with recent immigrants (arriving after 2011) experiencing higher rates of poverty (31.4 per cent) and living below the low-income cut-off (Statistics Canada 2017a). Economic hardship also follows women into their "golden years"—32 per cent of single women over the age of 65 live in poverty (Lambert and McInturff 2016). Such striking intra- and inter-gender economic disparity begs the question: Why is this the case? We now turn to consider this question by focusing on a number of interconnected processes, including the decline of the welfare state and the concurrent rise of neoliberalism; persistent embedded bias against some populations, including immigrant and racialized women; and the gender-segregated labour market.

The ethos of neoliberalism

We live in an era dominated by the philosophy of an unfettered market, deregulation, and privatization: **neoliberalism**. Neoliberalism is based in the understanding that "human well-being can best be advanced by liberating individual entrepreneurial freedoms and skills within an institutional framework characterized by strong private property rights, free markets, and free trade. The role of the state is to create and preserve an institutional framework appropriate to such practices" (Harvey 2007, 2). Deregulation of industry, a protracted war on organized labour, lower taxes for corporations, and a tattered social safety net are just some of the implications. At the same time, responsibility for social well-being is downloaded onto community groups and individuals (e.g., donor-funded food banks instead of livable social-assistance income).

This was not always the case. When the Great Depression (1929–1939) forcefully demonstrated the limits of liberalism, countries around the world, including Canada, embraced Keynesian economics as faith in the minimal state gave way to a conviction that the government was responsible for ensuring social and economic stability and ultimately the well-being of its citizens— that is, the welfare state. Between 1940 and 1970 an increasingly robust social safety net was established, which introduced such now taken-for-granted protections as old age security and universal healthcare. Justified by the needs of "the social," this also meant the state burgeoned, resulting in ever greater state apparatuses and bureaucracy. Such growth also increased state intervention (and therefore regulation) in the lives of citizens—particularly the poor or disadvantaged who were under the "care" of the "benevolent state." By the 1980s the welfare state was in decline, critiqued from the right as too costly and from the left as too regulatory (Rose 1996). In this context neoliberalism, characterized by a conservative, exclusionary approach that—in contrast to the ethos of the welfare state—accepts inequality and is more focused on social control than solidarity and social provision, gained purchase (Garland 2001).

In the context of neoliberalism, austerity measures are presented as a rational response to stabilize and grow the economy. Austerity is packaged in a narrative that reducing public costs will lessen the tax burden and thereby stimulate commerce, and eventually the wealth earned by corporations will trickle down in the form of increased jobs and a stimulated economy to the benefit of all. The impacts of these austerity policies are visible to us when, for example, we wait 12 hours to see an emergency room doctor, and when mental health funding disappears leaving us struggling to find help for a family member. However, the impact of austerity is profoundly shaped by intersecting social locations, including gender, class, ethnicity, and dis/ability. Vickie Cooper and David Whyte (2017) support their assertion that "austerity is a class project" (11) that has particularly detrimental impacts on racialized women by demonstrating that "austerity policies have been designed in such a way that target the most vulnerable and marginal groups in society, hitting them harder than any other income group.... It protects concentrations of elite wealth and power. The policies levelled at working class households have barely touched the elite" (10–11).

Recognizing the impact of austerity alerts us of the need to attend to what Johan Galtung (1969) called structural violence; he argued that when people are experiencing negative consequences that are "objectively avoidable, then violence is committed regardless of whether there is a clear subject-action-object relationship" (171). This immediately expands the parameters of the discussion; unlike physical acts of aggression, "the object of structural violence may be persuaded not to perceive this at all ... structural violence may be seen as about as natural as the air around us" (ibid.). A case in point is the way neoliberal capitalist market economics are virtually imperceptible, an unremarked upon reality. However, as we see throughout this book, like colonialism, neoliberal economic policies, including austerity measures that feel natural to us, are violence. Unlike the way violence is normatively understood (e.g., assault, terrorism; acts envisioned as enacted by working/underclass and racialized individuals), austerity is "a bureaucratised form of violence that is implemented in routine and mundane ways [and] de-politicized" (Cooper and Whyte 2017, 3). Indeed, the effects are profound and pervasive—simply put (and morosely illustrated by Kimberly Rogers's death; see Box 2.3 on page 52), austerity kills and maims (ibid.). A neoliberal government does not necessarily mean less regulation; rather, we see a decentred state characterized by the diffusion of regulation and government at a distance (Rose and Miller 1992), culminating in the entangling regulatory web that this book endeavours to (at least partially) untangle.

Moreover, neoliberalism has an impact well beyond the economic: It is also ideological and cultural. Under neoliberalism, citizens are reconfigured as rational, self-interested, responsible, free-choosing subjects; in short, the entrepreneurial model is extended and "the enterprising self is bound by specific rules that emphasize ambition, calculation and personal responsibility" (Elias, Gill, and Scharff 2017, 23). As Nicolas Rose (1996) writes, "the regulation of conduct becomes a matter of each individual's desire to govern their own conduct freely in the service of the maximization of their happiness and fulfilment" (59). In short, people are conceptualized as equally positioned choice makers (Rose 1999). Moreover, as we saw in Chapter 1 and will examine further in the next chapter, while the disadvantage experienced by social actors has long been explained by reference to the "innate" characteristics of their group (e.g., working class people are poor because they are unintelligent), under neoliberalism these meritocracy narratives come to operate in concert with **responsibilization**—individuals are tasked with managing risks and held to account when they fail to do so. What is obscured in this individualizing process, and therefore rendered invisible, is precisely the focus of the first section of this book—the social inequity and interlocking systems of oppression that determine the range of options available in the first place. Choices are constrained in unique configurations, so while individuals exercise agency, are able to make decisions, and have the capacity to resist, choices are always made in the context of economic, social, and ideological constraints that restrict what is doable—and indeed what is conceivable.

Understanding women's poverty in neoliberal times

The decline of the welfare state and the emergence of neoliberalism not only had a profound and far-reaching impact on women's everyday lives, but also conditioned the nature of and vulnerability to violence. One of the implications of neoliberalism is the unparalleled wealth disparity to which the Occupy movement's slogan "We are the 99%" drew attention. In Canada, as elsewhere, wealth is in the hands of fewer and fewer people. Internationally the richest 1 per cent now has more wealth than the rest of the world combined, and in Canada the top 1 per cent (comprised almost exclusively of white men) has greater wealth than the total held by the bottom 70 per cent of the population (more than 24.5 million people); this is markedly worse than it was even five years ago (Lambert and McInturff 2016). In short, the benefits of the economic recovery after the 2008 fiscal crisis—itself an artifact of the deregulation that characterizes neoliberalism—have not been evenly distributed, and real (adjusted for inflation) wages have fallen (Statistics Canada 2016a).

This is not coincidental: When a great deal of wealth is concentrated in a few hands it gives those individuals significant economic, social, and political power. For example, they have the capacity to lobby the same politicians to whose campaigns they generously contribute, and to mobilize expert knowledge in opposition to policies that would redistribute wealth (e.g., through fair taxation or guaranteed annual incomes) and against labour regulation that would hurt their profit margins but improve workers' wages, security, safety, and/or ability to organize (Snider 2015). Certainly it is hard to deny the influence of the wealthy few in—to name but one example—Canada's toothless climate change regulations, which are doing little to curb rising greenhouse gas levels, rapidly melting sea ice, and increasingly erratic weather patterns. How can we make sense of the disconnect between a narrative of improved economic stability and the reality of increased poverty and economic marginality for so many? Here we may consider that this elite 1 per cent of the population has the economic, social, and political capital to influence ideology, ensuring that a framing of the social and economic order that works in their interests becomes an unquestioned truth—in other words, that it becomes normative, and that the worldview of the dominant class comes to be accepted as common sense and in the interests of all. The continued sway of the disproven notion of trickledown economics (Dabla-Norris et al. 2015) is a case in point. This also reminds us that knowledge does not operate outside of power—rather, power relations constrain what is, and what is not, thinkable (Foucault 1980). These normative framings are the discourses circulated in and through the media, the education system, the government, and other political and economic apparatuses, assigning meaning to social practices and, in so doing, becoming dominant "truths" (ibid.).

As we consider gender income disparity, then, we must remain cognizant that the very policies, processes, and discourses that disadvantage women, racialized people, and the working class operate in the interests of the 1 per cent who wield such influence. Put another way, socio-economic inequity—for example, women not being paid what their work is worth; highly skilled immigrant women labouring in low-level jobs earning less than both immigrant men and Canadian-born women—"has become a perverse benefit in this upside down world" (Lambert and McInturff 2016, 1) in which the corporate bottom line is framed as being in our collective interests. Brittany Lambert and Kate McInturff (2016) go on to note that "higher levels of poverty are tolerated for the same reason—ensuring a steady supply of vulnerable people willing to take on poorly paid, precarious and unsafe work" (1). Box 2.1 provides a concrete example of how globalized neoliberal capitalism plays out in the profoundly gendered, raced, and classed exploitation of hotel housekeepers;

BOX 2.1: TOURISM'S DIRTY SECRET

In an economic climate of high competition, hotels are in a race to the bottom to scale profits at the expense of workers' rights, health and safety.... The systematic exploitation of these women is a clear example of how our economy is designed for the wealthy few, at the expense of the majority.... Contrary to the common assumption that housekeeping is domestic work and therefore easy, it is backbreaking and dangerous.... Housekeepers reported feeling invisible, undervalued and disrespected [and] are the victims of working conditions that silently destroy their health. Many are forced to exit the labour market prematurely, their bodies broken and their pockets empty. The hotel industry seems to view housekeepers as a disposable commodity. Rather than improve working conditions in a highly-competitive globalized industry, hotel companies have prioritized client satisfaction over worker safety. Beds are heavier than ever, cleaning chemicals are toxic, and stress levels and injury rates for housekeepers are rising, along with the number of rooms they must clean daily. Housekeeping is based on a room quota system, whereby housekeepers are expected to clean a certain number of rooms each day. The greater the room quota, the faster they must work, since they are not paid overtime to finish the quota.

Oxfam 2017, 2

in the Canadian context, these workers are overwhelmingly racialized immigrant women who, with the notable and telling exception of those labouring in unionized hotels, earn "poverty wages, enjoy little to no job security and face serious risks to their health and safety" (Oxfam 2017, 2).

The erosion of social security

To further elucidate the relationship between social, structural, and ideological processes and individual women's experiences we start with the erosion of social security before turning to examining the gender income gap. There is a plethora of reasons women are more likely than men to rely on social assistance programs. Some of these speak to structural impediments that exclude women from participation in paid work. For example, Canada's "colour coded labour market" (Block and Galabuzi 2011, 1) means racialized women are more likely to experience under- and unemployment; according to Statistics Canada, "visible minority women" have a 10.6 per cent unemployment rate compared to the 6.7 per cent rate for non-visible minority women (Hudon 2016). Furthermore, we see the lingering impact of colonization, generational trauma, and lack of economic opportunities in the 13.3 per cent unemployment rate of Indigenous women (Arriagada 2016). First-generation immigrant women, who may face significant obstacles (including language competence, racism, Islamophobia, limited professional networks, and a lack of recognition of their skills) experience extended periods of unemployment between (often precarious) jobs (Premji et al. 2014) and have labour force participation rates 7 per cent lower than Canadian women generally (Lambert and McInturff 2016). Trans women, in addition to discrimination and everyday transphobia, face major systemic barriers, including an inability to get employment references or academic transcripts with their correct name and gender; not surprisingly, trans women report significant underemployment (Bauer and Scheim 2015; see also Monica Forrester's narrative in Box 8.1 on page 182). Gender roles and the expectation that women assume responsibility as the primary caregiver also mean women are four times more likely to be sole-support parents than are men (Statistics Canada 2015b). Over and over again we see these and other systemic barriers (e.g., lack of federally funded childcare) constrain women's access to work and in turn perpetuate inequality.

In short, women are excluded from the paid labour market for a variety of structural factors at higher rates than are men. They are also less likely, because of unemployment reforms that deem many of those who contribute ineligible, to be able to access employment insurance (Mikkonen and Raphael 2010). Moreover, as we examine below, because women are more likely to work in non-standard precarious work they have less access to labour site protections (e.g., extended health benefits, long-term disability) should a health or personal crisis befall them. These women, who have little option but to turn to Canada's tattered social safety net, are always poor and live well below the low-income cut-off. As the quotes in Box 2.2 vividly demonstrate, the result is hunger, stigmatization, discrimination, poor health, and housing instability. The lack of secure housing, in turn, renders women exceptionally vulnerable to both interpersonal and state violence—issues considered in greater detail in Chapters 5, 6, and 11.

In the social assistance system, we see the full impact of neoliberal restructuring and ever decreasing levels of commitment to equity—the OECD (2016) ranked Canada 28th out of 35 member countries in welfare spending. As Luann Good Gingrich (2008) wryly argues, "due to 'welfare reform' launched [in the 1990s], what has been known as 'social assistance' in Canada has taken on a character that is neither 'social' in its emphasis nor 'assistance' in its delivery"

BOX 2.2: WOMEN ON SOCIAL "ASSISTANCE" SPEAK

If you have children at home and they're waiting for food or clothing to go to school, then you have to say no to them, and you also have to go to Salvation Army or Value Village to get clothing ... and then they feel less than a person at school, because their clothes are second hand and all the other children's clothes are brand new. If you don't get enough money, how do you look after your child's health, like their teeth and their everything, and then you want them to be in society, well if they're not looking like part of society, nobody accepts them.

First Nations woman, Vancouver

I was new in Canada, and at that time the money I was receiving was $402, and my rent was $750. And when I go out to search for a job, even to go for a cleaning job, they ask you for Canadian experience.

Immigrant woman, Calgary

I ended up living in a place that was extremely unsafe. I've been attacked several times. I'm scared to live there, and I have to move, and there's nothing out there. You can't even rent, you go into a rooming house and they're charging the welfare rate. My last three roommates have been strangers from the paper, and it's all resulted in disaster and them splitting and me spending all my food money to cover people's rent, or I get evicted.

Woman with disabilities, Winnipeg

Excerpts from CRIAW 2007, 3-4

(380). She recounts how the Canada Assistance Plan was retracted in 1995, since which time virtually all provincial governments have redesigned unemployment assistance into workfare programs (ibid.).

While we see the neoliberal language and emphasis on personal responsibility in the name change—welfare to workfare—it also (implicitly and explicitly) frames those who require assistance as cheats, thieves, and freeloaders. In real terms the shift from welfare to workfare is an austerity project that means fewer benefits, narrower eligibility, and punitive practices for clients who do not comply with program rules and requirements. For example, in Ontario these requirements include significant time spent searching for jobs, repeatedly proving financial eligibility, and participating in job or socialization (e.g., self-improvement) training or unpaid work placements, as well as pressure to accept the first available job (Pennisi and Baker Collins 2016). Moreover, because "work[ing] on employability does not lead to adequate employment for most clients" (Pennisi and Baker Collins 2016, 14), it locks marginalized women into cycles of part-time, precarious work.

Structural violence and women's social determinants of health

If women are subject to employment precarity, are underpaid, and must shoulder an unequal burden of domestic responsibilities (examined in more detail in the coming section of this chapter), their socio-economic position can lead to frustration and stress. Indeed, the stress of poverty, uncertainty, and overwork can be damaging to the body and can impact women's long-term health (CWF 2017b). In other words, as research on the **social determinants of health** has demonstrated, a woman's vulnerability to poor health is structurally determined (Mikkonen and Raphael 2010); at the same time, as we see repeatedly throughout this book, victimization increases women's poor health (Hutchins and Sinha 2013). The social determinants of health—which scholars have argued should be examined intersectionally and at the interpersonal as well as institutional and societal levels—include income, employment, education, housing, child development, healthcare, and social support networks (Montesanti and Thurston 2015).

The effects of poverty, lack of social support, inadequate housing, and restricted access to healthcare are among women's social determinants of health impacted by the reform of welfare. Exemplifying the violence of austerity measures (and the concurrent criminalization of poverty) is one tragedy that occurred in the wake of profound reductions and a "toughening up" of welfare under the neoliberal Mike Harris government of Ontario. In 2001, Kimberly Rogers was convicted of welfare fraud for claiming social assistance at the same time as she received student loans to cover the cost of her studies at Cambrian College in Sudbury. The penalty was six months of house arrest and three months' welfare ineligibility. Although her welfare was eventually reinstated by the courts, it was reduced, leaving her, after her rent was paid, with 18 dollars to buy food and all other necessities (Brooks 2002). In August 2001, 40 years old and eight months pregnant, suffering in the conditions described in Box 2.3, she completed suicide.

The link between socio-economic status, labour location, and health alerts us to another, broader way of thinking about gendered violence in neoliberalism—culminating in harm, excessive death, and violence that play out over years or decades. In this respect we can think about austerity as **slow violence** that "occurs gradually and out of sight, a violence of delayed destruction that is dispersed across time and space" (Nixon 2011, 3). While slow violence is examined in more detail in Chapter 8 (in relation to educational workers) and Chapter 12 (in relation to colonization), it is worth reflecting on the extent—certainly visible in Kimberly Rogers's story—to which austerity is not only implicated in violence, but is violence in its own right (Cooper and Whyte 2017).

BOX 2.3: KIMBERLY ROGERS'S CONFINEMENT

There's not much to look at out the narrow second-floor window of 286 Hazel St. in downtown Sudbury. The back yard is a grey gravel driveway strewn with litter. There's a rusted black Ford that looks as though it's been up on blocks for a decade, and a yellowed dishwasher that someone discarded years ago. And overlooking it is the ramshackle two-storey, five-tenant apartment building where Kimberly Rogers ... spent almost every hour of the past three months, after a judge ordered her confined to her home for all but three hours a week. Eight months pregnant, she was trapped inside her sweltering apartment for the duration of a record-setting heat wave. Temperatures were above 30 degrees for six days in a row the week she died.... She avoided eviction only through the grace of her landlord, and often relied on charity to pay for the prescription medication that kept her chronic depression under control. In a written affidavit submitted to the court hearing her case, Rogers described a life that spiralled downward as she was cut off from the outside world: "I have no one to turn to for money or a home if I am evicted," she said. "If I were evicted, I would have to go to a shelter. I would have no money to pay for storage of my belongings, and fear that I could lose everything." She worried about where every meal would come from, and feared for the future of her unborn child.

Excerpt from MacKinnon and Lacey 2001

Women in the paid labour market

Reliance on social assistance means a woman is poor, but participating in the paid labour market does not necessarily lift a woman out of poverty—indeed, most poor Canadians work (Oxfam 2016). Women have a long history of labour site engagement. Even as the narrative of the "angel in the house" (see Figure 2.1) idealized the "stay at home mom" and her unremunerated

FIGURE 2.1: General Steel Wares ad from *Chatelaine*, May 1946

parenting and housework, racialized and working class women were participating in paid work. Over the last 60 years, however, women have moved en masse into the labour market. Today, as noted in the Introduction, women make up 47 per cent of the Canadian labour force (compared to 21.6 per cent in 1950), participating at a rate of 82 per cent (Moyser 2017).

As we saw at the beginning of this chapter, in Canada not only is poverty gendered but there is also a significant intra- and inter-gender income gap. Since educational attainment is reliably correlated to higher income (Finnie et al. 2016), a logical assumption would be that women and racialized people have lower educational attainment. In fact, the reverse is true. Women are more likely to earn a high school diploma; are more likely to have a bachelor's degree (e.g., among young people aged 25–34, 40.7 per cent of women have bachelor degrees; this is true of only 29.1 per cent of men); and in 2016, for the first time ever, more women than men earned a doctorate (Statistics Canada 2017d). The same trend is evident when we look at the educational achievement of immigrant women; not only do 40 per cent of immigrants in the 25–64 age range have a university degree (compared to 25 per cent of the Canadian-born population), but "recent immigrant women were more likely than recent immigrant men to have a bachelor's degree or higher in 2016" (ibid., 6). Notably, while educational attainment is correlated to a decreased gender wage gap (e.g., women with post-secondary education earn 88 cents to the male dollar)—meaning working class women's gender income gap is greater than that of their upper and middle class counterparts—it increases for educated racialized, immigrant, and Indigenous women (Lambert and McInturff 2016). In short, by the conventional wisdom that education "pays off" in income, women, and in particular immigrant women, should as a group have higher incomes than men. This is evidently not the case. How can we make sense of this counterintuitive finding? In the coming section we reflect on women's disproportionate responsibility for childcare, non-standard labour arrangements and precarious work, and the gender income gap. Throughout we see how tenacious biases constrain the opportunities available to, and in turn limit the choices of, various groups of women.

Caregiving responsibilities

There is a persistent inequitable division of domestic labour in Canadian households, with women assuming disproportionate responsibility for managing and carrying out (unpaid) house, child, and elder care. It is not that men are not helping out more—they are; in fact, men's contributions have increased markedly since 1986, rising from 25 per cent of household work to 39 per cent in 2015—however, there remains a significant discrepancy with mothers doing nearly two-thirds (61 per cent) of household work and spending more time caring for children than do fathers regardless of the time they spend on paid work (Houle, Turcotte, and Wendt 2017). Interestingly, men's perception of their contribution is consistently skewed—they are considerably more likely to overestimate their share of the tasks performed (PRC 2015). In fact, the gendered domestic division of labour is stubbornly entrenched; not only do women do more work, they also assume primary responsibility for coordinating and planning the household tasks. Moreover, pivoting on the ascribed gender attribute that women are innately nurturing, they also continue to be the default caregivers. In social situations, when a child cries it is usually the mother who responds; failure to do so is met with contempt. By contrast, if the child's father engages he is praised—women are shamed as bad mothers if they are not hyperattentive; men are applauded as good fathers if they are merely observant. As psychologist Darcy Lockman (2017) notes, the unequal division of household care work reflects and ultimately reinforces structural relations of power and concomitant entrenched heteronormative gender roles: When mothers run around frantically while fathers read the news, children, who are "gender detectives," recognize power and "parse whose beliefs are more important and therefore worth adopting as their own." It is not surprising, then, that "men's attitudes about marital roles, not women's, are ultimately internalized by both their daughters and their sons" (ibid.).

Arguably the strain is increasing rather than lessening for women. Today's women not only face ever greater pressure to "do it all," but their mothering is surveilled, scrutinized, and held to an impossible ideal by themselves and others. Jeanie Keogh (2013) describes this as neoliberal responsibilization through "the perfect-mother myth." Moreover, with the dismantling of the welfare state, women's substantive burden has increased. Austerity measures have gutted many previously taken-for-granted services, including, for example, post-operative hospital care, support of seniors, and aids in schools. Removing funding does not eliminate need, it necessitates that *somebody* supply these services—either by purchasing them on the market (capitalism has certainly infiltrated this arena, as evidenced by the burgeoning service sector) or doing the work themselves, thereby "subsidiz[ing] the [Canadian] economy to the tune of approximately $192 billion per year" (Oxfam 2016, 11). Overwhelmingly it continues to be women who take on this responsibility, and while the burden of stepping up and filling the gaps in our increasingly frayed social safety net is felt more profoundly by poor women who lack financial resources, it impacts all women.

What are the implications of our society's reliance on women's unremunerated care work and the ensuing double day? It means women are less able to participate in labour organizing and, as we see in Chapter 3, in political engagement. It may hinder women's ability to invest in their career. The implications are clear and quantifiable: Canadian women with children earn 5 per cent less than women without children (Moyser 2017). The high cost Canadian mothers pay—sacrificing their long-term economic security—is a direct outcome of state policies. Looking internationally, we see that those countries where the gender income gap is the lowest are also countries where fulsome national childcare programs signal that the well-being of children (and the generational reproduction of the labour force) is a societal responsibility, not something to be downloaded onto mothers. Taking care of children and facilitating women's full integration into the paid labour market also makes good fiscal sense—universal access to low-fee childcare in Québec resulted in a 3.8 per cent increase in women's employment and raised Québec's GDP by 1.7 per cent (Oxfam 2016).

Non-standard and precarious work

We now turn to consider the relationship between the organization of women's work and their economic vulnerability. Neoliberal restructuring has fundamentally shifted the way we work, moving us away from the standard employment relationship (SER). This conventional approach calls to mind the image of a factory worker who brings his lunch to work in a metal lunchbox, is a proud union member who enjoys the benefits (including a living wage) organized labour has fought for and won, and retires with a pension after working his entire career for the same company. The SER is associated with job security and full-time, continuous employment with one employer that takes place on the employer's premises and under their direct supervision (e.g., not a contractual arrangement). In short, the SER is a year-round, 40 hours per week, 9-to-5 job (Vosko and Clark 2009). It is a model of work that is quickly disappearing. In its place we have non-standard labour: poorly paid part-time, seasonal, temporary, and/or precarious work sometimes masquerading as self-employment or contract work (OFL 2016). Not surprisingly this "gig" labour model, which allows employers to bring people into work only when they absolutely require them (and send them home early), pay low wages, and avoid the expense of benefits (e.g., health insurance, pensions) has been welcomed by those who own the means of production. For businesses, this access to a contingency workforce reduces their financial risks by allowing them to pay "lower wages and benefit costs during business downturns while also reducing their vulnerability to unfair dismissal lawsuits"; it is a neoliberal model that shifts "the burden of economic risk onto workers" (Friedman 2014, 171) at the same time as it de facto excludes workers from employment-based social security protections (e.g., employment insurance) that were developed in the context of the post-Depression welfare era with the SER in mind. All of which, of course, means these workers are in a perpetual state of insecurity and in turn are more likely to accept poor working conditions, harassment, and economic exploitation.

Who are these precarious workers? Many work in the service sector, where women workers cluster (Moyser 2017). They are servers, working late into the night at cafés, who can do little to guarantee a steady income because of the inconsistency of shift work and the unpredictability of gratuities (not to mention the potential for sexual harassment, which is further detailed in Chapter 10). They are store clerks, standing on their feet all day, whose managers ensure they always work slightly fewer hours than needed to qualify for full-time employment, thereby denying them the benefits that status would confer. They are on-call nurses, whose schedules routinely flip between night and day shifts, wreaking havoc on their bodies, and who labour in a stressful and hierarchical system in which they are disrespected not only by their patients but also by their colleagues and superiors (see Chapters 7 and 8). They are the non-unionized hotel housekeepers discussed in Box 2.1, whose scheduled shifts are routinely cancelled and who find themselves working harder, skipping their entitled breaks, and avoiding complaining for fear of being given fewer hours, or none at all (Oxfam 2016). Disproportionately, they are women.

The gendered racialized division of labour

Even though the labour market has moved away from the SER, the gender contract on which it relied—in which women took care of the children and home while men worked to support the family—has been much slower to change (Vosko and Clark 2009). We see this in the impact of both the lack of state-funded childcare and gendered care responsibilities; not only are women three times as likely as men to work part time, they are 19 times more likely to do so because of childcare obligations (Lambert and McInturff 2016). For these women workers their employment precarity engenders particular stress. On a day-to-day basis, for example, it may necessitate juggling childcare and family obligations (in a context where work hours are irregular), strategizing to make ends meet (without knowing exactly what one's pay will be), and navigating strained family life (where members see little of each other). Moreover, these workers do not meet the minimum thresholds for employment insurance. The net effect is women trapped in cycles of poverty: If they are ill there is neither sick leave nor long-term disability, and if they get pregnant they do not have access to parental leave (forcing them to turn to inadequate social assistance). Those who lose their job are not able to hold out for better, more secure employment, and when they retire there is no defined pension or savings upon which to rely.

Moreover, the rise of precarious employment has impacted racialized and immigrant women in particularly significant ways. One in four Canadian workers are immigrants (Statistics Canada 2017e); these im/migrants, most especially if they are racialized, are more likely than their Canadian-born counterparts "to end up in precarious, low-wage jobs … due to employers' discomfort with international experience and qualifications, and/or having different levels of language proficiency, and/or an absence of Canadian work experience (often nothing more than a proxy for xenophobia)" (Flecker 2016, 27). As a result, "internationally educated female immigrants (doctors, psychologists, teachers, engineers, forestry experts, chartered accountants, etc.) are ending up in low-paying gendered occupations such as hotel room attendants, personal support workers, daycare assistants, servers at fast food chains, front-line community workers, and office clerks" (Premji et al. 2014, 136). This is "what post-colonial feminists refer to as the 'racialized gendered division of labour' in which low-wage, socially undervalued or 'unproductive' work, and precarious types of jobs are systematically offloaded to women, particularly im/migrant women and women from racialized backgrounds" (ibid., 136). As we see in Chapter 7, in addition to being relegated to precarious work, racialized and im/migrant women experience systemic discrimination, racism, and microaggressions at the workplace as well.

The gender pay gap

So far we have examined the gender income gap considering the roles of women's childcare responsibilities, non-standard labour arrangements, and persistent structural biases. But what happens when we control for some of these variables and compare only those workers who are employed full time and year round? Doing so reveals that women still earn considerably less—26 per cent less—than men, or 74 cents to the male dollar (CWF 2017a). Disturbingly, it seems that women have hit a brick wall—in 2009 women earned 74.4 cents to the male dollar (Oxfam 2016). We can understand this by considering occupational segregation, gender pay bias, sexism and discrimination, and the assault on organized labour.

The Canadian labour force continues to be stubbornly gender segregated—divided into "women's jobs" and "men's jobs." Research consistently indicates that "women work in a narrower range of occupations than men and have high representation in the 20 lowest-paid occupations. About two-thirds of the female work force are concentrated in teaching, nursing, and health care, office and administrative work, and sales and service industries" (CWF 2017a, 2). Quite simply, women continue to work in jobs (care and service work) that are consistent with dominant gender stereotypes. How can we understand this? Gender stereotypes are telling in this regard and highlight how traditional, dichotomous notions of gender characterize women as naturally nurturing, fragile, and compassionate, while men are comparatively viewed as physically stronger, more rational, and with a greater propensity for math and science. Gender roles not only differentiate between women's and men's (presumed) skills and abilities, but their perpetual reiteration through cultural institutions also shapes individuals' self-perceptions, and in turn their choice of vocation (Weedon 1987). Moreover, female-dominated occupations (in both working class and middle class jobs, although more strikingly so in the former) are consistently less well paid. For example, a 2016 Oxfam report noted that the median annual wage for truck drivers (97 per cent of whom are men) is $45,417, while early childcare workers (97 per cent of whom are women) make $25,334. Since both sets of workers perform "important and challenging tasks" the explanation appears to lie in the resemblance to emotional labour and traditional care work that women are expected to provide for free; by extension it is not "real" or skilled work (Oxfam 2016, 8). This may, in part, explain why women make up 60 per cent of workers earning minimum wage—which, in every jurisdiction in Canada, is insufficient to meet life's basic necessities (ibid.). That this group disproportionately comprises single, racialized, and immigrant women provides a partial explanation for why racialized women experience an even greater pay gap.

Even after we factor in occupational gender segregation and the devaluation of women's paid work, a large portion of the wage gap remains: Women earn less than men in 469 of the 500 occupations monitored by Statistics Canada (Oxfam 2016). A large-scale study by Ross Finnie and his colleagues (2016) that used tax records from 2005 to 2013 to track the labour market outcomes of college and university graduates in four provinces found that the relatively small gender income gap evident upon graduation, with men earning $2,800 more than women, ballooned to $27,300 (44 per cent more) eight years later. A similar, if even more dramatic, pattern was evident among college graduates: Men earned $5,500 more than women upon graduation; eight years later it was $23,600, a staggering 56 per cent more (ibid.). A portion of this stark gender wage gap can be explained by the fact that women are more likely to take time off paid work to have and raise children and may prioritize family responsibilities over their career; that is, however, at best a partial explanation. Indeed, 10–15 per cent of the gap can be attributed to discrimination (CWF 2017a). Men are offered better starting salaries, higher-profile assignments, and faster rates of promotion than are women (Lambert and McInturff 2016); this gendered "glass escalator" applies even in female-dominated occupations (e.g., teaching, nursing) (Moyser 2017, 30). Here we, once again, come back to gender roles: All too often women's (potential and real) child-bearing and caring responsibilities are used to justify the failure to offer women the same career-furthering opportunities as men. The result: Not only are women over-represented in low-paying precarious work, they are under-represented among uppermost earners, of whom they make up just one in four of the top 5 per cent (Statistics Canada 2014).

These examples of gender-based discrimination demonstrate that labour and employment laws are failing to address "deep systemic discrimination" and neither protect women workers nor "ensure that they have a true voice in the conditions of their work" (OFL 2016). This draws our attention to the importance of organized labour. Research has consistently affirmed the union advantage. Organized labour affords workers a mechanism through which to challenge unfair labour practices (including gender discrimination and work-place violence) and assert their rights. Women workers in unionized jobs not only earn more, they also enjoy greater benefits, more job security (OFL 2016), and a significantly reduced gender wage gap (Lambert and McInturff 2016). Here again, however, we see how neoliberal laws and policies—in this case the assault on organized labour—operate in the interests of capital and against the interests of workers. For example, back-to-work legislation (that effectively denies workers the right to remove their labour power) is increas-ingly common; between 1986 and 2016, 90 pieces of back-to-work legislation were passed by the federal (19) and provincial (71) governments; these laws also often impose wage settlements (CFLR 2016).

Resistance: Making visible the value of women's contributions

The constraints examined in this chapter restrict not only women's economic power but also condition their ability to resist. This has not, however, stopped women from contesting the status quo. One remarkable example of a creative, collective, and effective action occurred on October 24, 1975, when 90 per cent of Iceland's women went on strike to protest the invisibilization of their economic and household contributions and the gender wage gap. Women marked the day, known as the Women's Day Off, by taking to the streets to demand equal rights (see Figure 2.2) and collectively withdrew their labour power—they did not go to their jobs, do housework, or mind their children. They made their point: "Banks, factories and some shops had to close, as did schools and nurseries—leaving many fathers with no choice but to take their children to work. There were reports of men arming themselves with sweets and colouring pencils to entertain the crowds of overexcited children in their workplaces. Sausages—easy to cook and popular with children—were in such demand the shops sold out" (Brewer 2015). The strike brought about increased awareness of the importance

FIGURE 2.2: Iceland's Women's Day Off, 1975

of women's work in all spheres of society, and, slowly, Iceland became a more equitable country: Women members of Parliament went from 3 in 1975 to 28 (out of 63) in 2015; they have elected a woman president and prime minister; and Iceland is at the top of the World Economic Forum's Global Gender Gap Index, in which Canada placed 35th in 2016 (Brewer 2015; WEF 2016). That said, even in Iceland women's socio-economic position continues to be hindered by gender norms and the factors explored in this chapter: enduring gender biases in workplaces, women's higher representation in part-time work, and women "choosing" lower-paid professions (Friedman 2016). Accordingly, in 2017 Iceland became the first country to introduce legislation ensuring that companies with over 25 employees must verify that workers are paid equally regardless of gender, ethnicity, sexuality, or nationality (Chapman 2017).

Iceland is not the only country where women have gone on strike in an effort to exert political power. Contrary to governance feminist Catharine MacKinnon's (1982) assertion that women's sexuality is "that which is most one's own, yet most taken away" (515), Kenyan Member of Parliament Mishi Mboko called on fellow women to deny their husbands sex until they registered to vote in the 2017 federal election, echoing the tactics of a 2009 week-long sex strike coordinated by a coalition of feminist organizations against civil unrest

(Pasha-Robinson 2017). Women also organized a sex strike in Liberia in 2003 to protest the civil war; and Colombia's Strike of Crossed Legs, through which women voiced their objections to violence, precipitated a crime drop of 26.5 per cent (Garau 2017). Like Iceland's Women's Day Off, such dramatic acts of resistance are powerful in part because they make a direct and poignant link between the personal and the political.

Concluding reflections

Throughout this chapter we have examined some of the ways neoliberal economic policies and labour relations, austerity measures, a disintegrating social safety net, and narratives of personal responsibility operate in relation to gender. We have also seen that the continued framing of women as (naturally) nurturing impacts women's share of domestic labour and childcare and restricts their employment options and opportunities. And we have seen the way socialization channels girls and young women into lower-paying professions in care work, education, and the service sector—economically and socially undervalued, gender appropriate "women's work." These interconnections lay bare the dialectical and mutually reinforcing relationship between economic and gender inequality (Lambert and McInturff 2016). Women's resistance and (albeit limited) gains, as well as their continuing struggles with the socio-economic aspects of inequality explored in this chapter, unfold in a broader crisis that "has its roots in a market fundamentalist narrative that insists that economic growth only comes from reducing public services and leaving markets to their own devices. However it is precisely these austerity policies that exacerbate gender inequality rather than narrow it" (Lambert and McInturff 2016, 2).

In real terms women's lack of economic power increases, as we see throughout this book, the risk of interpersonal, workplace, and state violence at the same time as a woman's particular socio-economic positioning and intersecting identities shape her vulnerability, the nature of the violence she experiences, and the options at her disposal to avoid or resist violence. As we see in subsequent chapters these relationships are neither linear nor simple; they are, however, pervasive. For example, women who are poor and reliant on public transit are exposed to more everyday intrusions on the street (Chapter 4); racialized women experience not only sexual harassment but also microaggressions at work at the same time as their ability to resist by resigning is undermined by their (constrained) access to employment (Chapter 7); low income is correlated to higher rates of sexual violence (Chapter 5); Indigenous women, one of the most economically disadvantaged populations in Canada, experience high rates of violence by the state and its agents but may well lack the resources to challenge those in authority (Chapters 11 and 12); im/migrant women whose labour is invisibilized are constrained in their ability to flee abusive worksites for fear of deportation (Chapter 9); working class women labouring in call centres tolerate verbal abuse, fearful that poor customer reviews will jeopardize their jobs (Chapter 8); mandated "sexy" dress codes in working class "feminine" occupations like waitressing increase women workers' vulnerability to sexual harassment (Chapter 10); and a woman's ability to leave an abusive partner is shaped by the resources at her disposal and the costs of leaving (e.g., whether she and her children will be obliged to turn to social assistance; Chapter 6).

The coming chapter considers the nexus of discourse, power, and knowledge that perpetuates the socio-economic constraints on women detailed in this chapter. As we will see, women's ability to address the structural context in which gendered violence from the state, from employers, from clients, from partners, and from peers emerges is restricted by mechanisms and narratives that constitute, regulate, and impede women's political representation and ability to influence law, the media, the corporate realm, and the sciences—the very apparatuses through which inequality and violence are reinforced and normalized.

EXERCISE: GENDERED ROLES AND RESPONSIBILITIES

Get into groups of 5–6 learners.

Each learner presents the following to the group:

- What chores are you responsible for at home?
- What kind of job do you have or have you had?
  - How much care or emotional work does/did the job entail?
  - Is/was there an official or unofficial dress code? Is/was it gendered?
- What is/was the gender of your co-workers? Your boss?
- What career to do you aspire to? Why?
  - Do you think your biological sex and gender presentation will help or hinder you in your career? Why/why not?

As a group reflect on the ways gender shapes our roles, responsibilities, and aspirations.

CHAPTER 3

REGULATORY DISCOURSES AND REPRESENTATION: HOW WOMEN ARE "KNOWN"

As we saw in the Introduction, one way women are known is as victims—of physical violence, of sexual violence, of men. Evidently the heart-wrenching imagery of the bruised and battered woman, a representation initially produced by mainstream feminist scholars and activists raising awareness about violence against women, is well-established. It has not, however, displaced other familiar tropes—the Madonna, the whore, the hysteric—each with its own set of assumptions about what women do, how they look, who they are. How do women navigate these archetypes? How do they influence women's presentation of self? What does it mean for the way women's behaviour and appearance are read? In order to set the stage for substantive elaboration of their impact on women, this chapter examines the power relations through which these conflicting cultural messages are established, reproduced, and come to exert influence. To this end this chapter explores how stubborn "truths" (stereotypes and myths) about women, including gender and sexual scripts, significantly and unrelentingly shape how women are perceived, represented, and treated—how women are *known*.

Conceptual tools: Power/knowledge and gender tropes

As Michel Foucault (1980) famously argued, knowledge and power are profoundly interrelated. Knowledge does not operate outside of power—indeed, normative framing and assumed "truths" speak to power relations that constrain what is, and what is not, thinkable. We see the power/knowledge nexus in one of the fundamental organizing principles of our society: gender. How else can we explain that ascribed characteristics continue to be justified on the basis of biological factors, including genitalia? For example, the ability to give birth is biologically determined, but the assumption that women are naturally nurturing is a social construct without scientific validity—quite simply, there are no intrinsic or essential gender characteristics (Fine 2017).

It would appear that decades of feminist activism and scholarship have failed to dislodge the deeply entrenched dualism—the binary framing of women as the opposite sex (e.g., men are rational; women emotional). Similarly, while women are no longer expected to be virgins upon marriage, the regulation of women's sexuality (a central tenant of **patriarchy**) endures. We see this in the Madonna/whore dichotomy that divides women into "good girls" and "bad girls"; the high price women pay for flaunting convention ensures widespread conformity—slut shaming remains a powerful gender-regulating tool.

Recognizing the dialectic relationship between knowledge and power helps us understand the persistence of gender tropes and fallacious myths. Knowledge is produced through **discourses**; discourses are more than groups of signs or statements—they are simultaneously "practices that systematically form the objects of which they speak" (Foucault 1972, 49). In this manner, discourse gives meaning to social practices. Discourses become dominant, or normative, when they are validated and circulate through relations of power—they are reproduced in and through political and economic apparatuses (e.g., the media, the medical and psy-professions, the legal system) as truths, dominant knowledges that in turn support the power relations through which they were constituted (Foucault 1979; 1980).

A critical take on knowledge alerts us to the regulatory nature of the norm and pushes us to reflect upon the ways that framing something as normal not only renders it an unquestioned truth but also defines its opposite—the deviant, the abnormal, that which requires intervention (Brock 2003). Here we can think about the ways stereotypes underpin and legitimate stigma (Goffman 1963). Stereotypes are precisely the common "truths" emanating from the perspective of those with the ability to name and define the "other." Bearing in mind the interplay between knowledge and power we can appreciate that "individual experiences of marginalized persons may not be incorporated into the body of accepted knowledge, particularly if such experiences challenge existing structures of power and social policies" (Hannem 2012, 16). In other words, stereotypes and the myths that support them, which may not be true in the empirical sense, are nonetheless real in their consequences. We begin by examining the way gendered stereotypes permeate medical discourse, practice, and policy before turning to consider law, the media, business, discipline, and politics.

Medicalization and the pathologization of women

Medicine provides a number of striking examples of how women are framed in terms of their deviations from the male norm—including through ascriptions of female infirmity or "craziness" that invisibilize social determinants of ill health, the medicalization of pregnancy and childbirth, and the perception of women as controlled by their hormones. To understand how deeply the framing and labelling of women as *ab*normal or deviant (in other words, **deviantiza-tion**) is embedded in cultural understandings of women, we turn back to the nineteenth century, a period when women were "known," through mutually reinforcing scientific, philosophical, and medical discourses, to be physically weak, overly emotional, and cognitively limited.

In the mid-nineteenth century a common diagnosis made by (virtu-ally always male) medical professionals was hysteria (derived from the Greek word for uterus, *hysteros*), a catch-all term applied to women's physical and psychological ailments and indeed any behaviour perceived as aberrant in its divergence from women's gender role expectations of domesticity (Hepworth and Griffin 1990). Some 50 years later the Western feminine ideal of thinness emerged, couched in a discourse of female emancipation articulated through athleticism, sexuality, androgyny, and independence (ibid.). Frustrated with their inability to embody the new ideal beauty or actually feel liberated, some women responded through extreme dieting, which came to be defined as anorexia nervosa (Vandereycken 1993; Hepworth and Griffin 1990). Julie Hepworth and Christine Griffin (1990) situate the discovery of anorexia in the Western framing of women as irrational and politically and sexually passive, based on its occurrence among those for whom these characteristics were imagined to be natural: white middle and upper class women. Through this lens, young women suffering from anorexia—just as those deemed to be suffering from hysteria—were viewed as typically feminine and pathologi-cally emotional. In addition to understanding anorexia as a personal failing (and thus overlooking the social context of its emergence), male medical professionals also viewed it as a moral defect. In response they prescribed treatment consisting of social segregation, institutionalization, and "education in moral rectitude" (ibid., 331). Contemporary media coverage continues to characterize extreme thinness (or "excessive" body weight) as a moral defect or proof of mental instability; for example, female celebrities, in addition to being shamed for being "too fat" (see Jennifer Aniston's quote on page 84), are demonized for being "too thin."

Women's bodies continue to be pathologized and regulated in contem-porary medicine; one clear example is the framing of premenstrual syndrome (PMS). While the cramping, discomfort, and bloating some women experi-ence the week prior to the onset of their menses is physiological, the associated moodiness and irritability is a specifically *Western* cultural phenomenon (Ussher 2012). Indeed "after five decades of research, there's no strong consensus on the definition, the cause, the treatment, or even the existence of PMS," yet it is "real" in Canadian society (De Luca 2014); indeed, the fifth edition of the *Diagnostic and Statistical Manual of Mental Disorders* (DSM-V) by the American Psychiatric Association now lists premenstrual dysphoric disorder (PMDD) (Browne 2015). Feminists have argued, however, that perhaps "premenstrual emotions are not a sign of women's madness. They are an understandable reaction to the stresses and strains of life … expressed at a time of the month when it's acceptable for women to be angry" (Ussher 2012). In this regard, Tamara Browne (2015) argues that PMDD is simply an updated diagnosis of hysteria that, along with PMS, shifts blame for a woman's oppressive circumstances (e.g., intimate partner violence) away from the victimizer and onto the woman herself, implying that she, not he, requires intervention.

The medico-scientific pathologization of menstruation also plays a role in criminal justice processes. In Canada, defence arguments have invoked menopause or postpartum depression; severe PMS has also been used to mitigate sentencing for women convicted of murder, effectively "support[ing] the idea that hormonal fluctuations can transform women into violent criminals" (Browne 2015, 316). The corollary is that women "cannot be trusted in positions of responsibility" (ibid., 317). Browne suspects PMDD will lead to comparable outcomes. Similarly, infanticide, a gender-specific offence (which is also a defence against the more serious crime of murder) certainly pivots on the (potential) pathology of women after childbirth. As defined in section 233 of the *Criminal Code*, infanticide occurs when the birth mother causes the death of her child within the first year of its life at a time when "she is not fully recovered from the effects of giving birth to the child and by reason thereof or of the effect of lactation … her mind is then disturbed." As Kirsten Kramer (2014) notes, the law came into effect in 1922, marking a recognition of the social context in which unwed mothers killed their infants to both protect their own reputations and to shield the child from the life of hardship endemic to being illegitimate; as such, the law created a space to read in social context as a mitigating factor, albeit one that nonetheless discursively affirmed women's fragile mental stability. The enmeshing of medical and legal discourses that pathologize women alerts us to their mutually constitutive regulatory power (Foucault 1979); what Carol Smart (1989) calls the "medico–legal discourse" (112).

Gender norms and the law: Constituting women

Smart (1989) famously applied Foucault's ideas to argue that the law disqualifies women's experiences; she demonstrated that the law's claim to truth, which "is indivisible from [its] exercise of power" (11), operates to reproduce patriarchal gender relations. Building on Mary Eaton's assertion that the law invariably constructs women in relation to men—"as family members, wives, divorcees, mothers, or daughters" (203)—Smart (1990) argued that the sexed body of woman is perpetually and dichotomously reproduced in law. In the above-noted binary framing, rationality, objectivity, culture, activity, and truth are associated with men and coded as masculine, while their opposites, emotionality, subjectivity, nature, passivity, and falsehood, are associated with women and coded as feminine. Thus, just as we see in the pathologization of women through medical discourse, law deviantizes and punishes women both for transgressing normative expectations of feminine conduct and for engaging in stereotypically feminine behaviours. Like Foucault (1979), Smart (1990) argues the law reaffirms other dominant (legitimated) discourses with which it interacts and is mutually constituted. One example she gives in this regard is that the law accepts the discourses of medicine and the psy-professions, and in so doing extends into, surveils, and regulates the lives of citizens. As Chapter 2 examines in greater detail, the interplay of law with medicine and psychology can significantly impact women in prison, who are disproportionately disciplined for "acting out" (i.e., exhibiting unsubmissive and therefore decidedly unfeminine behaviours), classified as mentally ill, isolated, and forcibly medicated.

Smart (1989; 1990) illustrates her argument that woman's sexed body is reproduced in law by analyzing rape trials, revealing how they construct women's sexuality as a valuable possession that men desire but one that is enjoyed only by those women who shirk their moral responsibilities—in other words by "bad" women. Further, Smart argues that consent is understood dichotomously, which excludes coercion or the overstepping of negotiated boundaries from consideration. Although laws relating to sexual assault and legal definitions of consent have changed over the past 30 years (see Chapter 5), these changes are not resulting in different outcomes. This is perhaps not surprising given the significant influence of gender tropes on Canadian culture and jurisprudence (Comack and Balfour 2004).

Rape myths (detailed in Box 5.2 on page 118), like other myths and stereotypes about women examined in this book—including women in abusive relationships, sex workers, and criminalized women—play out intersectionally. For example, in Chapter 1 we saw that the negative stereotype of Indigenous women as "dissolute, dangerous, and sinister" was created and propagated by the colonial Canadian state in the late 1800s to deflect responsibility from the state and its agents for violence and disease (Carter 1993, 148). These tropes live on not only in the everyday lives of Indigenous women, but also play out in the judicial arena. A deplorable example is the case of Cindy Gladue, a woman who bled to death in an Edmonton motel as the result of an 11-centimetre wound to her vagina. Since Gladue was deceased she could not testify, but her preserved pelvis, which had been cut off from the rest of her body in the autopsy, was admitted as evidence. Advocates for Indigenous and sex worker rights argued that this was the ultimate humiliation and would never have happened if Gladue had not been an Indigenous woman who earned money through the provision of sexual services (DiManno 2015). While the use of Gladue's dissected body for evidence is overtly and literally dehumanizing, the legal proceedings powerfully reinforced deeply problematic framings of Indigenous women as unchaste and thus unrapable. Although the Alberta Court of Appeal overturned the decision and ordered a new trial in 2017 (see Chapter 5 for more on this case), the accused, Bradley Barton, was initially acquitted of first degree murder—jurors concluded that the sex was rough but consensual and that Barton was not trying to kill Gladue (*R. v. Barton* 2017). Here we see how stereotypes about Indigenous women (e.g., witnesses, defence, and Crown council repeatedly referred to Gladue as a "native" girl or woman; ibid. at para 124) and sex workers intersect in a trope of disposability that made jurors unable to see Gladue as a victim; the focus on her income-generating activities reproduced a narrative linking her "risky lifestyle" to her victimization, framing her as a poor neoliberal subject.

Gender and sexual scripts in the media

The media focus on Cindy Gladue's sex work, like the responsibilization in the media framing of the street-based sex workers victimized by serial killer Robert Pickton as "drugged, dazed, deviant, dissolute, and corrupted" (Hugill 2010, 131), speaks to the complexity of power/knowledge by alerting us to the mutually reinforcing relationship between the media and the legal system. Whereas stereotypes and gendered representations can be obvious in news coverage of criminalized and/or victimized women, they also appear in gender and sexual scripts that function to regulate women's presentation of self (i.e., appearance, conduct).

Monica Longmore (1998) describes **scripts** as providing guidelines for people's performances in specific social contexts. Scripts can be understood as normative because they inform both the performance and interpretation of social roles. In turn, normative gender roles include **sexual scripts**, which William Simon and John Gagnon (1986) describe as cultural guidelines dictating how a (hetero)sexual encounter should play out. Gender and sexual scripts permeated cultural imagery long before contemporary media—John Berger (1972) has observed that in historical Western paintings, as in contemporary advertising, "*men act* and *women appear*" (47, emphasis in original). These presentations reflect (hetero)sexual scripts of masculine sexual aggressiveness (activity), and feminine timidity (not initiating) and beauty (presence rather than action). Simon and Gagnon (1986) further argue that scripted is not merely a synonym for learned behaviour but speaks to active engagement. This opens up the possibility of resistance, contestation, and subversion at the same time as it acknowledges that when conformity to normative sexual scripts elicits desire, those scripts—and relatedly, dichotomous gender roles—are reproduced.

Images of gender norms are inescapable; we are bombarded with representations of how women should look and how they should act—on television, in magazines, in movies. The pervasiveness of these images reminds us of the media's influence in entrenching normative expectations. We can, for example, consider how gender and sexual scripts pervade popular women's magazines: A woman is expected to be fit; be sexy in a fashionable and age-appropriate manner; please her man; be available and dedicated to her children; have a career but also practise conventional homemaking skills of cooking, baking, and crafting. In the 1970s, feminist scholars turned their attention to films, examining "images of woman under patriarchal society in which femininity and sexuality were displaced and distorted misogynistically" (Mulvey 2015, 25). Alongside the ubiquity of idealized representations is the narrowing and symbolic erasure of women. For example, the roles available to women on television and in movies are limited. The Bechdel Test, based on a 1985 cartoon strip by Alison Bechdel, has become a popular tool for assessing women's representation in film. To pass this test a film needs to have at least two female characters who talk to each other about something besides a man (Bechdel 1985). Thirty years after it was first introduced few films pass what appears to be a rather low bar; women comprised only 29 per cent of leading roles in the top Hollywood films of 2016, and only 32 per cent of all speaking roles (Lauzen 2017). As Martha Lauzen (2017) has observed, male characters are more often shown at work and as leaders; women appear in supporting roles to male heroes, reproducing the gendered ascription of leadership qualities (a matter explored below). This starts early: In 22 out of 30 Disney films examined men talk more, even when the movie features a female lead (Anderson and Daniels 2016). Moreover, women who are active protagonists—strong, smart, and empowered superheroes, for example—are still hypersexualized, sport completely inappropriate attire (e.g., high-heeled boots) and, unlike male heroes (or indeed any known fighting style), often conquer the villain using the "between-the-legs-takedown" (Nero 2017).

The response to the remake of the classic 1980s movie *Ghostbusters* that cast women in the title roles is telling. Even before it was released it was the object of derision, suggesting "the idea of a female cast taking up the mantle of a very male film series is just somehow wrong" (Sims 2016). Moreover, the egregious Twitter campaign of body shaming, homophobic, and racist abuse directed at Leslie Jones following the movie's release (Jenkins 2016) alerts us to the way movies not only limit the portrayal of women to the narrow aesthetic of slim, white, and youthful but also erase women of colour and reproduce racist stereotypes. In this respect one critique of the Bechdel Test is that it "disregards which women are granted dialogue, thus ignoring the silencing of women of colour, women of a 'certain age,' and those for whom English is not a first language" (O'Meara 2016, 1121). Indeed, a survey of the top 100 films of 2016 revealed racialized women to be under-represented: Asian women appeared in 6 per cent of movie roles, Black women in 14 per cent, and Latina women in just 3 per cent (Lauzen 2017). Further reflecting dominant beauty standards, women featured in film are also generally younger than men (Lauzen 2017), and speaking roles dip dramatically for women over 40 (Anderson and Daniels 2016).

Beauty remains important—and gendered—outside the film frame as well. Although some actors have begun to vocalize criticisms about the sexist focus on what they are wearing on the red carpet (O'Meara 2016), Hollywood performers continue to be featured in magazines and other entertainment media as little more than emblems of female beauty. Normative representations of women also permeate other facets of the media, including the news. On television newscasts, many female broadcasters conform to industry and normative beauty expectations: They wear shift dresses or feminized suits and (regardless of ethnicity) have long, silky hair. These women embody the professional feminine aesthetic: polished, moderately sexy, expensive, and therefore "classy."

Women are also collectively deviantized in the media backlash against feminism. At the same time as feminism is appropriated as a marketing tool in the beauty and fashion industries (see Chapter 10), the media is also a site through which anti-feminist narratives are spread. This messaging is articulated through a discourse of masculinity in crisis, frames feminism as no longer necessary (i.e., equality has been achieved), and, echoing the pathologization of women as overly emotional, dismisses feminists as too intense or aggressive (Silva and Mendes 2015). All too often, news coverage of feminist resistance focuses on the spectacle (e.g., protest) rather than the message (ibid.).

Women in business and the gendering of leadership

Given the representations examined in this chapter—of women as supporting characters, objects of beauty, or risky choice makers—it is not surprising that they are not "known" to be leaders in business or politics. Although, as we saw in Chapter 2, gender roles condition women's access to the labour market, women's economic and political success is additionally undermined through normative conceptions of leadership. There has been some progress among Fortune 500 companies—in which notions of leadership appear to remain strongly tied to the male archetype—with women occupying 22 (4.4 per cent) CEO positions in 2017, nearly a 12-fold increase from just 2 positions 20 years earlier (*Catalyst* 2017). We can make sense of this limited progress by examining the lasting relationship between masculinity and organizational authority that has long justified (white) men's over-representation in the managerial ranks (Collinson and Hearn 1996; Meister, Sinclair, and Jehn 2017). We see this in the qualities sought in corporate managers: "authoritarian, paternalistic, entrepreneurial, careerist, instrumental, ruthless, rational, unemotional and distant" (Whitehead 2002, 129). These attributes are so powerfully associated with masculinity that women's leadership qualities are read as gender deviant or not recognized at all. If women adopt agentic interpersonal tactics at work, akin to the above-mentioned masculine leadership style, their behaviour is read as transgressing gender norms and risks backlash (Smith et al. 2013)—in other words, they are likely to be perceived as "bossy." In male-dominated professions such as engineering, finance, and construction, women leaders are subjected to more scrutiny and stereotyping—as "battle axes" or "dragon ladies," for example—than men (Meister et al. 2017). As a result women, especially those from racialized and immigrant communities, continue to be under-represented in organizational leadership positions.

The progress that (some) women have made in reaching the upper echelons of organizational power begs the question: Why are these women seemingly unable to make a meaningful difference in dominant conceptions of leadership? Here Foucault's (1980) elicitation of the relationships between power, knowledge, and discourse is useful. The wealthy 1 per cent shape normative discourse through ownership of and advertising in the media; given the small proportion of women corporate leaders, and the framing of female leadership as oxymoronic, it becomes evident that the majority of this already small sliver of the population consists of privileged (white) men. For example, in the American film industry in 2017, "women comprised 18% of all directors, writers, producers, executive producers, editors, and cinematographers working on the top 250 domestic grossing films ... virtually unchanged from the percentage achieved in 1998" (Lauzen 2018, 1). Another example of the perpetuation of normative constructions of leadership is that men are more frequently referred to as sources and experts in news reporting, another industry that continues to be dominated by male leadership, decision making, networking, and ownership (Gross 2010).

Discipline: Navigating gender and class

Up to this point we have examined the representations—and absences—of women in medicine, law, business, and media. Recognizing that gender is not simply an imposed category but an interactionally realized process, we now turn to think about how women conduct themselves in such a way as to meet normative expectations while positioning themselves favourably in regard to gender tropes and myths. How can we understand the ways women act upon themselves to ensure they appear adequately feminine but not "too sexy" and, above all, "good" (virtuous) women? In other words, how do we, as social actors, "do gender" (West and Zimmerman 1987, 126)? And do our social performances, adapted in relation to gender and other scripts, reify these categories? One way to think about women's engagement and compliance is through the lens of disciplinary power.

Foucault (1979) described **disciplinary power** as targeting the soul to render the body docile in the interests of harnessing its productive value. We can look at schools as mechanisms of disciplinary power in which students' activities are determined, controlled, and tightly scheduled, and the students themselves are enclosed, partitioned, surveilled, hierarchically classified, rewarded or sanctioned, and perpetually evaluated in relation to the norm (the standard). Through the ongoing subjection of overt and suspected surveillance, the expectations are internalized, and disciplinary power eventually fosters self-discipline (ibid.). In this respect discipline inevitably entails both surveillance (by others) and self-regulation (in public and in private). Sandra Lee Bartky (1997) applies the concept of disciplinary power to women's negotiation of cultural expectations. Highlighting the extent of its reach, Bartky argues that even the movement of women's bodies is disciplined: They take up little physical space, avoid unabashed gazing, and smile more often than men. She illustrates the influence of these expectations with the archetype of the loose woman, or the slut, who violates normative gendered expectations not only of moral conduct but also of speech, movement, and how (public) space is inhabited. A telling example: Guidelines on how to exit a car gracefully (i.e., without flashing your underwear, or lack thereof) when wearing a short dress abound on the Internet. Gender role expectations, a theme revisited throughout this book, place the onus on women to self-regulate; if they fail to do so they face institutional sanction, harassment, and slut shaming; should they experience violence, they are blamed.

Of course gender intersects with class; here Albert Cohen's (1955) concept of the "middle-class measuring rod" (87) applied to women alerts us to the ways behaviour, language, and appearance are assessed in relation to normative middle class expectations of femininity, appropriateness, and propriety.

Not only do working class women's clothing styles continue to be associated with promiscuity (Armstrong et al. 2014), young women who flaunt normative (middle class) scripts by, for example, talking loudly, swearing, and dressing provocatively are deemed problematic (Skourtes 2016). Read as lacking in *class*, their clothing choices are held up as further evidence of their lacuna of style and taste—the antithesis of the middle class aesthetic of sexy, but not slutty, attire. Here, as we see repeatedly in this book, the fostering of advantage (and implicitly the entrenchment of disadvantage) between women is evident; as Angela McRobbie (2004) notes, "middle-class women have played a key role in the reproduction of class society, not just through their exemplary role as wives and mothers but also as standard bearers for middle-class family values, for certain norms of citizenship and also for safeguarding the valuable cultural capital accruing to them and their families through access to education, refinement and other privileges" (101).

The regulation of working class women's appearance in particular reminds us of the ways class has been (and continues to be) entangled with notions of respectability (Skeggs 1997)—indeed, middle class reformers' preoccupation with the propriety of working class women echoes throughout this book. Moreover, recognizing the interplay between cultural capital and gender draws our attention to the fine line women must navigate: a presentation of self that is simultaneously sexually appealing and adequately chaste. As such, young working class women are vulnerable to being "judged to be guilty of the crime of conducting feminine beautification to excess (too much makeup, too much fake tan, too little clothing)" (Buckley 2010, 221). In this context it is worth considering the classed nature of the ubiquitous slut label, which, in our post-sexual revolution world, has emerged as a regulatory device that, while drawing on tropes of female purity, has little to do with sexual activity. It also speaks to one way that social actors "do class." Elizabeth Armstrong and her colleagues (2014) suggest "high-status women employ slut discourse to assert class advantage, defining their styles of femininity and approaches to sexuality as classy rather than trashy" (101). Looking classy, "performing affluent femininity" (ibid., 112) requires middle class cultural capital as well as a significant investment of time and money—resources unavailable to working class women. In effect, a lack of disposable income and the ensuing inability to purchase expensive clothes and makeup is transferred from the products to the wearer—both are disdained as cheap.

Another tactic used to police appropriate gender presentation is clearly evident in schools. Young women (middle and high school students) are routinely sent home because their clothing contravenes gendered, classed dress codes: "too short" skirts, revealed bra straps, or midriff-baring tops. Gender regulation is evident in the extent to which it is overwhelmingly young women's clothing that is the focus of dress codes. Notably, heavier young women are read—and therefore regulated—as sexually mature and sanctioned for violations when wearing virtually the same outfit as a slimmer girl (see Box 3.1). Double standards are routinely justified by noting that "sexy" clothing is inconsistent with a positive learning environment because it is a distraction—what is left unsaid (or sometimes not) is that young men are assumed to be at risk of said distraction. It is a powerful example of a pervasive and dangerous narrative examined in greater detail in Chapter 5: Girls (and women) are passive but risky sexual seductresses; boys (and men) are unable to control their primal

---

BOX 3.1: SARAH FLORENCE ON FAT SHAMING

I've been big as long as I can remember. Even though I played soccer as a kid, danced in audition-only children's shows, and ran a nine-minute mile in PE, I was always big.... Elementary school went by well enough, but middle school came with the realization that I was terrifyingly different from the other kids. The vice principal targeted me for perpetual dress code violations like "too-tight shirts" and "glimpses of midriff," while my skinny, prepubescent friends wore booty shorts to school unscathed.

When my mother came to protest my detentions, she asked if I was being targeted because I had matured earlier than the other children. The school calmly said yes. It was my and my parents' responsibility, they told us, to ensure that my more mature body was appropriately covered up. The price of womanhood and fatness was that I was to be punished for my body.... Thankfully, my parents made sure to call bullshit.... They demanded that the school treat me the same as the other children, and they didn't take no for an answer.

Even so, when a friend's mom told my mother she was starting her 13-year-old on Weight Watchers, my mom asked me to join too. "You shouldn't have to change who you are, but I think you'll be happier if you look more like the other girls," she said. So I went.... The meeting ended in a paper-walled cubicle as I stripped myself of my socks, my shoes, and my dignity. Crying, I submitted to my weekly weigh-in. I was 12 years old.

... My whole life, people have told me that fatness is akin to failure. But my body is a success. It can run and jump and sing and laugh, and it can do all of those things while being fat.

Florence 2016

urges. Lauren Wiggins, sent home from her Moncton, New Brunswick, high school for wearing a full-length, shoulder revealing halter dress, drew attention to the troubling responsibilization of young women when she wrote a letter to the vice-principal of her school suggesting, "If you are truly so concerned that a boy in this school will get distracted by my upper back and shoulders, then he needs to be sent home and practice self-control." Ms. Wiggins earned national media attention, and a one-day suspension, for her resistant act of calling out institutional sexism (CBC 2014).

Case study: Women in politics

We now turn to examine how sexual scripts, gendered expectations, myths, and discipline coalesce in women's lives. In the following case study we examine political institutions and networks and their mutual reinforcement of other socio-political and economic apparatuses that perpetuate dominant "truths" about women. To this end we consider the relationship between dominant gendered framings and women's ability to participate in, and their experience of, the political arena.

According to Kay Richardson and her colleagues, the media treats women politicians as entertainment, subjecting them to relentless evaluation and commentary about their appearance, clothes, hairstyle, and how attractive they are—or are not (Richardson, Perry, and Corner 2013). In this context they are ridiculed if they do not conform to gendered heteronormative expectations of attractiveness and dismissed if they do. Men are not subject to comparable scrutiny—a double standard Richard Stewart, the mayor of Coquitlam, British Columbia, drew attention to when he purposely wore the same "boring" blue suit for 15 months. The response—"nobody noticed" (CBC 2016a)—would be unthinkable for a woman in politics. It is not only that women are subjected to gendered framing and discredited and/or trivialized, but that in the process their policies, arguments, and platforms are afforded less consideration. All of which, of course, undermines their credibility and ability to succeed.

Research has demonstrated that gender stereotypes and a sexist double standard are evident in the portrayal by the Canadian media of women who are campaigning for or who hold political office (Kittilson and Fridkin 2008). The embedded association of leadership with men means women politicians may adopt the "Iron Lady" persona, eschewing the markers of femininity (McIntosh 2013). While this offers some fragile protection from accusations of weakness, it increases the likelihood a woman will be demonized as unnatural and "too masculine." It is a no-win situation: The very qualities normatively valorized in (assumed to be male) politicians—ambition, confidence, forcefulness—are reframed in women as too ambitious, grasping, or shrewish. For women like Kathleen Wynne, the openly lesbian premier of Ontario from 2013 to 2018, gender bias intersects with homophobic tropes; social media comments attacked her competence as a leader, her looks, and her morality/sexuality, describing Wynne as a "subhuman dirty dyke," "sick," "wrinkly," and "bitch," demanding her resignation or her suicide, and threatening violence (Crawley 2017). Similar levels of verbal violence—in this case demonstrating intersecting xenophobia, Islamophobia, and sexism—were directed toward Liberal Member of Parliament (MP) Iqra Khalid, a Pakistani Canadian, when she introduced a motion to condemn "systemic racism and religious discrimination including Islamophobia" (Payton 2017). Powerfully demonstrating the need for her motion, Khalid read death threats and other commentary she had received to her colleagues in the House of Commons (inserting the word "blank" in place of stronger language). One message read "Muslim piece of blank terrorist.... Go back to your blank hole country where you came from"; another was explicitly threatening: "Blank you gently with a chainsaw, you camel-humping terrorist incubator blank" (Payton 2017).

Finally, even if a woman successfully navigates the plethora of roadblocks and challenges to win political office, she continues to confront sexism and misogyny—not only in the media but also from her constituents and colleagues. In 1985, when Justice Minister John Crosbie suggested Liberal MP Sheila Copps "quiet down, baby," the enraged Copps retorted "I'm not his baby and I'm nobody's baby." More than 30 years later it appears that little has changed—a House of Commons sexual harassment policy introduced on December 9, 2014, in the wake of accusations of serious misconduct on the part of male MPs notwithstanding. Women MPs from across the political spectrum have come forward to talk about the everyday sexism they confront (Giese 2016). On April 18, 2016, Conservative MP Michelle Rempel wrote an op-ed (see Box 3.2) clearly expressing her frustration with the misogyny she confronts both from her colleagues and from constituents. Similarly, other Canadian women politicians have been called "fat," "morbidly obese," and a host of other violent, sexist, and crude epithets (Giese 2016). The above-noted misogyny, some of which emanates from powerful men who make policy decisions that impact all of our lives, does not bode well for gender equity.

The experience of women in Canadian politics is not unique; an international study found that women parliamentarians are routinely the targets of sexism, harassment, and violence. In particular, an international survey found that psychological violence affects 81.8 per cent of women politicians; 44.4 per cent report threats of death, physical or sexual violence, or abduction; and 65.5 per cent report experiencing humiliating sexist remarks occasionally or often (IPU 2016). Women politicians also note that social and news media

BOX 3.2: MICHELLE REMPEL ON SEXISM IN POLITICS

Last week I found myself, once again, telling one of the young women on my staff that, "It's important to address sexism in the moment it happens."

Earlier, she witnessed another member of Parliament suggesting to me that we should talk about an issue we had been discussing, "when we were less emotional." She also watched as I asked him why he had chosen to use this particular phrasing. She then watched the conversation conclude with him giving me the very empowering and helpful suggestion of "(Be) nicer in the future." ...

Much has been written about sexism that's so systemic that it's referred to as "everyday." ... The everyday sexism I face involves confronting the "bitch" epithet when I don't automatically comply with someone's request or capitulate on my position on an issue, confronting assumptions that I have gotten to my station in life by (insert your choice of sexual act) with (insert your choice of man in position of authority), enduring speculation and value judgements about my fertility, and responding to commentary that links my appearance to my competency. It involves my ass being occasionally grabbed as a way to shock me into submission. It involves tokenism. It involves sometimes being written off as not serious when I've clearly proven I am....

The everyday sexism that I experience is grating. It angers me, and it makes me roll my eyes. Sometimes, when it's bad enough, it causes me to second guess myself. I address it. I speak out about it. That said, I've never lost a job because of it. I've never experienced violence because of it. I've never had to worry about feeding my family because of it.

So, who am I to tell other women how they should combat everyday sexism? ... While I applaud the efforts many women have made to empower other women to address sexism in the moment it happens, we should upend the table. The responsibility for combatting everyday sexism doesn't lie with those who live with it; it lies with you.

Rempel 2016

play a significant role in disseminating negative, sexist, and sexually charged comments and imagery about them (IPU 2016). Dismissive and disrespectful media coverage of women politicians dovetails with the challenges emanating from women's socio-economic and labour market location (discussed in

Chapter 2), presenting a significant barrier to women's political participation. Not only does a woman's ability to balance childcare responsibilities with the obligations of political office feature significantly in media coverage, women's disproportionate household and family care responsibilities restrict their availability (or willingness) to engage politically. In addition, the labour market sectors where women dominate (sales, service, education, and healthcare) do not lend themselves easily to taking the sort of extended leave necessary to run a campaign for political office. This is exacerbated by the lack of security and stability characteristic of the way many such "feminine" occupations are organized (e.g., non-standard, precarious, part time). In these respects women, as a group, have less access to the financial resources or networks needed to mount an election campaign. Moreover, as we saw in Chapter 2, racialized, immigrant, and Indigenous women may have even less social capital and economic resources as compared to white women. This is reflected in the makeup of Canada's 42nd Parliament—hailed as the most diverse to date—which consists of 88 women and 288 men. Of those 88 women, only 15 are racialized (3 Black, 7 South Asian, 3 East Asian, and 2 Middle Eastern women), and 3 are Indigenous—numbers comparable to the previous federal Parliament (Tolley 2015).

Moreover, gender norms continue to hold powerful sway on both women and men, diminishing the chances that women will be perceived by themselves and others as viable candidates (O'Neill 2015). Thus, in addition to systemic barriers there are also practices that maintain the gender status quo by effectively excluding women from or pushing them out of the political arena, including the nomination process. In order to be elected to political office one must first win the party's riding nomination. Most winnable or "safe" seats (where a given party can assume they will be victorious) are already filled by (usually male) incumbents; those that are vacant are hotly contested, and the party is more likely to put forward a male candidate. According to Joanna Everitt (2010), "The backroom boys (they are seldom girls) often decide in advance who they want as the candidate. Their decisions are based on their networks (more likely to be comprised of men than women), and on who they think is most likely to win. Given that winnable candidates in the past have most often been men it is no wonder that they often turn to other men to take up their party's standard." This reliance on informal networks and processes, and normative assumptions about what a "real" politician looks like, also play a role in the disproportionate exclusion of racialized women from politics.

Given that "the undersupply of women in Canadian legislatures is not due to any particular preference on the part of voters" (O'Neill 2015, 24), the intersecting factors of women's care responsibilities, stubborn gender income disparity and labour market segregation, gender bias in leadership, restrictive gender roles and myths, misogyny in the political arena, and sexism in the media evidently have deleterious effects on women's political engagement. As noted at the beginning of Chapter 2, however, in 2015, for the first time in our history, Canada had a gender-balanced cabinet. Moreover, women from across the political spectrum lead Canadian provinces, cities, and political parties. These milestones should be celebrated at the same time that caution is exercised. Women's most recent gains in federal representation, a historic best at 88 out of 336 seats (in 2015), still placed us well short of the 30 per cent benchmark identified by the United Nations as the minimum critical mass needed for women to have a significant impact on policies; when they do, women leaders often work across political divides to champion "issues of gender equality, such as the elimination of gender-based violence, parental leave and childcare, pensions, gender-equality laws and electoral reform" (UN Women 2012). Recognizing this, many countries, but notably not Canada, have introduced proactive strategies such as quotas and reserved seats to ensure more gender-equitable political representation.

The other side of the dualism: Gendered privilege and masculinity

Throughout the chapter we have seen that women are constituted—in mutually reinforcing discourses emanating out of medicine, law, media, business, and politics—as overly emotional and hysterical; intellectually inferior; lacking leadership qualities; naturally nurturing; physically weak; and biologically unruly. They must contend with the responsibility of being the gatekeepers of sexual morality through scripts of sexual passivity and are seen as irresponsible choice makers if they deviate from intersecting gender and class expectations. Women are also represented and socialized to act as silent and appropriately attractive supporting characters or love interests who enable men's independence and symbolize their status (as sexually virile or as responsible family men) in popular culture, politics, and family life. The corollary to the remarkable visibility of women's gender performance—deviantized through perceptions of behavioural or "natural" aberrance—is masculinity, the norm against which women are invariably compared. Men are constituted as *natural* leaders, sexual initiators, heroes, and speakers—their assertiveness read positively as strength and intelligence, their success celebrated and understood as self-made (ignoring the costs others shoulder to facilitate it).

As we see in later chapters, these qualities often justify and normalize gendered violence: For example, sexual violence is read as sexual prowess (Chapter 5); workplace bullying is framed as leadership (Chapter 7). Alternately, normative masculinity facilitates behaviours and contexts conducive to gendered violence—"tough" sports like football provide a trenchant example, as we see with Ray Rice in Chapter 6. Raewyn Connell (2008) characterizes commercial sport as a cultural institution in which "some of the most toxic" definitions and practices of masculinity are embedded and reproduced (133). Similarly, Michael Messner (1992) has shown that men's desire to fit in with peers in sports contexts is implicated in homophobia, sexism, harassment, and sexual assault of women (see also Godenzi, Schwartz, and DeKeseredy 2001). However, these behaviours are justified through the familiar "boys will be boys" narrative, the continued purchase of which alerts us to the invisibility of male privilege.

Subtle and pervasive: Symbolic violence and power

In this book we see over and over again that, even absent many of the explicitly exclusionary laws and regulations that litter our history (e.g., racially segregated school systems, the disenfranchisement of women), and indeed in the context where equity is not only rhetorically supported in endless statements by social and political leaders but also enshrined in law—not least in section 15(1) of the *Canadian Charter of Rights and Freedoms*, which guarantees everyone "equal protection and equal benefit of the law ... without discrimination based on race, national or ethnic origin, colour, religion, sex, age or mental or physical disability"—domination continues to exist (Krais 1993). This begs the question: Through what mechanisms are these stubborn stratifications maintained?

This chapter started, and indeed was oriented, around Foucault's insights, developed in the context of his archaeological and genealogical studies (e.g., Foucault 1978, 1979, 1982, 1991) about power/knowledge and discourse. Absent from the conversation, however, is "the bodily inscription of social structure as a habitus that is so at home with domination that it does not recognize it as such" (Burawoy 2008, 20)—a process we already explored in relation to class in Chapter 1. In order to extend the analysis and open up a space to think about these processes we can mobilize Pierre Bourdieu's (1990; 1998) work on symbolic power and **symbolic violence**. That it was, and is, predominantly upper class white men who, as medical experts, legal authorities, leaders in politics and business, decision makers, and media moguls, have established the norms we now take for granted alerts us to the gendered, raced, and classed nature of what Pierre Bourdieu (1990) refers to as symbolic power—"the power to define" (Hallett 2007, 149) and to create categories, ascribe value, and make distinctions. This is not a conspiracy theory but a recognition that—notwithstanding the democratization of knowledge dissemination ushered in with the Internet—representational authority and legitimacy continue to reside in those who are credentialled. In other words, it is skewed toward individuals who inhabit, and whose perspectives are informed by, privileged social locations. In this and preceding chapters we have seen many examples of these symbolic representations, the "di-vision" (Krais 1993, 158) of the world into two "opposing entities" (Bourdieu 1990, 210) along various axes of social differentiation. For example, the middle and upper class work ethic stands in opposition to the presumed lack of ambition of the working and underclass; the morality of middle class white women is constructed in relation to the promiscuity of Black and Indigenous women; the weakness of women is a foil to the strength of men.

Bourdieu argued that these representations permeate our social world and are incorporated into our habitus, the "ensemble of schemata of perceptions, thinking, feeling, evaluating, speaking, and acting that structures all the expressive, verbal, and practical manifestations and utterances of a person" (Krais 1993, 168). Put another way, these dichotomous and mutually affirming framings are so ubiquitous and pervasive that they permeate the patterns of thought and behaviour of social actors. Symbolic violence, then, is precisely the naturalization and acceptance as common sense of distinctions and the associated hierarchical ascription of value (e.g., the unremarked upon acceptance of the way the world operates in relation to privilege). Bourdieu's (1990) theory of symbolic violence has been criticized, most notably by Judith Butler (1999), for its deterministic tendency and assertion that symbolic violence operates with the complicity (albeit in complicated ways) of the dominated; others, however, take the position that symbolic violence is not an elaborate theorization of "blame the victim," nor does it imply false consciousness, nor, for that matter, does it mean that oppressed populations (e.g., women, racialized people, members of the working class) are cultural dupes (e.g., Krais 1993; McRobbie 2004; Weininger 2005). Rather, it acknowledges that gendered, raced, and classed representations percolate through our social world to such an extent that they inevitably inform (but do not determine) our worldview and our understanding not only of the "other" but also of ourselves—in spite of the fact that we may *know* better and even challenge these normative tropes. A case in point is Joanna Kadi's (1996) quote in Box 1.1 on page 34: "We hear, over and over, that our lousy jobs and living situations result from our lack of smarts. I internalized this lie. Rationally, I knew money and brains didn't go hand in hand. But on deep unconscious levels I believed in my own stupidity and in the stupidity of working-class people" (39).

Symbolic violence does not operate outside of or separately from other forms of violence but "is conceived in relation (not in opposition) to material and bodily violence. The two forms of violence, for Bourdieu, are complementary, go hand in hand, and can/do converge one into the other" (Ibrahim 2011, 634).

Indeed, while it is a central focus of Chapter 10, throughout the book we see that symbolic violence is not only implicated in the multiple incarnations and other forms of gendered violence, but is a significant thread running through and connecting the interpersonal and the structural.

Resistance: Challenging normative gender tropes

Of course, women challenge gender tropes—indeed, it is in acts of resistance that normative scripts and the power relations through which they are constituted are rendered visible (Foucault 1983). We have already seen instances of this in the chapter. Iqra Khalid, like so many political women, refused to be quiet—speaking up in the House of Commons she graphically proved wrong the hateful (anonymous) person who suggested she was a "little girl with very little intelligence, no personality, no strength in character, with no brave bone in her body" (quoted in Boutilier 2017). Michelle Rempel's op-ed (see Box 3.2) calls out the everyday sexism she experiences, while blogger Sarah Florence (see Box 3.1) sheds harsh light on regulatory fat shaming. These are just a handful of examples where women appropriated conventional and virtual platforms as mediums for resistance.

Women actors are also speaking out about the pervasive sexism in the film industry—everything from limited roles to pay inequity. Some leverage their star power to draw attention to gender tropes more broadly. For example, in July 2016 Jennifer Aniston penned a deeply personal op-ed that powerfully spoke back to the way women are portrayed in the tabloid press and addressed many of the topics examined in this chapter:

> We use celebrity "news" to perpetuate this dehumanizing view of females, focused solely on one's physical appearance, which tabloids turn into a sporting event of speculation. Is she pregnant? Is she eating too much? Has she let herself go? Is her marriage on the rocks because the camera detects some physical "imperfection"? ... Here's where I come out on this topic: we are complete with or without a mate, with or without a child.... I have grown tired of being part of this narrative. Yes, I may become a mother some day ... but I'm not in pursuit of motherhood because I feel incomplete in some way, as our celebrity news culture would lead us all to believe. I resent being made to feel "less than" because my body is changing and/or I had a burger for lunch and was photographed from a weird angle and therefore deemed one of two things: "pregnant" or "fat."
> (Aniston 2016)

Here we see how even conventionally attractive women who enjoy the wealth and privilege of celebrity cannot escape being perpetually measured against (unrealistic) standards; indeed, through the media they become targets of disciplinary power's normative judgment. It is, however, not only through acts of resistance but also the backlash they engender that we come to appreciate how the regulatory power of norms renders resistance fraught. All too often women are caught in delegitimation loops, and their acts of resistance are used to further validate gender tropes: See how hysterical and irrational women are? They are making such a big deal about women in movies, or a few tweets, or fill-in-the-blank. We see too how women, including Jennifer Aniston, are called out on their "hypocrisy" (Tam 2016)—as if any conformity to gender tropes renders a woman unable to think analytically. More commonly, critical/feminist assertions are negated as the sour grapes of unappealing women. The response to the 2017 Women's March discussed in Chapter 1 is a telling example. A Toronto woman's Facebook album of the event was flooded not only with sexist and body shaming comments (e.g., "how come 99% of the women on this march are fat?") but also homophobic and racist slurs (Chiasson 2017). On this theme Indiana State Senator Jack Sandlin's social media comments were unambiguous: "In one day, Trump got more fat women out walking than Michelle Obama did in 8 years" (Simons 2017). Very occasionally, backlash to resistance generates affirming (and ironic) ripples: John Carmen, a New Jersey Republican legislator, evoked gender roles when he "humorously" posted "will the women's protest be over in time for them to cook dinner?"; 10 months later he lost his seat to Ashley Bennett (a Democrat)—a woman whose entry into politics was inspired by his misogynist social media musings (Schmidt 2017). While operating within the bounds of normative structures (national governments, the entertainment industry), these examples of women's situated resistance to symbolic violence problematize and speak back to the dominant order, contributing (however momentarily) to a shift in the power to define.

Concluding reflections

In this chapter we have seen that women's bodies, social interactions, sexual practices, careers, and even their hobbies and habits (crafting, primping), are delineated and evaluated according to robust myths, traditional roles, and sexual and gender scripts, which together shape not only how women are perceived and represented but their self-perceptions. And we have considered how these notions are perpetuated as "truths" and reproduced in mutually reinforcing regulatory discourses and mechanisms through which women are framed as "other," in good (the Madonna), bad (the whore), pathological (the hysteric), or pathetic (the victim) ways.

Through the case study of women in politics we also saw how the interplay of social structures, institutions, and discourses limit women in another way: They must navigate the incompatibility of scripts that inevitably coexist in the multiple roles they inhabit. While, for example, a man can comfortably—and inconspicuously—be an organizational leader, a father, and enjoy his sex life, a woman authority figure is likely to be judged for the time she spends with her family, must manage her appearance and behaviour so as not to be read, and discredited, as a "slut," and negotiates the ongoing potential that she will be perceived as physically weak, too emotional, or governed by her hormones. That said, no matter the context, to be perceived as good, women are invariably expected to be visually pleasing, passive, and kind—behaviours that also restrict their options and responsibilize them when they are victimized; in effect, then, normative social expectations engender the double bind examined throughout this book. As we see in Parts B, C, and D, these limitations are not merely discursive; rather, they profoundly impact women's lives, including through institutional and regulatory sanctions that facilitate or restrict their access to state protection (e.g., police) and services (e.g., healthcare).

EXERCISE: MEDIA SENSITIZATION

For a week, take media, as a medium, seriously and critically consider news, entertainment, social media, magazines, and so on.
Pay attention to gender in the media:

- What do the women featured look like?
- What roles are women assigned?
- How are they described?
- What activities are they doing?
- Are they speaking? To whom? About what?

Did the shows and videos you watched meet the Bechdel Test?
In groups of 4–6 learners, share your observations.

PART B

Interpersonal Violence

Part B builds on the previous section of the book in which an intersectional lens was mobilized to consider women's (divergent but nonetheless gendered) social, economic, and political locations, and the ways women are discursively and institutionally constituted. It examines how myths about women—constructing them as, for example, physically fragile, overly emotional, and unfit to be leaders—not only reflect power relations that play out in social structures (e.g., the criminal justice system), representations (e.g., social media), and everyday activities (e.g., use of public transit), but also in the interpersonal violence women experience in different spheres: everyday intrusions on the street, on campus, and online (Chapter 4); sexual assault (Chapter 5); and intimate partner violence (Chapter 6).

EVERYDAY INTRUSIONS ON THE STREET, ON CAMPUS, AND ONLINE

Intrusions on women in public spaces are an everyday reality—a routine (if not usually welcomed) part of women's days. Rarely remarked upon, they are seamlessly woven into our cultural tapestry, a staple of everything from movies to videos to songs. They have also long been a marketing trope. While the harassment is sometimes a plot device (e.g., a man, watching a passing jogger instead of the road, drives his car into a pole in an Allstate insurance advertisement) more often, and ironically, ads use men's unwanted attention to sell women beauty products or clothes; presumably the leers and catcalls will convince women that with the help of the product they too will "turn heads."

In the previous chapter we saw a number of myths about women, the importance afforded sexual scripts, the capricious good girl/bad girl divide, and that women are routinely evaluated in relation to normative expectations informed by racial and class hierarchies. How do myths and scripts play out in women's everyday lives? And how do they inform women's interactions with strangers, or their efforts to avoid them? Normalized and even celebrated it is little wonder that intrusions are a predictable aspect of women's experiences of public spaces. Going out on the street, onto campus, or online renders a woman vulnerable to finding herself the object of unwanted attention, the recipient of unsolicited invitations for sex; subjected to having her appearance, "sexiness," and weight judged (and commented on); and told what she should do (smile, look up) and should not do (walk away, be like *that*). Racialized, gender non-conforming, or otherwise "othered" women find the script infused by, for example, racist, Islamophobic, and heterosexist tropes. Moreover, the imperviousness of power/knowledge is neatly on display: Women who complain are, as a matter of course, met with some variation of "accept the compliment," "have a sense of humour" or, evoking the slut shaming narrative examined in Chapter 3, "what did you expect looking/dressing/acting like that?" It is a normative response to women's victimization that, as we see throughout this book, simultaneously negates her experience and blames her for it.

While women sometimes find unsolicited comments or gawks affirming, other times they are embarrassing, annoying, or humiliating. Many are bewildered by the verbal and non-verbal attention—exasperated and mystified, women students regularly ask "What do these guys expect? Do they think I am going to sleep with them?" We can be fairly confident that men do not anticipate a relationship, sexual or otherwise, to be the outcome of these intrusions. Indeed, the anger and abuse that follows when women do not respond in accordance to the harasser's script makes it abundantly clear that these are not simply friendly interactions; for example, as one young woman explained "after me ignoring them, that's when it turns racial, that's when it might be 'you Black this' or 'you Black that'" (EVAW 2016).

Recognizing what it *is not*—a compliment or a sincere invitation—alerts us to what it *is*: a powerful gender (and race and sexuality) policing mechanism. It is also a problem hiding in plain sight—pervasive, visible, and absolutely normalized. Gender policing takes different forms in other public places: Online it manifests as cyber-misogyny; on campus, environmental and interpersonal sexism are pervasive. Very often accepted (by men and women) as just the way things are, the impacts of these intrusions are profound. In this, the first thematic chapter of the book, we start with a short socio-historical reflection before examining three spaces: the street, the campus, and the online world. In order to tease out commonality and explore specificity in each of these three spaces this chapter sketches the parameters of the issue and considers the nature of the interactions, the impacts on women, and state and social responses. Throughout we attend not only to victimization but also to women's resistance and refusal to cede these spaces, concluding with one particularly flashy example of collective resistance, Slut Walk, a movement critical of the myths about women and the ways they restrict women's public presence and sexual expression.

Socio-historic considerations: From mashers to online trolls

Unlike the other topics addressed in this section of the book—sexual assault and intimate partner violence—the issue of everyday intrusions on the street, on campus, and online has a much less robust history of feminist activism and engagement. This is not, however, to suggest that men approaching women was never the focus of legislative, feminist, and public attention. In the late 1800s and early 1900s, Canada's urban landscape was being transformed: Women were leaving their rural homes to find employment and adventure in urban centres, and shopping by middle class matrons became a respectable (and evidently profitable for merchants) pastime—in effect, women started to claim their right to public space. In this context of emergent "opportunities for gender and class mixing in public space" (Freedman 2013, 192), "the masher" caused considerable public outrage (Segrave 2014). Mashers were envisioned as white men (racialized men engaging in similar behaviour would have been read as sexual predators) who, singly or in groups, flaunted the Victorian chivalrous protector script by "loafing" on street corners and leering, ogling, and shamelessly approaching respectable women in public (Segrave 2014).

In Ontario, women turned to the courts for redress, and mashers could, among other things, find themselves being fined for their "smart remarks" (Dubinsky 1993, 39). Somewhat surprisingly, the protectionist narrative of risky urban spaces ran parallel to one that not only acknowledged women's right to enjoy public areas without interference but also celebrated their resilience and resourcefulness; in Canada there were a number of newspaper articles describing women hitting men over the head with umbrellas—others featured women administering resounding slaps (ibid.). Interestingly, in the United States it was not the umbrella but a considerably more robust weapon that took narrative centre stage: the hatpin. In the early 1900s women like Leoti Blaker—who used her hatpin (measuring almost a foot long) to stab the arm of a man who inappropriately draped his arm across her back in a New York City stagecoach on May 28, 1903—were applauded (see Figure 4.1). Within six years, however, celebration gave way to increasing levels of anxiety over the "hatpin peril" (Abbott 2014). The pleas of suffragettes like Nan Davis, who addressed Chicago's city council in 1910, asserting that "if the men of Chicago want to take the hatpins away from us, let them make the streets safe … no man has a right to tell me how I shall dress and what I shall wear" (ibid.), were ignored, and cities across the United States moved to regulate the length of hatpins. By the 1920s, in the face of changing social and sexual norms, protectionist and rights narratives were replaced by one that reframed such intrusions as harmless flirting, and "humorous representations of mashers supplanted feminist aspirations" (Freedman 2013, 192). The efforts of women in Washington, DC, who organized into an Anti-Flirt Club to "rid the city of the male pest" (Segrave 2014, 171) notwithstanding, the masher was soon relegated to the history books, and the normalization of men's everyday intrusions on women that we see today took hold.

By this time women in Canada and the United States were not only going onto streets to shop but going into universities to learn; there too they confronted antagonism between the sexes, sexual exploitation, and sexual harassment (Waller 1937). As on the street, university/college campuses became environments where men's aggressive sexual advances were normalized and women were blamed for taking offence, or if they were victimized, merely for

FIGURE 4.1: Leoti Blaker stabs a masher, 1903

being present (Kirkpatrick and Kanin 1957; Schwartz and DeKeseredy 1997). In this context the "academic arm" of the women's liberation movement concentrated its efforts on establishing women's studies courses and programs, in the face of considerable resistance from faculty and administrators (Bird 2002) as well as male students (Axelrod 1990).

While sexual intrusions on campus were not particularly high on their radar, second wave feminists were making important gains in publicizing women's experiences of sexualized harassment on the street. Throughout the 1970s and 1980s what came to be known as street harassment was a recurring theme at demonstrations and rallies, including Take Back the Night marches—protests that were (and continue to be) about sexual violence but, as the name implies, centre on women's ability to safely walk on the streets. That said the issue received considerably less attention from the movement than sexual assault and intimate partner violence, both of which lend themselves more readily to the legal reform/framing favoured by governance feminists (an issue examined in the coming chapters).

Since the turn of the twenty-first century the issue of harassment on campus and (more recently) online has increasingly been problematized; at the same time, everyday intrusions on the street have started to, once again, receive considerable feminist and activist attention. In 2014 *Hollaback!* "a movement dedicated to ending street harassment using mobile technology" (*Hollaback!* n.d.), with chapters throughout North America including in Halifax, Ottawa, and Vancouver, released "10 Hours of Walking in NYC as a Woman" (Rob Bliss Creative 2014). The 15-minute YouTube video—although widely critiqued for appearing to highlight comments by racialized men (Butler 2014)—went viral and reignited a conversation that had largely been dormant for a generation.

Everyday intrusions on the street

While the notion of harassment—everyday or otherwise—can be a useful sensitization device, it frames the issues in a specifically legalistic way that imposes a script inconsistent with third wave feminism's fluid engagement with sexuality. Fiona Vera-Gray (2016c), noting that the term "street harassment" is adapted from Catharine MacKinnon's and Liz Farley's efforts to address sexual harassment at work, argues that legalistic terminology does not adequately speak to some aspects of women's experiences. She suggests these instances "may be better captured through the language of intrusion. The deliberate act of putting oneself into a place or situation where one is uninvited" (ibid.).

The language of intrusions also sensitizes us to the range of experiences. While few women are likely to be pleased to be followed and subjected to disparaging remarks about their appearance, early research demonstrated that catcalls and appreciative looks are, at times, experienced as affirmation (Baker, Terpstra, and Larntz 1990; Cartar, Hicks, and Slane 1996); this is a more common response when the perpetrator is attractive and perceived to be of higher social status. Other women enjoy the banter and light flirting that can be part of the exchange (Perry 2007). Context is also important in conditioning how the experience is interpreted; research by Kimberly Fairchild (2010) found that nighttime intrusions by men in groups when women are alone are more likely to be perceived as threatening. As Imani Perry (2007) notes, "Although most sexual approach of women on the street may be harassment, not all of it is, and this is a worthwhile distinction to make" (112). She further maintains street harassment should be evaluated in relation to injury (to the target of the comments) rather than intent (of the putative harasser). Here she points out that a woman's culture, religion, sexual orientation, upbringing, and previous experiences shape her perceptions of sexual or gendered comments from strangers on the street; accordingly, comments a man assumes to be acceptable may or may not be interpreted as offensive by the subjects of his attention (ibid.).

The nature and extent of everyday intrusions

How common are everyday intrusions on the street? How often are Canadian women subjected to catcalls, taunts, or commentary on their appearance, body, and/or attitude? Anecdotally we know that this is a common experience—one that women, and most especially young women, often come to see as a routine part of being in public space. A survey led by Beth Livingston (2015) offers us a snapshot of the scope and nature of these intrusions. Of the 620 Canadian women under the age of 40 who took part, more than two out of every three (69.9 per cent) had experienced harassment before the age of 15; almost all (88 per cent) before the age of 17. The researchers found that while verbal and non-verbal intrusions (e.g., leering looks, ogling, hand gestures) were much more common than being touched—an activity that would meet the legal definition of sexual assault even if it is unlikely, as we see in Chapter 5, to meet the threshold for conviction—over half of respondents had experienced being groped or fondled. Disturbingly, 79 per cent reported they had been "followed by a man or group of men in a way that made them feel unsafe during the past year"; for 17 per cent of the research participants this had happened more than five times (ibid., 5). Livingston's research also unsettles common-sense notions of safe spaces: More than a quarter of respondents had experienced verbal intrusions on college campuses, in well-lit areas, on public transit, in places with lots of other people, and during the day.

The scripts of everyday intrusions are not only justified on the basis of gender tropes (all women want to be looked at) but also draw heavily on gendered expectations—women are evaluated on their appearance and how closely they approximate the heteronormative ideal. Of course street intrusions are not only a highly gendered form of victimization, but their nature and frequency are conditioned by intersecting identities. For example, trans people in Ontario "nearly universally report that they have experienced some type of 'everyday transphobia' … 96% had heard that trans people were not normal, [and] 73% had been made fun of for being trans" (Bauer and Scheim 2015, 3). Others in the LGBTQ community similarly report pervasive everyday discrimination; Doug Meyer (2012) reminds us this must be understood intersectionally: "homophobia does not merely amplify sexist violence … it makes certain forms of misogynist violence possible" (867).

Similarly, it is vital to consider how entrenched scripts of the "other" play out in sexualized/racialized harassment; as one woman explained, "my experiences are different as a Black woman than they are for my white friends. I should be 'up for it' or that I am 'fair game' or that I shouldn't care if my body is touched in a specific way" (EVAW 2016). We also see this intersectionality in Arij Elmi's (2017) piece in Box 4.1, which draws our attention to the ways verbal and non-verbal harassment of racialized women reflects and reproduces

BOX 4.1: I'M NOT AN ALARMIST—BUT AS A MUSLIM WOMAN I AM GENUINELY ALARMED

As a women's self-defence instructor, I teach Muslim and immigrant women to fight back and yell when faced with anti-Muslim and xenophobic violence.

I'm often invited to pass on the stories of the Muslim women who have been harassed on public transit, assaulted in the streets and discriminated against in their workplaces.... Many of these women have stopped taking the subway. Others have quit their jobs or don hats instead of hijabs. These were all choices they have had to make to remain safe in a country that is touted as being one of the safest in the world.

As a black woman who wears the hijab I too have faced Islamophobia and racism while shopping, driving and in my work as a social worker.

I will never forget the day I went to interview a client in our emergency department only to be informed that she would not work with a Muslim. It hurt even more to watch my colleague, a nurse, ask our client if she would prefer to be seen by someone else. My colleague never stopped to acknowledge the hatred that was on display moments before.

... When recalling these stories, I've learned to preface them with a statement downplaying their significance. I would always begin: "I don't want to overstate it," believing that if I made our hurt smaller, that if I softened our pain, our stories would be believed.... I soften and downplay the verbal and physical abuse we face as Muslims in the hopes of normalizing these experiences.

But it is not normal.

It is not normal to be told to go home. It is not normal to be called a terrorist. The stares are not normal. The comments online are not normal.

And more importantly it is not okay. It is not okay to vilify another person's faith. It is not acceptable to alienate and make us feel othered. And it was not okay for my colleague to not call this out.

Elmi 2017

stereotypes, the hyper-vulnerability of "othered" women, and the troubling minimization implicit in the acceptance of everyday verbal violence as normal.

Intersecting marginalizations come into sharp relief when we consider the experiences of street-based sex workers, a population in which Indigenous women—as the result of complex interlocking systems of oppression including colonization, entrenched social and economic inequality, and labour market discrimination—are dramatically over-represented (Benoit and Shumka 2015). Their labour location renders these women hyper-vulnerable not only to predatory violence but also denies them the ability to avoid harassment by neighbourhood residents and police (Benoit et al. 2015). Framed as moral, social, and health risks to the community and bearing the mark of the "whore," street-based sex workers appear to be "fair game" for particularly insidious and wide-ranging harassment from both men and (perhaps surprisingly) women. Echoing the class-based intra-gender policing noted in the previous chapter, Lynzi Armstrong (2016) suggests that female harassers "position themselves above the sex working women by publically scolding them for stepping outside of the boundaries of acceptable female behavior. In doing so, they could safely locate themselves within the category of 'good' women and be reassured that they were not like 'those' women" (291).

Navigating intrusions: Strategies and implications

Arij Elmi's comments in Box 4.1 remind us that everyday intrusions have direct and indirect impacts on the lives of women. Recognizing women's embodied reality necessitates we acknowledge the fear these everyday intrusions can evoke: According to Statistics Canada data, women are "less likely than men to feel safe in a variety of situations, including walking alone at night in their neighbourhoods … and using or waiting for public transportation alone after dark" (Hutchins and Sinha 2013, 77). Even when women rationally know that a small proportion of sexual assaults are committed by strangers (see Chapter 5), unwanted intrusions, particularly at night and in isolated spaces, remind women of the possibility. Not surprisingly, women report changing or curtailing their activities by, for example, not going out after dark, attending fewer events, and avoiding evening classes (Livingston 2015). Moreover, intersecting identities condition not only vulnerability and the nature of intrusions but also how the intrusion is experienced. For example, Muslim women who wear the hijab or niqab speak of running a gauntlet of everyday racism in the form of Islamophobic and xenophobic intrusions in public spaces (D'Souze and Kelly 2017); the fear that taunts will escalate into physical attacks (which, as we saw in Chapter 1, are increasing) creates an additional level of fear.

As women endeavour to minimize their vulnerability to unwanted intrusions they engage in what Vera-Gray (2014) calls "**safety work**" (237)—women's unseen and unacknowledged labour to avoid, prevent, or manage intrusions—that is "hidden, habitual, repeated over time and absorbed into the body" (Vera-Gray 2016b). Research has documented what women know, albeit not necessarily consciously so: that to minimize harassment they do a great deal of safety work both before and during their time in public space (see, for example, Fairchild 2010; Livingston 2015; Thompson 1993; Vera-Gray 2014, 2016c). Prior to going out a woman may, for example, reflect on her attire (is my skirt too short?) and makeup (am I wearing too much?); she may plan her route to avoid, to the best of her ability, "sketchy" areas. On her way she may be vigilant about such things as the route she takes, the seat she selects on public transit, and on what side of the road she walks. While in public she is likely perpetually scanning the environment, stealing herself for an intrusion, and mapping out her options should she be harassed.

She may also, as was discussed in the previous chapter in relation to Bartky's (1997) Foucauldian analysis, discipline her body, moderating not only where but also *how* she walks and adjusting her facial expression—endeavouring to hit just the "right" note between pleasant (to avoid being told to smile) and too friendly (to avoid being perceived as inviting interactions); or she may settle her face into an assertive "don't mess with me" expression in an effort to convey strength and signal her lack of vulnerability. A woman may also implement strategies to deter would-be intruders by, for example, wearing earbuds or appearing to speak on her mobile phone—rationalizing that if she cannot hear the demands for attention then she cannot be blamed for her failure to respond. And of course should she be intruded upon she is aware that too impetuous a response may engender anger and retaliation; too polite a rebuttal risks being read as encouragement. If, all her preventive efforts notwithstanding, the behaviour moves beyond the verbal to assaultive, she (and others) will berate her lack of good judgment—elucidating how entrenched tropes of appropriate behaviour make victim blaming a normative response (an issue examined in greater detail in Chapter 5).

Of course we need to factor in how privilege conditions access to mitigation or avoidance strategies; for example, while economic resources (associated with class status) do not protect women from being harassed on the street, they do afford some women the ability to insulate themselves by avoiding public spaces and instead, for example, driving to their destination. This option is not available to working class women who are reliant on public transit and more likely to reside, work, and engage in leisure activities in high-density areas where harassment is more pervasive (Popkin, Leventhal, and Weismann 2010). Moreover, it is precisely working class, racialized, and im/migrant women who are, as we saw in Chapter 2, more likely to be labouring in precarious jobs that demand shift work, necessitating they commute in the evenings or at night. Consideration should also be given to the identity and power of the harasser and how this conditions a woman's fears and in turn her safety work. For example, according to Human Rights Watch (2017) some Indigenous women limit their time in public spaces to avoid harassment by police; similarly, racialized women who are read through stereotypical tropes navigate interactions with law enforcement with care (see Chapter 11).

In short, then, just as women's experiences of everyday intrusions in public spaces are conditioned by intersecting identities, so are their management strategies shaped by interlocking systems of oppression. These variabilities notwithstanding, women have in common the fact that they consistently do a great deal of safety work (Vera-Gray 2016a). Moreover, not only is women's unfettered access to public space compromised by their fear, but their routine activities—walking down the street, window shopping, rushing to work or school—are disrupted and marked by stressful vigilance (Vera-Gray 2016c).

Regulatory responses

As we saw above, in the 1900s women resisted unwanted attention from street "mashers" by fighting back using the tools at hand—hatpins, their hands, or umbrellas. Today's women draw on mobile technology to, for example, capture images of harassers and post them on social media sites, or raise awareness by documenting their experiences on websites like Stop Street Harassment (see Stop Street Harassment 2017). While worth celebrating, Marissa Fessenden (2015) is undeniably right in asserting that "in each era, the instrument closest to hand, whether smartphone or hatpin, may work on an individual man, but has yet to stop catcalling entirely." To this end some women turn to more conventional mechanisms, making use of the handful of provincial laws (e.g., Nova Scotia's *Human Rights Act*, which under article 5(2) prohibits sexual harassment) or, in some cities, the municipal bylaws prohibiting disturbances (e.g., Winnipeg's *Neighbourhood Liveability Bylaw*).

While the ambiguous nature of street intrusions would appear to situate them outside criminal justice solutions, there are periodic calls for Canada to follow the lead of countries like Portugal and Belgium who have criminalized misogynist street harassment (Izadi 2016). As we see throughout this book, punitive solutions often feel intuitive in our carceral society; however, in practice such strategies reflect and reproduce class and race stratifications—not only are racialized and poor women unlikely to enjoy the benefits of legal protection, it is racialized men who are likely to be read as risky by criminal justice actors and subjected to criminal sanction (Comack 2012; Sapers 2015). The tragic 2016 death of Abdirahman Abdi, a mentally ill Somali man, at the hands of police is a cautionary tale in this regard—police had been called when

Mr. Abdi allegedly harassed and (in one instance) groped female customers at an Ottawa-area coffee shop (Helmer 2017).

Campus harassment: The continuing pedigree of white male privilege

In contrast to the "sketchy" areas that women may seek to avoid, university administrators have long promoted campuses as environments of liberal thought, civility, higher learning, achievement, and career preparation; Martin Schwartz and Walter DeKeseredy's (1997) assertion that campuses are not the havens they are made out to be has become more broadly accepted in light of the increasing publicity around sexual assaults on campuses over the past few years (examined more closely in Chapter 5). Among other factors fraternities, which scholars have identified as encouraging and facilitating sexist, assaultive, and racist behaviours, continue to have a significant presence on campuses in Canada as well in the United States (Axelrod 1990; Boyle 2015; Cabrera 2014; Sanday 2007).

"Panty raids" are a striking example of misogyny and its normalization by administrators a generation ago: "crowds of middle-class white men surround a women's dormitory and demand that each resident turn over a piece of intimate apparel…. The 'panty raids' were often supplemented by burglary, breaking and entering, and property damage. In cases such as these, the typical campus administrators' response was: 'Oh well, boys will be boys'" (Schwartz and DeKeseredy 1997, 4). Importantly, Schwartz and DeKeseredy (1997) attribute university administrators' perceptions of these and other crimes (e.g., vandalism) as "harmless prank[s] committed by exuberant fraternity men or a group of males 'cooped up' in a dormitory room" (4) to the privilege and social capital enjoyed by white middle and upper class students.

Recent examples of similar behaviour by young university men suggests that such beliefs continue to be held and transmitted; university campuses remain environments of white (upper and middle class) privilege in which misogyny figures prominently (Cabrera 2014). In 2014, university administrators and people in the surrounding community learned that young men in Dalhousie University's Faculty of Dentistry "had posted sexist, misogynist, and homophobic remarks and images on Facebook. Some of the posts focused on their female classmates, using derogatory, demeaning, and sexually violent terms" (Backhouse, McRae, and Lyer 2015, 1). That the comments were posted on December 6, the day of the Montréal Massacre—the horrific incident of misogynist violence at the École Polytechnique with which this book began—is a telling measure of how little attitudes among university-aged men appear to have changed (ibid.). News of other incidents soon followed: Professors in the faculty had exhibited sexist behaviour, fostering misogynist classroom environments (one "showed his students a video featuring scantily clad women to 'wake up' the early morning class"; ibid., 11); department administrators had allowed male students to contribute graffiti to a wall that had amassed sexist comments for so long it was a fond memory for returning male alumni to revisit. Initially, administrators responded with conventional excuses—it was "just locker room talk"; "boys will be boys." After garnering considerable negative national attention, however, the school struck a task force that characterized the culture of the Faculty of Dentistry as permitting "incidents of sexism, misogyny, homophobia and racism" (ibid., 3).

A similar incident occurred at the University of British Columbia (UBC) in 2013 when commerce students at the Sauder School of Business sang a chant about raping young women during frosh week. It began "Y-O-U-N-G at UBC, we like 'em young," and included the memorable "N is for no consent"; there were also "allegations that another chant was insulting to First Nations" (Sherlock 2013). When questioned, frosh leaders asserted that the chant helped create a sense of community and brotherhood among students and defended it as a well-established tradition (Fact Finding Team 2013). One student explained that, although hesitant, he was encouraged by frosh leaders and participated in what he interpreted as a rite of passage (ibid.). Scholars have characterized male students' adherence to misogynist traditions, including frosh leaders' desire to transmit them and new students' decisions to follow them without question, as forms of peer influence that engender sexist environments and facilitate sexual harassment and abuse (Godenzi, Schwartz, and DeKeseredy 2001). As we saw in Chapter 3, gender and sexual scripts are mutually reinforcing; in a context of increasing gender parity on campus (indeed, as noted in Chapter 2, more women than men now earn undergraduate degrees), young men may attempt to assert their masculinity and privilege by denigrating women and racialized people (Cabrera 2014; Godenzi et al. 2001).

Administrative responses

Both Dalhousie and UBC investigated the incidents that occurred at their institutions. While not exemplary, their responses at least demonstrate that university administrators' attitudes have changed somewhat with regard to sexist behaviours and environments. Dalhousie, in place of academic sanction, saw fit to resolve the matter through restorative justice and remedial training for the 12 male dentistry students who had been part of the Facebook group (Backhouse et al. 2015). Recognizing the systemic nature of the problem, the task force also recommended fashioning the Faculty of Dentistry into a less toxic and more inclusive and diverse environment (ibid.).

Similarly, UBC conducted an investigation and created a task force to respond to the frosh week rape chant. Three years later, few of the issues identified by the 2014 task force had been addressed (Benedet et al. 2016); in May 2017 UBC finally enacted a policy to respond to sexual harassment and assault. That these responses only came about after bad publicity evinces the reticence of university administrators to cede the mythic aura of enlightened thought shrouding the higher education experience (Schwartz and DeKeseredy 1997). However, the publicity did trigger important conversations about the prevalence of and strategies to reduce sexual harassment on campus. Illustrating the entwinement and pervasiveness of everyday intrusions, it is notable that some of the campus harassment discussed above happened online. In this respect, schools' social environment can also play a role in gendered cyberbullying, the issue to which we now turn.

Cyber-misogyny: Intrusions online

The Internet has transformed society in ways unimaginable just 30 years ago. As women have embraced online technologies, early fears that the Internet would be another "man's world" were quickly disproven; in fact, young women—who are more likely to be responsible for digital content than are young men—are heavily invested "in seeing and being seen through online media" (Bailey and Steeves 2013, 42). Women also, as highlighted throughout this book, use these new technologies to challenge the normative order, to mobilize, to put their stories "on the record." In short, the Internet is an important medium for women's individual and collective resistance.

The Internet has also opened up a new (virtual) space for women to navigate; like public space, the online world is rife with the potential for behaviour that is unambiguously gendered harassment, verbal abuse, and bullying. Indeed, the digital realm poses unique challenges: The omnipresence of mobile devices makes the potential for harassment ubiquitous as the private and public become ever more entangled; the ability to remain anonymous removes conventional deterrents and emboldens aggressors; the impersonality of the medium insolates perpetrators from the impact of "just words"; and the fact that the bullying is not confined to a fixed physical location and jurisdiction presents problems for legal and other regulatory responses (Broll and Huey 2015; Poland 2016).

What do we call this disturbingly normalized "ceaseless flickering hum of low-level emotional violence" (Haque 2016)? The term **cyber-misogyny** captures "the diverse forms of gendered hatred, harassment, and abusive behaviour directed towards women and girls online" (West Coast Leaf 2014, 5), including trolling, revenge porn, cyberstalking, cyberbullying, blackmail, and threats. The vulnerability of women to online bullying is well documented; we know, for example, that Canadian women between the ages of 15 and 29 report significantly higher rates than men (Hango 2016). Moreover, women who are public figures or engage with issues in a professional capacity, such as journalists and politicians, are routinely subjected to a particularly gendered form of online bullying (IPU 2016); as MP Michelle Rempel, featured in Box 3.2 on page 79, noted, "My male colleagues are not being threatened with rape, and they are not being called gendered slurs as a way to disempower them or harass them" (quoted in Singh 2016).

Powerful women like parliamentarians are subject to high rates of cyber-misogyny; statistics, however, alert us to the importance of factoring in intersecting identities that increase vulnerability to cyber violence—for example, young Canadian adults who identify as gay or bisexual are "more likely than their heterosexual counterparts to have experienced cyberbullying" (Hango 2016, 3), and individuals with mental health issues are disproportionately targeted (Fairbairn and Black 2015). Here, as in the other spaces we are examining, intersecting marginalizations condition not only vulnerability but also the nature of the abuse. We see, for example, how racism informed two of the cases discussed in Chapter 3: Leslie Jones, who was referred to as "King Kong" and "savage" (Bonazzo 2016), and Member of Parliament Iqra Khalid, who was referred to as, among other things, a "draper head Muslim" (Harris 2017b).

Cyber-misogyny is endemic, and it is not only women with public profiles, or marginalized women, or "othered" women, who are at risk—any woman who engages in social activism and speaks up can find herself the target of venomous attacks that draw on the same gender tropes and stereotypes we see on the street. One example, among myriad, was the experience of Wakefield, Québec, resident Amanda Dexter who, after publicizing her campaign calling for a boycott of Trump products, found herself the subject of ferocious online attacks; in addition to threatening physical harm, the cyber-misogynists engaged in completely extraneous body shaming, with tweets denigrating her as a "whiny and jealous fat ugly bitch" and "lard ass leftist" (Harris 2017a). If, as Bailey Poland (2016) suggests, these attacks are about signalling that women are interlopers in online spaces and aim "to silence women entirely or force them to conform to men's chosen norms for a specific space" (19), it is not self-evident they are successful—like their umbrella and hatpin wielding foremothers, women, including Ms. Dexter, show considerable resilience and, while acknowledging their fear and pain, are refusing to be silenced or to yield the space.

For some women, however, and particularly young women who "are most likely to experience online harassment in its most severe forms" (CWF 2014, 2), the porousness of the line between the virtual and real world denies them even the ability to disengage should they choose to do so. Two cases—Rehtaeh Parsons and Amanda Todd—illustrate the ways predatory behaviour, cyberbullying, and slut shaming are intertwined, sometimes with tragic consequences. Nova Scotia teenager Rehtaeh Parsons spoke of having been sexually assaulted at a house party by young men who took, and subsequently posted on social media, a revealing picture (Gillis 2013). At the time, in spite of her age, evidence of incapacitation, and an explicit photo that met the legal threshold for child pornography, no charges were laid. In his independent review of the case, Murray Segal (2015), while critical of the police investigation and the Crown's decision not to lay criminal charges against the young men, also signalled the impact of cyberbullying—it was when the image, reposted on social media by complicit peers, circulated widely throughout her school that Ms. Parsons's "inner turmoil became public knowledge" (Leah Parsons, quoted in Gillis 2013). Labelled a "slut," it was the subsequent harassment, social judgment, and peer exclusion she found unbearable; Rehtaeh Parsons died on April 7, 2013, three days after attempting suicide at the age of 17.

Like Rehtaeh Parsons, British Columbia teen Amanda Todd (age 15) also took her own life after years of teasing, social ostracization, and slut shaming; like Ms. Parsons, she too had been the victim of a crime—when she refused to comply with demands for "a show" her blackmailer (later identified as Aydin Coban) made good on his threat to widely disseminate a screenshot of her flashing her breasts (Todd 2012). In the heart-wrenching YouTube video she posted just weeks prior to her death, parts of which are transcribed in Box 4.2, Ms. Todd shared the "never ending" pain of social exclusion, the loss of friends, "name calling," and "judgement" (ibid.). The experiences of these two young women force us not only to acknowledge the symbiotic relationship between the cyber-misogyny and the peers who encouraged it and—through their retweets or "likes"—amplified the message, but also the enduring power of the slut epitaph to shame and control women.

Policing cyberspace, regulating girls

In the aftermath of the deaths of Rehtaeh Parsons and Amanda Todd, the federal and (some) provincial governments rushed to fill the perceived legislative void by enacting anti-cyberbullying legislation. The first such law, Nova Scotia's 2013 *Cyber-Safety Act*, is a classic example of knee-jerk legislative over-reach; it granted police broad powers, allowed victims to apply for protection orders that would limit an accused's access to electronic communication devices, and held parents of under-age cyberbullies liable. It was ruled unconstitutional two years later by Justice Glen G. McDougall of the Supreme Court of Nova Scotia (in *Crouch v. Snell*), who deemed the Act, largely on the basis of its exceedingly broad definition of cyberbullying, "a colossal failure" (para. 165).

BOX 4.2: AMANDA TODD'S ORDEAL

[I] got called stunning, beautiful, perfect, etc.... Then wanted me to flash ... So I did ... 1 year later ... I got a msg on Facebook. [...] It said ... If you don't put on a show for me I will send ur boobs. He knew my address, school, relatives, friends, family names. [...] my photo was sent to everyone. I then got really sick and got ... anxiety, major depression and panic disorder. I then moved and got into drugs & alcohol. My anxiety got worse ... couldn't go out. A year past and the guy came back with ... [...] a Facebook page. My boobs were his profile pic ... Cried every night, lost all my friends and [the] respect people had for me ... again ... Then nobody liked me. Name calling, judged [...] I started cutting ... [...] Didn't have any friends and sat at lunch alone. So I moved schools again ... Everything was better even though I still sat alone [...] a month later I started talking to an old guy friend. We back and fourth texted and he started to say he liked me ... led me on ... he had a girlfriend. [...] He hooked up with me ... I thought he liked me ... 1 week later I get a text get out of your school. His girlfriend and 15 others came including hiself ... The girl and 2 others just said look around nobody likes you. In front of my new school (50) people. A guy then yelled just punch her already. So she did ... she threw me to the ground a[nd] punched me several times. Kids filmed it. [...] Teachers ran over but I just went and layed in a ditch and my dad found me. I wanted to die so bad ... when he brought me home I drank bleach [...] Ambulance came and brought me to the hospital and flushed me. After I got home all I saw on Facebook—[was] she deserved it, did you wash the mud out of your hair? I hope she's dead. Nobody cared [...] I didn't wanna press charges because I wanted to move on. 6 months has gone by ... people are posting pics of bleach, clorex, and ditches, tagging me ... I was doing a lot better too ... [T]hey said ... she should try a different bleach. I hope she dies this time and isn't so stupid. They said I hope she sees this and kills herself. Why do I get this [treatment]? [...] life never gets any better... cant go to school meet or be with people ... constantly cutting ... Im really depressed [...] a month ago this summer I overdosed ... in hospital for 2 days. Im stuck [...] I have nobody.

Todd 2012

More measured, albeit still with an eye to punishment, has been the response of provinces who amended or expanded their education acts (which, generally speaking, already included prohibitions against cyberbullying) to increase potential sanctions (Department of Justice 2017). Moreover, since the *Protecting Canadians from Online Crime Act* came into effect on March 10, 2015, federal laws have criminalized anyone who "publishes, distributes, transmits, sells, makes available or advertises an intimate image of a person" without the consent of the person captured by that image (*CC* s. 162.1(1)). Here again we see gendered violence used to justify regulatory creep; the wide-ranging omnibus bill that introduced the law was critiqued for the expansion of police surveillance capacity and access to digital data.

The complexity and layers of the Parsons and Todd cases highlight the limits of criminal justice solutions to social problems rooted in gender inequality; none of these laws address the everyday harassment that caused these young women so much pain. Indeed, even some police officers frame the criminalization of what they describe as "meanness" as ineffective, a waste of government resources, or unnecessarily punitive, suggesting pre-emptive education would be preferable (Broll and Huey 2015). However, prevailing preventive approaches appear to pivot on the same myths about women that are critiqued when invoked in relation to sexual assault (see Chapter 5); for example, a *CBC News* documentary drawing attention to sexting as a social problem facing teens and tweens naturalized young men's sexual voraciousness and placed the onus on young women to protect themselves (CBC 2016b), while a resource published by the Canadian Centre for Child Protection (CCCP 2014) reiterates the "stranger danger" trope by framing online sexual predators as adults unknown to the victim.

Amidst the cultural anxiety around the online sexual victimization of teen girls—which can involve the non-consensual distribution of sexual images initially sent by the victim—Andrea Slane (2013) problematizes the failure to acknowledge the possibility that sexting can also be a healthy form of sexual expression, intimacy, and flirtation; she argues that both legal and popular conceptualizations of cyberbullying collapse sexting into online sexual harassment. In turn, solutions to sexting more closely resemble (sexual) abstinence approaches: preventive education urges teenage girls to police their own sexuality by refraining from sexting, which is framed as inherently risky—tellingly, another resource published by the CCCP refers to sexting as "self/peer exploitation" (CCCP 2017, 2). According to Lara Karaian (2012), news media and other popular culture outlets overwhelmingly "represent teenage girls who sext as lacking in sexual agency, having fallen prey to the 'pornification' of a generation" (58). Once again the policing of girls' sexual expression emanates from a desire to protect middle class, white, female sexual respectability, accompanied by the familiar tropes of sexual vulnerability, passivity, and victim blaming (ibid.).

Resistance: Contesting responsibilization and slut shaming

It is perhaps fitting that Slut Walk, a movement rejecting discourses that blame and shame women for not behaving "respectably" in public, was inspired on campus, began and spread online, and took to the streets—indeed, Amanda Todd's words in Box 4.2 powerfully illustrate how slut shaming pervades all three of the spheres addressed in this chapter. Slut Walk is an annual event inspired by comments made by a Toronto police officer placing the onus on women to prevent sexual assault; in response, two incensed students, Heather Jarvis and Sonia Barnett, used social media to mobilize, holding the first event in Toronto in 2011. It has since grown into a worldwide phenomenon that speaks back to the sexualized intrusions we have seen throughout this chapter—intrusions that illuminate the extent to which women continue to be evaluated in relation to their sexuality and ability to navigate the arbitrary line that divides the good girl from the *slut*.

Young women's rejection of the intrusive and pervasive regulation of their sexuality is evident in Slut Walk's statement of purpose, written by its organizers in 2011, who—in the long tradition of social justice movements reclaiming once-derogatory terms (e.g., the LGBTQ community's use of *queer*)—sought to rehabilitate the term *slut*: "We are tired of being oppressed by slut-shaming; of being judged by our sexuality and feeling unsafe as a result. Being in charge of our sexual lives should not mean that we are opening ourselves to an expectation of violence, regardless if we participate in sex for pleasure or work. No one should equate enjoying sex with attracting sexual assault" (quoted in Reger 2014, 50). Slut Walk marchers (cis women, trans women, gender queer people, and some men) wear ordinary clothes, or underwear, or flashy outfits, and carry signs with sex-positive and anti-violence messages. Overwhelmingly they are young adults (see Figure 4.2).

The desire to reclaim the term *slut*, along with the edgy sex-positive atmosphere that permeates the event, marks Slut Walk as a third wave feminist initiative; a decided departure from the Take Back the Night marches begun by an earlier generation. Further affirming the power of the label, Slut Walk has (like sexting) been criticized by anti-pornography feminists as a symptom of the false consciousness of young women who have grown up in a "pornified" culture and, through pressure to become hypersexualized, mistakenly equate sexual empowerment and freedom with "looking like a porn star" (Reger 2014, 62). At the same time, some racialized women, who contextualize the term *slut* in relation to the history of slavery and sexual oppression discussed in Chapter 1, are "troubled by the reclaiming of a word with such deep racialized meanings" (ibid., 63). The critiques powerfully illustrate how

FIGURE 4.2: Slut Walk, 2011

fraught resistance can be; it is an issue to which the organizers drew attention: "We have been discredited for our privilege, for our non-privilege, for being feminists, for hating feminists, for having the audacity to demand respect, for 'lionizing promiscuity', for doing too much, for not doing enough and almost every argument you can think of from every side" (ibid., 65). That Slut Walk continues in spite of these tensions demonstrates young women's commitment to resisting the subtext of everyday gender-policing intrusions.

Concluding reflections

In this chapter we have seen that as women venture into new spaces—onto the streets of urban centres in the late nineteenth century, onto campuses in the mid-twentieth century, and online in the twenty-first century—their everyday experiences of those spaces is characterized by disrupting and often destabilizing intrusions. Speaking to relations of power, it would appear that as new space opens up for women new exclusionary tactics emerge. Most recently we have seen that, for all the unprecedented changes the information age has wrought, there are powerful echoes of the themes we examined in terms of everyday intrusions on the street and on campus: the gendered and intersectional nature of the targeting; the scripts pivoting on sexuality and appearance;

the presumed inevitability that women will be victimized; and finally, for those cases where the situation escalates, victim blaming and solutions that use protectionist rhetoric and mobilize gender tropes to regulate women.

The very fact that these intrusions become a routine aspect of women's lives is significant. As we will similarly see in the following chapters in this section, it is here that the mutual reinforcement of interpersonal, symbolic, and structural violence becomes visible. Fear and stress in their everyday lives may shape not only women's routes and routines, but curtail their use of spaces, in turn reducing their involvement and visibility in public, political, and organizational leadership roles (see Chapter 3). This in turn impacts women's ability to shape responses and address regulation that perpetuates gendered and other forms of violence and discrimination. In this context some women's decision to, for example, wear a hat instead of a hijab (see Box 4.1) minimizes the risk of violence at the cost of reinforcing the "otherness" of Muslim dress. That this "otherness" is, in turn, encoded in xenophobic legislation such as Québec's *Act to Foster Adherence to State Religious Neutrality* (2017; detailed in Chapter 1) highlights the conditional nature of safety strategies that necessarily function within existing structures and relations of power.

EXERCISE: EVERYDAY INTRUSIONS AND SAFETY WORK

In this chapter we examined safety work, the unseen and unacknowledged labour undertaken to avoid, prevent, or manage harassment.

Spend a few minutes thinking about the safety work you engage in
- before entering a public space;
- when in a public space.

Get into pairs.

Interview each other about the safety work you do before you go out in public and when out on the street.

Compare strategies and tactics; reflect on differences and similarities.

Discuss what, if anything, this exercise illuminated.

CHAPTER 5

SEXUAL ASSAULT: LAWS, SCRIPTS, AND VICTIM BLAMING

On January 24, 2011, Constable Michael Sanguinetti of the Toronto Police Services told students attending a presentation at York University's Osgoode Hall Law School that "women should avoid dressing like sluts in order not to be victimized" (Rush 2011). His comment speaks to many of the issues examined in this chapter—persistent gender essentialism, deeply embedded rape myths, victim blaming, and the limits of the criminal justice system—as well as the themes of this book, most particularly the importance of structural analysis. The firestorm of controversy and mobilization that followed his comments (including the annual Slut Walk discussed in Chapter 4) alert us to an energized resistance against the normative framing of sexual assault.

Far from rare, sexual assault is shockingly common. An estimated 553,000 Canadian women are victims of sexual assault every year (Conroy and Cotter 2017), and approximately one in five female undergraduate students will be sexually assaulted during the course of her university studies (Task Force on Respect and Equality 2015). The overwhelming majority of these acts of aggression are committed by people known to the victim—acquaintances, friends, colleagues, and partners (Statistics Canada 2015a). How can we understand this? How can we even start to make sense of these numbers? The sheer volume speaks against psychological explanations of individual, "sick" perpetrators. But does that mean sexual assault is biologically determined, as Constable Sanguinetti's comment suggests? After all, if women must dress modestly to avoid molestation, then men must be controlled by their physiology and, implicitly, their inability to govern their sexual urges.

This surprisingly pervasive explanation, which normalizes sexual assault as natural and inevitable, quickly falls apart when we appreciate that sexual aggression is not equally prevalent in every society. Highlighting the importance of social context, cultural anthropologist Peggy Reeves Sanday (1981; 1996) divides cultures into rape free (low incidence of sexual aggression) and rape prone societies. Unlike those categorized as rape free, rape prone societ-ies are hierarchal, patriarchal, and characterized by a sharp division of labour; sex is understood as conquest; women enjoy less power, authority, and politi-cal participation; and "males express contempt for women as decision makers" (Sanday 1981, 24). The context laid out in Part A of this book—Canada has a gendered division of labour, women are poorer than men, women in posi-tions of authority are routinely disrespected, the media propagates sexualized and/or subordinate representations of women—suggests that Canada bears key markers of being a rape prone society. We can also think back to the sexual scripts introduced in Chapter 3. Not only do sexual scripts provide norma-tive guidelines for (hetero)sexual interactions (Simon and Gagnon 1986), they also influence cultural and individual understandings of consent. As Kristen Jozkowski and her colleagues (2014) note, according to traditional sexual scripts, women are expected to rebuff sexual advances or feign resistance to main-tain a virtuous appearance. Conversely, men are expected to actively pursue women until they succumb.

This is the point of departure for this chapter: We can only start to make sense both of gendered sexual violence and the (woefully inadequate) state and social responses if we situate sexual assault in the broader context of social structures and scripts. This point of entry also positions us to think beyond essentialist understandings and brings intersectionality into the conversation. For example, while all women are vulnerable to sexual assault, Indigenous women report rates three times higher than those of their non-Indigenous counterparts (Perreault 2015). Given that "the context in which indigenous women and girls are subjected to violence is one of **structural discrimina-tion** linked to social and economic inequality" (Human Rights Watch 2013), we see unambiguously how interlocking oppressions, which under neoliber-alism are framed as "risk factors"—homelessness, childhood maltreatment, and poverty—operate in conjunction with the racial tropes of promiscuity exam-ined in Chapter 1, to render Indigenous women hyper-vulnerable to sexual violence. Moreover, as we see in this chapter, from medieval law to present-day enforcement, responses to sexual assault have reproduced interlocking class, gender, and racial hierarchies.

Socio-historic considerations: From rape to sexual assault

Rape, as sexual assault was historically known, was long considered a serious capital crime and roundly condemned; right up until 1983 when the current laws came into effect those found guilty were liable to life imprisonment and whipping (*Criminal Code* s. 143). While on the surface sexual assault laws protected all women, a historic look at their enforcement highlights how deeply entrenched assumptions and gender norms limited the scope of legal protection to demonstrably modest, virtuous women. In medieval England, for example, rape was seen as a serious offence—punishable by castration and blinding—only if the victim was a virgin or a woman who was sworn to chastity (e.g., a nun); the offence was extended to include married women in the late thirteenth century, but continued to exclude women who were not seen as respectable (e.g., mistresses, prostitutes) (Greenberg 1984). A similar emphasis on sexual respectability is evident in early Canadian laws. For example, in 1886 the seduction of a girl between 12 and 16 years of age was criminalized, but only if she was "of previously chaste character" (Pilon 1999, 1).

As legal historian Constance Backhouse (1991) highlights, judges and juries in the nineteenth century were preoccupied with the character of the victim, and "women who were known to drink alcoholic beverages, frequent taverns, or indulge in extramarital sex were virtually guaranteed legal rebuff when they complained of violent rape. In the language of the courts they lacked credibility" (87). In addition, conviction pivoted on the victim's active and aggressive resistance. For example in *R. v. Flick* (1866), Justice Adam Wilson instructed the court that the victim must have been "overcome by force or terror, she [was] resisting as much as she could, and resisting so as to make the prisoner see and know that she really was resisting" (quoted in Backhouse 1991, 103). In other words, unconventional women cannot be raped, women lie, there is only one appropriate way to respond during a sexual assault, and the onus is on the victim to ensure that their non-consent is forcefully and unambiguously conveyed to their attacker. As we see below, these assumptions continue to hold sway today and profoundly impact all women, but most especially those who are sexually assaulted.

Prior to 1983 sexual aggressions were classified as sexual offences and codified in the *Criminal Code* (*CC*) as indecent assault on a female or male (s. 156) or rape and attempted rape (s. 143). Rape was defined as when "[a] male person … has sexual intercourse with a female person who is not his wife, (a) without her consent, or (b) with her consent if the consent is extorted by threats or fear of bodily harm, (ii) is obtained by personating her husband, or (iii) is obtained by false and fraudulent representations as to the nature and quality of the act." By the mid-1970s sexual assault and the state's response was very much on the mainstream feminist agenda. As women gathered in consciousness-raising groups in the 1960s and 1970s to share their struggles and experiences the pervasive nature of sexual violence (by acquaintances, not strangers) came to light (Johnson and Dawson 2011), and women in Canada (and the United States and Europe) took to the streets in protest. As Angela Davis (1983), writing about the United States, points out, in spite of Black women's long history of social activism they absented themselves from the anti-rape movement of the day, alienated by mainstream second wave feminists' confidence in the criminal justice system. Indeed, far from recognizing that the "myth of the Black rapist has been methodically conjured up whenever recurrent waves of violence and terror against the Black community have required convincing justifications" (Davis 1983, 173), key feminist anti-rape authors, such as Susan Brownmiller (1975), resurrected the spectre of the Black rapist arguing that Black men, denied access to other symbols of male supremacy, were particularly prone to committing sexual violence.

There is little evidence that the largely white middle class, mainstream second wave feminist movement north of the border was any more sensitive to diverse women's experiences—or any less carceral. That said, existing laws *were* profoundly patriarchal and heterosexist and spoke powerfully to the ways the legal apparatus reflected and maintained the normative order. Feminists were enraged that the law enshrined not only husbands' entitlement to sexual access but also demonstrated the significance of heterosexual (vaginal) penetration and not, for example, the experiences of women who are penetrated orally, anally, or with objects (Los 1994). More evidence of male centrism was identified in the assumption, encoded in law, that women (in addition to being intellectually inferior and hysterical, as discussed in Chapter 3) are naturally devious and malicious—prone to falsely accusing men of sexual misconduct. First, reflecting the normative framing of women as untrustworthy, conviction required collaboration: "No accused shall be convicted ... unless the evidence of the witness is corroborated in a material particular by evidence that implicates the accused" (*CC* s. 139. (1)). Second, the doctrine of recent complaint—pivoting on the assumption that women habitually fabricate rape scenarios when they regret their consensual sexual dalliances—meant accusations were invalidated if there was a delay in reporting the offence (Los 1994). Third, all (non-virtuous) women's unreliable character was invoked in the brutal re-victimization of complainants by defence council, who routinely badgered the victim using any suspicion of extramarital sexual activity to discredit her; indeed, prior to 1975 "the complainant's sexual conduct with men other than the accused was considered crucial in establishing if she had consented" (ibid., 25). As feminists of the day pointed out, sexually active women essentially forfeited their right to say no (Bowland 1994).

In 1982, endeavouring to meet the equality requirements of the newly enacted *Charter of Rights and Freedoms* (1982), parliamentarians introduced legal reforms that ostensibly responded to the demands of the mainstream feminist lobby (Los 1994). The new *Criminal Code* provisions defined "all incidents of unwanted sexual activities, including attacks and sexual touching" (Brennan and Taylor-Butts 2008, 7) as sexual assault, expanding the offence to include sexual assault (s. 246.1, now s. 271), sexual assault with a weapon, threats to a third party or causing bodily harm (s. 246.2; now s. 272), and aggravated sexual assault (s. 246.3, now s. 273). In addition to making the crime gender neutral (women could be perpetrators; men could be victims), these changes eliminated the recent-complaint doctrine, abolished husbands' legal immunity, and removed the need for corroboration. The law also defined consent in the positive (s. 244(3), now s. 273.1(2)), shifting the onus from the Crown proving the victim did not consent to the defence demonstrating that reasonable care was taken to ensure consent, while still allowing the "honest but mistaken" belief as a defence (s. 244(4)). At the same time, *CC* s. 246.6(1) (now s. 276), the "rape shield law"—which restricted when the complainant's sexual history with individuals other than the accused could be entered into evidence—was introduced.

These laws, with two significant changes, continue to govern sexual violence in Canada. First, in 1991 the "honest but mistaken" belief that consent was given (colloquially known as the "honest but stupid" defence) was replaced with an objective "reasonable person" test. Second, and more contentiously, in June 1991 the Supreme Court of Canada in *R. v. Seaboyer; R. v. Gayme* ruled the rape shield law infringed on an accused's right to life, liberty, and security of the person and the right to a fair trail and was therefore unconstitutional; in 1992, *CC* s. 276 was amended to ensure *Charter* compliance. Currently, *CC* s. 276(1) allows for a judge to determine whether specific instances of the complainant's sexual activity are relevant and significant enough to be admitted into evidence. This provision is tempered by *CC* s. 278.1, introduced in 1997 to conform to the Supreme Court of Canada's 1995 ruling in *R. v. Bishop*, "declaring that the trial judge must balance the privacy interests of complainants and third parties with the accused's right to a fair trial" (West Coast Leaf, n.d.).

The 1983 reforms moved away from the image of women as sexual and reproductive property and, by classifying it as an assault rather than a sexual offence, acknowledged that sexual aggression is an act of violence. In other words, at a symbolic level they are important. But do they address the more fundamental issue of sexual violence? Governance feminists of the day, while concerned that removing the term *rape* and making the law gender neutral depoliticized and minimized the offence (Majury 1994), were confident that replacing misogynist with feminist framing and enshrining a more equitable process would encourage victims to come forward, ultimately reducing the sexual victimization of women (Los 1994). This reflects profoundly normative assumptions, faith in legal and state rationalities/institutions, and in turn a failure to consider the very real class and racial biases in the criminal justice system. We now turn to the impact of the hard fought law reform by examining what we know about sexual violence in Canada today, how it is framed, and to what extent the objectives of the reformers have been realized.

Juxtaposing facts against myths

What do we know about sexual assault in Canada beyond its well-established prevalence? We know that women are predominantly (but certainly not exclusively) the targets, comprising an estimated 87 per cent of victims (Conroy and Cotter 2017); that, based on Statistics Canada data (which, as noted in the Introduction, is an incomplete measure), men are the perpetrators in 97 per cent of sexual assaults (Mahony, Jacob, and Hobson 2017); that approximately 75 per cent of women know their attacker (45 per cent as a casual acquaintance/friend; 17 per cent as an intimate partner; 13 per cent as another family member). We also know that most sexual assaults occur indoors; and that women who report 30 or more evening activities a month (e.g., for school, work, or leisure activities) have rates five times higher than women who participate in 10 or fewer (Sinha 2013). Finally, we know that women of any age, race, class, and body type are sexually assaulted.

We also know, however, that women between the ages of 15 and 24 are at highest risk, accounting for almost half (47 per cent) of all sexual assaults (Conroy and Cotter 2017). In this age group are, of course, college and university women, whom scholars have noted face significant risk of sexual violence. While alcohol is so prevalent on college and university campuses that 50 to 74 per cent of campus sexual assaults involve alcohol use by the offender and/ or the victim (Boyle 2015), consistent with Lawrence Cohen and Marcus Felson's (1979) routine activities theory it is sorority women who have been found to be especially vulnerable; they go out, consume alcohol, and interact with fraternity men—who in turn are more likely to be perpetrators of sexual assault (Boyle 2015)—to a greater extent than other students (Franklin 2016). That explanations of campus rape often highlight the role of alcohol (Johnson and Dawson 2011) evinces a thought fallacy that transforms a correlation into a causal factor: Correlation does not mean that alcohol or "risk taking" cause sexual assault, but it does speak to the context in which women are vulnerable and to the use of substances to facilitate sexual assault. It also speaks to the higher moral standard to which women are held—and men in turn exempted—in regard to sexual conduct.

We also know that while victims and perpetrators come from all class locations and ethnicities, socio-economic marginalization is correlated to higher rates of sexual victimization; further, "women with disabilities and those who are institutionalized, Aboriginal women, single women, and women who are unemployed or have low-incomes are at heightened risk of sexual assault" (CWF 2016, 2). This speaks to the way state policies not only increase vulnerability but also create conditions that render women at risk of sexual violence from those who should protect them. For example, disabled women face victimization at two times the national rate (Conroy and Cotter 2017), and women who are institutionalized are particularly vulnerable to sexual assault perpetrated by caregivers (Statistics Canada 2015a). We see similar dynamics in Indigenous women's experiences of sexual victimization at the hands of police. Comparing the level of apprehension to that in post-conflict zones, Human Rights Watch (2013) notes that "the palpable fear of the police was accompanied with a notable matter of fact manner ... reflecting a normalized expectation that if one was an indigenous woman or girl police mistreatment is to be anticipated" (34). In other words, structural inequality not only creates the conditions that increase marginalized women's vulnerability to sexual violence, it is sometimes directly implicated.

Further, we know there is no single response to violent victimization. Psychologists have documented three principal ways humans react to imminent danger: When individuals perceive they are able to overcome the challenge, they fight; when they deem this unlikely to be successful, they flee; but in "a situation in which [they've] concluded (in a matter of seconds—if not milliseconds) that [they] can neither defeat the frighteningly dangerous opponent confronting [them] nor safely bolt from it" people freeze and detach (Seltzer 2015). Leon Seltzer (2015) explains that freezing can be highly adaptive: "[B]eing physically, mentally, and emotionally immobilized by your consternation permits you not to feel the harrowing enormity of what's happening to you, which in your hyper-aroused state might threaten your very sanity." We see all of these survival strategies in instances of sexual assault: Some victims fight back aggressively, others struggle to flee, and still others "freeze up" or endeavour to minimize the physical harm by feigning compliance. Yet, echoing the experience of women in the nineteenth century, doubt is regularly cast on a woman's victimization if she does not flee or fight.

Finally, we know that victims' subjective experience will vary depending on the nature of the attack; the perceived danger; the response of family, friends, and first responders; and previous victimization. However, contrary to the myth that sexual assault does not really harm anyone, its impact is often profound and long lasting. In addition to "a multitude of emotions ... includ[ing] anger, confusion and frustration, shock and disbelief, self-blame, and fear" (Benoit et al. 2015, 26) and immediate concerns including physical injuries and sexually transmitted infections, there may be long-lasting struggles that include depression, anxiety, and mental health challenges that can have deleterious effects on self-perception, work, and relationships (Benoit et al. 2016; Johnson and Dawson 2011). For example, many victims experience increased fear, avoid social situations, have immobilizing flashbacks and recurring nightmares, experience personality and behavioural changes, and struggle to complete day-to-day activities—all possible symptoms of post-traumatic stress disorder (PTSD) (National Center for PTSD 2016). Arguably the attention paid to veterans of military conflict and first responders (who are overwhelmingly men) obscures the gendered nature of the affliction and speaks to the normalization of sexual assault. Women are 2.5 times more likely than men to develop PTSD, a statistic that can in part be explained by the fact that "women are more likely to experience sexual assault; sexual assault is more likely to cause PTSD than many other events; [and] women may be more likely to blame themselves for trauma experiences than men" (ibid.). Indeed, as we see in the powerful narrative of a survivor in Box 5.1, victims of sexual assault may experience any combination of the reactions and emotions discussed above during the incident, afterwards, and, as examined below, in interactions with criminal justice officials. Self-blame not only exacerbates the effects of sexual assault but is symbolic violence in its own right. The doubt, reproach, and questioning routinely experienced by women who rationally and consciously *know* they were not responsible for their victimization speaks to the deep entrenchment of rape myths and "real rape" tropes (see Box 5.2), as do the, however fleeting, thoughts of "why did she go there/do that?" in the minds of friends, family, and supporters.

What is perhaps most striking about the empirical data presented above is the extent to which it runs contrary to common knowledge about sexual assault, and how powerfully the facts contradict "real rape" tropes and myths delineating appropriate responses during and after an attack (see Box 5.2)—assumptions that are remarkably consistent with those held by jurists in nineteenth- and twentieth-century Canada. The disjuncture between these normative assumptions and their own experiences can be destabilizing for victims (Johnson and Dawson 2011). The data also challenge the victim-blaming narratives of *the kind of woman who is raped* (e.g., promiscuous, provocatively dressed, irresponsible). This and other rape myths are deeply entrenched, even among university students. For example, a University of Ottawa survey of 1,088 students found that more than one in four (26 per cent) agreed or were neutral that women who put themselves in risky situations are partly responsible if they are raped (Task Force on Respect and Equality 2015); and among the male respondents there was greater rape myth acceptance: 42 per cent were neutral or agreed that "rape accusations are often used as a way of getting back at men" (ibid., 12).

BOX 5.1: A SURVIVOR SPEAKS OUT

I was not only told that I was assaulted, I was told that because I couldn't remember, I technically could not prove it was unwanted. ... I had to fight for an entire year to make it clear that there was something wrong with this situation....

I was pummeled with narrowed, pointed questions that dissected my personal life, love life, past life, family life, inane questions, accumulating trivial details to try and find an excuse for this guy who had me half naked before even bothering to ask for my name. After a physical assault, I was assaulted with questions designed to attack me, to say see, her facts don't line up, she's out of her mind, she's practically an alcoholic, she probably wanted to hook up....

To listen to your attorney attempt to paint a picture of me, the face of girls gone wild, as if somehow that would make it so that I had this coming for me. To listen to him say I sounded drunk on the phone because I'm silly and that's my goofy way of speaking. To point out that in the voicemail, I said I would reward my boyfriend and we all know what I was thinking. I assure you my rewards program is non transferable, especially to any nameless man that approaches me....

This is not a story of another drunk college hookup with poor decision making. Assault is not an accident.... He has only apologized for drinking and has yet to define what he did to me as sexual assault, he has revictimized me continually, relentlessly. He has been found guilty of three serious felonies and it is time for him to accept the consequences of his actions....

He is a lifetime sex registrant. That doesn't expire. Just like what he did to me doesn't expire, doesn't just go away after a set number of years. It stays with me, it's part of my identity, it has forever changed the way I carry myself, the way I live the rest of my life.

Quoted in Baker 2016

The latter belief alerts us to another fallacy: Women routinely lie about being sexually assaulted, and even if they were assaulted are malicious in their pursuit of justice, most especially if the perpetrator is of high social or cultural status (e.g., a professional athlete). So entrenched is this trope (and the biological determinist belief that sexual offenders are "just being boys") that perpetrators

BOX 5.2: COMMON RAPE MYTHS AND "REAL RAPE" TROPES

Rape ...

- is a rare occurrence
- happens outside, at night, and/or in "sketchy" areas
- entails vaginal, anal, or oral penetration
- involves weapons or obvious physical injuries
- causes few long-term effects
- is a weapon used by women who routinely falsely accuse men when they have regrets or are angry

"Real" victims of rape ...

- are exclusively young, conventionally attractive/feminine
- are hysterical, visibly upset, crying, and bruised
- immediately report the incident to the police
- fight "tooth and nail" against their attacker; if they don't, they "wanted it"
- are "innocent"; if a woman is drunk, on drugs, or otherwise engaging in "risky" behaviour (e.g., hitchhiking, sex work), she is, at least partly, to blame
- are respectable; women who are provocative or promiscuous are "asking for it"

Perpetrators of rape are ...

- men motivated by sexual frustration, desire, or uncontrollable "natural urges"
- racialized and/or underclass men
- mentally ill men
- loners without partners and/or social networks
- strangers (e.g., *not* the victim's husband, partner, friend, or co-worker)
- deviant men; not the "guys we know"

are regularly transformed into the harmed parties while the victims' experiences are erased. For example, when two Steubenville, Ohio, high school football players were found guilty of sexually assaulting a 16-year-old woman incapacitated by alcohol, CNN reporter Poppy Harlow grieved the one- and two-year sentences, describing the hearing as "incredibly emotional, incredibly difficult" as "these two young men who had such promising futures, star football players, very good students, literally watched as they believed their lives fell apart" (CNN 2013).

In the face of pervasive victim blaming, rape myths, and persistent "real rape" tropes, it is not surprising that less than 3 per cent of victims report the assault to the police (see Figure 5.1). Far from making false accusations, many women do not report the crime, citing a range of reasons, including shame, privacy, and the perception that it was too minor (e.g., not "real rape"). Many women are also fearful that the police will be biased and the process will be too taxing with little chance of the offender being convicted or sanctioned (Perreault 2015). In the next section, as we turn to the response of state actors to sexual assault, it quickly becomes evident that victims' fears are well founded.

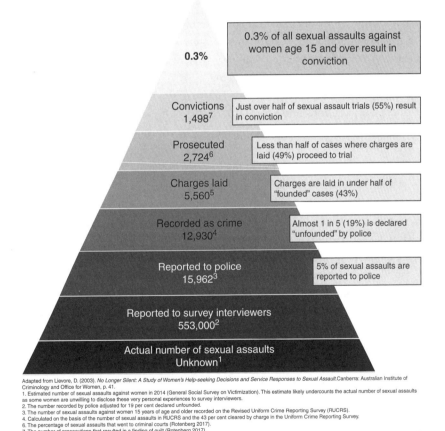

Adapted from Lievore, D. (2003). *No Longer Silent: A Study of Women's Help-seeking Decisions and Service Responses to Sexual Assault.* Canberra: Australian Institute of Criminology and Office for Women, p. 41.
1. Estimated number of sexual assaults against women in 2014 (General Social Survey on Victimization). This estimate likely undercounts the actual number of sexual assaults as some women are unwilling to disclose these very personal experiences to survey interviewers.
2. The number recorded by police adjusted for 19 per cent declared unfounded.
3. The number of sexual assaults against women 15 years of age and older recorded on the Revised Uniform Crime Reporting Survey (RUCRS).
4. Calculated on the basis of the number of sexual assaults in RUCRS and the 43 per cent cleared by charge in the Uniform Crime Reporting Survey.
5. The percentage of sexual assaults that went to criminal courts (Rotenberg 2017).
6. The number of prosecutions that resulted in a finding of guilt (Rotenberg 2017).
7. The number of prosecutions that resulted in a finding of guilt (Rotenberg 2017).
Sources: Perreault, S. 2015. "Criminal Victimization in Canada, 2014." *Juristat,* Catalogue no. 85-002-X. Ottawa: Statistics Canada; Uniform Crime Reporting Survey, 2014 special request; Rotenberg, C. 2017. "From Arrest to Conviction: Court Outcomes of Police-Reported Sexual Assaults in Canada, 2009 to 2014." *Juristat,* Catalogue no. 85-002-X. Ottawa: Statistics Canada.

FIGURE 5.1: Attrition rates for sexual assault in Canada, 2018

Criminal justice response

Standard in any first year criminology textbook is the criminal justice funnel, demonstrating the limits of official statistics by illustrating the process through which cases get weeded out of the criminal justice system: in order for a crime to be measured, it must first come to the attention of the police; be registered as an offence; a person identified as the offender; sufficient evidence collected to justify a criminal charge; a trial held; and a conviction obtained (Winterdyk 2005). The attrition rate for sexual assault is particularly dramatic with a paltry 0.3 per cent sexual assaults resulting in a conviction (Rotenberg 2017). Why might this be the case? Part of the explanation appears to be that, while the 1983 amendments gave sexual assault victims formal equity, the application of those laws by agents of the criminal justice system continues to be conditioned by normative assumptions, gender tropes, and the stubbornly persistent rape myths and "real rape" narratives. In the coming pages we focus on four aspects: rape myth adherence by police resulting in spurious classification of assaults as unfounded, the exploitation of stereotypical assumptions by defence attorneys to undermine the credibility of sexual assault victims, judicial and jury bias, and discriminatory sentencing.

Police: Gatekeepers and moral guardians of "real rape"

The few victims who do report their sexual assaults to police are, for the most part, motivated less by a desire to have the perpetrator arrested than to protect other women and to ensure the individual is held accountable—mindful of the way sexual assault victims are discursively constituted, most make the decision to report with considerable trepidation (Johnson 2017). Their apprehension is certainly warranted. Research by Robyn Doolittle (2017) has determined that in Canada—notwithstanding that only 2 to 8 per cent of all sexual assault allegations are spurious—almost one in five sexual assault complaints are categorized as unfounded. This means police believe the offence did not happen or was not attempted; put another way, over 5,500 times a year police think the individual laying a complaint is lying! By comparison 11 per cent of physical assaults are categorized in this way (ibid.). Moreover, there is striking variation across the country: Over a five-year period in Saint John, a shocking 51 per cent of cases were categorized as unfounded; in Yellowknife it was 36 per cent; in Halifax it was 13 per cent; and in Winnipeg it was just 2 per cent (ibid.). These numbers tell us more about police practices, beliefs, and the role they play as gatekeepers than they do about sexual assault in a given city.

While distressing, these findings are not surprising. There is widespread evidence that police responses are conditioned by their stereotypical beliefs about what constitutes a "real rape" and what a "real victim" looks and acts like

(Johnson 2017; Randall 2010). Holly Johnson's (2017) research found that while some sexual assault victims had positive experiences with law enforcement, many described it as "traumatizing" (18), reporting that they were not believed, told they were using the term *rape* too liberally, questioned why they did not fight back more aggressively, and in a number of cases, threatened with criminal charges of public mischief for making a false claim. Victims' credibility increases (for police) the closer the case resembles a "real rape" with a "good victim" and a stereotypical offender, as detailed in Box 5.2; for example, "cases involving strangers, White women, ethnic minority and low status perpetrators, a weapon, physical injuries, vigorous resistance, recent complaint, emotional upset, forensic evidence, no prior complaints of sexual assault, and a sober respectable woman with no prior sexual relationship with the suspect and no history of psychiatric or intellectual impairment" (ibid., 4). Here we see, once again, how scripts regarding appropriate gender behaviour and interlocking systems of oppression play out in women's lives—women who do not conform to the white middle class ideal of virtuous womanhood, who dress in an "inappropriate" working class style, who are Indigenous or Black (and therefore stereotyped as hypersexual and promiscuous), who do not speak English or do so with an accent or working class vernacular, or who are sex workers or otherwise engaged in "disreputable" behaviour are disproportionally having cases deemed unfounded by police. Devastating in its own right it also denies marginalized women criminal justice redress and, if they are fearful of the perpetrator, protection.

In short, it would appear that police continue to believe the age-old adage that women routinely make false allegations—the same myth that underlay the corroboration requirement of the pre-1983 rape law. In addition, adherence to the "appropriate response" narrative means doubt is cast when a woman appears calm and rational—in other words, when she is not stereotypically hysterical. At the same time victims who are unable to provide detailed or linear accounts are discredited by police even though episodic memory is a well-documented outcome of trauma (Doolittle 2017)—as we see in the testimonial featured in Box 5.1, not only is this destabilizing and distressing it can significantly impact interactions with criminal justice actors. Often police are not familiar with the symptoms of PTSD, which may manifest as emotional numbness or irritability (National Center for PTSD 2016)—behaviours that are not consistent with the imagined "appropriate response" (DuBois 2012). At the same time victims who are perceived as too hysterical (e.g., who cry while talking to police) or who have a history of mental illness are also subject to police suspicion for lying (ibid.). Thus, women are constituted not only in law (see Chapter 3), but also through its enforcement, as unreliable, manipulative, overly emotional, or immoral—in other words, as enduringly and inherently pathological.

Defence attorneys: "Whacking" the complainant

It would appear that, in spite of the 1983 legal reforms and a 1999 Supreme Court of Canada decision prohibiting the practice (*R. v. Mills* 1999), defence attorneys continue to relentlessly deploy every discursive tool at their disposal (e.g., lifestyle, past "misdeeds," substance consumption, inability to recall details) to destroy victims' credibility. The brutality of this tactic, which "exploit[s] the stereotypes and vulnerabilities inherent in sexual assault cases to secure a favourable outcome," is reflected in its colloquial name: "whacking" the complainant (Tanovich and Craig 2016). The following barrage of questions directed at a young woman who was sexually assaulted by four men, one of whom she had briefly dated, is illustrative:

> Defence counsel asked her why she did not just run away. Why did she not call out for help? Why did she not tell the police immediately? Why did she tell her friend before she told the police? Why did she wait six days to tell her mother? Why did she not tell the first person she saw in the elevator after the attack, or the bus driver, or the shopkeeper, or any of the other strangers she crossed paths with on the way home? ... Defence counsel called her a liar. They said she was evasive and outright dishonest. She was accused of perjury. It was suggested that she made the whole thing up out of animus against one of the accused, who had broken up with her a few weeks before her birthday. (Craig 2014, 429)

Here we see that complainants are not only required to recount their ordeal repeatedly and graphically in court (not to mention to other criminal justice officials before the trial begins), but are further re-victimized by defence lawyers viciously attacking their character and credibility. As law professors David Tanovich and Elaine Craig (2016) recognize, "some of the brutality of our adversarial process is inevitable"; they conclude, however, that "it is intolerable and shameful that our [legal] profession permits these unavoidable harms to be compounded by conduct that is neither ethically nor legally permissible." Tactics such as these highlight the onus placed on the complainant to perform—indeed to exude and embody—respectable femininity, an expectation that also influences the perceptions of judges and juries (Rayburn 2006).

Judiciary and jury bias

It seems that rape myths are not only held by police and exploited by defence attorneys but also reproduced by members of the judiciary. In 2014 Justice Robin Camp, then of the Provincial Court of Alberta, explicitly and repeatedly reiterated "real rape" tropes while presiding over *R. v. Wagar* (2015).

For example, he asked the 19-year-old victim (whom he repeatedly referred to as "the accused") "why didn't you just sink your bottom down into the basin so he couldn't penetrate you?" and "why couldn't you just keep your knees together?" Justice Camp further noted the victim failed to explain "why she allowed the sex to happen if she didn't want it" and suggested the victim's request that the accused wear a condom implied consent (Woolley et al. 2015, 5). He also showed disdain for the legal reforms and bemoaned the revocation of the doctrine of recent complaint, repeatedly suggesting that the victim's failure to report the assault immediately spoke against her credibility. Finally he passed moral judgment on the young woman who was homeless, poor, and a drug user, calling her "unsavory" and noting that her "sense of values, leaves a lot to be desired" (ibid., 8). He also engaged in explicit victim blaming: "She knew she was drunk. Is not an onus on her to be more careful?" (ibid., 8).

When his conduct was reviewed at a hearing in 2016, the victim testified that Justice Camp "made me hate myself and he made me feel that I should have done something" (Martin 2016). In March 2017 Robin Camp submitted his resignation after the Canadian Judicial Council recommended he be removed from the bench (Crawford 2017). While the Camp case is a particularly egregious and explicit example of judicial bias, it is not an isolated incident; for example, in Chapter 11 we consider the experience of Angela Cardinal, a young Indigenous woman who was incarcerated for a week when Provincial Court of Alberta Judge Ray Bodnarek became frustrated with her inability to present a clear narrative of the violent sexual assault she had experienced (*R. v. Blanchard* 2016). In short, Justice Camp's behaviour exemplifies a broader problem: judicial rape myth adherence that conditions the comments, instructions to the jury, rulings, and the sentences handed down by judges (Craig 2016).

The problem, however, extends beyond judges, sexual scripts, and myths; it also informs jurors' perceptions of, and decisions regarding, sexual assault complainants. Melanie Randall (2010) notes that intoxication significantly undermines the credibility of the victim in the eyes of jurors, even when she testifies the accused interfered with her drinks. Here we see the enduring double standard of sexual–social conduct: Illicit or excessive consumption of intoxicants is used to blame women and excuse men (Johnson 2012). Corey Rayburn (2006) similarly outlines a number of racial, gender, and class scripts that inform jurors' interpretations of complainants' character: the cold and calculating gold digger; the (presumed) promiscuous racialized or underclass woman; the angry, vengeful liar; the tease (reflecting the expectation of feigned refusal); and the virtuous Madonna, generally reserved for victims of stranger rape. Provocatively, Bennett Capers (2012) argues that the latter script is reinforced by rape shield laws, which maintain a shroud of secrecy—and implicitly, distaste and moral condemnation—around a woman's sexual experience.

How parties are assessed in relation to normative scripts impacts conviction rates as well. Here too judges' adherence to rape myths, and failure to understand the sexual assault laws, are implicated; in striking down the lower court's acquittal of Bradley Barton for the death of Cindy Gladue (see Chapter 3), the Court of Appeal of Alberta (in *R. v. Barton* 2017) noted the inability of "jurors to discharge their duties impartially if trial judges fail to warn them about relying on improper myths and stereotypes when jurors have been implicitly or explicitly invited to do just that" (para. 1). Finding the judge erred in both law (including non-compliance with *CC* s. 276) and his charge to the jury (including improper instruction regarding consent), the justices also spoke to systemic issues in sexual assault trials: "The time has come to push the reset button for jury charges in this country for cases involving an alleged sexual assault.... Key provisions in some jury charges have fossilized concepts Parliament sought to remove a quarter century ago.... Myths and stereotypes continue to stalk the halls of justice in cases involving sexual offences" (*R. v. Barton* 2017, para. 8).

Conviction

Even when the case goes to trial it is perhaps not surprising that, given the issues plaguing the criminal justice system examined above, including the "whacking" of complainants and judicial rape myth adherence, convictions are lower for sexual assault than for other crimes (Rotenberg 2017). Reflecting the myth that rape does not cause harm, when the police do lay charges they are overwhelmingly (98 per cent) labelled as the least serious (level one) sexual assault (*CC* s. 271) rather than the more serious sexual assault with a weapon (s. 272) or aggravated sexual assault (s. 273) even when these elements are in evidence; indeed, the proportion of less serious charges has been increasing since 1983 (Johnson 2012). Conviction is also more likely the closer the case resembles the "real rape" trope: reported within a day of the assault and committed by a stranger (Rotenberg 2017). Moreover, while there is a greater chance sentences will be custodial for sexual than for physical assaults (ibid.), sentences are shorter when the victim is a racialized woman (Chan and Chunn 2014), if there is a conviction at all.

Examining convictions also reveals *who* is criminalized, and by extension, who is *not*. In Canada a quarter of all men incarcerated for sexual assault are Indigenous (Benoit et al. 2015), underscoring the discriminatory way racialized and marginalized men are held to account by the criminal justice system while middle and upper class white men are "given a pass." Here too we see lingering fears of the Black rapist (Davis 1983), a myth that has roots as deep in Canada as it does in the United States. For example, in 1868 Prime Minister John A. Macdonald urged the retention of the death penalty for rape because of "the frequency of rape committed by negros ... [who] are very prone to felonious assaults on white women" (quoted in Backhouse 1991, 98). Indeed, both contemporarily and historically, racialized and poor men pay the highest price in the criminal justice system and through harsh vigilante punishment; they are also more likely to be falsely accused (nevertheless a rare occurrence given the stigma surrounding sexual assault)—something that mainstream second wave and governance feminists, with their preference for carceral solutions, did not acknowledge (Davis 1983).

At the same time, cultural justifications are sometimes invoked to diminish the sentences of racialized immigrant men when their victims are also racialized. Highlighting a Canadian case in which two Haitian men were sentenced to 18 months to be served in the community for having taken turns restraining and sexually assaulting a screaming young Black woman, and showing no remorse for their violence, Pascale Fournier (2002) suggests that Black women's bodies become naturalized as (acceptable) targets of sexual assault when men's actions are culturally excused. Not only does this reproduce harmful stereotypes about rapacious Black men and promiscuous Black women, it also reinforces stereotypes about racialized/immigrant communities as misogynist or "backward" (ibid.).

Resistance and prevention initiatives

In spite of the problematic tactics and "blind spots" detailed above, mainstream second wave feminists nonetheless organized and precipitated meaningful responses to sexual assault. Since the 1970s women's groups have been engaging in public education, lobbying for more victim-centred policing, providing support for sexual assault victims through rape crisis centres and crisis lines, offering counselling, and accompanying women to the police station and court—services that continue to be offered by sexual assault centres today (albeit, as we saw in Chapter 1, not all of which are welcoming to trans women). While Carol Smart's (1989) critique of legal reform as a limited strategy may not have been taken up by the mainstream women's movement of the day, her argument for feminist agitation that decentres law's power is embraced (albeit not completely or consistently) by contemporary feminists.

Indeed, conventional strategies endorsed by police and other institutional parties to protect women from sexual assault have been critiqued by feminists on the basis of their enthusiasm for restricting/regulating women's behaviour (e.g., don't walk alone at night, lock your doors, never hitchhike); newer situational crime prevention (or environmental design) approaches are similar but more subtle in the ways they endeavour to minimize the conditions facilitating (stranger) sexual assault. For example, many universities have emergency call alarms in public places, provide accompaniment to students walking across campus at night, and have installed lighting to eliminate shadowy areas. Notably, while lit walkways may make women feel safer, such strategies fail to address sexual assault perpetrated by acquaintances, which as we have seen is more common than stranger rape, in turn affirming the "real rape" trope and keeping the onus on women to take adequate safety measures (Sheehy and Gilbert 2015). In response, young feminists have mobilized to challenge the narrative and, like their foremothers, have taken to the streets in protest. A powerful example, highlighted in Chapter 4, is Slut Walk. Students have also demanded change from their institutions; in response, universities and colleges across Canada have introduced policies to address sexual assault on campus. While symbolically significant, for the most part these policies echo aspects of the criminal justice system insofar as they involve an investigation, an adversarial process, and punitive sanctions.

There is also a great deal of public education emanating from both grassroots and governments. Many of these campaigns use social media to mobilize and amplify messages that speak back to rape myths and challenge "real rape" tropes. Some of these initiatives are intended to educate on specific issues, such as, in the case of the "no means no" campaign, the meaning of consent. Others, like the multimedia #WhoWillYouHelp campaign (part of the Ontario government's "It's Never Okay" action plan), focus on bystanders, ending with the tag line "if you do nothing, you help him" (Feng 2015). Still others use clever slogans, images, and gender reversal to challenge rape myths and convey the (surprisingly *not* self-evident) message that rapists are responsible for rape; for example, the "Don't Rape" campaign challenges the biologism at the root of Constable Sanguinetti's comment by offering Anne Bartow's (2012) cheeky "helpful advice" including: "if you pull over to help a woman whose car has broken down, remember don't rape her," and "if you are not able to stop yourself from assaulting people, ask a friend to stay with you while you are in public." Similar to the "Don't Rape" messaging, the "Don't be that guy" campaign (see Figure 5.2), launched in 2011 by Sexual Assault Voices of Edmonton (SAVE), self-consciously abandons the conventional approach of changing women's behaviour and instead targets "the individuals responsible for preventing sexual assault: potential offenders" (SAVE n.d.). The poster campaign, which has spread to cities across Canada, is lauded as an effective prevention tool (Beres 2014; Matas 2012).

Increasingly, we are also seeing mobilization in the face of inappropriate or inadequate institutional responses to sexual victimization. Of course, given the prevalence of stigmatic assumptions about rape victims, speaking out and identifying as a victim is, in and of itself, a powerful (if fraught) way to challenge stereotypes about the *type of woman who is raped*. In the context of the widespread speculation that the women who accused former CBC host Jian Ghomeshi of sexual assault were lying because they had not spoken out earlier, journalists Antonia Zerbisias and Sue Montgomery started the hashtag #BeenRapedNeverReported. Many women took to Twitter to share

FIGURE 5.2: "Don't be that guy" campaign

their stories; within days almost 8 million people viewed the tweets and a national conversation was launched (Francis 2015). The hashtag, along with #IBelieveSurvivors, re-emerged on March 24, 2016, when Ghomeshi was acquitted of all sexual assault charges.

Concluding reflections

The widespread denunciation of Constable Sanguinetti's unscripted comment with which we started this chapter speaks to a paradox: Sexual assault is universally condemned at the same time it is a pervasive and shockingly common character-istic of Canadian society. As we have seen, much of this contradiction pivots on what is defined as "real rape"; who is perceived as a victim or merely discounted as an irresponsible or immoral woman; and how men's actions are perceived (and justified or vilified) according to gender, sexual, racial, and class scripts. Nor is anything new in this state of affairs. Indeed, we have seen that the same themes (with minor adjustments) echo across the centuries. The remarkable resilience of the narrative tropes, the persistently high rates of sexual assault, the ongoing re-victimization of women by agents and apparatuses of the state, and the fact that vulnerability is conditioned by intersecting marginalizations alerts us that sexual assault cannot be understood (or meaningfully addressed) in isolation.

In short, we need to shift our focus to power relations and the social, cultural, and discursive context in which sexual assault occurs, is experienced, and in which it is framed by perpetrators, institutions, and the state. This brings us back to the interconnections between power, knowledge, and discourse presented in Chapter 3. The hard fought 1983 legal reforms are a cautionary tale: While laws (and politi-cal announcements) are symbolically important, they do not get at the root of the problem. The rape myths and "real rape" tropes, reflecting and reinforcing gender scripts and roles, are too firmly entrenched, institutionally supported, and inte-grated into our habitus; quite simply, we cannot legislate (or wish) away symbolic violence. What is needed are changes that move us toward the characteristics of the rape free societies introduced at the beginning of the chapter—societies in which "women are treated with considerable respect, and prestige is attached to female reproductive and productive roles" (Sanday 1981, 16) and where there is "little division of labor by sex" (ibid. 17).

EXERCISE: TAKING ON RAPE MYTHS AND "REAL RAPE" TROPES

Get in groups of 4-6 learners.

Half of the groups go online and identify prevention initiatives or social media campaigns that challenge rape myths and/or the "real rape" trope.

The other half of the groups go online and identify material by rape apologists or men's rights groups that reproduce rape myths and/or the "real rape" tropes.

Each group should identify one element or product (e.g., a poster, press release, hashtag) that best captures the position.

Share your pick with the broader group or class and discuss the strategies employed and populations targeted.

Together, identify the strengths of anti-sexual assault education campaigns and how they could be more effective.

CHAPTER 6

INTIMATE PARTNER VIOLENCE: BRUTISH HUSBANDS AND PASSIVE WIVES

In 1982 when Margaret Mitchell, the NDP member of Parliament for Vancouver East, rose in the House of Commons to speak about domestic violence, male MPs laughed and jeered. Her furious response, "I don't think this is very much of a laughing matter" (Mitchell [1982] 2017), captured the media's attention and mobilized the nation. In the intervening decades we have seen a series of criminal justice reforms, a range of support services established, reams of scholarship published, and a much more nuanced and comprehensive understanding of the phenomenon developed. We have cycled through names: wife battery, family violence, domestic violence and, now, intimate partner violence (IPV). Nonetheless, rates of IPV remain stubbornly high: roughly 1 in 3 Canadian women (35 per cent) will experience IPV at some point in their lifetime (Wathen et al. 2014); moreover, the rate of IPV for Indigenous women, disabled women, and those who identify as LGBTQ is considerably higher (Burczycka 2016). On average, every six days a woman is killed by her intimate partner and "on any given night in Canada, 3,491 women and their 2,724 children sleep in shelters because it isn't safe at home" (CWF 2014, 2). While members of Parliament would be unlikely to find IPV a source of humour today, myths, misconceptions, and a general societal apathy continue to prevail. This begs the questions that guide this chapter: What is the social and state response to IPV today? And how much has really changed?

The Ray Rice case is a telling illustration of how little progress we, as a society, have made. When a surveillance video showing then Baltimore Ravens running back Ray Rice delivering a knockout punch to his fiancée, now wife, Janay Rice in an Atlanta casino elevator was leaked to the media it sparked outrage, including a campaign calling for a "CoverGirlcott" until the cosmetics corporation stopped sponsoring the NFL. Although eventually bowing to public pressure and removing Rice from the team, the Ravens executives, in spite of having seen the video (Van Natta and Van Valkenburg 2014), initially vigorously defended him: The team's head coach, John Harbaugh, lauded the star athlete's "character"; the franchise expressed concern that Rice was being maligned, stating "we know there is more to Ray Rice than this one incident" and tweeting that "Janay Rice says she deeply regrets the role that she played the night of the incident"; and fans and teammates rushed to his defence (Maine 2014). When Janay Rice spoke publicly about the man she married the day after he was arraigned on assault charges, drawing attention to his childhood, exceptionalizing the violence, and providing a series of rationalizations for the incident (Hill 2014), she was quickly vilified as a suspect character. The Twitterverse exploded with demonizing questions about why she married him, stayed with him, defended him—essentially asking, *what is wrong with her?* The efforts of survivors of intimate partner abuse to counter the stigmatic assumptions embedded in the emerging narrative through #WhyIStayed (Grinberg 2014) nuanced the conversation—it did not, however, rehabilitate her image.

The Rice story highlights many of the gendered myths that condition the societal response to IPV. The reactions of the Ravens franchise, the NFL, and many fans echo what we saw in the previous chapter when esteemed men are accused of sexually assaulting women; evoking a mythical *kind of man who assaults his partner* means that high-status men are "given a pass"—men who have "character" cannot possibly be guilty of assaulting their wives. All too often the devious woman myth is used to explain women's—presumed to be false— assertions of IPV. We see too that the victims of assault are assumed to be guilty of *something*; indeed, Janay Rice was, along with her husband, initially charged with assault (McLaughlin 2014). Moreover, narratives about the *kind of woman who experiences IPV* shift (at least some) responsibility onto her; at a minimum, she is perceived as having exceptionally poor judgment and wilfully ignoring the (presumed to be evident) warning signs. Again we see gender tropes evoked, and although the 1970s story that "she must like it if she stays" has been displaced by one that asks "why does she stay?" the central assumption—there must be something wrong with *her*—speaks to her deviance and lingering questions about her mental stability; her status as a victim is tainted. In this chapter we examine how this individualistic framing of IPV by state actors, by the media, and (inadvertently) by second wave governance feminists invisibilizes the broader social context in which IPV occurs, as well as the diversity of experience among different groups of women—to the detriment of us all.

Socio-historic considerations: From "judicious" discipline to masochistic wives

Traditional patriarchal Judeo-Christian society ideologically supports men's violence against their partners. After all, women, according to gendered readings of the Bible, are the physically and intellectually weaker sex: Made from the bent rib of Adam and responsible for original sin, they are ordained by God to obey their husbands. Even though by the 1500s the Catholic Church assumed a position against *excessive* violence, corporal punishment was nonetheless assumed to be a potentially necessary course of action "not out of anger but for the good of her soul" (Garcia and McManimon 2011, 68). Centuries later the same entitlement to "judicious" discipline for the purpose of correction lingered but was premised on the doctrine of marital unity (through which women forfeited their legal entitlements to their husband), which meant that since husbands must "answer for her misbehavior, the law thought it reasonable to entrust him with this power of restraining her, by domestic chastisement" (Siegel 1996, 2123). This doctrine, established in British common law, was also applied in Canada. Throughout the early and mid-1800s petitions for support, one of the few avenues available to women fleeing abusive men, were routinely denied by judiciary committed to protecting the patriarchal family unit and men's unquestioned authority. For example, in 1826 Chief Justice William Campbell, ruling in a case involving whipping, explained "however ungallant such conduct might be considered, yet a man has a right to chastise his wife moderately—and to warrant her leaving her husband, the chastisement must be such as to put her life in jeopardy" (quoted in Backhouse 1991, 174). As Constance Backhouse (1991) documents, judges, who were exceptionally critical of women "deserting" their marriage, "searched scrupulously for particulars that would justify a husband's behavior" (176), meticulously evaluating her conduct, character, and attitude.

By the 1870s, however, "wife beating" had begun to shift from a private "family broil" to a subject of public concern (McLean 2002), thanks to the concerted lobbying of temperance advocates who valorized the moral authority of faithful wives and mothers, and for whom violence in the home was tied to the consumption of alcohol. As Lorna McLean (2002) argues, while an effective strategy to expose the fallacious legal logic (if alcohol was at the root of the violence, then it was not legitimate chastisement), this discursive framing also diminished the responsibility of the abuser, who was under the influence of "demon rum," and affirmed cultural assumptions about brutish working class men, effectively framing male violence as a "lower" class problem rather than a symptom of gender inequality.

The incremental gains Canadian women were making toward personhood in the late 1800s did, however, open up a few avenues through which women could escape violence-filled homes. For example, working class women (who, unlike their middle class counterparts, were often engaged in income-generating activities) were able to seek protection orders to prevent their husbands from seizing their earnings (Fingard 1993); those who were "good women"—frugal, attentive mothers, and modest—could also turn to anti-cruelty and child protection agencies for support (Gordon 1988). Revealingly, as tentative gains against men's (excessive) violence were being realized, legislators moved in 1892 to encode what had hitherto been assumed: men's right to sexually assault their wives (Backhouse 1991)—a legal principle that, as we saw in the previous chapter, remained in force until 1983.

By the turn of the century, as women reformers shifted their attention to winning the vote, IPV largely disappeared from public awareness. Women continued to resist violence to the best of their ability—calling on family to intervene or turning to social service agencies. These (albeit fragile) tactics dissipated in the post–World War II era as the ever-more-idealized nuclear heterosexual family replaced extended family networks (reinforced by the "angel in the house" narrative; see Figure 2.1 on page 53), leaving women increasingly isolated. It also created a situation where women were routinely blamed for provoking "marital discord" (of which violence was a symptom) and urged (by counsellors, clergymen, and family) to stay lest their children be deprived of their father. Psychologists of the day were confident that "good wives don't get beaten and those that are must have flaws in their personalities" (Walker 2000, 101)—masochistic tendencies "gratified by her husband's violence" was the standard diagnosis (Martin 1978, 122). Powerfully demonstrating the power/knowledge nexus, researchers sought the etiology of wife battering by studying victims, perpetuating stigma by faulting abused women regardless of their behaviour: "[I]f they are passive, they are doormats that invite abuse. If they are aggressive they invite the beatings that put them in their place" (Martin 1978, 125).

The 1970s saw mainstream second wave feminists, alerted to the pervasiveness of IPV in their consciousness-raising groups, start to mobilize (Martin 1976). Early mechanisms to ensure the safety of women—places of refuge including drop-in centres and private homes—gave way to grassroots, volunteer-run, and donor-funded safe houses; by 1979 there were 75 battered women's shelters in Canada (Tutty 1998). It was not until 1980, however, when Linda MacLeod's report, "Wife Battery in Canada," was released that the issue gained national attention (including, as noted above, in the House of Commons); at that point provincial and eventually federal monies started to be allocated. On the one hand, funding requirements necessitated a much more formal structure and professionalization—abused women were transformed into "clients" receiving services in what became "transition houses." On the other hand, state funding enabled increased services (e.g., counselling, court support, second stage housing) and vastly expanded shelter networks in urban, rural, and northern areas (ibid.). It also entrenched what was intended to be an interim measure—after all, displacing women and children into crowded shelters might secure their safety, but it destabilizes and stresses the victims while leaving the perpetrator in the family home.

At the time the criminal justice response (or lack thereof) was seen by mainstream feminists as a significant stumbling block to realizing equality. Although wife battery had been prohibited by the *Criminal Code* since 1909 (McLean 2002) and physical cruelty grounds for divorce were available in all provinces once the federal *Divorce Act* was proclaimed in 1968, women's ability to call on the state for protection was limited. Not only did neighbours, friends, and family turn away (MacLeod 1980), but law enforcers were loath to intervene in "private matters between a husband and his wife" and (consistent with their training) police routinely ignored domestic violence calls or, if they responded, took the perpetrator outside to cool off, laying charges only in the rare instances when they witnessed the assault (Cole 1982). Moreover, Crown attorneys were decidedly ambivalent and rarely prosecuted cases; when they did, findings of guilt were rare (ibid.). Harking back to the 1800s, men pleaded provocation—common knowledge, affirmed by the courts, further legitimated the victim precipitation narrative; at the extreme she "provoked her own demise" (Edwards 1987, 161). Susan Cole (1982) argued not only that "men beat their wives because they are permitted to do so" (57) but that the criminal justice system's (non)response exacerbates the violence: "[A]s the police and courts continue to be lenient, the wife batter is convinced that the home is truly his castle and that no one, not even the uniformed cop or the robed judge, will brook his authority" (58).

At this time, as a result of "political choices the battered women's movement made in attempting to secure support, resources, and legislative and systemic change" (Goodmark 2008, 82), the image of the IPV victim shifted "from a low-income woman of color to a passive, middleclass, white woman cowering in the corner as her enraged husband prepares to beat her again" (ibid., 77). And by the early 1980s "wife battery" was effectively transformed from a private trouble to a social problem. In this context the state (supported by the governance feminist narrative) reframed IPV as a criminal justice problem, introducing a series of pro-charging and no-drop prosecuting reforms. By 1985 most police forces had policies in place mandating charges in cases of domestic assault (Brown 2000), and by 1986 all Canadian jurisdictions required "prosecution of spousal assault cases where there was sufficient evidence to support the prosecution, regardless of the victim's wishes" (FPTWG 2002, 10). At the same time, the weapons of the court started to be used to compel women to testify against their violent partners: women were routinely charged with contempt of court (and, by extension, threatened with incarceration) if they recanted their statements or refused to testify (Snider 1999).

These reforms, premised on the assumption that criminal justice intervention will change behaviour, sought to reduce IPV by increasing reporting, charging, prosecution, and sanctions (FPTWG 2002) and were largely supported by women's groups who (ignoring the critiques presented by socialist feminists) advocated not only for the application of the law but also for harsher penalties and the imposition of minimum sentences (Currie 1990). As such, governance feminists, in spite of a well-developed analysis that wife assault was rooted in structural inequality, implicitly supported the state, and in turn punitive and individualistic solutions (Abraham and Tastsoglou 2016). In the next section a brief overview of IPV in Canada today is presented before reflecting on the implications of this framing and the use of criminal justice solutions that ignore the intersections and interlocking systems of oppression conditioning women's experiences.

Intimate partner violence: Contemporary scope

IPV is profoundly gendered. The research is unequivocal: The gender symmetry implied by the roughly equal rates of IPV reported by men and women (Burczycka 2016) obscures the fact that "the frequency, severity, consequences and context of IPV are gender-specific with distinct victimization experiences for women and men" (Johnson and Dawson 2011, 65). According to self-report data collected by the General Social Survey (GSS), women are more likely to suffer physical injuries, have higher rates of long-term PTSD-like effects, and are "twice as likely as men to experience being sexually assaulted, beaten, choked or threatened with a gun or a knife" (Burczycka 2016, 7). Moreover, roughly "half (49%) of all female murder victims in Canada are killed by a former or current intimate partner. In contrast, only 7% of male murder victims are killed by intimate partners" (CWF 2014, 3). As Michael Kimmel (2002) suggests, based on his extensive review of the research, men use physical violence to restore their gender domination when they perceive they are losing control in the relationship; in contrast "women's violence toward male partners … is far less injurious" (1355). Offering a similar nuancing of the gender symmetry thesis, Joan Kelly and Michael Johnson (2008) differentiate between chronic, coercive, controlling behaviour (predominantly by men), situational violence emerging out of specific conflict (an issue examined in Chapter 8 in relation to workplace violence), violent resistance or self-defence (which women may be more likely to engage in), and separation-instigated violence.

IPV does not necessarily cease when the relationship ends; 41 per cent of individuals who separate from their abuser suffer physical or sexual violence post–break-up (Burczycka 2016). Indeed, leaving an abusive relationship can be exceptionally dangerous; 26 per cent of women murdered by partners are killed after they have ended the relationship, and "women are 6 times more likely to be killed by an ex-partner than by a current partner" (CWF 2014, 6). In this sense we can appreciate that in some cases remaining in an abusive relationship is perceived to be a rational harm-reduction strategy. IPV is also not contained in the home—it has a profound effect on workplaces, costing employers an estimated \$77.9 million annually (Zhang et al. 2012), and a pan-Canadian study found that 34 per cent of abusive men report emotionally abusing and/or monitoring their (ex) partners during work hours (Scott et al. 2017). Similarly, a large-scale survey by the Canadian Labour Congress (CLC 2015) found that for the 53 per cent of respondents who were or had been in a violent relationship, at least one act of abuse had occurred at or near the workplace (including abusive calls/texts/emails, stalking/harassment, violent confrontation, and/ or contact made with the employer or co-workers) (ibid.). It follows that women in abusive relationships, who like all women are disadvantaged in the labour market (see Chapter 2), face additional barriers in realizing financial stability. Moreover, abuse impacts more than victims' ability to get to their jobs, the quality of their work, their ability to focus, and their capacity to meet workplace demands; it also affects colleagues aware of the abuse, who experience concern, stress, interruptions, increased workload, harm, and/or threats (ibid.).

Definitions and dynamics of intimate partner violence

What do we mean by IPV? We see many of the same manifestations of violence that we examine throughout this book take on a particular dynamic in the context of an intimate relationship. Physical aggression (e.g., hitting, slapping), sexual abuse (e.g., sexual violence, unwanted sex acts, use of penetrating objects), and harassment (e.g., surveillance, repeated phone calls/texts) resemble the forms of violence we see in other chapters; however, as intimate partners are already socially and economically enmeshed in their victims' lives they can also exert control through financial abuse (e.g., sabotaging efforts to acquire or sustain employment, interfering with educational endeavours, limiting and controlling financial resources). Verbal abuse (e.g., put downs, name calling, accusations of infidelity) and emotional abuse (e.g., threatening suicide, harming pets, sleep deprivation), which are receiving increasing attention (Adams et al. 2008; CWF 2014), are similarly shaped by the physical and emotional intimacy of the relationship.

Though less visible than acts of physical aggression, psychological abuse (including emotional and verbal abuse) can be devastating; abused women report profound long-term effects that rival or exceed those of the physical violence they endure (Johnson and Dawson 2011). It is also often, as we see in Maria Fitzpatrick's testimonial (Box 6.1), the first manifestation of violence in a relationship—the victim is belittled, isolated from friends and family, and her confidence undermined (ibid.). We now see considerable attention paid to one particular tactic used by abusers: gaslighting. Named after the 1944 Ingrid Bergman film Gas Light, in which a husband isolates his wife and then systematically manipulates the environment (e.g., hiding objects) to inspire self-doubt and push his victim to question her recollections and mental competence, **gaslighting** is defined as "the process of driving a person to question their own sanity through deliberate psychological manipulation" (Johnsen 2017). In abusive relationships, normative gender tropes (e.g., women as irrational, emotional) and entrenched victim-blaming narratives (e.g., the provocation myth) are manipulatively drawn upon by the gaslighter to undermine the target's confidence and incite doubt in her own perception, making the individual feel "wrong, stupid, paranoid" (Simon 2014). These tropes work in another way that speaks to symbolic violence: Women in relationships characterized by IPV are also social actors who, even if they *know* better, have nonetheless absorbed into their habitus the cultural message that there is something wrong with women who stay in violence-filled relationships—embarrassment, guilt, and self-doubt are predictable responses; isolation and secrecy the foreseeable outcome (Johnson and Dawson 2011).

Explanatory frameworks

The mutually reinforcing nature of physical and psychological abuse underlies one of the most widely accepted explanatory frameworks—the "battered woman's syndrome." Lenore Walker (1979) put forth this psycho–social model that combines the cycle of abuse (see Figure 6.1) with the notion of learned helplessness (characterized by an inability to conceptualize alternatives, feelings of powerlessness, and being paralyzed with fear) to explain why women do not leave. Framing the experiences of women in abusive relationships in this way glosses over differences and negates resistance and agency, at the same time as it individualizes the problem and suggests there is a uniform psychological response to abuse that manifests in recognizable

BOX 6.1: MARIA FITZPATRICK'S HARROWING EXPERIENCE OF IPV

On September 5, 1972, five days after I was married, I realized there was a problem but could not put my finger on it. Words were spoken and I felt a shiver in my back and a knot in my stomach....

Broken bones, black eyes, sexual assault and two miscarriages as a result of this abuse were only some of the physical atrocities I had to endure.

... I finally got away to a women's shelter.... [T]he limit at the shelter was two weeks and I had nowhere to go. At the end of the two weeks I was forced to return.

The next time I left I was a little more prepared.... I met with the lawyer but I couldn't get a court date for a month. The time in the shelter was only three weeks. Again, I had to go back.... This time the abuse was so bad that I thought I would be killed, especially when I awoke from a very tentative sleep with a gun to the back of my head and the clicking sound of the hammer as the trigger was pulled. There were no bullets in the gun and he laughed hysterically.

He beat me. He raped me. And then he threatened that the next time there would be bullets, and he would kill our daughters first to hurt me and then kill me.... I called the police as soon I could and he was arrested and then released on his own recognizance and a restraining order was put in place.

... I called the police 16 times in two weeks before he was arrested again. Not so much for assaulting me but because he broke the restraining order.... In court he was found guilty and sentenced to a year in jail. But this sentence was suspended ... as he was leaving the courtroom, he said he would kill me.

I asked the judge how could he let him go, and the judge said to me it's a marital issue, get a divorce and leave. He proceeded then to give me a lecture on how much it was going to cost to keep him in jail.

When I returned to my house, he was there, holding my children and my mother-in-law at the point of a gun. At the end of a four-hour ordeal, his mother rose and asked God to help us, and he ran from the house. We spent a few more days barricaded in the house before we finally had the opportunity to get out and get on that bus and run for our lives.

Quoted in Ibrahim 2015

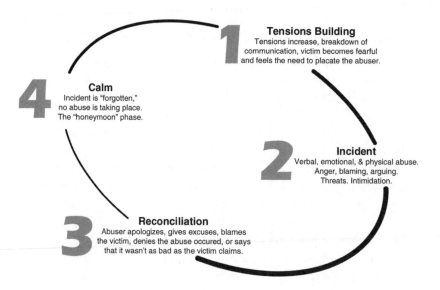

FIGURE 6.1: Cycle of abuse

symptoms. The theory was, however, adopted by mental health professionals (since 1980 it has been a subcategory of PTSD), social workers, and some feminist scholars and activists. In 1990 the Supreme Court of Canada (in *R. v. Lavallee*) expanded the legal doctrine of self-defence to include the battered woman's defence (an issue discussed in greater detail below). This pathologizing explanatory framework's focus on a woman's inability to make the "right" choice also reinforced the narrative of the helpless, lone, and usually white and middle class battered woman (Goodmark 2008)— the oft-repeated image of the "ideal victim" in need of salvation examined in the Introduction.

Though the battered woman's syndrome continues to resonate in the criminal justice system, it has been supplemented in the academic and activist literature by more sociological and (critical) feminist analyses that shift the focus from the individual to the social, economic, and discursive context. After an extensive review of the literature Margaret Abraham and Evangelia Tastsoglou (2016) concluded that "the root causes of intimate partner violence are structural" (572)—poverty, patriarchy, gender inequity. Quite simply, men have greater access to social, economic, and political power than women and hence are more likely to be in a position to abuse power; it follows that women's experiences of IPV must be viewed in relation to the social, structural, and economic inequity and normative scripts sketched in Part A of this book.

Thinking about IPV as rooted in power relations allows us to rethink the narrative: The power and control wielded by abusive partners is embedded in, reflects, and reinforces broader stratifications and discursive framings. For example, gendered expectations that women are passive, caring, and nurturing, and men are aggressive and dominant; the continued assessment of women in terms of their relationship status; pressure to conform to the two-parent heteronormative family ideal; even the beauty imperative examined in Chapter 10 provides a powerful taunt for abusers to undermine women's confidence and sense of well-being. We can think too of the ways economic inequity limits a woman's options. This may explain why financial abuse is so prevalent—diminishing a woman's capacity to support herself and her children restricts her ability to leave the relationship (CLC 2015). Here we see that thinking about IPV in terms of power relations destabilizes assumptions of (her) deviance and allows us to recast a woman's decision to remain in an abusive relationship not in terms of her pathology but, for example, as a rational assessment of her personal and social position. In other words, rather than look to individualized explanations reflecting an inability to make the right choice, we need to "address power dynamics defined by many intersecting forms of systemic oppression, including sexism, heterosexism, transphobia, racism, classism, and ableism" (Gillis and Diamond 2012, 219).

Looking closer: Intersections and interlocking oppressions

The insight that abuse is rooted in power also alerts us to the importance of thinking beyond gender and reflecting on intersections and interlocking social, economic, legal, and discursive factors that increase some women's susceptibility to IPV, shape the nature and form of that abuse, restrict (viable) options, and condition the ability to resist. The importance of taking an intersectional approach is highlighted by the Disabled Women's Network of Canada (DAWN 2014), who assert that "violence against women and girls with disabilities is not just a subset of gender-based violence—it is an intersectional category" (1). Women with disabilities experience high rates of IPV and particular forms of violence (e.g., the withholding of assistive devices), at the same time as concerns about "discriminatory action, retribution … or loss of economic and other supports, financial dependence and fear of being institutionalized" are powerful disincentives to reporting abuse (ibid., 2). Moreover, when they do report, they are disadvantaged by police officers' stereotypical assumptions about women with physical or cognitive impairments—assuming they do not have partners and/or treating them in an infantilizing and patronizing manner. And should they flee, shelters may not be an option; only 1 in 10 is accessible for women with disabilities (ibid.). These vulnerabilities reflect critical disability studies scholars' position that the problem with disability resides in the societal response and structural context—not in the capacities of those labelled disabled (Goodley 2013; Reaume 2014).

Im/migrant women

Im/migrant women, who as we saw in Chapter 2 disproportionately inhabit a precarious economic location, are particularly vulnerable to domestic violence. Fewer fiscal resources, and perhaps lack of familiarity with the language, increases their likelihood of being economically dependent on their spouse. They may also be isolated, displaced from their family, friends, community, and support networks at the same time as they lack knowledge about and access to social services. These socio-economic constraints intersect with immigration status, making im/migrant women—scared that the family will be torn apart and concerned about their refugee or immigration status—less likely to report abuse (Abraham and Tastsoglou 2016). Moreover, "newcomers who arrive in Canada traumatized by war or oppressive governments are much less likely to report physical or sexual violence to the authorities, for fear of further victimization" (CWF 2014, 8). Women whose immigration status is tied to that of their husbands are particularly vulnerable to threats of forced removal from Canada, while migrant women who come to Canada through irregular channels are unlikely to turn to either social service agencies or police for fear of being deported—a factor that was implicated in the decision by some cities, including Toronto, Montréal, and Vancouver, to declare themselves sanctuary cities. Migrant women with precarious status may also find themselves ineligible for "safety-net programs including social security, housing, education, and healthcare" (Bhuyan et al. 2014, 11) that could assist them in leaving an abusive relationship. In short, immigration and refugee policies, as well as anti-im/migrant sentiments (discussed in Chapter 1), directly impact im/migrant women's vulnerability to IPV.

LGBTQ intimate partner violence

That women from the LGBTQ community, like disabled women, report rates of IPV at least double the national average (Burczycka 2016) immediately destabilizes gender essentialism—indeed, it brings into sharp relief the heterosexism (and heteronormative assumptions) of the prevailing narrative and lingering language of wife battery. As such, the linguistic shift to intimate partner violence speaks to a more expansive understanding consistent with the way violence is being conceptualized throughout this text. Examining abuse in LGBTQ relationships pushes us to think through intersections and the way power differentials manifest. We see, for example, that while the types of violence and abusers' motivations mirror those of heterosexual couples, we also need to factor in cultural heterosexism (Gillis and Diamond 2012) and the ability of abusers to mobilize homophobia, biphobia, transphobia, and transmisogyny (St. Pierre and Barrett 2015). For example, abusers may use transphobia to increase isolation, shame, and question, control, or mock trans women's gender identity (ibid.). Similarly, in a lesbian relationship an abusive partner can exercise control by threatening to out a closeted partner—a strategy that is especially potent in rural, small, and northern communities (Ristock 2002)—or belittle her as not a "real" lesbian (AVP 2003). The effectiveness of these strategies may be further compounded by isolation from families of origin coupled with the relative importance of the LGBTQ community, resulting in reticence to risk exclusion from a vital support network. There may also be a fear that disclosure would reflect poorly on the community and further legitimate assumptions of pathology and/or deviance (Gillis and Diamond 2012).

The conventional framing of domestic violence may also operate to inhibit recognition of the behaviour as abuse on the part of women in same sex relationships who, like everyone else, have been inundated with heteronormative tropes (Brown and Herman 2015). Moreover, in light of the history of repression and outright aggression by police against LGBTQ individuals, there is often a deep distrust of law enforcement; while norms are changing, police violence against gender non-conforming women, and most especially trans women, suggests these concerns are not without merit (McInnes 2017). Further, police arriving at the scene are likely to either arrest both parties or dismiss it as a "cat fight," and services and counselling may not be appropriate, gay positive, or, in the case of trans women, even available (St. Pierre and Barrett 2015). In short, even though the language of IPV no longer centres on heterosexual relationships, the attitudes of police and social workers speak to a deeply ingrained heteronormative frame of reference. As Janice Ristock (2002) points out, unlike heterosexual IPV, power dynamics among lesbians shift because discrepancies in physical strength are (relatively speaking) minimal, and unlike masculinity, femininity is not fearsome—factors that complicate the distinction between abuser and abused and demonstrate the importance of understanding IPV in LGBTQ relationships on its own terms.

Indigenous women

Indigenous women, too, confront particular risks and vulnerabilities in regard to IPV. Not only do they experience twice the rate of IPV as their non-Indigenous counterparts, but also, according to the 2014 GSS, suffer more severe violence, including beating, choking, threats with a weapon, and sexual assault (Burczycka 2016). As Chapter 12 further elaborates, this heightened vulnerability has been attributed to the intergenerational effects of colonial violence, including the legacy of residential schools—something that, along with feelings of powerlessness emanating from unrelenting racism, also contributes to IPV among Indigenous lesbians (Ristock 2002). Not only has colonization entrenched patriarchal norms in Indigenous communities, engendering IPV and the dismissal and blaming of victims, it has also informed the attitudes of community leaders who depoliticize IPV, relegating it to a private concern (Kuokkanen 2015). The ramifications of these interlocking oppressions on Indigenous women's access to justice and resources are powerfully illustrated in the testimonial by Juanita Perley in Box 12.4 on page 282.

Like other women experiencing IPV, Indigenous women may hesitate to report abuse because they do not wish to see their partner charged or are reliant on their partner's income. However, Indigenous women may also fear they will lose their children (Corrado, Cohen, and Cale 2013), which is a well-founded concern since Indigenous children continue to be disproportionately apprehended by the state (TRC 2015a; see also Chapter 12). In addition, as we saw in Chapter 5, Indigenous women have a deep distrust of state actors; according to Human Rights Watch (2017), they are reluctant to call the police, and when they do officers are more likely to disregard their claims of IPV or respond with "scepticism and victim-blaming" (15); along with other racialized women, they are also more likely to be criminally charged for their acts of self-defence (Balfour 2012). In addition, the dearth of culturally appropriate social services can impede Indigenous women's ability to access support in urban settings (Corrado et al. 2013).

The question of progress

So how far have we, as a society, come? At least in terms of physical violence, sexual abuse, and stalking, IPV is down to 4 per cent from 7 per cent a decade earlier (Burczycka 2016). At the same time, we continue to see women beaten, killed, and maimed—in 2014 "victims of intimate partner violence accounted for more than one quarter (27%) of all victims of violent crime reported to police or 88,600 incidents" (Ibrahim 2016, 23). This number does not capture the many women, in particular those who are Indigenous, disabled, migrant, or LGBTQ, whose ability to turn to police, as we have just seen, is structurally and discursively restricted. This begs the question: How much progress have we made, and what are the limits of said progress? We now turn to critically reflect on the impacts of neoliberalism and the limits of governance and carceral feminist solutions, and to consider the ways the prevailing framing of IPV aligns with, reproduces, and reinforces gender tropes integral to inequality.

Certainly since mainstream second wave feminists first drew attention to "wife battery," arguing that "the facts tell us that the words 'home sweet home' are the fabrication either of a deluded fabulist or a skilled propagandist" (Cole 1982, 56), we have seen an explosion of scholarship about IPV. Moreover, transition houses have become an established part of the social service landscape. That said, after decades of expansion neoliberal austerity measures have meant these places of refuge have started to close. As a result, the needs of women fleeing abuse are not being met and every day 200 women are turned away from shelters because they are full (CWF 2014). The reduction of services has, and will continue to have, the most profound impact on women whose access is already restricted—rural women, disabled women, Indigenous women, and gender non-conforming women—the most marginalized women. This is yet another example of how the downloading of responsibility from the state onto communities and individuals that characterizes neoliberalism most directly harms those women with the least social, cultural, and economic capital by removing even the fragile security of transition houses. Truly, austerity kills and maims (Cooper and Whyte 2017).

We have also seen increasing recognition of IPV by provincial governments, including the introduction of civil domestic or family violence legislation to facilitate protection orders (Johnson and Dawson 2011). Moreover, some provinces are seeking to address particular challenges. For example, Ontario and Manitoba have amended their occupational health and safety regulations to mandate employers ensure that workers are protected from IPV at the labour site (Wathen et al. 2014). In March 2016, Manitoba revised its *Employment Standards Code*, becoming the first province to guarantee victims of IPV paid and unpaid leave to deal with safety, criminal justice, health, housing, and/or other issues. Alberta passed legislation ensuring victims can break their leases without penalty after Maria Fitzpatrick, then a newly elected member of the Legislative Assembly, stood up and recounted her own experience of IPV (see Box 6.1) (Purdy 2015).

The above-noted changes notwithstanding, for the most part progress appears to centre on improving the criminal justice system's response. As Holly Johnson and Myrna Dawson (2011) have documented, in most Canadian cities, trained multidisciplinary domestic crisis intervention teams (composed of social workers and police) respond to domestic assault calls, police officers receive sensitization training, and special domestic violence courts with trained personnel endeavour to expedite the court process. Over the years the *Criminal Code* has expanded (e.g., in 1993 criminal harassment, also known as stalking, was added) and sentencing guidelines have been put in place (e.g., in 2002 a history of domestic violence became an aggravating factor in sentencing) (ibid.). In other words, criminalization has become entrenched as a solution to a social problem that is rooted in inequality. As with the 1983 introduction of the sexual assault laws, while the recognition of IPV as a serious criminal issue is symbolically significant, there is, perhaps not surprisingly, little evidence that the repressive, androcentric justice system (Smart 1989) is an effective mechanism for deterring or preventing interpersonal violence (Johnson and Dawson 2011).

Moreover, as Laureen Snider (2014) writes, "middle-class white women have benefited the most from feminist efforts to compel the state to take attacks on women seriously; Aboriginal, marginalized, poor women the least" (275). Indeed, there have been significant detrimental effects. As we saw above, from the onset regulation specified that pro-charging and no-drop policies would be implemented "regardless of the victim's wishes" (FPTWG 2002, 10). While removing responsibility (and blame) for the decision to lay charges from the victim may well have been motivated by the desire to protect women from pressure or retaliation, the explicit override of victims' self-identified needs speaks to a criminal justice agenda and astounding paternalism. In consequence the victim may be disempowered and re-victimized by, for example, compelling her to testify. Moreover, many abused women are motivated by a desire to have the abuse stop—not retribution. In this sense intervention by the criminal justice system may exacerbate the violence by increasing stressors (e.g., economic challenges brought about by lost wages and legal fees).

If mandatory charging and no-drop policies do not work to the advantage of many women, for women who have physical or cognitive impairments, are gender non-conforming, are new to Canada, have a precarious immigration status, or are Indigenous or racialized, they add an additional barrier. This alerts us to the power of entrenched narratives of the weak, passive, and respectable "ideal victim." As Leigh Goodmark (2008) notes, it is an image that is not only profoundly raced but also classed; pivoting on scripts of appropriate femininity, it renders the experiences and constrained choices of "othered" women invisible and their responses illegitimate: "Women who fight back are those with the fewest other options for addressing the violence against them. They are women who lack access to resources, women who may be afraid or unwilling to turn to the police or other professionals for assistance, and women whose marginalized status may deprive them of the ability to make choices other than retaliation" (77; see also Ms. Cree's testimonial, in Box 11.1 on page 253). Moreover, as the analysis of Ontario Domestic Violence Court decisions by Holly Johnson and Ashley McConnell (2014) demonstrates, judges, echoing the approach taken by those who sat on the bench 150 years ago, meticulously evaluate the victim's behaviour, character, and attitude: "[W]omen were constructed as responsible and deserving [of violence] when judges viewed them as failing to exercise the appropriate level of agency by staying with the violent partner, not staying in contact with the police, or delaying reporting the incident" (153). Those women who failed to make the "right" choice and avail themselves of the aid of the "benevolent" court are seen as forfeiting their right to assistance.

The "ideal victim" and prescribed gender scripts also permeate the battered woman's defence, a classic illustration of the medicalization of women that we examined in Chapter 3. Use of the defence necessitates the woman is diagnosed as suffering from battered woman's syndrome (now called battered person's syndrome), a subcategory of PTSD; symptoms, as noted above, include an inability to envision alternatives and being paralyzed with fear. This not only constructs women's behaviour in terms of mental disorder as assessed by psy-professionals, but also renders women's individual experience relevant only to the extent it supports the medico–legal discourse; it neither centres the experiences of women nor sheds light on underlying dynamics and causes of abuse (Williams 1992). In real terms, women who have fought back in the past are by definition excluded. Moreover, it would appear that "ideal victims" must not only be passive but read as "good women," a reading that is entangled not only with class-based notions of respectability (Skeggs 1997) but also racial stereotypes: "[T]he passive, gentle white woman is automatically more like the 'good' fairy tale princess stereotype than a Black woman, who as the 'other' may be seen as the 'bad' witch" (Allard 1991, 194). Additionally, although the court's acceptance of the battered woman's defence (if nothing else) speaks to an acknowledgment of intimate partner violence, this recognition is restricted to a psychological, as opposed to sociological, framing. A case in point is the Supreme Court ruling in *R. v. Ryan* (2013), which acknowledged Nicole Doucet Ryan's years of abuse and harassment at the hands of her husband and recognized that her attempts to use the criminal justice system and other protections were repeatedly thwarted by the perception that it was a "civil matter" (para. 9); the court nonetheless denied her the defence of duress.

What about alternative strategies? Feminists remain divided on whether to abandon punitive criminal justice solutions in favour of restorative justice. As Melanie Randall (2013) recounts, caution and skepticism among some feminists emanates from a perception that restorative approaches do not account for gendered power imbalances and are "too easy" on the abuser. However, building from Indigenous practices and feminist principles, Joan Pennell and Gale Burford (2000) developed a restorative approach called family group decision making that was found to be effective in reducing violence among 32 families of various cultural backgrounds in Newfoundland and Labrador. This process continues to be offered in Ontario, countering the common knowledge (and as we have seen, sometimes spurious) assumption that separation is the best means to safety (George Hull Centre for Children and Families 2011). In these family group decision-making processes, or conferences, a coordinator confirms that the victim feels safe and that the abuser is included (whether in person, through a representative, by a letter, or by phone), and also ensures everyone in the group, which includes immediate and extended family, has the opportunity to be heard. The family group then privately negotiates and makes a safety plan, which must be approved by legal and social service officials before being formatted into an actionable plan distributed to all family members by the coordinator (ibid.). Family group conferencing is also available in Manitoba, and programs are being developed in other provinces as well (ibid.).

Resistance: Women fighting back

As we have seen throughout this chapter, women's movements have engaged in a long and protracted, if sporadic, battle to lift IPV out of the shadows, from the temperance movement's fight against brutish men, to the second wave governance feminist agitation for law reform, to the Twitter and media campaigns we see today. For all the limits examined in this chapter it is hard to deny that their efforts have been successful to the extent that there is a general, if periodically grudging, recognition that IPV is a social problem. We have also seen female politicians subversively insist that IPV be put on governments' agendas—a dynamic that speaks to the importance of female political representation noted in Chapter 3. Here too we see a measure of success: Margaret Mitchell's 1982 assertions were greeted with laughter and derision; 33 years later when Alberta MLA Maria Fitzpatrick (NDP) recounted her own story (see Box 6.1) to demonstrate the importance of legislation that ensured abused women were able to break leases without penalty, "she received a 30-second all-party standing ovation" and the law passed with unanimous support (Ibrahim 2015).

When we shift from collective resistance and public assertions and look at the micro-interactional level, we see that women use the tools at hand to protect themselves—tools that are always conditioned by their cultural, social, and economic capital. Historically, women withdrew into convents, "deserted" their families (either by leaving or by suicide), and badgered child protection associations to expand their mandate to include domestic violence (Gordon 1988); others endeavoured to change their partner's behaviour and to that end called on family and/or publicly shamed their husbands (Backhouse 1991); some women stood up for themselves by fighting back. That the costs were (and are) high—including forfeiture of financial security, loss of children, violence, and imprisonment—negates neither their efforts nor their agency. Instead it offers a powerful counter-narrative to the "ideal victim" trope that continues to haunt the criminal justice system today.

As we have seen, there are many reasons why women do not turn to the criminal justice system for support, but as Linda Gordon (1988) writes these "heroes of their own lives" have "always resisted battering" (251). One way women assert their right to protect their family, personal, and financial well-being is by resisting mandatory charging policies. Johnson and McConnell (2014) note a failure in the criminal justice system to recognize that women may call the police in a momentary push back against their abusers without wanting to pursue the matter any further. We see women's rejection of the framing of IPV as a criminal justice matter in the striking 40 to 65 per cent of Ontario victims who subvert mandatory prosecution policies by recanting their testimony or otherwise not participating in the prosecution of their abusers—an act of resistance to state intervention that puts women at risk of contempt of court charges and therefore incarceration (ibid.).

Faced with prolonged or severe violence, some women resist the tyranny of an abusive partner by retaliating with lethal force. Women like Jane Hurshman (Figure 6.2) who, in 1982, shot Billy Stafford—a man who had terrorized her for six years, subjecting her to horrific physical, sexual, and psychological abuse (Vallée 1986). Like many women in abusive relationships Ms. Hurshman knew from experience that neither the police nor the community could protect her from Billy (ibid.). Fuelled by the knowledge that there was no escape from a man who threatened to hunt her and her family down and kill them (an assessment supported by the above-noted statistics demonstrating the increased risk of leaving an abusive partner, as well as Maria Fitzpatrick's narrative in Box 6.1), Ms. Hurshman reached the apparently rational conclusion that "I'd

Figure 6.2: Jane Hurshman

die here, or he'd die here; one of us would" (quoted in Vallée and Gartner 2007). In many ways murder is the ultimate subversive act; women take justice into their own hands because there are no other options. The criminal justice system, demonstrably unable to protect women like Ms. Hurshman, nonetheless frowns upon such actions: When a jury acquitted her on a murder charge, the Crown appealed; before going to trial for a second time, the Crown accepted her guilty plea for manslaughter. Justice Merlin Nunn of the Appeal Division of the Supreme Court of Nova Scotia, while recognizing the horrific violence Ms. Hurshman had endured, was nonetheless adamant that, even in such circumstances, "wives don't have the right to kill their husbands" (quoted in Vallée 1986, 199) and sentenced her to six months in jail with an additional two-year probation.

Concluding reflections

As this chapter has demonstrated, public, personal, and legal responses to IPV are complex and contradictory. As we saw in the Ray and Janay Rice case, people continue to defend violent partners as otherwise "good guys," while women who do not follow the "right" steps—leaving the relationship, initiating and cooperating with the criminal justice process—are framed as both irresponsible neoliberal subjects and responsible for their own victimization. We have similarly seen symbolic violence in the internalization of heteronormative tropes by LGBTQ women that renders their victimization at the hands of their partner invisible, and in abused women's internalization of the trope that something must be wrong with women who stay in violent relationships.

At the same time as women's victimization is minimized and invisibilized, there is, undoubtedly, a deep-seated and age-old lust for revenge that continues to be sated through punishment (if only of those perceived as the *type of man who abuses his wife*) in both criminal and vigilante justice. Indeed, thinking about Jane Hurshman's (however constrained) decision to kill her monstrously abusive husband we may darkly delight in thinking *he deserved it*. This in turn relates to the abundance of criminal justice solutions—and mainstream feminists' support of them—and while these communicate the state's disapproval it is troubling that they are the only acceptable actions a woman can take.

As Kirsten Kramer (2014) notes, "when progressive or emancipatory rationalities are disciplinary, they often result in the solidification of governmental structures that are difficult to untangle once established" (322). This means that if we embrace carceral solutions and see more cops, courts, and corrections as the answer, we are less motivated to address the root causes of the problem: gender inequality, poverty, and lack of access to resources. It also justifies increased budgets for police and other sectors of the criminal justice system—money that is not being used for things that would actually help women, like increased government transfer payments, public housing, employment equity, and shelters/support. In this regard it should certainly give us pause that welfare supports have eroded, meaning that leaving an abusive partner is likely more difficult today than it was 20 years ago. At the same time, we have arrived at an acknowledgment that IPV arises from and occurs in a context of not only gendered power imbalance but also the interlocking oppressions that manifest in diverse ways among differently situated groups and relationship configurations. This broadened analytical scope has allowed for the recognition of manifestations of gendered violence that occur outside the home, and it is to this we turn in Part C.

EXERCISE: IPV CASE STUDY—THINKING THROUGH SOLUTIONS

A friend has just disclosed to you that, as you had suspected, she is in an abusive relationship. The violence, which started with put-downs and gaslighting, now includes physical and sexual violence. Your friend is scared and believes her partner's threats that he will kill her if she leaves; she does not, however, want to go to the police for fear her partner (whom she loves) will, because he is a Black man, experience violence at the hands of the police.

In groups of 3–5 learners:
- Fill in the back story.
- What advice would you give your friend?
- What resources (economic, cultural, social, etc.) will your friend need to address the situation?
- What are the limits of the solution you propose?

PART C

Workplace Violence

The previous section of this book elaborated on interpersonal forms of violence in diverse contexts, both public and private—streets and community spaces, university campuses, and homes—that are conventionally understood under the umbrella of violence against women. Part C draws on the same tools and concepts presented in Part A and nuanced in Part B to examine how gendered violence unfolds in the workplace. Focusing on sexual harassment, bullying, and microaggressions (Chapter 7); predatory, situational, and slow violence (Chapter 8); and invisibilization and under/over regulation (Chapter 9), this section demonstrates that manifestations of violence at the workplace are at once interpersonal (e.g., occurring between people who interact at the labour site), institutional (e.g., facilitated through organizational policies and practices), structural (e.g., grounded in and perpetuating the racial, gender, and class hierarchies shaping the distribution of labour and, in turn, labour protections), and symbolic (e.g., when women workers blame themselves for the workplace violence they experience).

CHAPTER 7

NOT "JUST A JOKE": WORKER-ON-WORKER SEXUAL HARASSMENT, BULLYING, AND MICROAGGRESSIONS

Almost 40 years ago, the film *9 to 5* (see Figure 7.1) was sardonically hailed as "a militant cry for freedom" in a *New York Times* review that characterized the comedy's biting social critique of capitalist exploitation and workplace harassment as secondary to more important social issues including inflation, the price of gold, and (not sarcastically) "the disappointing sales of the Chrysler 'K'," even going so far as to declare the famously busty Dolly Parton to be a poor casting choice for the role of practical and modest Doralee Rhodes (Canby 1980). Although the film has since received considerable acclaim, it is ironic (but not surprising) that the reviewer used humour to belittle women's issues. Tellingly, *9 to 5* attempted to use comedy as a vehicle through which to offer social critique without alienating audiences (Murtha 2015). Tara Murtha offers a description:

> The plot of *9 to 5* feels nothing short of radical, even (and perhaps especially) today. Mr. Hart spends his days harassing Doralee by telling her she's much more to him than "just a dumb secretary." He lies about sleeping with her, and purposefully knocks pencils on the floor so she'll lean over and pick them up. He insults Judy, and bullies Violet by demanding she fix his coffee. After learning she lost out on a promotion to a man she trained, Violet confronts Mr. Hart [only to have her points dismissed as feminist claptrap] ... Mr. Hart is soon made to pay.... Hijinks ensue, and eventually they kidnap him. In order to hide the fact that they're holding their boss hostage, the women have to run the business as best they can, which, it turns out, is much better than Mr. Hart. They implement flexible schedules and a job-sharing program, set up a daycare center and ensure equal pay.

As Murtha points out, and as we saw in Chapter 2, programs conducive to workplace equality remain nearly as radical and as unrealized today. So too,

FIGURE 7.1: *9 to 5* publicity shot

it would appear, are nuanced representations of women in the workplace. Shows like *Scandal*, which stars a Black woman occupying a powerful role in Washington's political scene, notwithstanding, contemporary pop culture offerings appear to be less progressive than the women in *9 to 5* would have envisioned in 1980. Humour continues to be used, not to challenge gendered structural impediments, but to negate and normalize them. All too often sexual harassment at work is—like the street intrusions examined in Chapter 4— dismissed as a joke, a harmless expression of sexual attraction, flattery, or perhaps even clumsy courtship. It is a framing that negates the reality of power rela- tions: Sexual harassment is not flirting, precisely because the victim cannot ward off the aggression or decline the "invitation" without fear of reprisal. It also creates a discursive space to blame the victim: She is either responsi- ble for sending out the "wrong signals" or a hypersensitive "uptight" woman evidently lacking a sense of humour. As we have seen in previous chapters on sexual assault and intimate partner violence, such myths and stories add one more disincentive to reporting victimization.

What has changed, then, since the 1980s in regard to workplace harass- ment, sexual and otherwise? And how is it that hostility directed at co-workers continues to be dismissed as a joking matter? This chapter discusses impor- tant changes in the awareness of and regulation regarding worker-on-worker violence (LeBlanc and Barling 2004), which includes violence among colleagues (horizontal), by senior workers toward their less experienced counterparts (quasi-horizontal), and by supervisors, managers, or bosses (vertical). It begins with a consideration of sexual harassment before shifting to other modes of workplace violence and exclusion: bullying and microaggressions. Using examples from a range of occupations and labour market sectors, including the military, nursing, sex work, and office work, the chapter illustrates how these forms of violence are not only gendered but intersectional and have significant psychological, financial, organizational, health, and even physical impacts. These examples show that although occasional (or frequent) aggression appears to be endemic to contemporary capitalist labour sites, women use the tools at their disposal to exercise agency, and to resist interpersonal and environmental workplace violence.

Socio-historic considerations: From social norm to social problem

Workplace sexual harassment is by no means a new phenomenon, merely one that was not seen as a social problem, even by women activists, until relatively recently. Middle class reformers in the early twentieth century were certainly preoccupied with the morality of young women (see also Chapter 8), who were abandoning the family farm and rural life for the excitement and independence of the city and finding employment in factories as well as in emerging "white blouse" jobs—telephone operators, office clerks, and shop girls (Pedersen 1986, 23). However, while Progressive Era reformers fretted about the "inappropriate attentions" the young women received from employers and co-workers (Backhouse 1991), their solution to the "girl problem" focused on restricting women rather than, for example, securing rights (Pedersen 1986). For the most part, however, the unwanted sexual attention women experienced at work was "ignored, denied or even considered a natural or inevitable consequence of integrated workplaces" (Crocker and Kalemba 1999, 542). Little changed in the ensuing decades; it is precisely this context of overt sexualization that *9 to 5* depicts. Here we can think not only of secretaries but also other "feminine" professions such as flight attendants, who were eminently visible in airline ads that featured beautiful women in revealing uniforms characterized by short skirts and boots (see Figure 7.2). Some, like the 1971 National Airlines innuendo-dripping "fly me" ad campaign—complete with text promising to "help you have fun getting there. With movies. And Stereo. And good food and cocktails. And lots of personal attention. Fly me" (in Ortega 2012)—seemed to invite sexual harassment.

It was a(nother) problem with no name until feminists coined the term *sexual harassment* in the 1970s; as Liz Farley (2017) notes the response was telling: "[W]omen immediately took up the phrase.... No longer did they have to explain to their friends and family that 'he hit on me and wouldn't take no for an answer so I had to quit.' What he did had a name. Now women could

FIGURE 7.2: Southwest Airlines flight attendants, Texas, circa 1968

share stories and strategies." Moreover, as feminist activism and, subsequently, scholarly research began to draw attention to women's experiences of sexual harassment at work, the issue gained a measure of acknowledgment (McDonald 2012). In Canada, under the tutelage of labour activist Grace Hartman (the first woman to lead a North American trade union), the Canadian Union of Public Employees (CUPE) launched a program to end sexual harassment and in 1975 released the film *Don't Call Me Baby* (CUPE 2014; 2015). Since that time, workplace sexual harassment has become increasingly recognized in Canada and globally—nearly 50 countries have introduced prohibitive legislation, and international bodies such as the United Nations have officially addressed the issue (McDonald 2012).

As Paula McDonald (2012) notes, there is mixed evidence as to whether sexual harassment has increased or decreased over time. Surveys conducted in the 1980s and 1990s revealed that approximately half of all women in paid employment experienced some form of sexual harassment at the workplace, making it the most prevalent form of sexual victimization experienced by Canadian women (Crocker and Kalemba 1999); worryingly, a Government of Canada (2017b) survey conducted some 30 years later found that 60 per cent of respondents had been sexually harassed during the preceding two years. Of course, shifts may speak to increased identification and reporting, and methodological and jurisdictional inconsistencies make it hard to draw conclusions about long-term trends (McDonald 2012). There are also important sector-specific differences; for example, the Canadian Armed Forces did not recognize sexual harassment until the 1990s—this is perhaps not surprising given that the military was relatively late to gender integration; barriers to women's participation were only fully removed in 1987 (Standing Committee on the Status of Women 2014).

Research and awareness about workplace sexual harassment have also precipitated regulatory developments in Canada. In 1985, alongside the equality provision (s. 15) of the *Canadian Charter of Rights and Freedoms*, the sexual harassment provisions in the *Canada Labour Code* came into force (Standing Committee on the Status of Women 2014). Shortly thereafter, in *Robichaud v. Canada* (1987), the Supreme Court of Canada (SCC) found that an employer, including the federal government, could be liable for sexual harassment by its employees. Two years later, in *Janzen v. Platy Enterprises* (1989), the SCC defined workplace sexual harassment as "unwelcome conduct of a sexual nature that detrimentally affects the work environment or leads to adverse job-related consequences … an abuse of both economic and sexual power … a demeaning practice, one that constitutes a profound affront to the dignity … and self-respect of the victim both as an employee and as a human being" (para. 57). This remains the definition of sexual harassment in Canadian case law. Recognizing that power imbalances may discourage employees from reporting sexual harassment perpetrated by their superiors, in 1998 Parliament amended the *Canadian Human Rights Act* to prohibit retaliation. As we see below, various levels of regulation currently govern sexual harassment in public and private workplaces. In short, in Canada and around the world, we have seen important recognition of sexual harassment. Indeed, a 2014 report by the Standing Committee on the Status of Women declared that sexual harassment ought no longer to be considered strictly a "women's issue," but rather something that is illegal, immoral, and harmful to everyone in the workplace, and that can happen in any workplace environment (3).

Contemporary experiences of sexual harassment and its regulation

In Canada, workplace sexual harassment is regulated provincially through labour provisions (that notably exclude sexual assault, which remains a criminal matter). Though they vary across jurisdictions, these mechanisms are similar insofar as they endeavour to attribute liability to and prevent retaliation by employers and require (with some exceptions) a policy pertaining to sexual harassment at the workplace. The terms *vexatious* and *unwelcome* are usually included in provincial definitions; in their application, vexatiousness is tested subjectively (i.e., was the behaviour concerning, annoying, or distressing to the complainant?), whereas unwelcomeness is typically tested objectively through a "reasonable person" test (i.e., would a reasonable person consider the same conduct unwelcome?) (NSHRC n.d.).

There are some variations between provinces. For example, Ontario's *Occupational Health and Safety Act*, which addresses harassment alongside violence in the workplace, also considers other risks faced by workers (e.g., situational violence, which we examine in Chapter 8) as well as intimate partner violence in the workplace. Nova Scotia's approach to workplace violence is also expansive: While the province's *Human Rights Act* prohibits discrimination and defines sexual harassment, the provincial government additionally includes bullying as a form of harassment in its human resources policy for civil servants (Nova Scotia 2012). By contrast, other provinces take a more ambiguous approach. For example, Alberta's *Human Rights Act* prohibits discrimination, which includes sexual harassment (AHRC 2012), albeit without explicitly stating so. Similarly, s. 81.18 of Québec's provincial *Act Respecting Labour Standards* prohibits "'psychological harassment' [which] means any vexatious behavior in the form of repeated and hostile or unwanted conduct, verbal comments, actions or gestures, that affects an employee's dignity or psychological or physical integrity and that results in a harmful work environment for the employee" and is generally understood to be applicable to sexual harassment (*Barreau du Québec c. Laflamme* 2015).

Exceptionally, federal government workers fall under the purview of various federal statutes, including the *Canada Labour Code*, which defines sexual harassment as "any conduct, comment, gesture or contact of a sexual nature (a) that is likely to cause offence or humiliation to any employee; or (b) that might, on reasonable grounds, be perceived by that employee as placing a condition of a sexual nature on employment or on any opportunity for training or promotion" (s. 247.1). The code, along with the *Canadian Human Rights Act*, prescribes rights and obligations, policies and mechanisms for addressing sexual harassment, which are administered by the specific government department (e.g., the Canada Revenue Agency) or arm (e.g., the military) in which a worker is employed (Standing Committee on the Status of Women 2014). In short, much as we saw with sexual assault, there is robust and comprehensive legislation addressing sexual harassment. However, its seeming inability to diminish the persistently high rates noted earlier speaks to the impact of structural and institutional factors—something that is eminently visible in the military.

Case study: Sexual harassment in the military

Sexual harassment occurs in a variety of workplaces and may emanate from one problematic senior worker whose behaviour goes unsanctioned—an issue discussed in greater detail below and highlighted in Box 7.2 (on page 170). Sexual harassment can be particularly challenging when it occurs in an environment that is encouraging of such behaviour; here the military is a poignant example. Reflecting on her external review of sexual misconduct in the Canadian Armed Forces (CAF), former Supreme Court Justice Marie Deschamps (2015) notes "there is an underlying sexualized culture in the CAF that is hostile to women and LGBTQ members, and conducive to more serious incidents of sexual harassment and assault" (i). She describes this culture as fostering a perception "that it is permissible to objectify women's bodies, make unwelcome and hurtful jokes about sexual interactions with female members, and cast aspersions on the capabilities of female members," and furthermore, that such conduct is ignored or condoned by superiors (v)—factors researchers have characterized as constituting a poisoned or toxic environment (Crocker and Kalemba 1999). Moreover, there appears to be a low level of awareness about what constitutes sexual harassment and how, for example, it differs from fraternization (Deschamps 2015).

Given that numerous scholars describe sexual harassment in the military as systemic (Standing Committee on the Status of Women 2014; see also d'Arge 2013; Lucero 2015), it is perhaps predictable that a significant number of instances of sexual harassment go unreported. Why do so few women make use of existing workplace mechanisms to report their experiences of sexual harassment? Victims express concern about negative career repercussions, not being believed, stigma, and not wanting to be perceived as a trouble maker (Deschamps 2015). In this context, in spite of the above-noted protective legislation that endeavours to eliminate precisely these barriers, it is hardly surprising that victims of sexual harassment also express concern about retaliation by peers and superiors, that their confidentiality would not be protected in the complaint-reporting process, and that their superiors would fail to take their complaints seriously. The sexualized workplace culture of the military, along with the lengthy, cumbersome, and onerous resolution process, also discourages victims from reporting sexual harassment (Deschamps 2015). Indeed, the CAF harassment complaint tracking system has been critiqued for having unclear instructions and a lack of accountability in the chain of command to respond to and investigate complaints (ibid.). Would-be complainants are deterred by the inconsequentiality of sanctions meted out in the military in the rare event that complaints are successful—the completion of an online sensitization training program, for example (ibid.). Finally, military women's fears that they will be perceived as weak and "diagnosed as unfit for work" (ibid., iii) speak to the particular vulnerability of women in non-traditional occupations—something that is brought into sharp relief with the experiences of women in the RCMP considered below (Bronskill 2016).

Workplace bullying

It is certainly laudable that sexual harassment has attracted the attention of the public and government even if, as we saw in the case study above, the effectiveness of preventive strategies and resolution processes remains questionable. When we consider women's experiences at the workplace we see, however, that verbal abuse and psychological violence are not limited to sexual harassment. For example in the movie *9 to 5* with which the chapter started, Mr. Hart's repeated put downs, threats of dismissal, insults, and negation of the women's skills and competencies, while certainly gendered, are examples not of sexual harassment but of workplace bullying and verbal abuse. Notably, while most provinces have workplace violence protections, provisions prohibiting bullying and mandating employers to take preventive and remedial action are relatively new. For example, while Québec introduced its *Act Respecting Labour Standards* in 2004, it was not until 2010 that Ontario amended its *Occupational Health and Safety Act* to oblige employers to ensure their workplaces are free from bullying; and only since 2013 has British Columbia's *Occupational Health and Safety Regulation* detailed the duties of workers, employers, and supervisors in regard to preventing and addressing workplace bullying (Hudson 2015).

Workplace bullying is "a repeated and patterned form of psychological violence that involves power over another that is employed to victimize, undermine or intimidate [and] incorporates … incivility, harassment, counterproductive behaviour and aggression" (Hutchinson 2013, 563). Examples of these behaviours include belittling, yelling, intimidation, threats, spreading rumours, over- or underworking someone, persistent criticism, blocking access to advancement opportunities, withholding information, and undermining work (CCOHS 2017). The distinguishing characteristic of bullying is that it is systematic in nature—frequent and ongoing—and often personal insofar as it occurs between people who know each other (Lutgen-Sandvik and Tracy 2012). It is a remarkably common feature of workplaces: Research has found that 40 per cent of Canadian workers are bullied weekly (Hudson 2015). Moreover, there is reason to believe that bullying may be becoming more prevalent. Randy Hodson and his colleagues explain that job insecurity—a direct impact of the neoliberal restructuring examined in Chapter 2—increases bullying because it "diminishes worker power and creates a pressure-cooker environment in which civility is replaced by bullying as supervisors and managers seek to intimidate and blame employees for their mutually held fears about the future security of their jobs" (Hodson, Roscigno, and Lopez 2006, 386).

How can we understand this everyday violence at work? Doing so necessitates that we first acknowledge that workplaces are saturated in power relations. It follows that workers with less relational power are vulnerable to bullying—even in the absence of job insecurity (Hodson et al. 2006). Reflecting on the power relations and constraints in Part A of this book provides a point of entry to understanding workplace bullying as a gendered and intersectional phenomenon. As we saw in Chapter 2 women, and especially racialized and im/migrant women, are over-represented in low-paying jobs and more likely to be working in precarious, non-standard labour arrangements; in real terms, this means women are not only less likely to exercise organizational authority but have fewer labour site protections and restricted ability to resist. Their vulnerability is further compounded by the systemic barriers that condition employment options and access to social security protections (e.g., employment insurance) should they leave their jobs. Moreover, as Pamela Lutgen-Sandvik and Sarah Tracy (2012) explain, stereotypes and stigmatic assumptions—such as the myths we have been exploring throughout this volume—make women and racialized people "easy targets" for mistreatment and bullying by aggressive members of an organization. Here we see that racial or ethnic identity, gender, social and economic capital, labour location, and organizational hierarchy intersect to increase the vulnerability of some women to supervisory bullying as well as sexual harassment (Roscigno, Hodson, and Lopez 2009). In short, women, and in particular working class and "othered" women, are not only more vulnerable, but with less social and economic capital their ability to resolve the issue is constrained.

The following case studies illustrate general and specific aspects of workplace bullying; the accompanying textboxes provide yet more examples. As we will see, women may not turn to existing workplace or other institutional, provincial, or federal complaint mechanisms for a variety of reasons. In addition, management may be reluctant to enforce their own provincially mandated policies (Bernier 2014), especially in an organizational or professional culture in which the behaviour is tolerated or normalized.

Nurse on nurse bullying: "Nurses eat their young"

Workplace violence is not exclusive to male-dominated workplaces. Demonstrating the need to contextualize violence and factor relations of power into the analysis, the perpetrators may be women as well. To illustrate this, we consider nursing—a profession comprising 92 per cent women (CNA 2015)—in which lateral violence, or bullying among peers and colleagues, is so deeply entrenched that the expression "nurses eat their young" has been in use for over 30 years (Gillespie et al. 2017). Moreover, according to the Canadian Nurses Association (2014), "bullying, as a form of violence, has increased significantly in the workplace in recent years. This type of violence (lateral/horizontal and vertical) affects more than half of all nurses and nursing students" (4). To make sense of the counterintuitive fact that workers in a caring profession are experiencing violence not only at the hands of patients and their families (a situation examined in the next chapter) but also from other nurses we need to consider context. Neoliberal restructuring and wide-ranging austerity measures have resulted in drastic cuts to healthcare spending, ever-changing policies, rapidly evolving managerial expectations, and greater job insecurity (Eggertson 2011), which as we saw above, correlates to increased workplace bullying. Beyond this, however, we also need to bring power into the discussion of horizontal or quasi-horizontal victimization. Researchers, building on the pioneering work of Kathleen Bartholomew (2006), suggest nurses are enacting oppressed group behaviour: Subject to the authority of administrators and doctors, struggling with overwhelming (and sometimes competing) demands, obliged to navigate aggression and violence from patients and their families (see Chapter 8), and afforded less and less autonomy, nurses experience increased levels of stress and escalating feelings of powerlessness. In this context nurses may take their frustrations out on other nurses through bullying and other oppressive behaviours (Gillespie et al. 2017).

The influx of immigrant and foreign-trained workers has made nursing a more diverse field; in this respect nursing provides an example not only of bullying but also of intersectional discrimination, violence, and incivilities targeting racialized, immigrant, and young women. Godfred Boateng and Tracey Adams's (2016) study of Ontario nurses found that most racialized nurses report both subtle and direct racism from their colleagues, including "racial abuse, excessive scrutiny and monitoring, and being excluded" (39). Nurses also describe being disproportionately sanctioned, marginalized, and having their expertise discounted by colleagues. Similarly, newly licensed nurses, who are at particular risk of horizontal violence (Gillespie et al. 2017), report shaming and verbal abuse by older colleagues (Boateng and Adams 2016). However, unless the bullying is severe, nurses do not make use of institutional policies or union support to stop the behaviour, relying instead on individual strategies, including staying positive, emotional dissociation, and focusing on career goals (Leong and Crossman 2016). Moreover, nurses may not interpret bullying behaviour from supervisors—such as sarcasm, criticism, insults, and angry scolding, even if it causes considerable emotional distress—as violence, instead framing it as "tough love," a well-intentioned albeit still hurtful strategy employed to acclimatize new workers into professional and organizational

culture (ibid.). In short, it appears nurses interpret and often respond to bullying as an unavoidable part of the job.

Bullying by bosses in the public service

Whereas lateral bullying may occur among colleagues lacking in significant
organizational and professional power, workplace bullying can also emanate
from a more explicit abuse of authority. In a telling example of the ineffectiveness of reactive laws and policies, a report by the Office of the Public
Sector Integrity Commissioner on the bullying behaviour of a senior executive at the Public Health Agency of Canada (Friday 2017) gives an idea of
the apparently common occurrence of workplace harassment in Canada's
federal public service (Rice 2017)—a conclusion supported by a 2014 Public
Service Employee Survey that found 19 per cent (or almost one in five) of
public service employees had been the victims of this form of harassment in
the previous two years (Government of Canada 2015). The report details an
executive loudly verbally abusing workers—at times reducing them to tears—
sometimes for extended periods, using expletives, and targeting workers in
groups and individually. This mistreatment also included threats and physical
displays of anger: "slamming hands down on the desk, throwing files or paper,
leaping upright and leaning forwards towards staff in an angry and aggressive
posture" (Friday 2017, 8). As the following account attests, workers reported
feeling scared, physically unsafe, and upset: "I have never seen an explosion
like that [the individual] absolutely went ballistic … just totally decimated my
whole character … like total rage … I took my things and went quietly out
of the office but as soon as I was by [the executive's] windows, I ran all the
way back to my desk" (ibid.).

Although confidentiality concerns preclude knowing the gender of the
targets (or the perpetrator) in the commissioner's report, it is worth considering that 55 per cent of Canada's public servants are women and roughly
two-thirds of senior leadership are men (Morris 2016). That the behaviours
noted above are an evident display of stereotypically masculine aggression—
an extreme version of the leadership qualities celebrated in men that we saw
in Chapter 3—speaks to the significance of the organizational culture and
structure of the federal public service. As Marika Morris (2016) notes, this
environment is not conducive to more open, egalitarian, and collaborative
leadership styles (more commonly embraced by women and minority men).
All of this suggests that, statistically speaking, women are more likely to be the
targets of bullying among public servants and that the structures in place do
little to mitigate relational power. Moreover, while it may be, as it appears in
the integrity commissioner's report detailed above, that bullying and aggressive outbursts are indiscriminate, there may be a failure to engage with subtler

forms of sexism, racism, and other varieties of discrimination. Looking at workplace microaggressions allows us to consider this possibility.

Microaggressions: Subtly reinforcing stereotypes and other myths

As the above discussions have shown, workers may perceive workplace anti-violence policies (around sexual harassment and bullying) as difficult or undesirable to apply even where they do exist. We have also seen that the application, suitability, and effectiveness of such policies are hindered by the same myths examined in previous chapters—that women lie or exaggerate, are too emotional or too sensitive; once again, they simply cannot take a joke. We see the same thing with subtler behaviours that may not necessarily fall under the catchment of sexual harassment or bullying, but that nonetheless "other" and alienate women, and especially racialized women or those perceived as unconventional. These behaviours are called **microaggressions**. Originally defined as "brief and commonplace daily verbal and behavioral indignities, whether intentional or unintentional, that communicate hostile, derogatory, or negative racial slights and insults toward people of color" (Sue et al. 2007, 271), the term is now applied to describe subtle forms of discrimination toward a wide array of marginalized people, including "hostility or indifference toward women" (Basford, Offermann, and Behrend 2014, 341). As such it names modern manifestations of discrimination that, compared to "old fashioned" forms of overt racial hatred and gendered bigotry, are ambiguous and covert (Sue et al. 2007); for example, assumptions, to return once again to the movie *9 to 5*, that women are not really "management material" but rather are more suited to preparing coffee and purchasing supplies.

Microaggressions can include racist, sexist, ableist, homophobic, or intersectional verbal, non-verbal, or visual insults that pivot on stereotypes—the kind of everyday slights such as the failure of a colleague to even acknowledge the racist hatred described by Arij Elmi in Box 4.1 on page 95. Other workplace examples include being overlooked, under-respected, and devalued because of one's race or gender expression. Verbal microaggressions include such things as a white middle class person remarking on the articulateness of a working class person (communicating an unspoken assumption of inferior intelligence or education) or on the lack of accent of a racialized colleague (an assumption they are foreign born) (Sue et al. 2007). It may also include a male colleague commenting on a woman's attire or looks, as we saw with women politicians (see Box 3.2 by Michelle Rempel on page 79). Microaggressions also manifest through dismissive looks, gestures, and tones. These examples highlight the porousness of the line between sexual harassment, bullying, and microaggressions and the limits of sharp classifications. According to Derald Wing Sue and his colleagues (2007), "the power of microaggressions lies in their invisibility to the perpetrator and, oftentimes, the recipient" (275). Although they can be relentless, because they are subtle and may or may not be intentional, microaggressions can be hard to prove, and, as is the case for sexual harassment, some victims do not see pursuing the matter as worthwhile or viable—indeed, many of these comments and behaviours would be unlikely to meet the legal threshold of workplace harassment.

In workplaces where microaggressions are tolerated and flourish, they can be described as environmental. Furthermore, sexist, racist, or classist microaggressions can exact a psychological impact on women even in jobs that can be characterized as overtly sexualized (see Erickson 2010); strip clubs are illustrative in this regard. In one study, Ontario erotic dancers who were otherwise untroubled by the sexual nature of their job described a work environment conducive to sexist and racist microaggressions that negatively affected their morale, noting that staff and management made inappropriate comments to dancers even though they were colleagues—for example, one racialized dancer described being called "China girl" by doormen (Law 2016, 181). Illustrating the intersection of gender and class, dancers also reported some male managers and colleagues treated them as "silly" and irresponsible "girls," failing to recognize them as professionals (ibid.).

Microaggressions can also impact job candidates, exacting a toll on people even before they get a job (and whether or not they end up getting it). As research by Sabine Koch and her colleagues demonstrates, women's exposure to sexist behaviour by men that can be characterized as both sexual harassment and microaggressions—including intrusions of personal space like sitting uncomfortably close and touching exceeding a handshake, dominating interpersonal tactics such as interrupting and arguing, and ogling—diminishes their performance in work tasks for which women are stereotyped as weak, such as math tests (Koch, Konigorski, and Sieverding 2014). The researchers suggest that this may contribute to the under-representation of women in occupations that do not conform to traditional gender role characteristics (e.g., professions in science, technology, engineering and math)—another (albeit subtle) way the gendered division of labour examined in Chapter 2 is reinforced. We can extend Koch and her colleagues' research to racist and intersectional microaggressions to explain the limited effectiveness of employment equity legislation (Ng, Haq, and Tremblay 2014). Indeed, Black women working in Toronto report feeling frustrated, depressed, and stressed by the stereotypical assumptions they routinely encounter both in interviews and at the workplace (see Box 7.1).

BOX 7.1: THE QUIET PAIN OF PREJUDICE

Sheena Blake can still remember the feeling in the pit of her stomach when she was offered the job. At first she thought she had beat out the other candidates, but she soon learned that she was on top of the list for a different, much more insidious reason. "Someone asked me to work for them so they could meet their quota of having a multicultural space," Blake told *CBC News*.

That was years ago. But it's just one example of the countless quiet, hidden abuses that she says happen daily to black women, especially when it comes to the workplace.... Verlia Stephens knows that strain all too well. Stephens, who has worked as a social worker with black women for about 20 years, says she often sees that frustration in her clients in the form of depression or high blood pressure. "It does kill from within," she told *CBC News*. "It's like a pimple that grows and gets infected. You get ill." Many would expect when they go to work that they were hired because the hiring managers thought they were best for the job, she says.

"But it's not the same for us. We go into our jobs with, 'Thank you, I got the job, I got a pay cheque, however I have to do this additional work to show you, to prove to you that you made the right decision with me—as if you did me a favour'." It's a quiet kind of prejudice that also travels beyond the workplace, Stephens says. Despite being a social worker and a university-level lecturer, Stephens says she's often mistaken by others for a client.

Quoted in Nasser 2016

Microaggressions also intersect with structural discrimination. This happens, for example, when an employer characterizes employment equity legislation as unfair (Sue et al. 2007), thus leading to minimal adherence to the *Employment Equity Act*—ironically, so named in Canada to avoid the negative backlash directed toward affirmative action in the United States (Ng et al. 2014). This foreseeably results in people who "fit in" to the organizational culture (in professional environments, most likely white men) being hired (Green 2005). The question of "fit" is perhaps most evident in tech start-ups, which Dan Lyons (2017) characterizes as steeped in "bro culture": "A 'bro co.' has a 'bro' C.E.O., or C.E.-Bro, usually a young man who has little work experience but is good-looking, cocky and slightly amoral—a hustler.... Bro cos. become corporate frat houses, where employees are chosen like pledges, based on 'culture fit.' Women get hired, but they rarely get promoted and sometimes complain of being harassed. Minorities and older workers are excluded." This example also demonstrates how, in a toxic work environment, microaggressions coexist with and bleed into other forms of workplace harassment.

The spectrum of gendered workplace harassment

Acknowledging that all workplace harassment—ranging from subtle to purposely targeted aggression—can be sexual and/or gendered, and also racist, ethnocentric, Islamophobic, homophobic, transphobic, or conditioned by class, alerts us that this is an intersectional problem. We also begin to see the limits of regulation and accompanying definitions. Of course, while legal and administrative sanctions have been developed to protect Canadians from workplace sexual harassment, bullying, and discrimination, behaviours such as microaggressions are relatively newly acknowledged and remain under-recognized. Online harassment is another form of gendered workplace violence that, as with the other kinds of cyber-harassment discussed in Chapter 4, goes beyond the temporal and spatial confines of work.

Thinking about these experiences on a spectrum is useful in this regard. Indeed, as Kathryn Borel describes in Box 7.2 (on page 170), sexual harassment, bullying, and other problematic behaviour including verbal abuse and even gaslighting can coexist. A spectrum accounts for overlap between definitions used by scholars; for example, exclusion, criticism, and undermining have been characterized as "masked forms of bullying" (Hutchinson 2013, 564) as well as microaggressions (Sue et al. 2007). This also expands our understanding of vulnerability; for some women workplace violence is intersectional and a daily occurrence. McDonald (2012) situates sexual harassment alongside other counterproductive and abusive workplace behaviours, all of which emanate from hierarchical power relations within, and outside, the workplace (e.g., structural oppression such as racism). In general, women perceived as unconventional or vulnerable—including "divorced or separated women; young women; women in non-traditional jobs; women with disabilities; lesbian women"—are disproportionately targeted (ibid., 7).

Effects of gendered workplace harassment
As with their social position and identity, women's experiences and interpretations of—and as we see below, their resilience and resistance to—workplace sexual harassment, bullying, and microaggressions can vary, but all have potentially significant emotional, psychological, physical, financial, and organizational impacts. A workplace environment that is conducive to, or tolerant of, one form of violence also likely engenders others. The military is a prime example

of a workplace in which bullying, discrimination, microaggressions, and sexual harassment flourish (Statistics Canada 2016c). In this regard it makes sense to talk about the effects of gendered violence as resulting from any of the behaviours on the spectrum.

As we saw in previous chapters, there are interconnections between emotional, psychological, physical, and social impacts. Gendered worker-on-worker violence can also have career and financial implications. Victims experience diminished professional reputation, impaired concentration, decreased motivation, and lower job satisfaction. Psychological and emotional effects can include stress, irritability, anger, fear, nervousness, feelings of disempowerment, self-doubt, loss of self-esteem, burnout, anxiety, depression, PTSD, and suicidal thoughts (Standing Committee on the Status of Women 2014; Cleary, Hunt, and Horsfall 2010; Crocker and Kalemba 1999; Leong and Crossman 2016). The impact of worker-on-worker abuse can also manifest physically as "fatigue, headaches, gastrointestinal disorders, teeth grinding, eating disorders and nausea" (Standing Committee on the Status of Women 2014, 5). Moreover, navigating toxic environments creates stress which, as we saw in Chapter 2, is related to a host of health problems and even death.

The duration and intensity of the abuse also play a role in its impact: If the victimization occurs frequently and/or over an extended period of time, women may engage in self-blame or increased alcohol and drug use (Cortina and Leskinen 2013). For example, Leanne Nicolle (2017), the former executive director of the Canadian Olympic Committee (COC), whose sexual harassment complaint ultimately resulted in the dismissal of the COC president, highlighted a conspiracy of silence, cover-up, and wilful blindness in the organization, describing her experience as "a death by 1,000 cuts: Not until I could not sleep without medication, until I was dependent on alcohol to get through my day, until I was a shell of my former self, did I realize that I was entirely broken by this man—and by those abiding by the *omerta* of the COC."

Finally, like so many other forms of gendered violence, workplace harassment ripples well beyond the confines of the worksite and the victim: It can harm victims' family relationships (Standing Committee on the Status of Women 2014) and elicit fear in witnesses as well as victims (Friday 2017). There can also be implications for those receiving services, including health-related outcomes for patients, when nurses are being bullied (Lee et al. 2014). Potential organizational costs include absenteeism, decreased performance, lowered morale, and professional shortages; and when victims quit their job, change professions, or retire early, employers confront higher staff turnover and subsequently increased training costs (Boateng and Adams 2016; Standing Committee on the Status of Women 2014; Cleary et al. 2010; Crocker and Kalemba 1999; McDonald 2012).

Resistance: From "soldiering on" to speaking out

As we have seen, regulatory mechanisms—both at the state and workplace levels—are not responding adequately to women's experiences of sexual harassment, workplace bullying, and microaggressions. In this context, what options do women have? This chapter started with conventional examples of collective resistance in feminist and union activism: awareness raising, dissemination of educational materials, and policy development. But how do women resist harassment *at work*? At the individual level women can occasionally subversively draw on their labour capital; for example, some erotic dancers respond to sexual harassment (e.g., leering, inappropriate comments) as an opportunity to manipulate managers into giving them desirable schedules or allowing them to break workplace rules (Law 2016). Some women withdraw their labour power by quitting; others, like Sheena Blake—who in response to the racist microaggressions detailed in Box 7.1 turned down a job she had been offered "so they could meet their quota" (Nasser 2016)—refuse offers of employment. In the socio-economic context sketched in Chapter 2, however, this course of action is not always realistic.

Women, most especially those who are im/migrants, racialized, Indigenous, or transgender, have fewer labour market options, making the consequences of resistance potentially devastating—neither filing a complaint nor removing their labour power by resigning may be a viable option. Predictably, in this context of constrained choice, women workers today, much like the women at the beginning of the movie *9 to 5*, draw on their personal strengths as they endeavour to navigate toxic, abuse-filled environments. For example, racialized nurses, who, as we saw above, are particularly vulnerable to bullying, manage challenges and conflicts through various individual strategies, including standing up for themselves, "working harder, carefully selecting colleagues to help and mentor them, and assuming a demeanour of competence and confidence" (Boateng and Adams 2016, 41). Of course "soldiering on," while demonstrating impressive levels of resilience, autonomy, and creative problem solving, can extract a heavy emotional, psychological, and physical toll on workers. Moreover, these strategies do not challenge or change the environments or structures facilitating the problematic behaviours in the first place, nor do they address predators' ability to mobilize their male (and often class and race) privilege and social capital to circumvent regulations governing workplace harassment. Indeed, it was precisely CBC's lack of accountability and their willingness to prioritize Jian Ghomeshi's "whims" over her well-being to which Kathryn Borel's public statement (see Box 7.2) draws attention—her public calling out is a powerful act of resistance.

BOX 7.2: KATHRYN BOREL: SEXUAL HARASSMENT AT CBC

Every day over the course of a three-year period, Mr. Ghomeshi
made it clear to me that he could do what he wanted to me and
my body. He made it clear that he could humiliate me repeatedly
and walk away with impunity. There are at least three documented
incidents of physical touching. This includes the one charge he just
apologized for, when he came up behind me while I was standing near my desk, put his hands on my hips and rammed his pelvis
against my backside over and over, simulating sexual intercourse.
Throughout the time that I worked with him, he framed his actions
with near-daily verbal assaults and emotional manipulations. These
inferences felt like threats, or declarations like I deserved to have
happening to me what was happening to me. It became very difficult for me to trust what I was feeling. Up until recently, I didn't
even internalize that what he was doing to my body was sexual
assault. Because when I went to the CBC for help, what I received in
return was a directive that, yes, he could do this and, yes, it was my
job to let him. The relentless message to me from my celebrity boss
and the national institution we worked for were that his whims were
more important than my humanity or my dignity.

Borel 2016

Other women have managed to realize justice through the courts. As with
internal complaints mechanisms, however, this strategy can impact complainants'
careers and reputations. One group of women who courageously stepped up—
at considerable cost to themselves—were members of the RCMP. Like many
working women they first attempted to "soldier on," adjust their behaviour, and
use the internal processes, only to find themselves ostracized, subjected to more
abuse, and their careers stalled or derailed (while, in some cases, their abusers
were promoted) (Woo 2016). Frustrated, angry, and suffering the health consequences of prolonged harassment a number turned to the courts. As women
started to come forward others, recognizing that their experience was not in fact
unique—as the narrative of uptight women unable to take a joke would have
them believe—joined them; by 2016 there were two class action suits in progress
representing over 500 women (Bronskill 2016). As evidence of systemic problems
mounted, the RCMP, after years of steadfast denial, earmarked $100 million for
compensation to the estimated 1,000 victims and, on October 6, 2016, (then)
RCMP Commissioner Bob Paulson issued an apology. His words validated the
accusations and acknowledged many of the issues examined in this chapter:

> Instead of succeeding and thriving in a supportive and inclusive workplace, many women have suffered careers scarred by gender and sexual discrimination, bullying and harassment. Some of these women left the RCMP, heartbroken, disillusioned and angry. Others stayed and were forced to find ways to cope with this inexcusable condition since they did not see an organization that was willing to change. Still others courageously tried to make themselves heard by management only to find they were denied movement and opportunity or judged adversely and punished within the RCMP for their efforts. The impact this has had on those who have experienced this shameful conduct cannot—must not—be solely understood as an adverse workplace condition for which they must be compensated. For many of our women this harassment has hurt them mentally and physically. It has destroyed relationships and marriages, and even whole families have suffered as a result. Their very lives have been affected. (Paulson 2016).

After Commissioner Paulson's apology, Janet Merlo, the lead plaintiff in the British Columbia class action suit, expressed her hope that this was a "turning point" and the beginning of a "new era" (Bronskill 2016). There is reason for optimism to the extent that his comments acknowledge context. In this regard they are consistent with recommendations made by governmental inquiries, which—reflecting the fixation on reactive and punitive responses we saw with sexual assault in Chapter 5—still largely focus on policy recommendations, but also emphasize the importance of changing workplace culture, the need to educate workers about worker-on-worker violence, the importance of responsible leadership, and the imperative of fostering respect, diversity, and inclusiveness in the workforce (Friday 2017; Rubin and Nikfarjam 2015; Standing Committee on the Status of Women 2014). Notably, the RCMP appears to have made an important change in this regard: In April 2018, Brenda Lucki became the first woman to be named permanent commissioner of the RCMP; she has vowed to hold bullies and sexual harassers to account (Leblanc and Bailey 2018).

Concluding reflections

As this chapter has shown, gendered workplace harassment is pervasive across different professions, organizational relationships and power differentials, identity configurations, and workplace cultures. It manifests in different forms, both overt and covert, that are variously referred to as sexual harassment, bullying, and microaggressions. These forms of gendered worker-on-worker violence persist in spite of provincial labour standards and rights mechanisms, as well as the *Canadian Human Rights Act*, which mandates equal pay, and the *Employment Equity Act*, which requires equal opportunity. In practice, however, women, and in particular Indigenous, racialized, and disabled workers, continue to be limited by a persistent glass ceiling and disproportionately represented in lower-paying occupations (Ng et al. 2014). Sheila Block and Grace-Edward Galabuzi (2011) attribute this continuing gap in wages and quality of employment to ongoing discrimination. In this respect the factors shaping women's socio-economic position discussed in Chapter 2 can be seen as contributing to the context in which these forms of violence occur and as mechanisms that perpetuate it. Once again demonstrating the ways power/knowledge binds the structural and the personal, microaggressions, harassment, and bullying not only recirculate (and in the process further entrench) gender, racial, and class tropes but also emotionally, physically, and financially hurt the people they target. Moreover, they reinforce existing hierarchies and privilege by upholding, through discrimination and exclusion, the gendering of leadership as male.

This pervasiveness illustrates the interlocking oppressions of neoliberalism, class discrimination, racialization, and gender norms in action, begging the question, is worker-on-worker violence—like work itself and the unequal power relations it entails—an inevitable part of life under capitalism? Future efforts toward preventing and ridding workplaces of intersectional, gendered violence—such as those recommended by scholars, activists, and government investigators—will tell whether or not capitalist relations can be untethered from the other systems of oppression with which they are intricately intertwined.

EXERCISE: REFLECTING ON MICROAGGRESSIONS

In groups of 3–4, identify the subtexts of the following statements and reflect how they might reinforce stereotypes and stigmatic assumptions about women or "othered" populations—even if not intentionally so.

- Aren't you hot in your hijab?
- You are really good at math for a girl.
- If you would just smile more things would be smoother at work.
- I can show you how to apply your makeup so it looks classy.
- You are so articulate!
- That is so gay.
- Wow, lucky for you there are employment equity laws.
- But where are you *really* from?

- So what do your people think about this issue?
- I feel sad sometimes too. You just have to pull yourself out of it.
- In Canada we are not like the United States; race does not matter.
- That dress kind of makes you look like a whore.
- You're really irritable. Are you on your period?
- I prefer "he" or "she"—it's more grammatically correct.
- Don't be such a sissy.

CHAPTER 8

JUST PART OF THE JOB?
PREDATORY, SITUATIONAL, AND
SLOW VIOLENCE AT WORK

When we think about dangerous work, certain occupations immediately come to mind—police officers, firefighters, and perhaps correctional workers usually top the list—jobs that are, historically and today, dominated by men. Turn to the Internet and you quickly find that while law enforcement and firefighting are notable in their absence, logging, fisheries, construction, and steel work virtually always appear on any "ten most dangerous careers" list (Barton 2014). This makes immediate and intuitive sense—these are exactly the labour sites we associate with tough working class men doing physically demanding, high-risk jobs. Indeed, according to official statistics, women are dramatically less likely to be killed at work than are men; for example, in 2015, 40 women were killed at work in Canada—for men the number was 811 (AWCBC n.d.). At first glance it would appear that if workplace risks are a gender issue it is one that disadvantages men; perhaps, if nothing else, the insidious segregated labour market examined in Chapter 2 reduces women's vulnerability to injury and death at work!

What happens, however, when we consider not only fatalities and injury but also violence and victimization? When we consider the work of women in the shadow economy? And when we problematize the casual (often normalized) everyday violence women experience at work? Even excluding women's vulnerability to sexual and other worker-on-worker harassment and abuse examined in the previous chapter, a very different and counterintuitive picture emerges. Much of this violence is excluded from the oft-cited statistics based on reported incidents covered by provincial compensation boards—it is simply not "counted" (Chechak and Csiernik 2014). When we examine Statistics Canada data, however, we see that "one-third of incidents that occurred in the victim's place of work involved a victim working in the fields of education, law, social and community services (18%) or health (15%), despite these occupations representing small proportions of the working population (12% and 6% respectively)" (Perreault 2015, 17). In other words, 33 per cent of workplace violence occurs in female-dominated sectors that represent just 18 per cent of the workforce (ibid.). It would appear, then, that workplace violence is decidedly gendered. Here too an intersectional lens sheds light on diversity: Workers' vulnerability to violence is further conditioned by, for example, racialization and class location.

Moreover, the same myths, discourses, and relations of power evident throughout this book shape not only women's vulnerability to victimization and the nature of the violence they experience but also state and institutional responses. In principle there is robust recognition of what the *Canada Occupational Health and Safety Regulations (COHSR)* define as "any action, conduct, threat or gesture of a person towards an employee in their work place that can reasonably be expected to cause harm, injury or illness" (s. 20.2), including "teasing, and abusive and other aggressive behaviour" (s. 20.3(b)). Not only does the *COHSR* specify both preventive and remedial actions, so too do the *Canada Labour Code* and provincial occupational health and safety regulations across the country. However, as this chapter will demonstrate, even in standard labour arrangements where such regulations apply, workplace cultures and gender scripts normalize and invisibilize (sometimes even to the victim) workplace violence at the same time that real or feared sanctions for standing up undermine the ability of workers to access those mechanisms.

Our discussion of the range of experiences that fall under the umbrella of workplace violence as well as their specificity is informed by what Mireille Leblanc and Julian Barling (2004) refer to as the "four major types based on the perpetrator's relationship to the workplace" (42). We have already examined two of these: Type III, or worker-on-worker violence, was the focus of the previous chapter, and type IV, personal relationship violence, was considered in terms of intimate partner violence in Chapter 6. In this chapter three additional types of workplace violence are examined: type I, stranger-initiated violence, or what John Lowman (2000) calls **predatory violence**—criminal acts committed by individuals who have no legitimate relationship with the workplace; type II, customer/client/patient violence, or **situational violence**— aggressive acts perpetrated during the course of a work-related exchange (see also Chechak and Csiernik 2014). The final type, slow violence, is not part of the conventional typology but emerges out of Rob Nixon's (2011) work on environmental injustice. Unlike the other types it is incremental: "a violence of delayed destruction that is dispersed across time and space.... [V]iolence typically not viewed as violence at all" (Nixon 2011, 3). Uniquely, there is no readily identifiable perpetrator; rather, slow violence is the outcome of decisions made by state and/or non-governmental actors (e.g., neoliberal austerity measures) that set the stage for harm, sometimes years or even decades later (ibid.)—a devastated planet, eroding health of the poor, or an act of aggression at work are all possible outcomes.

This chapter examines predatory, situational, and slow workplace violence through an intersectional lens. In each section we start with an overview that unpacks the characteristics of each type and the occupations in which workers are particularly vulnerable. In order to tease out specificity and shed light on experiences, case studies of four female-dominated occupations are presented: sex workers (predatory violence), call centre workers and nurses/nursing assistants (situational violence), and teachers/educational aids (slow violence). We then move on to consider the dispersed implications of this workplace violence, and strategies and tactics of resistance. We begin, however, by briefly reflecting on the history of gendered workplace protections.

Socio-historic considerations:
Protectionism, rights, and risky work

The plight of working women is a long-standing concern for social reformers, one that has, as noted in the previous chapter, historically been characterized by maternal protectionism and class bias. As Constance Backhouse (1991) documents, in the late nineteenth and early twentieth century middle class women were alarmed for the *reproductive* health of shop girls (whose employment required extended periods of standing) and women factory workers (facing hazardous working conditions and long hours). Alongside other middle class observers they worried that women's participation in waged labour exacerbated their vulnerability to sexual violence (ibid.), and because they earned low wages and shared workspaces with men, also had the potential to lead to immorality and prostitution (Frances, Kealey, and Sangster 1996; Johnson 2007). In the face of medical "evidence" and persistent mobilizing, provinces introduced protective labour legislation, beginning with the *Ontario Factories Act* (1884), which restricted the number of hours women could work (10/day, 60/week), prescribed gender-segregated lunch rooms, and decreed hour-long lunch breaks. Notably excluded from these protections were domestic workers and nurses (Frances et al. 1996); moreover, the laws did not address income inequity—women at the time earned between one-third and one-half of men's wages (Backhouse 1991; Frances et al. 1996).

Although, as Backhouse (1991) wryly notes, "there is little record of what working class women thought of [protective labour] legislation" (276), it would appear their main preoccupation was insufficient earnings; moreover, they quickly found ways to circumvent their new-found entitlement to longer (unpaid) lunch, preferring to leave work earlier. Middle class women reformers were dismayed, chastising the women for their "poor economy" and maternalistically insisting "in this matter the girls themselves are not the best judges" (Jean Scott, quoted in Backhouse 1991, 276). Similar indifference was shown in 1912 when over 1,000 Eaton's garment workers (a third of them women) protested the unjust firing of (male) workers—who, in solidarity with their working class sisters, had refused to take on tasks that would have eliminated the women's jobs—by going on strike. Working class feminists and unions mobilized a boycott, and "customers from across the country mailed back their Eaton's catalogues in protest" (Fagen 1986, 96). As Ruth Fagen (1986) reports, however, "meaningful solidarity between women appears to have stopped at the class border" (97). When Alice Chown, a women's rights and union activist, attempted to enlist the support of middle class women's groups she found no sympathy for the demands for better working conditions and reasonable pay; indeed, she was obliged to evoke the spectre of morality to elicit any sympathy for the strike: "I had to tell over and over the old, old story of the bosses who favoured the girls whom they would take out evenings, girls who had to sell themselves as well as their labour to get sufficient work to earn a living" (quoted in ibid., 97). The strike failed to win concessions. Over the next decades the labour conditions and wages of the "weaker sex" improved little; rather, in the interests of preserving women's reproductive and sexual purity—sometimes with the support of male-run organized labour—they were ideologically and legislatively excluded from an expanding list of occupations (Backhouse 1991).

Seventy years later women's occupational health and safety emerged as a very different sort of social problem. When the decline of real wages coupled with changing gendered expectations pushed and pulled middle class women into the paid labour market in the 1970s (Maroney and Luxton 1997), they were soon sensitized to the realities of the gender-segregated labour force and joined their working class sisters (who had, of course, never left their jobs in factories, shops, and upper class homes) in calling for access to *good* jobs and equal pay (Fitzgerald et al. 1982). In this context protectionist rhetoric justifying occupational regulation was challenged by feminists like Marianne Langton (1982), who not only problematized the exclusion of all potential mothers from certain manufacturing jobs on the basis of the damage to their hypothetical fetuses but also the double standard; employers routinely "turn a blind eye to reproductive threats which abound in traditionally 'female' jobs" (187), including, for example, the exposure of nurses to radiation. Framing the issue as a right to a safe workplace for all workers (including men, whose hypothetical offspring should also not be endangered) transformed it into one of labour rights and helped mobilize organized labour (ibid.). In spite of these hard-won environmental hazards protections, the collusion of the state and capital considered in Chapter 2 ensures that workers' protection from, and compensation in the case of, corporate wrongdoing (e.g., failure to implement mandated safely protocols) continues to be wholly inadequate (Bittle 2012).

The above gains notwithstanding, unlike the rich history of female agitation to transform women's personal troubles into public issues that characterizes the fight for labour market access and many of the other topics in this book, mainstream second wave feminist engagement with workplace violence has been circumvent save for the mobilization against sexual harassment examined in the last chapter, which resulted in complaints mechanisms—however inadequate—being put into place. The limited attention paid to other forms of workplace violence may speak to the framing adopted by governance feminists: If women's victimization is envisioned as men's violence against women, then gendered violence against women perpetrated by both men and women in the context of the capitalist labour market is outside the parameters of the conversation. It is not only feminists who have largely ignored workplace violence. Indeed, the inequitable working conditions and poor occupational health and safety practices engendering victimization highlight the low regard workers labouring in occupations coded as feminine and/or working class are afforded. Perhaps it is not surprising then that, as we see throughout this chapter, it has been left to organized labour to mobilize and raise public awareness about the issue.

Predatory violence

Predatory or criminal intent violence is, generally speaking, premeditated acts of aggression by individuals who have no relationship to the victim or the organization. The violence may be secondary to another crime (e.g., robbery) or it may be opportunistic violence where the victim is perceived to be a convenient target (Leblanc and Barling 2004). Among the workplace factors that increase risk to predatory violence are "handling or exchanging money with the public, working alone, working at night or early in the morning, working in secluded locations" (Chechak and Csiernik 2014, 57), and having a mobile workplace (CCOHS 2012). The victim of predatory workplace violence is the bank teller or store clerk injured or killed in the course of a robbery, or the taxi driver robbed by an individual posing as a client. Predatory workplace violence periodically receives national media coverage when the victim is a police or correctional officer or when the violence is fatal. For the most part, however, notwithstanding that "incidents of purely 'criminal' violence by intruders into the workplace against retail and service employees in restaurants, stores, gas bars, banks and taxis are shockingly frequent" (Edwards 2010, 2), the injury and suffering experienced by victims—who are doing the sorts of jobs dominated by working class and im/migrant workers—receive little attention. Provincial legislation (e.g., Alberta's *Occupational Health and Safety Code*, s. 393, 394) does mandate employers implement risk mitigation strategies (e.g., security cameras) when workers labour by themselves in a context where assistance is not readily available. Notably, however, workers who are classified as self-employed or contract—part of the growing category of precarious workers examined in Chapter 2—generally speaking fall outside the scope of these protective labour laws.

Sex work: Violence in the shadow economy

The vulnerability of (predominantly male, disproportionally racialized) taxi drivers to predatory violence (assault and robbery) at work is well documented (Facey 2010). But what about workers in female-dominated occupations? One segment of marginalized women workers—those who provide sexual or erotic services in the commercial sex industry—are particularly vulnerable. As John Lowman (2000) explains, in this context the violence "may be financially motivated—a planned robbery—and it may be misogynist, sexual and serial" (1005). Much like individuals intending to rob a convenience store or a bank will enter establishments under the pretense of being a customer, predators pose as clients but are "not a client as such, because he sets out with a different agenda.… He knows where to find victims: the unregulated strolls of a city" (Lowman 2000, 1005).

Sex workers' vulnerability to violence, ranging from "violations of sexual boundaries (i.e. attempting to engage in sexual acts that the worker has not consented to) to serious physical and sexual assaults," is common knowledge (Hannem 2016, 33). Indeed, while sex workers, labouring in the shadow economy, would have been excluded from the workplace violence statistics cited in the introduction of this chapter, according to Statistics Canada 2 per cent of all homicide victims between 1991 and 2014 were sex workers (96 per cent of these 294 victims were women); in 57 per cent of the cases the death was work related (compared to 16 per cent of homicides more generally) (Rotenberg 2016, 11). How can we understand this? Prevailing narratives that sex work is an inherently risky activity that should be abolished are routinely put forward by state actors, as we see below, and legitimated by carceral feminists who support criminalization of clients and third parties (e.g., receptionists, security personnel, managers) but not sex workers (who are understood to be victims)—a position that not only erases sex workers' agency and diverse circumstances but ignores evidence that "anywhere from 60–80% of indoor workers report never experiencing any work-related violence" (Benoit and Shumka 2015, 14; O'Doherty 2015). In other words, risk can be significantly mitigated and is conditioned by the workplace setting (Lowman 2014).

Moreover, the argument that sex work is inherently violent—resembling the arguments (which we saw in Chapter 5) that sexual assault is inevitable and, therefore, to avoid victimization women should not dress like *sluts*—normalizes the violence and absolves the state of any responsibility. At the same time it obscures interlocking systems of oppression by negating the need to interrogate the social, legal, and discursive contexts; it is the poorest and most marginalized women working in the street-based sector—which represents, at most, 20 per cent of the sex industry (Belak and Bennett 2016)—who are at greatest risk of violence at the hands of predators (Benoit and Shumka 2015). It is also the sector where racialized, Indigenous, and trans women—who, as Monica Forrester (Box 8.1) explains, are often unable to access safer indoor spaces such as massage parlours and brothels—are over-represented (ibid.). Here again we see that colonialism, discrimination, and other interlocking systems of oppression have tragic consequences: Despite accounting for just 4.9 per cent of Canada's population (Statistics Canada 2017b), 34 per cent of the victims of fatal sex-work-related violence are Indigenous women (Rotenberg 2016).

Throughout this book we see that gender tropes intersecting with racial stereotypes construct racialized women as "other"; we also see the enduring power of the slut discourse and the continued judgment of women who transgress normative sexual scripts, the way risks (e.g., of sexual assault, cyber-misogyny) come to justify constraining women's movement and actions, and that when women resist restrictive protectionism they are dismissed through myths of feminine intellectual inferiority, incompetence, or naïveté. All of this is evident in the way sex workers, and in particular street-based sex workers, are constituted in social and legal discourse as both victim and victimizer, risky and at-risk (Bruckert and Hannem 2013). These tensions permeate the *Protection of Communities and Exploited Persons Act* (*PCEPA*) introduced in 2014. The protectionist rhetoric implicit in its name notwithstanding, *PCEPA* not only criminalizes clients (*CC* s. 286.1), "procurers" (s. 286.3), and third parties who either materially benefit from the sale of sexual services (s. 286.2) or advertise sexual services (s. 286.4), but also sex workers. Defined as victims under the legislation, they are nonetheless vulnerable to being criminally charged under *Criminal Code* section 213 if they stop a motor vehicle, impede pedestrian or vehicular traffic, or communicate for the purpose of prostitution "in any place open to public view, that is or is next to a school ground, playground or daycare centre." While indoor sex workers have reported increased surveillance and police interactions under the new legal regime (Belak and Bennett 2016)—most especially, as we see in the next chapter, workers from Southeast Asia—enforcement efforts continue to focus on the street-based sector, and workers are being charged with sex work, drug, or civic disorder offences (Karim 2017).

BOX 8.1: MONICA FORRESTER ON THE CHALLENGES OF BEING AN INDIGENOUS, TRANS SEX WORKER

I am a woman of colour from Curve Lake reservation in Ontario. I am a trans woman and a street sex worker of 25 years. I have been stigmatized because of my identity, race, class and circumstances.

For many years I was homeless. I had no other options but to do sex work to survive and get the basic necessities of life and to access community. Sex work was where I found community with people dealing with the same discrimination as me....

A lot of trans women like me can't find jobs, because they don't have basic human rights. Recently a trans woman said to me about sex work, "How else would I pay my rent, go to college or transition so I can get another job?"

Aboriginal women in remote areas are working along the highways in order to get from town to town. Survival sex work is necessary to feed their kids and themselves. They face added stigma within their communities because of ongoing colonization....

When there is more policing and surveillance, sex workers get isolated from essential services, such as education about safer sex, safer work areas, the law, policing and community support.... [P]eople are more fearful of sharing information and supporting each other. We end up taking whatever clients we can and are not able to screen for safety.

Police push outdoor workers away from residential areas because of the restriction on clients being near anyone under 18 years old. This leads to an increase in residential surveillance and harassment. Marginalized sex workers like people of colour, trans women, Aboriginal women and two-spirit women are more likely to be street based and face extreme criminalization under this new regime....

Right now, when we face violence, we can't call the police because our sex work status is recorded in the system. I have never been able to call police for help even after I was sexually assaulted.... The new sex work laws would not have helped me then and they don't help me now.

Forrester 2016

Based on their review of post-*PCEPA* research, Brenda Belak and Darcie Bennett (2016) argue these laws have "dire consequences for sex workers' health and safety" (6). For example, to minimize their vulnerability of coming to the attention of police (and risk criminalization under *CC* s. 213), street-based sex workers solicit in poorly lit or industrial areas where neither assistance nor witnesses are likely to be at hand in case of trouble; rather than taking time to assess clients (e.g., Are they intoxicated? Is someone else in the car?) they get into vehicles quickly; and instead of working collectively (e.g., taking licence plate numbers of each other's clients), they work alone (Hannem and Bruckert 2014). Clients' behaviour also changes when they are targeted by laws or enforcement practices—clients are more likely to "seek out street-based sex workers working in more isolated areas and to pressure them to get into cars quickly" (Belak and Bennett 2016, 41). Adina Landsberg and her colleagues (2017) found that after the Vancouver police focused its enforcement efforts only on clients, sex workers increasingly rushed negotiations. Shorter negotiations in turn restrict sex workers' ability to adequately communicate the services they will, and will not, provide; indeed, the laws criminalize precisely those conversations essential to ensuring consent is communicated. Finally, the materially benefiting provisions (s. 286.2) target sex workers' professional and personal relationships, restrict access to security mechanisms (Gillies and Bruckert 2018), and undermine street-based sex workers' ability to work in what Andrea Krüsi and her colleagues (2014) call "unsanctioned safer indoor sex work environments" (e.g., supportive housing that permits women to see clients in their rooms) (1154).

As Monica Forrester explains in Box 8.1, this legal context not only exacerbates the vulnerability of street-based sex workers to predatory violence, it also increases these workers' hesitancy to turn to police either for fear they will face criminal sanction (for sex work or other activities) or, mindful that sex work stigma intersects with rape myths, concern that they will not be believed (Hannem 2016). The real or perceived inaccessibility of criminal justice protection or redress ensures that acts of predatory violence are virtually never brought to the attention of police—instead, aggressors victimize, and continue to victimize, with virtual impunity. This legal and criminal justice context in concert with the media, police, and political "discourse of disposal" (Lowman 2000, 978) that posits street-based sex workers as a social problem to be eliminated creates a "perfect storm of danger for prostitutes" (*Canada v. Bedford* 2012, para. 364). This may in part explain why sex workers are disproportionately victims of serial killers: 29 per cent of the sex working women killed between 1991 and 2014 were murdered by an individual accused of killing three or more sex workers (Rotenberg 2016). Robert Pickton is a telling example in this regard; moreover, that 12 of the 33 women whose remains were found on Pickton's farm were Indigenous (Oppal 2012) speaks to the particular risks faced by Indigenous women—risks that are informed by the colonial stereotype of "sexually licentious savages" (Hunt 2013, 85). Not only is their over-representation in the street-based sex industry itself an artifact of poverty and racism borne of colonialism (TRC 2015a), but they are reticent to call law enforcement mindful that, as Indigenous women, they are vulnerable to violence and mistreatment at the hands of police (Human Rights Watch 2013; 2017; Oppal 2012) (see also Chapter 12). In short, racism, intersecting with misogyny, classism, and stigma, shape motivations for, and women's vulnerability to, predatory violence. As we see in the coming section, racism can also factor into situational violence.

Situational violence

Unlike predatory violence, situational or client-initiated violence erupts in the course of an interaction between a client, consumer, or patient and a worker (Leblanc and Barling 2004). Predictably, it is workers in jobs that require interactions with the public, "in the service industries, such as health care, social services, retail, and food services, that are most likely targets of these incidents" (ibid., 46)—in other words, workers in female-dominated occupations. Who is victimized? It is the social worker whose frustrated client lashes out physically, or the daycare provider who is verbally attacked by the parents of one of her charges, or the waitress slapped by the intoxicated customer angered at being refused service. It could also be the call centre clerk for whom (as we see in Box 8.2) verbal abuse and racial, misogynistic, classist, ableist, and homophobic comments—that range from microaggressions, such as callers demanding they speak with a man or a white person or "someone from Canada," to lewd behaviour, to death threats (Lu 2016)—can become so routine that workers are desensitized and "don't even notice how terrible customers are" (Silliker 2017). It was only after the United Steelworkers (USW) launched the "Hang Up on Abuse" campaign in 2016 that the extent of the "dehumanizing abuse" at call centres—New Brunswick's "flagship industry" (Stevens 2016, 119) and a significant working class labour sector employing 150,000 Canadians (USW 2016)—received national attention. The campaign highlights the poor and exploitative working conditions and calls "on employers to introduce policies to allow call centre workers to hang up on abusive callers, which many employers currently prohibit" (USW 2016). In fact, in the context of restricted employment options, competitive labour markets, and a "customer is always right" culture, even when employers have zero-tolerance policies workers are fearful of losing their jobs and mindful that poor post-call survey results can have a negative impact on their performance appraisals and compensation (Silliker 2017; see also Box 8.2).

BOX 8.2: TESTIMONIES OF EVERYDAY ABUSE AT A CALL CENTRE

I get an abusive or troubling caller every week at work.... Here I am trying to help a customer who is verbally abusive. Then they end up giving me a poor survey and my managers get me in trouble because maybe I could have been nicer to them. So I can't hang up on this customer who is telling me I am disgusting and to fuck myself, but then I get in trouble by management for not using "kid gloves" when handling them or being nicer to them. Never do they say, "Oh wow, that was a terrible experience for you."

I have been called an "f***ing faggot" multiple times, been told that there is a rifle being aimed at my head through the window.... It cuts me to the core of my being. I have stood up against violence and bullies my entire life. To have to face it as part of my job devalues my self worth, fills me with anxiety and makes me question my value.

She told me, "You better clear the fucking charges! You're a piece of s**t! You guys are all the fucking same!" She proceeded to tell me I was a puppet and that I for sure had no education to work in a place like employer XXX. I'm a university graduate.

The customer replied by saying, "You are talking kinda slow—do you have Downs Syndrome or something?" I responded by saying, "Even if I did, that wasn't an appropriate comment to say." He replied, "You are a fucking cunt!" Then he said, "You can stick your mother's pussy somewhere." ... I felt sick to my stomach, my heart started racing; my anxiety level was extreme and I was terrified that I would get him again as he had called in ten times prior the same day. I felt completely unprotected and vulnerable.... I was a sitting duck. I felt it was a psychological assault on me because I was a woman. I felt helpless to defend myself and I felt unprotected; my mind started racing and I was worried about this man escalating and harming women like Marc Lépine.

Quoted in USW n.d.

Nurses and nursing assistants: Caring work, risky work

Healthcare professionals, specifically nurses and nursing assistants, are another female-dominated occupation that is endeavouring to bring attention to the workplace violence they experience. These workers not only risk exposure to chemical, biological, and physical hazards, predatory violence, and, as we saw in the previous chapter, worker-on-worker violence, they also experience exceptionally high rates of situational violence at the hands of patients and their families. Indeed, nurses are subject to more workplace violence than any other occupational group (including police and prison guards) (Brophy, Keith, and Hurley 2017). In British Columbia, for example, healthcare and social service workers comprise an astounding 61 per cent of all incidents of reported workplace violence (WorkSafeBC 2015). Furthermore, the BC Nurses' Union (BCNU 2017b) insists that violence is under-reported by up to 70 per cent and that the numbers significantly underestimate the scope of the problem. In response to what appears to be a growing crisis (WorkSafeBC 2015), in 2017 the BC Nurses' Union implemented a "nurses' violence support hotline," reminding its members that "violent behaviour from patients, clients, family members and members of the public has somehow been accepted as part of our normal work environment. But no form of workplace violence is acceptable" (BCNU 2017a). The same year the union launched a powerful campaign to pressure British Columbia's health authorities to act, evoking a slogan that should be self-evident: "Violence. Not part of the job" (BCNU 2017b) (see Figure 8.1). That these campaigns are necessary speaks to the normalization of violence not only from colleagues (as we saw in the previous chapter) but from patients and their families.

All of this raises a number of questions: Why are (predominantly women) healthcare providers subject to violence from their patients and the family members of those to whom they provide care? Why is the reporting rate so low? And how has this become "somehow accepted"? Thoroughly documented contributing risk factors include interventions requiring close physical contact, interactions with patients and family in what can be stressful and emotionally challenging circumstances, and the impact of medical conditions (e.g., Alzheimer's, dementia) or medication on patients (CCOHS 2016). However, an Ontario study found that patients who verbally abuse nurses are for the most part neither overly medicated nor mentally ill (Brophy et al. 2017). This suggests there are no simple (individualistic) answers but that we must consider the context in which the violence occurs.

We can start by thinking about the environment in which nurses and nursing assistants labour. In the age of austerity, successive governments have made deep cuts to healthcare funding, slashing budgets and demanding hospitals do more with less, resulting in understaffing, increased likelihood of working alone, and additional stress for patients in regard to wait times, quality, and availability of care (CUPE 2016). Consequently, short-staffed shifts, time-crunched working, and a focus on budgets means workers are obliged to "skimp" on patient care. In long-term-care facilities—whose workers are disproportionately immigrant and racialized women (Armstrong et al. 2011)—this includes,

FIGURE 8.1: Poster from the BC Nurses' Union

for example, diapering patients because there are no staff to toilet them, not completing foot care (vital for diabetic patients), and providing only rudimentary grooming (Armstrong et al. 2011; Daly et al. 2011). Not only are frustrations on the part of patients inevitable, but nurses and nursing assistants are so pressed that they are unable to interact with their patients, and therefore less able to recognize the signs of agitation; even if they do, they are simply too busy to intervene. All of these factors correlate to increased violence (Daly et al. 2011).

   In addition to these austerity-precipitated structural factors we need to factor in intersectionality. Tellingly, and reflecting racial and gender hierarchies, female nurses are victimized more than male nurses (Brophy et al. 2017), and racialized nurses are targeted more frequently than their white colleagues (Boateng 2015). Here we also see how gendered expectations condition women's experiences of violence. Women have long been constructed as nurturing and as having a natural ability for care work. Moreover, as we saw in Chapters 2 and 3, gender scripts inform women's occupational opportunities and choices, self-perception, and interactional approaches. It is not surprising then that female nurses are more likely than their male counterparts to normalize violence as part of the job and to perceive incidents as resulting from their own incompetence and professional inadequacy (Moylan, Cullinan, and Kimpel 2014); when administrators express or imply that nurses must have done *something* wrong, their self-doubt is affirmed. It also provides abusive patients (and families) a powerful weapon—one that is exploited when aggression is composed of, or accompanied by, threats to report nurses to their superiors (Boateng 2015).

As with the low reporting rates of sexual harassment and other forms of worker-on-worker violence seen in Chapter 7, efforts of unions to ensure their members report instances of workplace violence are undermined by factors that inhibit workers' ability and/or willingness to do so, which in turn help perpetuate a culture of silence. Some of these are bureaucratic (e.g., limited or absent policies, exceedingly complex procedures, inadequate staff training or support); some are institutional (e.g., perception that nothing will come of complaints); others are pragmatic and related to already excessive demands on the worker's time (i.e., the time-consuming task of documenting frequent violence is not feasible); and others are cultural (e.g., perceptions that violence is part of the job) (CCOHS 2016). Furthermore, the same process we see in relation to interpersonal violence—responsibilizing women for preventing violence and ascribing blame when they are unable to do so—operates as a powerful disincentive for nurses to report situational workplace violence.

Slow violence

There are other ways that workplace violence slips under the radar. The silence of nurses and the absence of police and community concern about sex workers signals a need to expand the discussion to include structural factors that either create or exacerbate conditions that culminate in violence. The "oxymoronic concept of slow violence" (Nixon 2011, 8) alerts us to how a broad range of factors can coalesce, move, and change slowly over time, and to the need to consider not only the context in which workers labour and experience violence, but also the way structural violence such as austerity measures is "often a catalyst for more recognizable overt violence" (ibid., 11). The concept of slow violence allows us to strip away the rhetorical veneer, exposing the perverse way neoliberal discourse—in conjunction with gender scripts—normalizes violence against women workers while simultaneously responsibilizing victims for failing to manage the violence precipitated by neoliberal policies in the first place. Schools are illustrative of this process.

Teachers and educational assistants

Violence in schools is usually framed in relation to student-on-student violence, but schools are also workplaces for (predominantly female) teachers and educational assistants (EAs); workers who, in principle, are entitled to a violence-free workplace. In practice this right is all too often not realized; as is the case for nurses, female teachers experience higher rates of victimization than do their male counterparts (Wilson, Douglas, and Lyon 2011). Teachers report sexual harassment (e.g., condoms thrown at them, suggestive remarks), such rampant verbal abuse that it is "pointless to send students to the office or to reprimand them in any way," and threats of physical harm from both students and, to a lesser extent, aggravated parents (Younghusband 2010, 49). They also confront the threat of physical aggression, even at the elementary level: A 2017 survey of elementary school teachers in Ontario found that 70 per cent of teachers had experienced or witnessed violence, most often at the hands of students (83 per cent); overwhelmingly, respondents perceived that the violence was increasing both in terms of number of incidents and severity (79 per cent and 75 per cent, respectively) (Stratcom 2018). Similarly, a 2015 survey of 700 elementary school teachers in the Durham region of Ontario found that 15 per cent (106 teachers) wore Kevlar clothing (i.e., constructed with the same high-strength fabric used in bulletproof vests) during the previous school year, a third had had their classroom evacuated at least once during the year, and a shocking 94 per cent of teachers sometimes or always felt unsafe at work (Szekely 2017). Graphically demonstrating not only how pervasive but also how absolutely normalized violence in schools has become, in 2016 an Ontario EA experienced escalating physical abuse (see Box 8.3) at the hands of a developmentally delayed 8-year-old boy, which was framed by the Workplace Safety and Insurance Appeals Tribunal as "expected in the course of her work as an educational assistant and was not traumatic" (2016 ONWSIAT 250 at para. 7). Apparently sometimes violence really is part of the job!

How can we understand this situation, how did we get here, and how can we explain the apparent societal indifference? Conventional framing and crime narratives collapse—after all, a distraught child of 5 or 7 or 9 is not a perpetrator. Thinking of this as slow violence alerts us that the child's act of aggression is the consequence of violence—violence that may have proceeded the act by decades (Aggarwal, Mayorga, and Nevel 2012); we recognize the

BOX 8.3: EVERYDAY VIOLENCE IN THE CLASSROOM

[12] ... For no reason that was apparent to the worker or her co-workers, the student was "targeting" her and going after her "constantly." The student was extremely violent and there were incidents "every day, all day long," including:

- objects were thrown at the worker, hitting her in the face;
- she was bitten;
- she could not turn her back on the student because he would hit her in the back;
- she had been punched in the breast, arms, abdominal area, and face;
- she had been slapped in the face; and
- the student would chase the worker to kick or punch her.

[14] ... [T]he various forms of assault occurred in the context of a classroom in which there were other children with special needs. She could not prepare for the constant attacks from the particular student if she were assisting another student. Behaviours requiring attention from other students could include taking one's clothes off and urinating in the classroom or smearing feces on one's face. The worker did not indicate that she had any difficulty with these tasks, but they required attention and prevented her from antici-pating attacks from the particular student. It was her responsibil-ity to handle these types of incidents because it was in her job description, rather than the teacher's.

[15] The worker described that she reported her concerns to the principal. The principal advised her to take "stress" days.... She was eventually given protective equipment in the form of gloves. She had some meetings with the administration, including the head of Special Education. She was told that they did not know what to do about this situation.

Workplace Safety and Insurance Appeals Tribunal, Decision 177/16, 2016

child who is biting, kicking, and hitting the teacher or EA is also a victim, as are other students in the class. For example, in the Ontario context (although a similar analysis could be done in other provinces) we can appreciate the impact of the 1980 *Education Amendment Act*, which was (rightfully) cele-brated as a victory for children with disabilities because it mandated their unrestricted inclusion in public education (Elkin 1982). Fifteen years later the neoliberal "common-sense revolution" of the Mike Harris government set in motion a series of events that swept away the mechanisms (e.g., small classes, EAs to provide the necessary support) that initially helped ensure the success of this mainstreaming. In 1995 Mike Harris came to power, promising a "better and brighter Ontario" (Harris [1995] 2010) realized through lower taxes financed by deep cuts to welfare (the impact of which we considered in Chapter 2 in relation to the tragic death of Kimberly Rogers), dramatically reduced healthcare spending (which engendered the violence experienced by nurses/nursing assistants examined above), a more "efficient" educational system, and the gutting of unions.

The attack by Mike Harris (who, ironically, was himself a former teacher) on the education system, like those of other proponents of neoliberal education reform, used assessments that asserted "weak student outcomes to frame the teaching community as ineffective and, along with their unions, only concerned with the interests of teachers at the expense of the needs of children" (Aggarwal et al. 2012, 158). In Ontario the rhetoric of "excessive spending and scholastic mediocrity" (Rose 2002, 101) was accompanied by dramatically slashed budgets, starting with "a reduction of $400 million in the education budget and the introduction of user fees for junior kindergarten" in 1996 (MacLellan 2009, 60). A year later the *Education Quality Improvement Act*, which aimed to remove "an additional $600 million in 'waste' out of the education system" (Rose 2002, 106), was introduced. Among other things the Act increased teachers' workloads, decreased administrative support, restricted the scope of union bargaining, undercut teachers' labour rights, and prohibited school boards from accessing property tax funds (ibid.). Scrambling to balance ever-shrinking budgets, school boards increased class sizes, made deep staffing cuts (e.g., fewer EAs and administrative staff), and outsourced services, which effectively privatized elements of publicly funded education (OFL 2002). When demoralized but resistant teachers across Ontario took to the streets for 10 days of protest (see Figure 8.2), the "useful crisis" that Minister of Education John Snobelen had called for two years earlier was realized (MacLellan 2009, 52). In response, the government ramped up its rhetoric of a broken system, evil unions, and uncaring teachers. Already vilified as overpaid and unprofessional individuals operating against the interests of innocent students, their act of resistance was reframed as self-serving; teachers who were protesting devastating austerity-inspired cuts that undermined the education system were labelled "law breakers" unwilling to spend "a little more time with their students"; the closing frame of an attack-ad style video asserts "our kids deserve better" (Harris [1997] 2010). Here we see how gender scripts permeate stigmatizing narratives of women workers in feminized labour: Teachers' relationships to

FIGURE 8.2: Ontario teachers' strike, 1997

students are not framed as professional but rather as pseudo-maternal—expectations of unconditional love, care, and availability override the notion of the finite work day and professional competence; those who assert their labour rights are demonized.

In Ontario today we see the outcome of the slow violence—of education reform and also the deep cuts to healthcare—enacted under Mike Harris. For example, in spite of clear evidence that at-risk children who receive services and support have better educational outcomes and fewer behavioural problems (Olds et al. 2004), "less than 1% of potential early childhood clients [are] reached" by Ontario's Healthy Babies Healthy Children program

(Public Health Ontario 2014, 10). Even if a child is identified as having problems (e.g., hearing and/or developmental delays) and requires support (e.g., speech or occupational therapy), costs can be prohibitive (certainly for working class parents) and wait times for funded services—which may or may not be available in rural regions—can stretch months or even years (Sachgau 2015). The result is frustrated, struggling children in classrooms who, in the absence of support, lash out. Moreover, the problems created by the "Harris-initiated funding formula" (Mackenzie 2015, 14) are compounded by inadequate funding overall and the failure, on the part of the provincial government, to earmark funding for at-risk students (Mackenzie 2017). In this context large classes, understaffing, and insufficient resources have become the new normal. As elementary schools "struggle to provide adequate services for students with high risk behaviours" (ETFO 2017, 2), it is women workers—in particular poorly paid and working class EAs at the centre of this particular austerity-induced perfect storm—who pay the price.

Impact and implications

In the absence of a commitment to address the root causes of situational violence at work, we see that (all too often) women workers are expected to handle difficult behaviour through gendered expectations of caring, or (in the case of sex workers) are responsibilized to manage the dangers of their participation in a "risky" activity. These framings normalize the violence, attributing a lack of professionalism or responsibility to workers who are victimized. What are the effects of the violence and accompanying victim-blaming narrative? As we see with other kinds of violence throughout this book, the harm of workplace violence is not restricted to physical trauma but also includes the impact of stress and anxiety on victims' emotional well-being, home life, and physical health. The assertions by the unions highlighted in this chapter are supported by research noting that while situational violence is less likely to be fatal than predatory violence, verbal, physical, sexual, and psychological violence can have profound long-term effects that reverberate through victims' lives (Leblanc and Barling 2004). When workers' experiences are not validated, when policies are absent or not followed, and when violence or abuse is dismissed or ignored, isolation and feelings of stress are exacerbated (Younghusband 2010). In these respects, the impacts of workplace violence are similar to those of the various manifestations of violence from colleagues or superiors we saw in Chapter 7.

There are also, inevitably, secondary victims of workplace violence—the (other) patients who do not receive the care they require (Boateng 2015);

students, who are destabilized by routine evacuations and unnerved by seeing authority figures attacked while wearing personal protective gear, feel unsafe in their classrooms (Szekely 2017). There are also broader societal costs, including lost productivity, absenteeism, highly trained workers abandoning their careers, and increased illness due to stress (Wilson et al. 2011). These costs demonstrate that the neoliberal narrative that taxes (and subsequently services) can be cut without sacrifice is a compelling but ultimately irrational myth—"there is no free lunch" (Mackenzie 2015, 34).

Resistance: Workers mobilize and organize

As we have seen, violence against women at work, with the notable exceptions of sexual harassment and intimate partner violence that spills into the labour site, has not been taken up as a cause by organized feminism. Consequently, there is no flashy equivalent to the Slut Walk rallies or the creative posters that "talk back" to rape myths, and no courageous political women standing up in Parliament as we saw with intimate partner violence. In short, there is no broad-based collective feminist movement to highlight. At the same time the ability of individual women to resist is, as discussed in the last chapter, undermined not only by precarious labour status but also by pervasive gender scripts that obscure violence through characterizations of failed professionalism and irresponsibility. In this context the importance of organized labour's commitment to lifting the "veil of silence" (Younghusband 2010, 48) and ability to mobilize in workers' collective interest comes into sharp relief. The United Steelworkers, nurses' unions, and teachers' federations have all campaigned to bring attention to the workplace violence their members experience and to lobby for policy changes. The action taken by these unions has resulted in workplace violence being problematized in relation to specific occupational sectors—and not as a broader issue of gendered workplace violence. However, there are also collective voices (e.g., umbrella organizations such as the Canadian Labour Congress [CLC]) that do draw attention to gendered workplace violence including, as we see in the next chapter, that experienced by migrant domestic workers (CLC 2011; 2015).

Organized labour's engagement with the violence experienced by sex workers has been more circumvent, restrained, and inconsistent. At times some Canadian unions have articulated their support for sex workers' rights through official statements, opinion pieces published in national newspapers, and by raising the issue of sex worker rights in relation to the marginalization of women and LGBTQ persons (Clamen and Gillies 2018). For example, in 2001 the Canadian Union of Public Employees penned a resolution calling for the decriminalization of sex work, and the Provincial Women's Committee of the Ontario Public Service Employees Union voiced its support for decriminalization in 2015 (ibid.). That said, organized labour was notable in its absence throughout the *PCEPA* hearings. Acknowledging the ideological and bureaucratic barriers, Jenn Clamen and Kara Gillies (2018) conclude that "overall the labour movement in Canada has failed to vigorously and meaningfully engage with legal and social reforms for the advancement of sex workers' basic rights, including labour rights" (309).

Absent the powerful voice and resources of organized labour, sex workers have embraced grassroots methods to draw attention to workplace violence, police indifference, and problematic laws and policies that increase their vulnerability. For example, the International Day to End Violence against Sex Workers was started by the Sex Workers Outreach Project in Seattle in 2003 as a vigil for the victims of Gary Ridgway, known as the Green River Killer (December17.org 2017); Ridgway confessed to murdering 48 sex workers, whom he targeted because "they're not valued" (Alvarez and Bachman 2016, 109). Sex workers and their allies similarly petitioned for a memorial to commemorate Vancouver's West End stroll, a safe haven for sex workers from the 1960s to 1984, at which point local residents—middle class homeowners worried about "their" neighbourhood and property values—organized to expel them (Hamilton and Ross 2016; Ross 2010). Notably, this exodus was spearheaded by gay men who, like the nineteenth-century matrons whose interventions into working class women's labour conditions was informed by moral suspicion, could have recognized their shared sexual oppression but instead disavowed the "other"; street-based sex workers were relegated to the more dangerous Downtown Eastside, where many died at the hands of serial killer Robert Pickton (Ross 2010). The memorial—a striking Victorian-style lamppost complete with red light (see Figure 8.3)—unveiled in the fall of 2016, speaks powerfully to the importance of community and the tragic consequences of exclusion articulated by Monica Forrester in Box 8.1.

Concluding reflections

We don't often think of the banal routines and mundane jobs we do every day in terms of danger, yet earning a living can be a risky endeavour for workers in Canada, and as we examine in this book's Conclusion, internationally. If we don't often think of work in terms of danger, then we most certainly do not think of the threat work poses to our health, safety, security, and well-being as a "violence against women" issue. Yet selling one's labour power for a wage is the very heart of capitalism, so the exchange is necessarily imbued

FIGURE 8.3: The West End Sex Workers Memorial, Vancouver, British Columbia

with power relations, which, as seen across this book, are intricately intertwined with gendered violence.

Certainly the nature of risks and how they unfold is gendered as well as classed and raced. We see too that while this chapter has employed a workplace violence typology as a convenient mechanism to tease out specificity, categories are not mutually exclusive and distinctions are murkier in practice than they are in principle: Sometimes forms of violence are co-occurring, mutually supporting, and/or overlapping. For example, the predatory victimization of an Indigenous sex worker is clearly also an outcome of policies and narratives that date back centuries and the slow violence of colonialism examined in Chapter 12. These layers and complexity once again bring the importance of an intersectional lens into sharp relief. In other words, much as we saw in regard to interpersonal violence in Part B of this book, we need to attend to the structures, narratives, and processes that increase some women's vulnerability to workplace violence.

As we have seen, class, race, and gender condition not only vulnerability to violence but also state and civic responses. Moreover, while federal and provincial occupational health and safety laws acknowledge violence in mainstream work, responsibility for ensuring workplace safety is downloaded onto employers (although in practice onto workers) at the same time as underlying causes, rooted in capitalism and neoliberal policies, remain unacknowledged and untouched.

EXERCISE: RESPONDING TO VIOLENCE AT WORK

Write about one incidence of violence you have experienced in the workplace from a client/patient/consumer or predator; fold the sheet of paper and submit it to the instructor.

The instructor randomly selects stories to read out loud.

As a group, discuss the following points:

- How should the person have responded in the moment?
- What are the risks and potential benefits of responding in this way?
- What could be done to reduce or eliminate violence like this in the workplace?
- Who should ultimately be responsible for dealing with work-place violence?

CHAPTER 9

INVISIBILIZED MIGRANT WOMEN: OVER-REGULATED AND UNDER-PROTECTED WORKERS FROM THE GLOBAL SOUTH

In the last two chapters we saw that gendered violence is not only a real and pervasive risk for women workers in Canada but that state policies, including austerity measures, have a profound impact on the extent and nature of the verbal, physical, and psychological violence women experience at the workplace. That said, we also saw that protective labour legislation, while inadequate and of questionable effectiveness, at least demonstrates awareness among decision makers that workplace violence exists. But what about those workers whose precarity denies them access to even the fragile protections afforded by employment standards—those who are not included because we do not see their work as work, or we do not think about them at all? What happens to migrant workers hidden from view, for example in the home or in the shadow economy (Budd 2016)? As Winifred Poster and her colleagues argue, **invisible labour** is work that is not "seen" and where neither the labour nor the workers who perform it are valued (Poster, Crain, and Cherry 2016). Working in invisibilized sectors or jobs not only impacts perception but also workers' capacity to organize and resist. Invisibility of the workers also translates into invisibility of the problem's scope—for example, those who arrive in Canada through irregular channels evade the radar of statisticians and researchers. This, in conjunction with definitional inconsistencies, can result in widely divergent numbers of, for example, human trafficking victims (Toupin 2013).

This chapter examines the intersections of class, race, gender, and im/migration in relation to the gendered violence experienced by women workers doing invisible labour. To do so we juxtapose two populations of exceptionally vulnerable and "othered" migrant women workers: the first, domestic workers, about whom we rarely think; the second, migrant sex workers, who are the focus of a great deal of police, media, and public attention at the same time that their work is obscured by narratives of vulnerability or victimization. We see how, in divergent discursive and legal contexts, migrant women workers from the Global South navigate the nexus of over- and under-regulation, migration status, stereotypes, socio-economic constraints, discrimination, xeno-phobia, racism, and exclusion. Here the importance of an intersectional analysis is once again brought into sharp relief—interlocking systems, including laws, policies, and practices, violent in themselves, also create vulnerability to phys-ical, sexual, and psychological gendered violence at the hands of upper and middle class employers in the case of domestic workers, and employers, third parties, clients, and predators in the case of migrant sex workers.

Although Canada portrays itself as a multicultural nation welcoming of immigrants, an examination of historical and contemporary policies toward migrant workers uncovers the exclusionary and racist practices that underpin and maintain the national identity of the "nice," middle class, *white* Canadian. Indeed immigration—who is allowed to cross the borders, who is allowed to stay, for how long, and under what conditions—has long been governed by percep-tions of riskiness, constructing a racial hierarchy in which non-Europeans have remained at the bottom (Bakan and Stasiulis 1997; Sharma 2002; Walia 2010). The desirability of migrant workers has often also hinged on their race, ethnicity, religion, and nationality. In other words, whereas Canadian workers' suitability for a job may be assessed in terms of whether they are perceived to "fit" with the organization's culture (which operates, as we saw in Chapter 7, as a subtle form of racial and/or gender exclusion), migrant workers' entry into and status in Canada have been conditioned—sometimes overtly—by how they do or do not "fit" with Canada's national self-image. In the process, migrant women, with a few notable exceptions, have been erased from Canada's national narrative.

This chapter unfolds in two parts: The first sketches the broad socio-historical context of migrant work in Canada and then turns to consider the contempo-rary regulation and treatment of migrant domestic workers; the second teases out the challenges faced by migrant women in the sex industry emerging from historical and contemporary narratives of slavery and trafficking. The end of the chapter brings the experiences and resistance of these two groups—which have been discursively constituted as separate and facing distinct contexts and challenges—into conversation with each other. We begin, however, by consid-ering the invisibilization of processes and factors of labour migration and exploitation by unpacking the loaded (and gendered and raced) term *trafficking*.

Migration, trafficking, unfreedom, and precarity in the global labour market

Who are the workers who navigate the unique challenges of over-regulated and under-protected invisible work? And why do they migrate in order to do so? As we see in Box 9.1, women migrate for a wide range of reasons. Many, as

BOX 9.1: THE NANNY DIARIES

Sheila Calica, aged 49, from the Philippines, arrived October 2008; salary: $1,720 per month

My father died from a cardiac arrest when I was 17. As the eldest girl in my family, I became a stand-in mother and father to my four siblings while my mom worked to put us through school. Thanks to her, I now have a degree in industrial technology.

In Toronto, I found work with a family with three kids. On my third day, they were running around the house with knives in their hands, and I couldn't control them, so I just sat down and cried. They fired me the next day....

I applied for permanent residency in October 2011, and I was told that my application would take 36 months to be processed.... After 36 months, I called, and they told me that my application would now take a total of 39 months to process.... Last summer, my white blood cell count plummeted, and I had to take two weeks off work. The doctor's diagnosis was stress.... The family fired me last June. I've since found part-time work in a factory and am hoping to find a new, full-time caregiver position when my health improves. It has been 45 months since I applied for permanent residency, and still no response.

Rosalinda Umpad, aged 49, from the Philippines, arrived June 2009; salary: $2,200 per month

I taught home economics and English literature in the Philippines for almost 20 years. My husband was a mechanical engineer. In 1997, he was diagnosed with skin cancer. I spent $22,000 on treatments over the next six years and still have $5,000 to pay off.

I made only $300 a month as a teacher, so when my husband died, I didn't have enough money to support my two children and my mother. In 2006, I left for Dubai. Though my girls were only nine and 16.... Leaving them was the hardest decision I've ever made. The family that employed me in Dubai had a newborn child with bad asthma, so I was like his nurse. When I decided to move to Canada in 2009, they bought my plane ticket and gave me $2,000.

... I haven't been home to see my kids in almost 10 years. When I left, my younger daughter hung a photo of me inside the mosquito net that surrounds her bed. She would talk to my picture before she went to sleep. I try to keep myself busy so I don't think about how much I miss them. I rent an apartment at Victoria Park and Lawrence, which costs $575 per month, and until I was let go, I would commute about an hour each day.

Gonzales 2015

direct or indirect victims of transnational corporations and greed, have been pushed out of their countries of origin by poverty and/or discrimination; others have suffered the devastation of their traditional economic activities (through, for example, the loss of land either to developers or climate change); and some are driven by a desire for a "better life," adventure, or new experiences (Lam and Gallant 2018). These women, in the context of constrained choice including the unequal global distribution of wealth, weigh the costs of diminished bargaining power and the limited labour and geographical mobility temporary or illegal status entails against the benefits of leaving their country of origin, where they may face structural and/or physical violence (e.g., war, corruption, discrimination, poverty), and determine that migrating for work is their best alternative (Strauss and McGrath 2017). In short, like other workers labouring in the context of the dependence and compulsion characteristic of advanced capitalism (Westcott, Baird, and Cooper 2006), women make strategic decisions to migrate through formal or informal channels to work as domestic workers, as sex workers, or as workers in other labour sectors. They are neither exclusively exploited nor wholly agentic; rather, their decisions are constrained by the complex interplay of global, national, social, and economic factors. Personal characteristics also factor in; often lost in the narrative is the courage, resourcefulness, and resilience individuals exhibit in leaving their home country, and social and familial support networks, to make their way to a country in which the laws, customs, climate, and language may be foreign.

How do we understand the experiences of these migrant women workers? Kendra Strauss and Siobhán McGrath (2017) argue that the term *trafficking* is not particularly useful, as it "does not exhaust the range of unfree labour relations to which migrant workers are subject" (199). Without denying that exploitation and victimization happen, these authors suggest the framing and focus on trafficking "may in fact elide and invisibilise pervasive forms of institutionalized unfreedom that are 'less than' trafficking" (ibid., 200). Expanding on factors affecting women's labour that were considered in Chapter 2, the authors argue that unfreedom should be analyzed along with precarious labour and immigration status as a continuum of labour exploitation—which not only is financial violence but also increases workers' vulnerability to physical, sexual, and verbal violence (ibid.). As such, the notion of unfreedom alerts us to the role of the state and interlocking systems of oppression that create and maintain inequity and, thereby, produce the conditions of possibility for gendered violence.

The concept of a continuum of labour exploitation also provides a point of entry to think about the often long and difficult journey to the destination country, a process that is largely absent from media and popular culture representations. Indeed, while we often hear of trafficking, political and media debates focus overwhelmingly on *sex* trafficking of women and children; in fact, research has demonstrated that many migrant domestic labourers fit the designation of trafficked persons (ibid.). For example, some domestic workers are exploited by employment agencies that charge exorbitant fees of $3,500 to $5,000 (exclusive of travel and setup expenses) (Galerand, Gallié, and Ollivier-Gobeil 2015), resulting in debt bondage, a situation that evokes images of servitude. In some cases workers arrive in Canada only to find they have been deceived about the nature or even the existence of the job, but are nonetheless obliged to repay their debt (Strauss and McGrath 2017).

In striking contrast to the indifference we collectively exhibit regarding the abuse of racialized migrant women working in the homes of privileged Canadians, the narrative of exploitation in the sex industry is so robust that unsubstantiated claims and estimates about trafficking are unquestioningly accepted as facts (Weitzer 2012)—they also drive enforcement practices that disproportionately target sex workers and leave the exploitation of other migrant workers unacknowledged (Maynard 2015; O'Doherty et al. 2018). International sports events are telling. Local and national authorities and media outlets invariably devote funds and attention to preventing sex trafficking at the World Cup: For example, estimates of 40,000 victims of sex trafficking were circulated for both Germany in 2006 and South Africa in 2010; 0 and 5 cases, respectively, were found. By contrast, migrant construction workers related to the Qatar 2022 World Cup preparations only attracted attention after hundreds had died (Gibson and Pattison 2014; Ham 2011). Thus, the mainstream anti-trafficking narrative obscures the struggles faced by other migrant workers—whose labour and contributions, as we see in the coming section, have long been minimized—at the same time as it engenders regulation that fails those it putatively aims to help: migrant women in the sex industry.

Socio-historic considerations: Migrant workers and Canadian nation-building

Historically, racialized men and women have been "welcomed" not as landed immigrants but as **migrants**, which, in a labour context, refers to non-immigrants whose temporary status is conditionally tied to their employer and employment; in turn, they lack workplace and other legal protections, have limited rights, and confront significant barriers accessing healthcare and social services (CCR 2016a). This lack of protection can be seen as an extension of Canada's long history of treating migrants as foreign and "other"—un-Canadian and unwelcome—at the same time as their (invisible) labour played a pivotal role in Canada's physical and ideological nation-building efforts. For example, the labour of migrant men figured prominently in the geographical expansion of Canada and the annexation of Indigenous lands. As Harsha Walia (2010) recounts, an estimated 17,000 Chinese men came to Canada in the late 1800s to build the Canadian Pacific Railway: "[F]orced to work in dangerous and deplorable working conditions … an estimated 1,000–3,500 died during the railway's construction" (74). The ethnocentric fear of the "yellow peril" was used to justify the requirement that these men return to China once the work was completed, and to impose an exorbitant head tax; as a further precaution- ary measure to prevent them from staying, they were not allowed to bring their families (Mohanty 2003; Walia 2010). In 2006, then Prime Minister Stephen Harper issued an apology for this "unjust treatment," noting their contribu- tion to "the most important nation-building enterprise in Canadian history" (Harper 2006). By contrast, racialized migrant women have never been invoked for their noble contributions to the nation. Their work—like the unpaid work of women in the home—was and remains largely unacknowledged, save for the recognition afforded by some dedicated unions (e.g., the Canadian Labour Congress) and social justice movements (e.g., No One Is Illegal).

Historically, as was the case for migrant men, the value of migrant women workers was explicitly hierarchically categorized by race and ethnicity. Abigail Bakan and Daiva Stasiulis (1997) highlight how "ideas about the superiority of the 'Anglo-Saxon' race, and race-specific notions of womanhood" (32) were embedded in Canadian immigration policy: Until 1947, Canadian nationals were not defined as Canadian citizens but rather as British subjects, establish- ing a white, British norm against which potential migrants were assessed and subsequently accepted or rejected according to their degree of racial/ethnic similarity. This ethnocentrism, intersecting with class, is evident in the history of paid domestic work in Canada. In the nineteenth century, working class Canadian women started to abandon domestic service in favour of employ- ment in factories, shops, and eventually offices that offered better pay, fewer hours, and more autonomy (Backhouse 1991; Segrave 1994). In response to the loss of their household "help," upper and middle class women "organized in associations, such as the National Council of Women, to encourage the state to fill the new void in the domestic labour force by recruiting overseas" (Hsiung and Nichol 2010, 767). From the 1890s to the 1920s, young women who came to Canada from Great Britain to work as domestics "were granted landed immigrant status on the stipulation that they would provide live-in service for six months"; envisioned as eventually becoming wives and moth- ers, they formed part of the nation-building project (Bakan and Stasiulis 1997, 33). Restrictions subsequently increased when other groups of women from demographics less highly valued than "British stock" were accepted as migrant domestic workers. Women fleeing from Eastern Europe in the 1940s were required to live with their employers for one year before being eligible for landed immigrant status. In the 1950s, although the Canadian government began to allow German, Italian, and Greek women in, applicants from these even less "desirable" groups were subject to increased levels of scrutiny. However, racialized workers from the Global South were subjected to Canada's most restrictive and coercive regulation (ibid.). Policies excluding Black Caribbean domestic workers from Canadian immigration drew heavily on racist tropes of inability to adapt to Canada's climate and assumptions of sexual promiscuity (ibid.) as well as mental and social inferiority (Calliste 1993). For example, the *Immigration Act* of 1952 allowed people to be barred from immigrating to Canada on the basis of their race, class, nationality, "peculiar customs" or lifestyle, or general unsuitability (ibid., 90).

Domestic work, however, became "specifically associated with women of colour from the Third World, and no longer understood as primarily European women's work" when, in 1955, Canada began to admit domestics from the British Caribbean (Hsiung and Nichol 2010, 767). The shift, which conveniently helped maintain favourable trade relations with the Caribbean region, was necessary to meet the ongoing demand in the face of dwindling supply; it also reflected the stereotype of the loving and generous Mammy (Bakan and Stasiulis 1997)—the "fictionalized celibate and idealized good Black woman" who is subservient, devoted, and loving (Maynard 2017, 117). Nonetheless, reflecting the complementary Jezebel trope highlighted in Chapter 1, Canadian authorities compelled Caribbean domestic workers to undergo medical testing for sexually transmitted infections. From the perspective of the government, the program was a success; racism ensured "Caribbean workers stay[ed] in their positions longer because of restricted occupational mobility" (Hsiung and Nichol 2010, 767). By the 1970s the Mammy stereotype gave way to that of the West Indian "island girl"; Canadian recruiters now perceived Caribbean women as unintelligent, un-motherly, hypersexual, and possibly criminal (Stasiulis and Bakan 2003). This, alongside the growth of the stereotype of Asian women as docile and nurturing, contributed to a shift from the Caribbean to the Philippines as the source of migrant domestic workers (ibid.). Today demand—driven, at least in part, by the lack of a national childcare program and tattered social safety net necessitating, as we saw in Chapter 2, that Canadians purchase not only childcare but also elder care—continues to outstrip supply. And today this labour continues to be done by racialized women from the Global South— disproportionately women from the Philippians (Lu and Hou 2017).

Over the past five decades policies regulating migrant domestic workers have continued to undergo revisions—the common thread of each incarnation being the creation of an exploitable labour force to meet the demand of upper and middle class Canadians for domestic workers, thereby also contributing to the gendered and racial segregation of the labour market (Strauss and McGrath 2017; Walia 2010). In 1981 the Foreign Domestic Movement program introduced a two-step process that enticed migrant workers with the possibility of permanent residency, for which they could apply only after two years of working for and living with one employer. Under the program, domestic workers, unlike other migrant workers at that time, had to prove self-sufficiency to be eligible for landed immigrant status through social participation, volunteering, and financial security (i.e., savings)—arduous demands in light of their long hours and low pay (Bakan and Stasiulis 1997).

When the program was revised in 1992, becoming the Live-in Caregiver Program (LCP), these additional requirements were dropped. However, entry criteria were made more restrictive: completion of high school education and six months related occupational training or one year of practical experience (Bakan and Stasiulis 1997). As its name suggests, the LCP required domestic workers to reside with their employers, appealing to prospective migrants with the promise that they would be eligible for landed immigrant status after 3,900 hours (two years) of live-in service, during which time they had to work for the same employer for at least six months. That workers who wanted to change employers could only do so upon paying a $1,000 fee restricted the freedom of movement to which they were, in principle, entitled (Strauss and McGrath 2017). Returning to the idea of costs and benefits in the context of the inequitable global distribution of wealth, the program attracted workers by offering a pathway to permanent residency (with the eventual possibility of bringing their families to Canada); migrating for work also offered the more immediate benefit of being able to send money home.

In 2014, amidst the recurring narrative of "foreigners taking our jobs," the Conservative government of the day introduced changes "intended to 'put Canadians first', ensuring they are prioritized for jobs over the migrant workers participating in the program; the changes did little to address the situation of Temporary Foreign Workers themselves" (CCR 2016a, 6). Later that year the Live-in Caregiver Program was rescinded; new migrant care workers are now subject to the Temporary Foreign Worker Program (in-home caregiver stream). For the roughly 7,500 migrant domestic workers (IRCC 2016) who enter Canada under this program every year this change further narrows their ability to transition to permanent residency by imposing new language and licensing requirements, limiting permanent residency spots to 5,500 per year (CGSP 2017), and effectively revoking the "previously guaranteed access to permanent residence for caregivers" (CCR 2016a, 6). While the live-in requirement was also removed, migrant domestics' work permits continue to be tied to a single employer; in principle, workers can change employers, but in practice significant barriers continue to inhibit their ability to do so (e.g., the need to secure a record of employment, a new contract and employer, and a new work permit) (Government of Canada 2017a).

Invisible work, invisible violence: Contemporary migrant domestic work

---

While the rhetoric of migrant domestic worker programs has changed over the years from overtly distinguishing between "preferred" nationalities and races and undesirable "others" (Sharma 2002) to subtler modes of systemic discrimination, such as narrowing eligibility criteria and increasing bureaucratization (Strauss and McGrath 2017), today migrant domestic workers continue to occupy a deeply unequal position in relation to those who employ them. As non-immigrants, their visas are conditional on having an occupation and employer; even their temporary status in Canada is continually haunted by the spectre of deportation. As a result, their ability to realize their rights, already difficult because of barriers including language, isolation, and limited or absent settlement services (ibid.), is further impeded; in practice workers are reluctant to risk the potential consequences of accessing even the limited labour standards enforcement mechanisms for which they are, in principle, eligible. Although, as we see in Box 9.1, migrant domestic labour is not inevitably or inherently abusive, economic and labour exploitation are shockingly common. For example, research by Elsa Galerand and her colleagues (2015) found the average hourly wage for migrant domestic workers in Canada is $6.00. In the words of Kristina Torres, a Toronto-area live-in caregiver, "Any two-step process or path to permanent residency is really a path to exploitation" (quoted in Thompson 2016). The Canadian Council for Refugees (CCR 2016a) similarly asserts that migrant domestic workers' "temporary status is at the root of the precariousness and vulnerability they experience in Canada" (11). Indeed, the reliance of migrant workers on their employers (e.g., for references, paperwork, eligibility to remain in Canada) creates exactly the sort of power imbalance that, as we see in relation to intimate partner violence and indeed throughout this book, is at the root of gendered violence. The power relations in this employment relationship pivot on migration status, race, and class. In addition to illegally low pay and mandatory overtime, migrant domestic workers report a range of abuses, including threats of deportation; physical violence (e.g., throwing objects, physical ejection from the residence); sexual violence and harassment; accusations of misconduct (e.g., theft, violence); gendered, racist, and ethnocentric insults and verbal abuse (e.g., bullying, microaggressions); and emotional and psychological abuse (e.g., confidence-destroying insults) (Galerand et al. 2015). Sometimes the abuse includes de facto confinement when a worker's travel and work documents are confiscated and held by employers (CLC 2011). Here again we see the social determinants of health: Substandard working and (sometimes) living conditions in conjunction with these abuses take a toll on the women's physical and mental health; they report weight loss, fear, decimation of self-esteem, stress, feelings of powerlessness, and a sense of unfreedom (ibid.). As we see in Sheila Calica's narrative in Box 9.1, in addition to being engendered by stressful working conditions, ill health can lead to termination and in turn further stress and financial hardship.

Moreover, even though under the Temporary Foreign Worker Program domestic workers are not required to live with their employers, they may still reside with them if both parties agree (CLC 2011). Migrant women in these arrangements have reported invasions of privacy, inadequate heat or ventilation, being prohibited from having visitors, and restricted freedom of movement (e.g., having to ask permission to leave the house) (ibid.). The following account is one among many:

> A caregiver from Peru suffered one year of abuse in the hands of an employer who was also abusive to his own wife and children. He would walk, unannounced, into her room and wake her up by pulling away her blanket. She was not given sufficient food. She was not allowed to go out, not even to go to church. She was physically assaulted when she asked for time off. When it became obvious she was going to leave, the employer called the police on her, accusing her of theft. (CLC 2011, 14)

Although it may be surprising, even shocking, that Canadian families would subject the women who labour in their homes and care for their children or aging parents to such unreasonable demands and violence, we can make sense of this by considering the gender scripts that continue to invisibilize women's labour in the home. Indeed, being on-call 24 hours a day, working from early in the morning to late into the evening, tending to children, and preparing meals are tasks that have long been obscured by their framing as women's natural duties and skills (Bakan and Stasiulis 1997).

Regulatory tools to address these manifestations of violence are woefully inadequate. Although workplace sexual harassment provisions are in principle inclusive of a broader swathe of workers than those in conventional employment relationships, as we have seen migrant women's experiences of workplace violence and harassment are complicated by their intertwined immigration status and dependence on their employers, making them unlikely to report complaints (Welsh et al. 2006). Inspections of labour abuse are also few and far between: In 2014–2015 there were a mere 340 labour inspections, even though there were 177,704 temporary foreign workers in Canada at the time.

Moreover, if immigration officials deem the employer's treatment abusive the work permit is suspended, and the victimized worker is left without legal status in Canada (CCR 2016b).

In sum, we see that state policies create the conditions that render the labour of migrant domestic workers precarious and the workers themselves vulnerable to physical, sexual, financial, and psychological abuse. At the same time the structural and interpersonal violence faced by migrant domestic workers is invisibilized and outside of dominant narratives of exploitation. We now turn to another population of very differently framed migrants—sex workers—to consider how state policies, pivoting on protectionist and racist rhetoric informed by myths about naïve Asian women, similarly increase their vulnerability to violence and exploitation while also invisibilizing their labour.

Migrant sex work and the "white slave trade" narrative

The term *trafficking* calls to mind images of enslaved women living in sordid conditions controlled by evil men who force them to provide sexual services. It is a compelling, evocative, and, above all, pervasive image. Representations of sex trafficking often look strikingly familiar to the battered woman problematized in the Introduction: a woman, or sometimes a girl or teenager, alone and without context, except perhaps a hand over her mouth. This woman is sometimes also in chains or marked with a bar code. It is an image that unfailingly negates the labour of sex work, the context of women's migration, and their agency—an image that, at best, partially captures a complex reality that includes various forms of victimization that may or may not overlap, including kidnapping, coercion, sexual assault, and debt bondage. It also excludes aspects of labour and migration that are not so easily classified as either exploitative or agentic, including human smuggling, survival sex work, and abusive working conditions.

Turning back to the nineteenth century we see that, as is the case today (see Chapter 7), prostitutes and prostitution were framed as risks to public health and morality and as threats to the carefully policed boundaries of gender, class, and race. In the 1870s and 1880s, in the context of a vibrant eugenics movement and purity crusades (Toupin 2013), Europeans were becoming increasingly concerned about the "white slave trade"—a framing that appropriated the suffering of Black men and women in the transatlantic slave trade (Maynard 2015). British journalists and fiction writers alike described in salacious detail the gruesome sexual exploitation of women and girls (Ringdal 2004; Walkowitz 1992). The most well-known of these accounts, *The Maiden*

Tribute of Modern Babylon by W. T. Stead, "exaggerated the role of children in the social economy of prostitution and misrepresented the way young girls were recruited for the streets" (Walkowitz 1992, 83). That these stories were not supported by evidence collected by the British police—a few dozen young women had migrated over a few years, of their own volition, to work in brothels on the continent; most were 17 or 18; one was 14 (Ringdal 2004)—made little difference. The tales precipitated both protectionist and repressive legislation: Britain's age of sexual consent for girls was raised from 13 to 16, and police powers to persecute street-based sex workers and brothel keepers were expanded (Walkowitz 1992).

In the appeal of these victimization narratives we also begin to see the spectre of the trafficker—the underclass, foreign man who seduces and exploits impressionable young girls. In Canada, *The Black Candle* (1922) by Emily Murphy—a woman celebrated as one of the petitioners in the "famous five" persons case that paved the way for (some) Canadian women's emancipation—provides a striking articulation of the discursive interweaving of racial purity, nationhood, morality, immigration, risky foreign men, and prostitution. In it, Murphy describes young (white, working and underclass) women—"nimble of body, empty of mind"—as easy targets for the "sharks" who provide drugs "against [whose] power no girl has a chance" (ibid., 303). Subsequently, the girls inevitably "gravitate to Greek or Assyrian candy joints, Chinese cafés, cabaret-bars, negro opium houses, or to disorderly houses" (304). At the same time as Murphy chastises young women for putting themselves "in the way" (233), she constructs them as victims. Tropes of the "lowest classes of yellow and black men" (17), "many [of whom] are obstinately wicked persons, earning their livelihood as free-ranging pedlars of poisonous drugs" (189) loom large in Murphy's xenophobic (and exceedingly well-received) text; indeed, Black and Asian men are constructed as not only the instruments of women's downfall but also emblematic of their debasement—as the victim "descends lower on the social scale she doesn't work for anyone but the negro who buys her for the price of opium" (302; see Figure 9.1). The imagery is unambiguous: white women—and therefore the moral purity of the nation—at risk from dangerous racialized men; the solution (for Murphy and others of her day) was the prohibition of prostitution and drugs as well as strict restrictions on immigration.

For all the social changes we have witnessed since white upper and middle class women mobilized to save their "fallen sisters" from traffickers in the nineteenth century, the trafficking narrative and the image of the evil trafficker echoes across the centuries, and the contours of the conversation remain remarkably consistent: "[W]omen are seen as eternal victims to be saved from the clutches of their predators … rehabilitated and returned

"When she acquires the habit, she does not know what lies before her; later she does not care."—Chapter I, Part I.

FIGURE 9.1: Image from *The Black Candle*

home" (Toupin 2013, 112). In the late 1970s mainstream second wave feminists like Kathleen Barry (1979) unambiguously reproduced the white slave trope (complete with the racialized, dangerous "other") arguing, for example, "that many of the several thousand French teenagers who disappear every year end up in Arab harams" (56). For many years this narrative was relatively marginal and had limited impact on public discourse or state policy. By the late 1990s, however, as the direction of the envisioned routes reversed, the sex trafficking narrative became widely accepted (Durisin and Heynen 2016). Now pivoting on a "colonizing and infantilizing image of women" (Toupin 2013, 112), the modern incarnation of the narrative not only negates the agency of "othered" women and their ability to operate in their best interests but obscures the socio-economic context, including the global inequity of wealth and the myriad factors that push and pull women to migrate.

In the Canadian context, for example, Canadian and American erotic dancers enjoyed relatively easy movement between the two countries in the 1970s and 1980s, applying for and receiving work permits at the border (Macklin 2003). In the 1990s, however, Eastern European women seeking economic opportunities in the aftermath of the collapse of communist regimes increasingly migrated to work as erotic dancers. The media portrayal of these women as forced (or duped), mistreated, and passive victims of organized crime networks run by depraved Eastern European men while also being "active agents engaged in nefarious activities" (Durisin and Heynen 2016, 11) ultimately "came to shape the regulation of sex work, labour migration, and the policing of borders" (ibid., 10). By 1997, justified on the basis of "protecting the women" (ibid., 14) erotic dancers were required to provide documentary proof of their credentials and employment to Canadian authorities in their home country (Macklin 2003). After another bout of sensationalistic media coverage in 2004, the federal government rescinded the visa program altogether.

Alongside fears regarding Eastern European women in strip clubs, collectively known as the "Natashas," ran concerns of Asian women working in massage parlours—an issue that first came to national attention in 1997 when 23 Thai and Malaysian women were arrested in Toronto on prostitution-related charges (Suthibhasilp, Petroff, and Nipp 2000). Here again the ethno-sexualized dyad of racialized, "othered" women and dangerous foreign men was in evidence (Durisin and Heynen 2016) with similar themes to the ones considered above emerging in the bifurcated framing of Southeast Asian women—as either culpable criminals (who migrated willingly) or innocent, naïve victims (who were trafficked)—and the looming threat of "international/'foreign' criminal syndicates" (Brock et al. 2000, 5). In this context tougher immigration policies were "equated with protecting women and protecting the Canadian nation, simultaneously, from the (usually masculine) foreigner" (ibid.). In a rather striking example of what Juliet Stumpf (2006) calls "crimmigration"—the merging of criminal and immigration law (377)—in 2001, both the *Criminal Code* and the *Immigration and Refugee Protection Act (IRPA)* were amended to, among other things, increase penalties against smugglers and traffickers, enable the state to seize proceeds of crime, and deny admission to suspected smugglers and traffickers; provisions for victims were conspicuous in their absence (Jeffrey 2005). In the intervening years—as a result of the concerted mobilization of evangelical Christians, carceral feminists, and conservative politicians (Bernstein 2010)—the trafficking narrative has become a normative common-sense framing, precipitating the exponential expansion of punitive responses. In 2005, the anti-trafficking provisions of the *Criminal Code* (s. 279.01 (1)) came into effect; the law has since been amended four times, with progressively harsher penalties being specified in each incarnation (O'Doherty et al. 2018).

Moreover, in 2012—once again evoking protectionist rhetoric—the Government of Canada passed into law Bill C-10, a large omnibus bill that included amendments to the *IRPA* with the articulated goal of attempting "to preclude situations in which foreign nationals might be exploited or become victims of human trafficking in this country" (Introduction, para. 10). The bill gave border guards sweeping powers to refuse entry if "in the opinion of the officers, the foreign nationals are at risk of being victims of exploitation or abuse" (10.1). Here we see not only an infantilization of "othered" women—who, unlike Canadian women, are deemed incapable of making labour-sector decisions (CASWLR and Pivot 2016)—but also the "easy slippage from protecting victims to measures that invoke stronger barriers against immigration" (Jeffrey 2005, 37). At the same time, the *IRPA* was amended to prohibit any migrant, including those with valid open visas, from entering "into an employment agreement … with an employer who, on a regular basis, offers striptease, erotic dance, escort services or erotic massages" (183(1)(b.1)). In other words, not only are migrant sex workers operating in a criminalized context because of prohibitionist prostitution laws (see Chapter 8), they also face the additional threat of deportation—even if they are working in legal sectors of the sex industry (e.g., strip clubs).

Crimmigration and migrant sex workers: The impact

Who are these migrant sex workers? Research suggests that like domestic workers they are often mothers "working to support their families and/or build a better life" (Millar and O'Doherty 2015, 68) who may have come to Canada (through regular or irregular channels) to labour in the Canadian sex industry, or they may be im/migrants who, as is highlighted in Box 9.2, are confronted with significant obstacles, including language competence and a lack of credential recognition (ibid.), or they may be trans women whose ability to access mainstream employment is impeded by "barriers to obtaining gender-congruent identity documents for non-citizens" (Butler Burke 2018, 205). In any of these contexts, "working class racialized women from the Global South are still making decisions for themselves and, for some, sex work is their best economic option as it can offer better working conditions, higher pay, and greater flexibility than other work available to them (e.g., live-in caregiving)" (Lam and Gallant 2018, 296). As one anonymous migrant sex worker explained, "I look for work in a restaurant but they did not want me. They think I wasn't strong enough for lifting [and] [m]y language skills was not strong enough" (Butterfly, n.d., 3). Another woman expresses pride in her self-sufficiency: "I can rely on myself. I have a job and I take care of my family. I contribute to the economy. It's a blessing. It doesn't matter what industry I work in. I don't embarrass myself or others" (ibid., 2). In short, the journeys that bring women to Canada and into the sex industry are varied, filled with hardship—as we see in Blue's story (Box 9.2)—but also tenacity, resilience, drive, and creativity.

What does the discursive, regulatory, and historic context sketched above mean for these women? The tension between perceptions of migrant

BOX 9.2: BLUE'S STORY

After graduating from university in Asia, Blue decided to move to Canada to further develop herself and her education by attending a university in Ontario.... After Blue's first year in Canada her family back in Asia experienced an unexpected financial crisis and were no longer able to provide her the same kind of support. Blue's program requirements only allowed her to work 10 hours a week. On top of that, her experience with racism and language barrier meant that she could only find work making minimum wage. Also, Blue needed to spend a lot of time volunteering and interning in order to gain the experience necessary to find a job in her field, especially as a woman in a male dominated profession. Blue started working in a massage parlour ... to better meet her financial needs and balance her school and internship.

In 2015 there was a raid in Blue's place of work.... The police failed to find any evidence of illegal activity. After completing the search the police officers asked Blue for her immigration documents. Blue showed the officers her working permit ... Dissatisfied, the police called CBSA. While waiting for CBSA to arrive three police officers ... asked her questions like, why she came to Canada and why she worked in a massage parlour. Blue felt overwhelmed, insulted and started to cry.... The police made her sit still for almost two hours and would not let her move, not even to get a coat to cover herself. When CBSA arrived they continued to interrogate Blue and would not allow her to make a telephone call. The police told Blue to leave the massage parlour immediately and warned her that if she returns to work she will get arrested and deported....

After the incident Blue was too afraid of law enforcement to return to work in a massage parlour, and instead, she started to work indoors where she felt like she needed to provide full sex services. The new working environment is much more stressful for her.

Blue updated her working permit at the beginning of this year. The updated version of the permit restricts her from working in employment of any sex work related activities. Given the added risk this places on Blue's immigration status, Blue had no place to turn after recently being robbed by a client.

Elene Lam, in Butterfly 2016, 9

women as both at risk of sexual exploitation and as risks to the host nation (O'Connell Davidson 2006) plays out when "sex workers who are targeted in anti-trafficking investigations are labeled as victims but treated as criminals" (CASWLR and Pivot 2016, 9). Indeed, after victims are "rescued," they are often deported. The migrant sex worker rights organization Butterfly documents one case:

> The RCMP, local police forces, and the Canadian Border Services Agency (CBSA) have conducted periodic investigations and raids.... Racialized and migrant sex workers are often subjected to surveillance, harassed, arrested, detained, and deported.... For example, in 2015, 11 women were deported in an anti-trafficking investigation in Ottawa. The RCMP failed to provide justification and information for their claim that there were 500 "victims" who were involved in a "Canadian-wide prostitution ring." (Butterfly 2015)

According to research undertaken by Hayli Millar and Tamara O'Doherty (2015), such law enforcement practices based on "erroneous and racially-based assumptions about im/migrant sex workers" (70) have significant impacts—some of which are evident in Blue's story (Box 9.2)—including the displacement of workers into unlicensed work spaces that isolate them and increase their feeling of vulnerability, hesitancy on the part of managers to have safer sex supplies on the premises for fear these will be used as evidence of commercial sexual activity, and greater reticence by workers to access health or social services. These practices also create an antagonistic relationship with police (Anderson et al. 2015). As we saw in Chapter 8, Canadian sex workers are already hesitant to call on law enforcement in the context of criminalization (Krüsi et al. 2014). For migrant workers, most especially those who are undocumented or whose documents expressly forbid them from engaging in sex work, the fear of detention and deportation is an additional powerful disincentive against reporting theft, sexual assault, or physical violence (CASWLR and Pivot 2016; Maynard 2015). In this context their vulnerability to predatory violence increases.

These factors also complicate their relationships with third parties—the people who organize, supervise, or facilitate the labour of sex workers (or, in this case, possibly their migration) in a managerial, collegial, or contractual capacity. Being denied access to work permits "pushes sex workers into the hands of third parties, or 'smugglers,' who will help them to travel through informal channels ... these voyages can be exploitative or violent, yet migrant sex workers frequently have few other options" (Lam and Gallant 2018, 297). Once in Canada, their lack of language skills and unfamiliarity with the Canadian sex industry or laws means migrant sex workers are often dependent on third parties for work space, clients, equipment, and other services (Lam 2014). At the same time, not only are they, like all sex workers, de facto excluded from protective labour laws by virtue of the criminalization of their work and workplace, but their ability to challenge unfair labour practices is further undermined by their precarious migration status, fear of being exposed as a sex worker, and the ever-present risk of deportation (CASWLR and Pivot 2016).

The trafficking narrative not only increases the vulnerability of the very women it endeavours to "save," it also justifies laws, policies, and practices that cast a long shadow on all women—and most especially racialized women from Southeast Asia (as well as racialized men). In a rather classic example of regulation creep, surveillance has moved beyond border agents and police officers to include flight attendants, hotel clerks, and the general public who are urged (and in some cases trained) to spot human trafficking victims in, for example, "if you see something, say something" campaigns sponsored by police departments across Canada, the United States, and Britain. Another example is a Halifax poster that mobilized the gender tropes we saw in Chapter 3 to inform transportation industry workers to report people who, among other things, "rarely smile" and appear "disheveled" or "made up to look older than they really are" (Halifax Regional Police, n.d.). In this context women, and especially Asian women—read as either hyper-vulnerable trafficking victims or as potential or actual sex workers (criminals)—emerge as "gendered suspects" subject to elevated levels of surveillance and exclusion (Ameeriar 2012, 172). The ensuing racial profiling restricts the mobility of these gendered suspects. A striking illustration occurred in 2016, when a New York couple, Kathleen Chan and Jay Serrano, were questioned prior to being allowed to disembark a plane in New York—the flight crew had flagged the Asian-American woman, travelling with her Puerto Rican partner, as a potential victim of trafficking (Murphy 2016).

Moreover, targeting and criminalizing sex trafficking is unhelpful not only to migrant sex workers but also to those women who identify themselves as trafficking victims. As Julia O'Connell Davidson (2006) has observed, the language and practices of law enforcers and social workers—who speak about *catching* victims of trafficking—reflects the reach of neoliberal individualizing narratives and myths regarding the *kind of women who end up in the sex industry* (even if involuntarily): They are damaged, vulnerable to temptation, and make poor choices that facilitate their own exploitation. This is, of course, especially visible in criminal justice solutions that ultimately result in deportation and do nothing to address the issues (e.g., poverty, political instability) that make women vulnerable to being trafficked in the first place (Bruckert and Parent 2004).

Resistance: Fighting for rights and recognition

Migrant workers' capacity to resist is conditioned by the precarity of their immigration status. In this regard, for migrant workers and especially migrant sex workers, who face the additional hurdles of criminalization and restrictions under the *IRPA*, allyship and support from privileged individuals who enjoy more expansive civic rights and access to resources is important to collective resistance and advocacy. A laudable example of this is Butterfly, a network of migrant sex workers and allies who offer support and legal resources, as well as an important counter-narrative to the dominant sex trafficking discourse. Canadian sex worker organizations, like the Canadian Alliance for Sex Work Law Reform (national), Maggie's (Toronto), Peers (Victoria), S.H.O.P. (St. John's), SPOC (Ontario), and Stella (Montréal), have also been vocal about the harms of anti-trafficking and prostitution laws (see, for example, CASWLR and Pivot 2016).

Similarly, there are a number of domestic and care worker rights organizations in Canada comprising current and former migrant workers, their allies, and supporters. Early organizing efforts were evident in the engagement of the Canadian Black community; by 1954 a coalition of organizations came together in the Negro Citizenship Association, which lobbied against racist immigration policies (Calliste 1989). Caribbean domestic workers also organized social support networks among themselves in Montréal, Toronto, and Ottawa (ibid.). In 1986, in response to the influx of Asian migrants to Western Canada, the West Coast Domestic Workers' Association was founded by two allies and law students, Kyong-ae Kim and Janet Patterson. It focuses on legal advocacy and support, research, the provision of legal education, tax clinics, and legal services to migrant domestic workers (WCDWA 2015). Much like a national trade union, there is also a broad national organization, the Coalition for Migrant Worker Rights Canada, which brings together various migrant workers' organizations, including domestic and farmworkers' groups, to advocate for mobility, voice, and equality for migrant workers. The coalition has a membership of "hundreds of thousands of Canadian-born and migrant workers" (CMWRC 2017).

The work of groups like these is starting to shift the discourses surrounding migrant work, not only nationally but internationally as well. For example, in 2011 the International Labour Organization (ILO) passed the Domestic Workers Convention, marking an important step toward rendering the labour of domestic workers visible. In its preamble, the convention recognizes "the significant contribution of domestic workers to the global economy," noting that paid domestic work "continues to be undervalued and invisible and is mainly carried out by women and girls, many of whom are migrants or members of disadvantaged communities and who are particularly vulnerable to discrimination in respect of conditions of employment and of work, and to other abuses of human rights" (ILO 2011). The convention asserts that ILO member countries should not oblige domestic workers to reside with, or remain in, their employers' household; that employers not be permitted to keep workers' identity or travel documents; that workers be entitled to "at least 24 consecutive hours" of time off per week (ibid., Article 10); and that domestic work be subject to the occupational health and safety and labour standards enjoyed by other workers. Unfortunately, only 23 countries have ratified this convention; Canada is not among them (ILO n.d.).

Concluding reflections

In this chapter we have seen how two groups of migrant women—those working as domestics and as sex workers—are obscured through mutually supporting regulations and discourses framing their work as unskilled or as non-work through gender scripts of "natural" caring responsibilities and sexual (im)morality. We have also seen myths about women from the Global South; Asian women in particular are perceived as docile, both in relation to their suitability for childcare and their vulnerability to sexual exploitation. Deeply devaluing women's labour and agency through racial, classed, and gendered tropes, to the extent that they are accepted, these myths can be understood as symbolic violence that shapes and is perpetuated by social and government apparatuses, including the media and the law.

In a regulatory context that does not recognize the value of their labour, migrant women workers are disqualified from the (albeit fragile) protection of labour regulation, inviting exploitation in jobs characterized by already poor working conditions (Maynard 2015). Historically, regulations limited prospective migrant workers' entry to, and status in, Canada according to their race, and contemporary laws and policies continue to limit the rights and status of women from the Global South by focusing on their putative lack of skills and/or agency. In this respect the emphasis has shifted but the result is the same: regulation that perpetuates the middle class values and whiteness of the Canadian state. Moreover, because their labour is not valued, any attention by government officials (e.g., investigations into labour conditions for domestic work or police raids for sex work) can lead to loss of official status or deportation.

This chapter has also shown that women migrate for many different social, personal, and economic reasons. Women show agency not only in deciding to migrate and dealing with the challenges on the journey and at their destination (whether or not the job is what they expected), they also demonstrate courage in organizing and seeking allies to speak up against harmful and exclusionary criminal and immigration policies. Their resistance, along with the recognition they have garnered, can be seen as mobilizing a discourse of value—that their work is important, that they contribute to the economy, that they should be valued as workers and as people—something that Poster and her colleagues (2016) argue is an essential precursor to public attitudes and regulations that lift workers out of invisibility, and a notable claiming of symbolic power. Unfortunately, however, as we see in Part D, state regulation and social norms stubbornly continue to facilitate structural gendered violence.

EXERCISE: PRACTISING ALLYSHIP

Get into groups of 4–6.

Develop a social media campaign that brings attention to the issues confronting either migrant domestic workers or migrant sex workers.

- Develop three main points you want to convey about the challenges these workers confront.
- Consider what would be the most effective strategy and medium to convey your message.
- How would you mobilize support and "visibilize" this sector of the economy without drawing on the conventional gender tropes or protectionist rhetoric?
- Do a mock-up or story board of your campaign (time permitting).

Share your ideas with the larger group or class.

PART D

Structural Violence

Part A of this book laid out the social, economic, political, and discursive contexts in which Canadian women are situated and through which they are constituted. As we saw in Parts B and C, this lens renders visible how broader structures and discourses play out in women's lives. It also positions us to move beyond documenting disadvantage to teasing out intersections and interlocking systems of oppression. Part D shifts the focus by foregrounding three forms of what Galtung (1969) calls structural violence. In Chapter 10, Bourdieu's (1990) concept of symbolic violence—the violence of naturalized categories and ascribed (hierarchical) values—is used to examine the beauty imperative. Chapter 11 focuses on state violence—governmental policies and practices that are detrimental to women, most especially "othered" women. Chapter 12 employs Nixon's (2011) concept of slow violence—delayed destruction dispensed over time and space—to examine colonization and violence against Indigenous women.

CHAPTER 10

MORAL REGULATION, DISCIPLINE, AND THE BEAUTY INDUSTRIAL COMPLEX

In 1949 feminist philosopher Simone de Beauvoir ([1949] 1997) famously asserted "one is not born, but rather becomes, a woman" (295). Of course, de Beauvoir was not talking about biology (i.e., the gradual development into the sexual maturity of adulthood) but of the social process through which a woman is created. This draws our attention to gendered expectations and further suggests that the embodiment of femininity is an ongoing process. As we saw in Chapter 3, scholars have elaborated how femininity—indeed, gender altogether—is never achieved, rather it is a perpetual performance (Butler 1990; West and Zimmerman 1987) necessitating invisible, unacknowledged cost and labour (Wolf 1991). Social expectations and pressures are not only distinguished by gender but also by race, socio-economic class, and other modes through which women's bodies are read according to and compared against beauty norms, gender stereotypes, and sexual scripts. We have already seen how these scripts can precipitate interpersonal and institutional violence. For example, women read as "too sexy" are both targeted for and dismissed when they are victims of gendered intrusions, harassment, and violence; derided as unprofessional, they are also more likely to be excluded from, or marginalized in, "white collar" occupations. But how do the normative expectations constructing feminine beauty relate to broader socio-economic structures and processes? How can we make sense of women's embodiment of, and exclusion from, aspects of normative beauty? And what are the impacts on women's everyday lives?

Examining more abstract conceptions of gendered violence and governance positions us to understand the interplay of moral regulation and capital profit in creating and perpetuating beauty as a moral and social imperative. As we readjust the lens and focus on structural violence in this section of the book, the links become murkier, the relationships messier, and the ability to identify *the* perpetrator increasingly difficult. At the same time, the complexity and insidiousness of the regulatory web come into sharper focus. In this, the first of three chapters focusing explicitly on structural violence, we foreground what is perhaps its most ethereal form: symbolic violence. Pierre Bourdieu's (1984) concept of symbolic violence draws attention "to the subordinating effects on people of hidden structures that reproduce and maintain social domination in covert ways. This involves the numerous mechanisms through which overall social domination is achieved from institutions to ideologies" (Colaguori 2010, 389). More particularly, it refers to the way oppressive social structures and relations are maintained, perpetuated, and legitimated, becoming normalized, internalized, and unremarkable—perceived as "just the way things are." Gender studies scholars like Angela McRobbie (2004), who employs the concept to make sense of the "process of social reproduction [through the] spatial and temporal framing of female individualization, the body, and the world of cultural objects" (103), remind us that these gendered appearance norms are profoundly classed and raced.

This chapter builds on these insights, reflecting on how the beauty imperative is mobilized by, and perpetuated in, the interests of capital—the beauty industrial complex—and examines on how expectations are (re)configured and negotiated in the context of neoliberalism. Throughout we consider the implications of social, discursive, and structural factors that entrench stratifications and make "us *all* 'aesthetic entrepreneurs'" (Elias et al. 2017, 6, emphasis in original) at the same time as they trivialize and negate women for doing so. The chapter begins with the historical interplay of capitalism, beauty practices, and moral regulation before moving on to consider how the beauty imperative pervades state and social regulation, disciplinary tactics, and marketing practices. We then turn to examine the complexity that emerges when we recognize that these gendered framings are part of our habitus (i.e., as social actors we cannot escape or exist outside of the pervasive messaging) and at the same time appreciate that women are not cultural dupes; rather, they navigate the tropes and experience normative expectations—sometimes simultaneously—as discrimination, (self-) governance, violence, economic opportunity, pleasure, and spaces of resistance.

Socio-historic considerations: Regulating beauty, regulating morality, making money

Looking to history allows us to see the mutually constitutive nature of beauty, gender, race, and class. This relationship was, and as the rest of the chapter demonstrates, continues to be, characterized by **moral regulation** operating through the encouragement of forms of expression consistent with the dominant ideology and the framing of non-compliant behaviours as harmful, wrong, and risky (Corrigan 1981; Hunt 1997). Indeed, moral regulation underlies the governance of women's appearance by state actors, institutions (including, as we saw in Chapter 3, the school and the medical establishment), and individuals (women's peers, social and organizational superiors, and women themselves). While de Beauvoir focused on how society creates woman as "other," as we have seen throughout this book women are constructed as "others" in particular ways depending on their intersecting identity characteristics. Examining this process of differentiation through a socio-historical lens renders visible the interplay between sexual scripts, racism, classism, heteronormativity, moralization, and beauty.

The debate surrounding dress reform and corsets tellingly illustrates the role of class in the symbolism of European women's fashion, how "race purity" was invoked as a regulatory device by middle class white women (Valverde 1989), and how those narratives were mobilized by capital. In the mid-1800s early women's rights activists, including Elizabeth Stanton, embraced dress reform and rejected corsets, mindful that "women could never be fully emancipated until they no longer displayed their oppression in the clothes they wear" (Banner 1983, 87). By the turn of the twentieth century, however, middle and upper class women were rejecting corsets and critiquing fashion not in the name of emancipation, but in the interests of social purity, urging middle class girls to dress in the new "proper" fashion to avoid (working class) vulgarity and at the same time preserve their "race" (Valverde 1989). Increasingly concerned about their waning business, corset manufacturers responded by evoking a strikingly similar discourse of morality and racial purity, intertwined with youthfulness, heterosexuality, and national security (Fields 2001). Manufacturers and other proponents conjured the image of the "grotesque squaw" to position corsets as protecting white women from the threat of thickening waistlines of middle age and racial impurity (ibid., 121–2).

The 1800s also saw the emergence of department stores selling cosmetics (which needed to be rehabilitated from their association with underclass, stigmatized, and sexualized "painted women") and ready-to-wear fashions (ending the monopoly previously enjoyed by dressmakers); this marked the beginning of capital's aggressive deployment of beauty in the interests of profit. It also, thanks to the gendered division of labour, created a space for women workers and entrepreneurs, including shop girls and corsetieres (Banner 1983; Fields 2001). In this context some Black women, "whose race caused them to be excluded from or relegated to the bottom rungs of most forms of employment[,] became beauty entrepreneurs providing hair care services to other Black women" (Craig 2006, 171). These salons became spaces of community-building and opened up avenues of social mobility for women like Viola Desmond (see Figure 11.1 on page 249)—whose resistance to racial segregation is highlighted in Chapter 11—who started a beauty school that

FIGURE 10.1: Miss America protest, 1968

drew Black students rejected from whites–only academies across Eastern Canada (Backhouse 2001).

While first wave feminists took on dress reform including corsets, the second wave was marked by more radical politics vis-à-vis the beauty imperative, in which race and capitalist profiteering were narratively front and centre. Robin Morgan, one of the organizers of the infamous 1968 Miss America Pageant protest in Atlantic City, New Jersey (see Figure 10.1), described a picket line with signs declaring "No more beauty standards, everyone is beautiful" and "If you want meat, go to the butcher"; not particularly subtle gorilla theatre featuring a live sheep being crowned; and a "freedom trash can with instruments of woman-torture—bras, curlers, false eyelashes, steno pads, dishcloths and issues of women's magazines" (Morgan 1968). Morgan asserted the beauty pageant "neatly combines all the good old American values: racism, capitalism, militarism (the winner tours Vietnam), competition, vulgarity, puritanism, male chauvinism AND, lightheartedness, a protection from anyone taking it seriously and maybe doing something about it" (ibid.). Indeed, the objectification of women and "beauty as a tool of patriarchal domination seen to entrap women in narrow and restrictive norms of femininity," as well as how both contributed to women's subjugation, depression, and anorexia (Elias et al. 2017, 5), were key arguments (albeit less theatrically disseminated) of the mainstream second wave feminist movement.

At the same time as women were picketing the Miss America pageant and distributing pamphlets denouncing it as "racism with roses" (Welch 2016) there was another protest a few blocks away that focused not on the beauty imperative as much as its exclusionary framing—the first Miss Black America pageant. As Paige Welch (2016) explains, while Miss America regulations no longer specified, as they had in the 1930s, that contestants had to be of the "white race," the parallel contest made "a pointed public criticism of the Miss America pageant's discriminatory practices. But they were also challenging racist standards of beauty in order to fully afford black women their humanity and belonging in the nation." That Saundra Williams, the winner of the first Miss Black America, wore her hair in a natural style speaks to another profoundly embodied way Black women challenged white normativity and beauty scripts: In the context of the Civil Rights and Black Power movements, natural hair became not only an expression of political affiliation but a reclaiming of beauty and a visceral challenge to its racialized framing (Craig 2006).

Since the turn of the twenty-first century the issue of beauty has once again emerged as a subject of feminist engagement. Scholars today, many writing from an intersectional point of departure, are largely rejecting reductionist interpretations that read women's engagement with beauty practices as evidence that they are cultural dupes—as symbolized by the sheep crowned by the Atlantic City protestors. As Ana Sofia Elias and her colleagues (2017) observe, "increasingly writers argue for the need to 'complicate' established positions on beauty … and, above all, to examine everyday cultural practices of beauty and women's experiences of them" (12). At the same time these authors note that "it would be naïve to ignore the vast power of the beauty-industrial complex in promoting and selling particular looks, and the products, labour or services to achieve them" (ibid., 12). Moreover, the role of the neoliberal state in perpetuating and affirming gender presentations must be integrated into the analysis. To this end we now consider the way state regulation of women's bodies and appearance is informed by racist, Islamophobic, and classist tropes.

State regulation: Policing "deviant" bodies

Morality continues to inform state and institutional policing of women's appearance. Although no longer accompanied by the eugenicist and classist rhetoric of preserving (white) racial purity espoused by women like Emily Murphy (see Figure 9.1 on page 211), the ideal remains white middle/upper class, heterosexual, cisgender, and non-disabled. Just as the focus of moral regulation shifts with changing social conceptions of risk and morality, so too does its rhetoric and approach. We have seen moral regulation emanating from state actors already in this text, for example when police officers admonish women not to dress "like sluts" in order to minimize their risk of sexual assault. In this section, to shed light on underlying race and class narratives, we focus on two manifestations of intersecting ascriptions that construct women as inadequate or "other"—the clothing choices of some Muslim women and the policing of "too large" bodies.

Regulating Muslim women's bodies

As Sherene Razack (2008) argues, Muslim women's bodies are imagined by Westerners as confined and violated, their modesty read through a white middle class, pseudo-feminist lens as unempowered and emblematic of patriarchal oppression. While the visibility of Muslim women who wear hijabs or niqabs makes them, as we saw in Chapter 1, vulnerable to hate crimes, Muslim women's bodies, and more specifically modest Islamic dress, have also become a focal point of state regulation through ethnocentric and gendered rhetoric of secularism and national security. The attention paid to the burkini (see Figure 10.2) is telling in this regard. Aheda Zanetti, an Australian Muslim woman, designed the garment to encourage Muslim girls' participation in swimming and other sports. Importantly, Ms. Zanetti, who named the suit a burkini not as a burqa for the beach but as a practical middle ground between a burqa and a bikini, describes it as "a garment to suit a modest person, or someone who has skin cancer, or a new mother who doesn't want to wear a bikini, it's not symbolising Islam" (Zanetti 2016). Her invention was certainly not interpreted this way, and in 2016 enforcement of a burkini ban by French cities in the interests of "secularism and security" empowered armed police officers to demand women disrobe (Dearden 2016).

There have been regulatory efforts to disrobe Muslim women in Canada as well. During the 2015 federal election, then Prime Minister Stephen Harper pronounced the niqab to be contrary to Canadian values and emblematic of "a culture that is anti-women" (Harper 2015). This debate arose when Zunera Ishaq, a permanent resident of Canada, challenged the government's 2011 ban against wearing the niqab at (public) citizenship ceremonies. Similarly, as we saw in Chapter 1, in Québec as of October 18, 2017, the movement and civic participation of Muslim women who wear the niqab are potentially subject to restrictions under the auspices of a religious neutrality law that requires individuals providing or receiving public services (e.g., taking

FIGURE 10.2: Burkinis on the beach

public transit, studying at university, receiving medical attention in a hospital) to show their face. In addition to non-consensually (and ironically)
imposing Western notions of gendered and sexual freedom onto Muslim
women's bodies, these state actions read over women's diverse reasons for
wearing the hijab or niqab (or indeed the burkini), which can include religious observance, cultural identification, rejection of Western beauty norms,
and defence against the male gaze (Clark 2014).

Body size: Class, health, and slovenly women

Both women and men are shamed, (morally) regulated through the neoliberal language of risk, medicalized (with designations such as "morbidly
obese"), stigmatized for being "overweight," and persistently urged—by
doctors, family, and friends—to lose weight; a process that starts in childhood, as we saw in the stirring testimonial by Sarah Florence (Box 3.1 on
page 76). Moreover, clusters of class-based stigmatic assumptions mean

personalities are read off of women's "too large" bodies: She is lazy, slovenly, self-indulgent, and weak; her "excessive" weight is proof that she is a bad neoliberal subject who has failed in the entrepreneurial project of the self. Indeed, that low income is a risk factor for becoming obese, and more so for women than men (Kpelitse, Devlin, and Sarma 2014), speaks powerfully to environmental factors—and the social determinants of health—including not only the ability to purchase "nutritious food and safe, inexpensive places to be active" (Raine 2004, 37) but also the physiological impact of cycles of food insecurity (e.g., binge and starve), and the effect of chronic stress (correlated to low socio-economic status) on how the body metabolizes food (ibid.). At the same time the class implications of having a "too large" body are gendered: Women are disproportionately evaluated according to their physical appearance—women whose body mass index (BMI) is classified as obese face discrimination in hiring and have lower hourly and annual incomes, trapping them in cycles of poverty (Laros 2014).

Furthermore, as Ximena Ramos Salas (2015) points out, Canada's (ineffective) public health "war on obesity"—a term that in itself attests to the moralization of fat—is a neoliberal project that prioritizes individual solutions. Notably the focus on weight rather than health results in "unintended consequences, such as excessive weight preoccupation among the population, which can lead to body dissatisfaction, dieting, disordered eating, discrimination and even death from effects of extreme dieting, anorexia, and obesity surgery complications, or from suicide that results from weight-based bullying" (Salas 2015, 80). In addition, the tactics of the "war on obesity"—which include menu calorie labelling and tax incentives promoting physical activity—disproportionately favour higher income individuals and families at the same time as they responsibilize individuals and obscure structural factors (ibid.).

The beauty imperative

It is of course not only, or even principally, the state that polices women's bodies; as we saw in Chapter 3, the media circulates gender and sexual scripts in the news, television, film, and advertising. There we also saw how these scripts impact not only how women are perceived and the scrutiny to which high-profile women are subjected, but also women's sexual interactions, career choices, leisure pursuits, and ability to succeed in entertainment, business, and politics. Media representations also perpetuate normative beauty expectations; as Elias and colleagues (2017) note, "in contemporary media culture we are relentlessly incited to surveil other women's bodies, a project that is enhanced by textual features such as magazine close ups, magnification, red circles and highlighted areas (e.g., to draw attention to cellulite or un-depilated hair or other aesthetic 'transgressions')" (14).

As images of ideal female beauty increasingly permeate both the physical and the virtual world, ever more expansive sharing, and subsequent scrutinization, of images has given rise to heightened sensitivity and vigilant horizontal or peer surveillance and critique (Elias et al. 2017). Whether at work, at school, or on social media, women are subject to relentless inspection and judgment in relation to gendered appearance expectations—in other words, beauty is an imperative. This intensification also includes a broadened scope in terms of age, including "demands that 6-year-olds look like 12-year-olds and 70-year-olds like 40-year-olds" (Orbach 2017, viii); young girls are told to "watch their weight," and older women are exhorted to engage in ever more expensive and invasive interventions (from anti-aging creams to injectable "fillers" to face lifts). Similarly, pregnancy and postpartum, once a period during which women escaped conventional beauty pressures, has emerged as a time of scrutiny and censure—most especially if a woman should fail to regain her pre-pregnancy body with the speed of media personalities (Elias et al. 2017).

The beauty imperative means that regardless of their skills, credentials, and accomplishments, women are assessed in terms of their ability to conform to gendered expectations vis-à-vis appearance in the context of a culture that "always finds a way to comment on a woman's appearance, no matter how irrelevant it is to the matter at hand" (Engeln 2017, 8). It means the costs of non-compliance are high. Women's clothing and beauty choices elicit evaluation that can potentially discredit them in professional settings: Does she look too sexy? Too frumpy? To old? Too young? Perhaps the most inadvertently overt articulation of the work and the artifice of women's gender presentation: Is she *well put together*? These questions routinely asked about women are virtually never applied to men. Class discrimination, sometimes intersecting with moralization (i.e., the slut shaming examined in Chapter 3), is also visible in the epithets used to describe "inappropriately" dressed or "overly" made-up women: cheap, trashy, hooker (on its own or as an adjective, e.g., hooker boots). Perhaps it is not surprising that body dysmorphia and appearance obsession, or what Renee Engeln (2017) calls "beauty sickness"—when women's "emotional energy gets so bound up with what they see in the mirror that it becomes harder for them to see other aspects of their lives" (7)—is, if not epidemic, then certainly disturbingly common.

Doing gender: Disciplining the body

How does the context sketched above impact women? According to Judith Butler's (1990) theory of performativity, people maintain a stable gender identity through the repetitive enactment of gender, which includes beauty practices and clothing. Similarly, Candace West and Don Zimmerman (1987) argue that people "do gender" in ways that sustain and legitimate normative social and institutional arrangements (126). In other words, the ongoing process of performing, or doing, gender in particular normative or non-normative ways allows people to be understood through, and categorized according to, social norms.

Although expectations regarding men's gender presentation have, over the past few decades, increasingly come to emphasize a pleasing aesthetic associated with fitness and engagement with fashion trends, the beauty imperative continues to feature disproportionately in women's lives. Sandra Lee Bartky (1997) addresses this by adapting Michel Foucault's concept of disciplinary power (examined in relation to the policing of women's bodies and conduct in Chapter 3) to cultural appearance expectations imposed on women. Perhaps the epitome of Foucault's (1979) internalized panopticon is the woman who perpetually checks (and fixes) her appearance, ever conscious of herself as an object to be observed—the external eye is internalized. Today, the ubiquity of cellphone cameras and the widespread dissemination of photos on social media has rendered this a considerably more entrenched process, requiring women to be perpetually camera ready (e.g., looking her best, makeup in place). The result is an "utter routineness—particularly among young women—of practices of magnification and scrutiny when looking at images of the self and others" (Elias et al. 2017, 26). We can think too of the increasingly popular apps that enable the airbrushing of these "candid pictures" (Engeln 2017), creating an "improved" digital version of the subject (e.g., skin tone evened out or lightened, the nose made smaller, features slimmed down, pores eliminated) that affirms our "imperfections" while supporting an unattainable (e.g., skin has pores) ideal of what we should look like. Indeed, Siân McLean and her colleagues (2015) found a mutually reinforcing relationship between posting (and manipulating) selfies on social media and "body-related and eating concerns" (1139) among teenaged girls.

Disciplinary parameters have also expanded beyond the physical (without actually lessening that imperative). As Rosalind Gill and Ana Sofia Elias (2014) note, today's "love your body" narrative is a "new cultural scaffolding for the regulation of women" that has extended the disciplinary reach to include "suitably upgraded and modernised postfeminist attitudes to the self. Women must makeover not simply their bodies but … their subjectivity as well, embracing an affirmative confident disposition" (185). Viewed through the lens of moral regulation, an inability to exude what Laura Favaro (2017) calls "confidence chic" (283) becomes a moral failing. Put another way, disciplinary power has been supplemented with the imperative to meticulously work on, in order to correct, our own subjectivity—what Foucault (1982) referred to as technologies of the self.

Aesthetic labour

What does the beauty imperative and its prescribed weight, size, and appearance mean for women's everyday lives? Bartky (1997) highlights cultural and

gendered obsessions with weight as disciplining women's bodies through dieting (from "watching one's weight" to anorexia and bulimia), exercise, and even
holding one's face in a particular way so as to diminish visible signs of aging.
She also describes the discipline of ornamentation: smooth skin from various
hair removal strategies, including the removal of pubic hair; creams to tighten,
even, brighten, and (for brown and Black women) lighten the complexion;
makeup to perfect the features, applied with enough expertise to look neither
overly nor inappropriately made up; smooth, styled hair.

An easy way to illuminate the discipline of the beauty imperative—whether
women conform to it wholesale or not—is to simply list the components of
women's everyday beauty regimen. Getting ready for work in the morning, for
example, can consist of a staggering number of steps and the use of innumerable
products (all of which, of course, have to be purchased). For the face: cleanser,
toner, serum, moisturizer, sunscreen, followed by skilfully applied foundation,
concealer, eyeliner, mascara, eyeshadow, blush, highlighter/bronzer, lip liner,
lip stick or balm or gloss. For the hair: shampoo, conditioner, heat protecting cream, mousse or gel, then curling or straightening and styling. Corporeal
upkeep may also pervade a woman's day: monitoring calorie intake, choosing artificial sweeteners, going to an exercise or yoga class. And then there are
the occasional, or regular, trips to the beauty salon for waxing, haircuts and
colouring, eyebrow shaping, manicures, and pedicures. Even if women do not
do all of these things, virtually all women, regardless of income, likely do a
combination of some of them *every day*.

The pain of beauty: Just suck it up (or in)

If conforming to appearance criteria takes time and work and, as examined in
greater detail below, costs money, it is also sometimes exceedingly painful, as any
woman who has ever experienced waxing or electrolysis to remove "unsightly"
body hair can attest. This reminds us that while women self-discipline their
bodies and endure the discomfort of treatments and fashion in the interests
of being (or feeling) beautiful, sometimes the body is, literally, tamed and/or
controlled. Even as women's garments have become less physically restrictive
than the long skirts and bustles that impeded their active movement in the
1800s, it appears fewer layers of clothing have precipitated new ways of regulating women's ever more visible bodies (Fields 2001). In some ways, changing
styles and improvements in manufacturing technologies have resulted in little
more than occasional updates—seen, for example, with the corset, renamed a
girdle, and then shapewear, and now waist trainer. Regardless of its incarnation, performing femininity can exact long-term damage on women's health;
scholars have argued for well over a century that corsetry is harmful to the
organs (Lewis, Stanton, and Chadwick 1882). Similarly, tight and/or heeled
shoes can damage feet and posture; indeed, wearing high heels daily can "result

in chronic muscle shortening associated with discomfort, compromised muscle efficiency, increased fatigue, reduced shock absorption, and increased risk of strain injuries" (Zöllner et al. 2015, 309).

Why, then, do women continue to engage with beauty practices that can be characterized by the (flippantly) oft-repeated maxim "beauty is pain"? It is here that we see the insidiousness that is the mark of symbolic violence. While selectively engaging with fashion and beauty routines can be a pleasurable activity and even, as we see below, an act of resistance that subverts normative tropes, the high costs of non-compliance in terms of economic opportunities (Hamermesh 2011) and social judgment suggest an element of obligation (or a beauty imperative)—women must at least *try* to approximate an appealing middle class presentation of self. Moreover, if failure to approximate the ideal costs, then conforming, at least in part, to the beauty standard *pays*; here again we see that the natural corollary to the disadvantages it bestows (in this case by virtue of class- and race-infused "lookism") is the privilege enjoyed by those who are assessed as being conventionally attractive (young, white, slim, non-disabled, with a nice smile). Indeed, appearance is an arena where corporally inscribed cultural capital directly correlates to economic capital—individuals, especially women, who approximate the white, heterosexual, middle class ideal are not only afforded more economic opportunities, they are remunerated more generously (Gordon, Crosnoe, and Wang 2014; Kpelitse et al. 2014).

Capital: Harnessing the beauty imperative for profit

The modes of discipline described above are also, given the time and the number of products and services they require, expensive. As such the socio-economic aspect of the beauty imperative is also a mechanism that visibly communicates class standing. This is evident in the value ascribed to outrageously priced designer brands, not to mention luxury beauty products, exclusive spas, and private fitness training. Perhaps the clearest class marker is the financial means to straighten and whiten teeth.

Similarly, while slimness has been a feature of the Western beauty ideal (albeit in different incarnations) for over a century, its more recent turn toward fitness, along with medical and state discourse promoting a healthy diet and lifestyle, highlights the fluidity and the financial toll of the beauty imperative. It requires both disposable income and leisure time—going to the gym, consuming and being knowledgeable about nutritious food, routine and professional beauty care, staying on top of the latest fashion trends, investing in and mastering a range of tools—for a woman to "take care" of herself. This investment of time necessarily comes at the expense of other activities (e.g., leisure, education). Moreover, the beauty ideal—light-skinned, slim, straight haired, and youthful—immediately excludes most women, certainly any woman who is full figured, over 40, disabled, or racialized. The latter point is powerfully imparted in the stirring speech given by Lupita Nyong'o (Box 10.1) upon being awarded the Breakthrough Performance Award at the 2014 Black Women in Hollywood luncheon (Paris 2014).

It is here that we see how moral regulation and gendered expectations governing feminine beauty have been mobilized in the interests of profit by the beauty industrial complex. In 2015, the late Carrie Fisher, facing criticism for "not aging well," famously tweeted "youth and beauty are not accomplishments, they're temporary happy byproducts of time and/or DNA" (in Carbone

---

BOX 10.1: LUPITA NYONG'O ON THE POWER OF REPRESENTATIONS

I remember a time when I too felt unbeautiful. I put on the TV and only saw pale skin, I got teased and taunted about my night-shaded skin. And my one prayer to God, the miracle worker, was that I would wake up lighter-skinned. The morning would come and I would be so excited about seeing my new skin that I would refuse to look down at myself until I was in front of a mirror because I wanted to see my fair face first. And every day I experienced the same disappointment of being just as dark as I had been the day before. I tried to negotiate with God: I told him I would stop stealing sugar cubes at night if he gave me what I wanted; I would listen to my mother's every word and never lose my school sweater again if he just made me a little lighter. But I guess God was unimpressed with my bargaining chips because He never listened.

And when I was a teenager my self-hate grew worse, as you can imagine happens with adolescence. My mother reminded me often that she thought that I was beautiful but that was no consolation: She's my mother, of course she's supposed to think I am beautiful. And then Alek Wek came on the international scene. A celebrated model, she was dark as night, she was on all of the runways and in every magazine and everyone was talking about how beautiful she was. Even Oprah called her beautiful and that made it a fact. I couldn't believe that people were embracing a woman who looked so much like me as beautiful.... When I saw Alek I inadvertently saw a reflection of myself that I could not deny. Now, I had a spring in my step because I felt more seen, more appreciated by the far away gatekeepers of beauty, but around me the preference for light skin prevailed. To the beholders that I thought mattered, I was still unbeautiful.

Quoted in Paris 2014

2015). The beauty industry invests heavily in asserting the opposite—not only that women are not thin enough, or pretty enough, or light-skinned enough but that through consumption such "defects" can be addressed. At the same time, the continued capitalization of the beauty imperative rests on its unattainability. As Laura Kipnis (2006) pithily argues:

> The drawback to femininity, as currently construed, is that it can never be successfully attained. Or not since consumer culture got into the act, since in this configuration, femininity revolves around the anxiety of female defectiveness to perpetuate itself.... In fact, a better name for contemporary femininity would be *the feminine industrial complex*, a vast psychocommercial conglomerate financed by women themselves (though any sex can profiteer) and devoted to churning out fantastic solutions to the alarming array of psychological problems you didn't know you had ("Are You a Love Addict?"; "Do You Have Night Eating Syndrome?"); social hazards you hadn't even considered (dangerous infections from unsanitized pedicure bowls, the sociopath who could be living next door); and bodily imperfections previously overlooked ("poor pore management," unkempt pubic hair).... Eager to feel minimally less agonized about themselves, the subjects in question enlist in ongoing and usually rather pricey labouring, improving, and self-despair in service to the elusive feminine ideal.... [N]eedless to say, your self-loathing and neurosis are someone else's target quarterly profits. (8–10)

Indeed, since Kipnis wrote these words the growth of the beauty industrial complex has accelerated. Not only are new problems that require "fixing" being identified, but capitalism has also "moved 'inside' the body with a range of products—starting with vitamins and minerals and now extending to heavily promoted daily 'drinks' that promote collagen [and] anti-oxidant defenses" (Elias et al. 2017, 30).

Beauty is certainly big business. In 2015, cosmetics and fragrances alone generated $2.89 billion in Canada (Statistica 2016); driven by young consumers, the cosmetics industry, unlike other sectors of the economy, is expanding (Creswell 2017). The pressure of the beauty imperative means that women spend considerably more of the 74 cents to the male dollar they earn on their appearance than do men—for example, in 2015 Canadian women spent $16,956.1 million on clothing and accessories; men spent $9,385.2 million (Statistics Canada 2016b). Not only do women earn less and invest more in their appearance, what they purchase is more expensive. Women are charged higher prices than men for equivalent products (e.g., clothes, grooming products) and services (e.g., dry cleaning, haircuts)—a quantifiable retail phenomenon colloquially referred to as "the pink tax." Indeed, a comparison of drug store personal care products such as deodorant, razors, soaps, and hair products conducted in 2016 found that, on a gram for gram basis, Canadian women pay 43 per cent more (Fomina 2016). In effect, then, women's actual wage (examined in Chapter 2) is diminished and their economic exploitation exacerbated by the hidden costs of the (essentially) mandatory investment in their physical appearance.

Marketing beauty: The role of advertising

Marketing has played a pivotal role in the beauty industry since the 1920s, when advertisers learned that "with proper timing and the correct perception of the public mood … they could sell almost anything," including products, such as vaginal deodorant sprays, that are "clearly detrimental to health" (Banner 1983, 273). Increasingly, and speaking to capitalism's capacity to adapt, corporations are mobilizing social media platforms by employing video bloggers and "influencers" to stimulate sales among millennials (Creswell 2017). Regardless of the medium, what remains constant is the manipulation of our desires and the affirmation of our perpetual state of imperfection; we are inundated with the manufactured images that stare back at us from billboards, glossy magazines, and our mobile devices. Not only do teams of beauticians, photographers, and lighting specialists ensure the model looks virtually flawless, but the ensuing images are further digitally "corrected" in myriad ways—tone and colour evened out, body contours reduced (or enhanced), facial features "improved," and wrinkles, blemishes, and pores erased. So profound is the transformation that supermodel Cindy Crawford famously quipped "I wish I looked like Cindy Crawford" (Kilbourne 2010). The regulatory nature of the beauty ideal is starkly evident in the growing disparity between ideal proportions (as reflected in the media) and actual women's bodies. For example, in 1993, fashion models weighed 8 per cent less than the average American woman; by 2013 the gap had grown to 23 per cent (Oakes 2013).

Women are not only inundated with images of unattainable female beauty, but the subtext is always that this is what women *should* (at least attempt to) look like: white, young, and slim. Comparing perceptions of female celebrities is insightful in this regard. After winning virtually every major tournament and outplaying her male counterpart Roger Federer, Serena Williams was described in 2017 as tennis's greatest athlete of all time (St. John 2017). The American tennis player earned $13 million in sponsorships in 2015 (Bains 2015), less than a quarter of what Federer earned and $10 million less than Maria Sharapova, who ranked considerably lower than Williams (Bains 2015). Journalist Marc Bains (2015) surmises that this is because Sharapova is "willowy, white, and blonde, while Williams is a Black woman with prominent, athletic muscles—as is often pointed out, sometimes disparagingly." In turn, sponsoring corporations perceive

Williams's aesthetic as unmarketable; after all, if they are in the business of perpet-uating the Western beauty ideal (even if they are selling sportswear), it is not surprising that they would foreground a female athlete whose body conforms to it. Negative online comments about Williams—for example, describing her as resembling a man or a gorilla—only further highlight the intersecting racism and sexism that exclude Black women from Western conceptions of beauty.

A little nip and tuck: The surgical solution to a manufactured problem

Beauty as a commodity to be purchased (and pain endured in its pursuit) is clearly evident in the more invasive interventions that, quite literally, reconfigure women's bodies. Cosmetic plastic surgery is overwhelmingly done on women (92 per cent), with the most popular procedures being breast augmentation, liposuction, nose reshaping, eyelid surgery, and tummy tucks (ASPS 2016). Here too we see fads and fashions—in 2014, the American Society of Plastic Surgeons reported a 28 per cent increase in buttock implants from the previous year; by 2015 they were the fastest growing cosmetic intervention (ASPS 2016). In South Korea, by contrast, the most common cosmetic surgery is blepharoplasty, a procedure that creates a double eyelid, something only 50 per cent of the East Asian popu-lation is born with (Z. Stone 2013). Increasingly, too, parents in Canada, as in other Western and Asian countries, are giving their daughters cosmetic surgery as a high school graduation gift—effectively celebrating scholastic accomplish-ment by signalling the (overriding) importance of (sexy, Western) appearance (ibid.). Marketing narratives that promote improved self-esteem for "these amaz-ing young women" who "have spent their high school career ashamed of their small bust or ridiculed because of their A or B cup bra" (Dr. Jeffrey Spiegel, Plastic Surgeon, Boston) affirm the "confidence chic" imperative that women not only look good but also *feel* good about themselves (Favaro 2017, 285).

Many of these medical interventions (e.g., liposuction, butt lifts, breast augmentation) are driven by a desire to approximate the shapely, slim ideal of low body fat, large breasts, and round buttocks (a body type that is exceedingly rare); others, however, are motivated by the desire to ensure all body parts are "normal." The dramatic increase in female genital cosmetic surgery, including labiaplasty, vaginoplasty, hymenoplasty, and G-spot augmentation (Dalal 2014) speak to the power of the norm (Foucault 1982)—and the ever-expanding tendency to define every nook and cranny of women's bodies as potentially abnormal and hence in need of correction. The costs, beyond the self-evident financial ones, range from psychological (e.g., disappointment with the fail-ure to achieve perfection) and social (e.g., colleagues who feel the woman is "cheating"), to physical, including botched surgeries and body alienation (e.g., a lack of sensitivity in the breasts after augmentation surgery), to infection and even death from medical complications (Goudreau 2011).

Women at work: Sexy attire required

The ability to profit from the beauty imperative extends beyond selling products, services, clothes, and operations to women; it also includes the deployment of beautiful "sexy" women to peddle everything from lawn tractors to hamburgers to men's shoes. This same premise informs dress codes imposed on women service-sector employees such as servers and bartenders—a working class labour sector employing nearly three times as many women as men (Statistics Canada 2017g). As the Ontario Human Rights Commission noted in 2016, "commonplace and normalized across the restaurant industry, sexualized dress codes reinforce stereotypical and sexist notions about women. Human rights decisions dating back to the 1980s have found these to be a violation of human rights laws. Yet they continue in 2016" (OHRC 2016). Gender-specific dress codes (e.g., short skirts, high heels, tight and/or low-cut tops) not only "exclude trans and gender-diverse people, some racialized people and some people who practice a religion," they impede women's ability to do the work, increase the difficulty of the job, and can inflict long-term physical damage (e.g., from wearing high heels) (ibid.). Moreover, given the reading of attire in terms of sexual availability we have seen repeatedly throughout this book, these women workers' vulnerability to unwanted sexual attention from customers may well be exacerbated by their mandatory sexualized presentation of self.

Femvertizing: "Empowerment" and capitalizing on the backlash

Perhaps nowhere is the ability of capital to exploit opportunities and adapt to maximize markets more evident than when corporations profit from the consumer backlash against the unrealistic beauty imperative—"femvertizing" (Elias et al. 2017, 31). For example, Dove has invested heavily in its "Real Beauty" campaign, marketing the importance of inner beauty and self-confidence in advertisements featuring "real" women that still conform to a fairly narrow aesthetic that is exclusionary of trans, hairy, disabled, and "overly" large bodies. The campaign also affirms the importance of beauty at the same time as it challenges the trope. Of course this is a marketing strategy, and occasionally the veil (if believable in the first place) slips; for example, "Dove was exposed placing an advert in *Craigslist* searching for 'flawless' non-models for the next commercial. The ad stated: 'Beautiful arms and legs and face … naturally fit, not too curvy or athletic … Beautiful hair and skin is a must'" (Elias et al. 2017, 32).

Moreover, and in spite of the disciplinary nature of the beauty imperative, the rhetoric of empowerment is frequently invoked in advertising directed at women. As Rosalind Gill (2008) has observed, "in affluent developed societies … women are invited to purchase everything from bras to coffee as signs of their power and independence (from men)" (36). Sarah Banet-Weiser (2017) points out that the ultimate goal of empowerment marketing initiatives is "to insure that women are better, more confident economic subjects, not feminist subjects" (280). This consumable version of empowerment also has a sexual component; rather than passive sexualized objects, women featured in advertising now appear as sexual agents, within still narrow margins: They embody a heteronormatively sexy aesthetic, they are sexually active or knowing subjects, and it is through these markers that their empowerment is constructed (Gill 2008). At the same time, the script of "empowered sexiness" only goes so far: Women continue to be read as "low" or no class and sanctioned when they are deemed to be dressing *too slutty* (ibid.).

Trivializing and negating women's angst

In Chapter 3, in the context of women and politics, we saw how even powerful women are required to be feminine at the same time that a "ladylike" presentation of self is invalidating. We see a similar tension in the disdain and trivialization of women's concern with aesthetics—women's preoccupation with fashion and physical appearance is one more indicator of their frivolity, lack of intellectual competence, and superficiality (Engeln 2017). In other words, women are bombarded with the message that appearance is important, but then invalidated for taking it seriously. Relatedly, marketers are increasingly reframing (and thereby rendering invisible) aesthetic labour as "easy, enjoyable," self-care or "girlish pleasures" to which every woman is entitled (Lazar 2017, 52). This negation of structure and accompanying responsibilization of the individual is, as we have seen throughout this book, symptomatic of neoliberalism. This particular version of gendered blaming imposes another challenge: creating a flawless appearance that looks natural and seems effortless. The commercialized empowered beauty narrative adds yet another level of responsibilization by blaming women for the insecurity that the beauty industry has so carefully and meticulously fostered (Kipnis 2006), thereby "suggesting that female body dissatisfaction is women's own fault" (Elias et al. 2017, 32). In this framing "women's (sometimes) difficult relationships to their own embodied selves are both dislocated from their structural constraints in patriarchal capitalism and shorn of their psychosocial complexity" (ibid. 33).

Resistance: Contestation, compliance, or complicity?

Can beauty also be a site of resistance, or does women's engagement with aspects of normative beauty mean women are simply, as the 1960s women's liberation activists seemed to suggest, sheep? Maxine Craig (2006) argues against such an interpretation, maintaining instead that women accept certain expectations or scripts while resisting others. This tension between contestation, complicity, and compliance also plays out in relation to beauty products and service provision; on the one hand, women's participation in the beauty industrial complex can be read as colluding with the oppressive beauty imperative, while on the other hand it can be seen as a source of personal and/or collective empowerment and a tactic to realize economic autonomy. Questions of complicity and culpability get even messier when we remember the women labouring (often in the context of deplorable working conditions) in the global production chain producing beauty and fashion products for Western consumers—something we consider in this book's concluding chapter.

Queer femme-ininity and fat activism: Contested sites of resistance

Tensions between resistance and compliance/complicity are evident in the narratives of queer and trans activists who challenge mainstream second wave feminists' framing of women who embrace normative beauty scripts as patriarchal dupes and argue that engaging with aspects of traditional femininity, by adopting a femme identity or aesthetic, can be resistant. For example, some women position themselves as queer femmes by assuming certain elements of femininity while flouting important aspects of its normative construction, namely heterosexuality. There continues to be disagreement among feminist and LGBTQ communities as to whether, and the extent to which, a femme aesthetic is resistant. There is also the potential for misperception: For example, a woman who identifies as a queer femme may be perceived as conforming to heteronormative expectations—her subversion read over. As bisexual femme trans activist Julia Serano (2013) has observed, even in LGBTQ communities, binary conceptions of gender mean femmes are routinely disregarded as unpolitical, and echoing the mainstream narrative noted above, femininity is perceived as frivolous and silly. She argues this evinces how sexism can remain stubbornly entrenched even in self-described radical queer communities: "Regardless of one's sex or identity, people who are more masculine in gender expression are almost always viewed as more valid and attractive than their feminine counterparts" (ibid., 2).

Queer femme activism overlaps with fat activism in the realm of fashion blogging, a platform in which women position themselves as reclaiming aspects of femininity through conscious political engagement with fashion. This practice is also fraught with contradictions, since queer sexualities and fat bodies challenge the heterosexual and thin aspects of the beauty imperative; at the same time, engaging with fashion inevitably involves consumption, perpetuating capitalism, and failing to challenge the socio-economic privilege the beauty imperative assumes. Here it is important to remember, as we saw in the Introduction, that resistance is always in a dialectical relationship to power. In this regard, Catherine Connell (2013) argues that queer fat fashion blogging can offer "a place of belonging in the context of the exclusive, elit-ist, and oppressive confines of mainstream fashion" (221), where bodies read as non-conforming and undisciplined are othered and excluded. As Cary Webb (2015) counters, however, "Fatshion" is part of the fragmentation of the size acceptance movement, which began as an explicit rejection of narrow femi-nine beauty standards and the cultural exaltation of thinness, but has become less political and in turn less inclusive over time.

Hair and Black women's resistance

The politics of aesthetics is perhaps most powerfully conveyed by the 1960s Black Is Beautiful movement (Taylor 2013). As the politics of Black women's hair gained traction, women started wearing their hair natural as an expression of their commitment to Civil Rights and a rejection of white beauty stan-dards embraced by both the Black community and society more broadly. Today, unstraightened hair is once again politicized in the debates over the "profes-sionalism" of natural hair; Black female media and political personalities have weighed in regarding their personal and political decisions. Notable among these is Michaëlle Jean, the twenty-seventh Governor General of Canada, who began her mandate with her hair styled straight and subsequently made the conscious decision to wear her hair natural. Jean (2012) urged Black women to reject the alienation of "caucasian standards of beauty," stating "how wonderful it was to conduct diplomatic missions—State visits—to Europe, China, Latin America, Africa, fully assuming my blackness!"

The politics of Black women's hair is, unsurprisingly, not without contro-versy. One issue is the potential for natural hair to become a normative obligation; Canadian television personality Arisa Cox (2014), who terminated her employment when she was told by a news executive that wearing her hair straight was not negotiable, not only acknowledged her privilege in resisting through the removal of her labour power, but also cautioned against a natural hair imperative, noting "any woman should feel the freedom to wear whatever hair makes her feel good." Maxine Craig (2006) raises another issue: In the 1960s, as women with large Afros—a style that necessitates the conventional feminine attribute of long hair—started to be perceived as more attractive in the Black community, it shifted but did not disrupt the evaluation of women in terms of their appearance. Angela Davis (see Figure 10.3), the brilliant scholar, Civil Rights leader, prison abolitionist, and former political prisoner cited repeatedly in this volume, became emblematic of this politicization of hair. She expressed frustration at being remembered as "the afro," stating that it was both humiliating and humbling "to discover that a single generation after the events that constructed me as a public personality, I am remembered as a hairdo. It is humiliating because it reduces a politics of liberation to a politics

FIGURE 10.3: Angela Davis, Raleigh, North Carolina, 1974

of fashion; it is humbling because [it] demonstrate[s] the fragility and muta-
bility of historical images, particularly those associated with African American
history" (Davis 1994, 37).

Concluding reflections

This chapter examined the relationship between capitalism and the beauty
imperative, endeavouring to tease out the complexity of women's relationship to normative appearance criteria. We have also seen how the contours
of the beauty industrial complex have shifted and expanded both in terms
of life stages targeted (e.g., youth, pregnancy, aging) and in relation to the
colonization of ever-increasing parts of women's bodies and subjectivities.
Profoundly regulatory, the beauty imperative is also a site and source of gendered
violence. Leaving aside the contentious question of whether beauty practices and interventions are violence against the self, we can return instead to
the expansive framing of gendered violence—including both structural and
symbolic violence—provided in the Introduction of this book. The notion
of symbolic violence alerts us to the subtlety and pervasiveness of the beauty

imperative. It is elusive but insidious, permeating our perceptions and affecting our actions even as we *know* better.

We can think too of the messaging implicit in marketing campaigns hinging on perfecting women's appearance and harking back to their construction as the "weaker sex": Never thin nor confident nor sexually empowered *enough*, women are inherently flawed. That women must overcome their intrinsic flaws through a disproportionate (as compared to men) amount of aesthetic labour reiterates the pathology of their natural state (e.g., body hair, natural hair texture, bare face). Through the lens of moral regulation we have also seen how not conforming to the beauty imperative becomes a moral failing: Fat bodies are perceived as wrong and risky; a lack of confidence or sexiness or relishing one's own beauty is seen as harmful to the self—a failed disciplining of the body and soul.

Symbolic violence also allows us to think through the ways women may well be expressing individuality and agency but at the same time reproducing class and racial stratifications—ultimately operating against their own best interests by positioning some women as more beautiful, and *valuable*, than others—which affords conventional women more opportunities and pay, but still less than men. The appropriation of the discourse of female empowerment in beauty and fashion advertising and the media blurs the line between conformist and resistant acts vis-à-vis normative beauty—this is the insidiousness of symbolic violence. Laura Favaro (2017) reflects on the profound irony in the trend given that "in our injurious patriarchal cultures, unconfidence is almost inescapable when inhabiting womanhood. However, recently the promotion of self-confidence has surfaced as the site for expanded, heightened and more insidious modes of regulation, often spearheaded by those very institutions invested in women's insecurities" (283).

EXERCISE: THE POWER OF BEAUTY*

Reflect on your ideal image of beauty.

How does your ideal image conform to, or differ from, the dominant beauty norm?

Imagine that you embodied your ideal.

What would your life be like, and how would it be different than it is now?

Reflect on what your answer says about the personal and/or social importance of beauty and appearance.

*Adapted from the work of Renee Engeln (2017)

CHAPTER 11

STATE VIOLENCE: WOMEN AND THE CRIMINAL JUSTICE SYSTEM

In Chapter 1 the concept of privilege was introduced—the unearned benefits conferred on the dominant group that feel natural, unremarkable, and inherent. One key marker of white privilege is the ability to call on the police, to be confident that police "serve and protect," and to feel secure in the conviction that laws are equitable and equitably applied. We have seen many examples of gender bias in this book that draw into question how *just* the justice system really is—and how gender, class, and race blind. For example, in Chapter 5 we saw rape myths reproduced when police classify a sexual assault as unfounded because the woman was consuming alcohol, when a defence attorney "whacks" a complainant, accusing her of "making the whole thing up," and when a judge asks a victim "why couldn't you just keep your knees together?" Nonetheless, we have also seen contemporary feminists, echoing mainstream second wave reformers' confidence that law is ideological in *content* and therefore amenable to reform (Currie 1990), advocating for legal modification and criminal justice solutions—in effect, more laws and harsher penalties. It is in the well-intentioned but privilege-blind reforms that we see the white middle class roots of today's governance and carceral feminisms. Indeed, what is obscured is the privilege derived from embodying the ideal woman victim—white, upper or middle class, cisgender, heterosexual, and *respectable*—and in turn how this reproduces the exclusion of "othered" women.

Highlighting interlocking systems of oppression, this chapter foregrounds the work of feminist criminologists and employs an intersectional lens. This allows us to consider the criminal justice system as gendered structural violence. This is not to suggest that women are more likely to experience state penal interventions than are men—such a claim is inconsistent with the empirical evidence; indeed, women comprise just 24 per cent of all individuals accused of committing *Criminal Code* offences in Canada (Mahony, Jacob, and Hobson 2017). Nor does this mean that women are never culpable of egregious acts—certainly the anomalous spectre of Karla Homolka (who, along with her husband, Paul Bernardo, was convicted in 1992 for the murder of two young women) haunts any discussion of female criminality (Kilty and Frigon 2016). However, an intersectional gendered lens allows us to ask some important questions: Who are the women who are criminalized? How do scripts, myths, and stereotypes coalesce with socio-economic location and racialization to condition women's vulnerability to, experience of, and ability to resist the violence of the criminal justice system? To what extent is the normative expectation of white middle class femininity implicated in the response to and treatment of criminalized women? And how has this changed in the context of neoliberalism and the emergence of the risk framework? In Chapter 10 we examined "soft," diffused regulation and how gender norms and scripts of femininity have been exploited (and propagated) in the interests of capital; in this chapter we consider "harder" regulation—the law and repressive criminal justice apparatuses: police, courts, and prisons—and its particular impacts on Black, Indigenous, working class, and trans women.

Structural violence and profiling

As we have seen, structural factors operate to restrict "othered" women's access to what is reputed to be a fundamental right: the ability to turn to the police for criminal justice protection or redress. For example, in Chapter 7 we saw that marginalized women such as sex workers are hesitant to file police reports, knowing that in spite of being discursively framed as victims the pervasiveness of the "just a whore" mentality impedes their ability to do so. We also saw that the response of law enforcement to intimate partner violence (IPV) is conditioned by broader social narratives and stigmatic assumptions; for example, police infantilize and patronize women with disabilities and dismiss violence in same sex relationships as a "cat fight" (Chapter 6). Similarly, as examined in greater detail in Chapter 12, not only are Indigenous victims of IPV vulnerable to being blamed for the abuse, but the insidious racist stereotypes of hypersexuality and substance abuse (Comack 2014b) play out in shaming and apathy toward missing and murdered Indigenous women (Human Rights Watch 2013). Such neglect and disinterest is not only state violence in its own right but also further entrenches narratives of worthlessness and disposability that are integral to the high rates of violence experienced by Indigenous and other racialized and marginalized women. Moreover, their victimization, read through the lens of intersecting race, class, and gender scripts, can bring them into contact with the criminal justice system. We saw this, for example, in the charging of racialized and queer women under mandatory charging policies for IPV (Chapter 6) and in the deportation and incarceration of migrant sex workers (Chapter 9). In short, when we shed race and class blinders we see that the criminal justice system is not a solution for all; rather, it is another potential site and source of violence.

This chapter, then, examines state violence, drawing on Johan Galtung's (1969) concept of structural violence—the injustices embedded in social institutions that cause harm and undermine people's ability to realize their potential—to build on the analysis developed throughout this book. We have seen, for example, that the law is a mechanism through which the interests of the powerful are furthered; as such, the law operates to retain class, gender, and racial inequity. We have also seen how law entrenches dichotomous and classed gender roles and characterizations (Smart 1989), distinguishing between credible and discreditable victims of sexual assault (Chapter 5). Moreover, if laws are about maintaining race and class distinctions, then police are the enforcers; for example, as historian Lorne Brown (1992) details, the North West Mounted Police (the forbearer of the RCMP) was developed with an eye to protecting the interests of capital by containing and controlling the labour union movement (e.g., ending the Winnipeg General Strike) and Indigenous peoples (e.g., enforcing the *Indian Act* pass system and ensuring prohibitions against traditional dances). A recent example of these twin pillars would be the police response to Indigenous resistance to resource extraction (see Figure 12.2 on page 289). Finally, as labelling theorists have long noted, criminalization is not about contravening the laws—which, after all, everyone does in some ways (e.g., Internet piracy, speeding, under-age drinking)—but about coming to the attention of the police, being charged, and ultimately convicted (Becker 1973). Here the possibility of **social profiling**—discrimination on the basis of visible signs of poverty or marginality (CDPDJ 2009)—which pivots on class-based stereotypes and stigmatic assumptions by police, social service workers, and officers of the courts, needs to be considered. So too does racial profiling: **Racial profiling** is defined by the Ontario Human Rights Commission (OHRC 2017) as "any action undertaken for reasons of safety, security or public protection that relies on stereotypes about race, colour, ethnicity, ancestry, religion, or place of origin rather than on reasonable suspicion, to single out an individual for greater scrutiny or different treatment" (94). Systemic bias that results, for example, in areas where poor racialized people live being identified as "high risk" or "priority" neighbourhoods and the inhabitants therefore subjected to hyper-policing also needs to be factored in (Cader and Amofah 2016). In the coming pages we see that while social and racial profiling and systemic bias result in certain populations being identified—and surveilled—as risky, these processes are also gendered. We start by considering this historically.

Socio-historic considerations: Unruly women, fallen girls, and middle class saviours

Throughout Western history, women who challenged or resisted (even if unintentionally so) the social order have been subjected to harsh repression at the same time as the laws and their enforcement have functioned as powerful mechanisms that entrench gender roles, class positions, and racial stratifications. The murder of what is conservatively estimated to be hundreds of thousands of wise women, midwives, lay healers, and independent though poor "spinsters" between the fourteenth and seventeenth centuries in the European witch hunts is perhaps the most explicit and graphic example (Ehrenreich and English 1973). The ability of the church and state to mobilize well-established religious mythology constructing women as sexual, and sexually threatening, rendered these women easy scapegoats for the challenges confronting a rapidly transforming feudal society; that such women undermined the burgeoning male discipline of medicine provided a further motivation to discredit them (ibid.). The dunking or confinement in gossip's or scold's bridles (see Figure I.1 on page 3) of women who challenged the patriarchal order by speaking out against their husbands or any other man is another powerful example of church and state authority enacted on the bodies of women in symbolic (albeit painful) sanctions meant to both change the "offender's" behaviour and "to serve as a moral lesson and deter those who watched" (Dobash, Dobash, and Gutterridge 1986, 20).

The law as reflecting and enforcing gender, class, and race relations is evident in other crimes against the social order as well. Notably in England from 1351 to 1828 a woman accused of killing her husband—or a servant their master—"was liable to be indicted not for wilful murder but the aggravated offence of petit treason" (Gavigan 1989/1990, 335). Working class women were also criminalized, along with working class men, when they protested industrialization and the subsequent erosion of their access to a living wage. For example, women were convicted for their participation in the 1919 Winnipeg General Strike; charges included unlawful assembly, disorderly conduct, assault, and intimidation (Horodyski 1986). We also see that women who resisted racist repression were harshly sanctioned for their non-compliance. The Mounted Police found that when Indigenous women refused to heed mobility restrictions imposed by the colonial state in the late 1800s, "the promise to take them to the barracks and cut off their hair had a wonderful effect" (Carter 1993, 156). In 1946 when Viola Desmond (Figure 11.1) refused to leave the "whites only" section of a New Glasgow, Nova Scotia, movie theatre she was forcibly removed, arrested, jailed, convicted, and fined $20 (Backhouse 2001).

FIGURE 11.1: Viola Desmond

Acknowledging the acts of resistance by women who explicitly contested or subverted gender, race, and class oppression is important; to frame criminalized women as revolutionary heroes would, however, be disingenuous. For the most part in the seventeenth, eighteenth, and nineteenth centuries women engaged in, and were charged for, petty property crimes and prostitution—behaviours motivated by economic need (Faith 1993). There is little evidence of leniency—women were subject to the same corporal and capital punishments men received; indeed, the first person officially hanged in Canada was a 16-year-old girl convicted of theft in 1640 (ibid.).

As states embraced prisons as a more efficient and effective disciplinary and regulatory mechanism than corporal and capital punishment (Foucault 1979), women were first housed alongside men and subsequently in separate wings of male institutions. However, by the mid-1800s the image of the female criminal as "wretched, depraved and unreformed" was being rehabilitated; she became the (infantilized) fallen woman "who could be redeemed through proper instruction and guidance" (Hannah-Moffat 2001, 53–4). These (women) reformers were mindful of the low wages and poor labour conditions that working class women endured (see Chapter 8), but "repeatedly returned to the theme of women's sexual vulnerability" (Freedman 1984, 44). Invoking the narrative of women's moral superiority they focused attention on sexual victimization by men as the root cause of women's criminality and petitioned for separate prisons run by and for women, certain that "the fallen could be redeemed and made into true women" (ibid., 45) with the predictable result that women spent long periods in institutions designed to "save" them (Brock 2003). Canada's first women-only prison, the provincial Andrew Mercer Reformatory for Women in Ontario (Figure 11.2), opened in 1879, was a state-initiated project informed by this "maternal penal reform" narrative (Hannah-Moffat 2001, 54). Matrons, envisioned as firm but caring motherly figures, were tasked with gender indoctrination reflecting deep class cleavages—the "ideal of the prim, sober middle-class woman" was the "goal for all destitute, criminalized women" (Faith 1993, 130). Women were instructed in hygiene, morals, and domestic training; those who successfully refrained from unseemly behaviours (e.g., swearing, chewing gum) were rewarded with badges and privileges, and those who rejected the middle class ideal of femininity fell outside the redemption narrative and were subject to harsh physical sanctions (ibid.).

For the next 50 years, "the regulation of young women in public space took on a decidedly classed and racialized edge" (Balfour 2014a, 159). The moral regulation of women was evident in increased charges for vagrancy, prostitution, and public drunkenness; Indigenous women were particularly vulnerable to coming to the attention of law enforcement and being sanctioned (ibid.). Working class women's supposed promiscuity also informed

FIGURE 11.2: Andrew Mercer Reformatory for Women

Canada's first *Criminal Code* (1892): Women in public spaces who could not give a good account of themselves were deemed to be common prostitutes and criminalized under vagrancy law. It appears Canadian legislators were concerned with the moral and public health menace posed by "risky," underclass women. Criminalized women, however, received little attention from reformers or scholars. Instead, the hypersexualized "women in prison without men" trope in popular culture constructed "good" (albeit lawbreaking) women as vulnerable to being seduced into "hard" criminality and lesbianism by "bad" women; exemplified by the 1950 film *Caged*, this narrative lives on, for example, in the HBO production *Orange Is the New Black*. To the extent that criminologists considered criminalized women at all, they too constituted them as doubly deviant—both as citizens and as women (Comack 2014a).

It was not until the late 1960s, when women criminologists "first called attention to criminology's amnesia when it came to women" (Comack 2014a, 12) and set about to systematically challenge the sexism of "malestream" criminological thought, that the image of the criminalized woman was once again rehabilitated—or at least nuanced. Throughout the 1970s and 1980s an extensive body of literature developed that was, in many ways, informed and inspired by the anti-violence against women movement. As Elizabeth Comack (2014a) writes, while some feminist criminologists and legal scholars supported carceral feminist calls for law reform, others like Dawn Currie (1990), Carol Smart (1990), and Mariana Valverde (1985) "engaged in critical treatises on the wisdom of engaging the criminal justice system to promote feminist concerns" (Comack 2014a, 25). In relation to criminalized women in particular a similar tension emerged in research. Some Canadian feminists trained in critical criminology argued that while women's path into, and experience of, the criminal justice system was undeniably gendered, the system itself was a violent mechanism of class and race repression (e.g., Faith 1993; Monture 1990; Morris and Elliot 1987). Other scholars, drawing on reformist criminological theories, focused their attention on pathways, endeavouring "to understand the lives of women and girls and the particular features that helped lead them to their criminal activity" (Comack 2014a, 27). Recognizing the high rates of victimization criminalized women experienced at the hands of the men in their lives (Johnson 1987; LaPrairie 1987; Shaw 1989), this literature blurred "the boundaries between offender and victim" (Comack 2014a, 31).

This victimization trope permeates *Creating Choices* (CSC 1990), a unique report (albeit one whose neoliberal orientation is evident in its name) by the Correctional Service of Canada (CSC) and the Canadian Association of Elizabeth Fry Societies (CAEFS) that examined the state response to women in the federal correctional system. The authors adopted a "woman-centered approach" (27)—notably, the word feminism never appears—expressing confidence that "women's needs" (109), including their "security needs" (110), could be met in a "supportive environment" (133). In short, they framed criminalized women as victims who could be healed and empowered in penal facilities and ultimately go on to live "productive and meaningful" lives (133). There are clear echoes of the essentialism that drove nineteenth-century reformers to become "their sister's keepers" (Freedman 1984, 2; see also Hannah-Moffat 2000, 2001); and like their foremothers, the *Creating Choices* authors sought to bring feminine influence to foster middle class sensibilities: "the presence of women staff particularly in key positions, provides a powerful message of self-sufficiency to women. Teaching strength and self-esteem to women can be achieved when women can daily observe these characteristics in other women" (CSC 1990, 109). It is a classed (and race-blind) narrative that Ms. Cree (Box 11.1) takes on with biting precision.

In the historical glimpses presented in the preceding pages, we have seen the "scolds" and "witches" of the Renaissance become redeemable fallen women under the watchful eye of social reformers in the nineteenth century, and elevated to the status of victims in the twentieth century. This demonstrates that, while framings and offences come into, and go out of, fashion, narratives about criminalized women consistently police gender, race, and class parameters and sexual conduct—women who pose a risk to entrenched social norms are deviantized and targeted. This brings into sharp relief the imperative to examine how the criminalized woman is constituted, reified, and sanctioned in and through interlocking systems of oppression. To that end we now turn to consider some of the ways this (structural) state violence is enacted in Canada today.

Women and criminalization

How do women come to be in trouble with the law? As we have seen, most criminalized individuals are men. Furthermore women are charged with a small portion of violent crimes. For example, women comprised just 11 per cent of those accused of homicide between 2001 and 2015 (Mahony et al. 2017, 28); in almost a third of the cases their victim was a current or former intimate partner (ibid., 29). As is the case for men, most women who appear before the courts are under the age of 34, and their crimes are predominantly property crimes—theft (35 per cent) and fraud (33 per cent) (Maxwell 2017). Who are these women? Disproportionally they are Indigenous women, Black women; most especially they are poor women (Sapers 2015). They are

BOX 11.1: MS. CREE ON BEING AN INDIGENOUS WOMAN IN PRISON

Those who assess us come from an opposite life-experience. The average case management person is Caucasian, married, has 1–2 children, a university degree, is from an upper-middle-class background with no comparable experiences to a Native woman....

When we come to prison, we need to adjust to greater and greater violence in our lives.... We forget how life once was, how blue the sky is, how good food tasted....

Trying to see a case management officer to get a call to our children is a major, major event. It is no wonder that so many of us cut our throats, lacerate our bodies, hang ourselves. It is no wonder we need to identify our pain onto our physical bodies, because our whole lives have been filled with incredible pain and traumatizing experiences—psychic pain, physical pain, spiritual pain.

When you ask a Native woman why she was placed in a foster home, she'll likely tell you it was because Children's "Aid" arrested her because her parents didn't send her to school regularly. When you ask a Native woman where she was sexually abused, she'll likely respond it took place in the foster homes. When you ask a Native woman why she killed somebody, she'll tell you she was a battered wife and she lost control of her senses when she was taking another beating. She didn't mean to kill her husband, her lover, her friend, she was just so spun out after each licking....

I am your typical Native woman and one who has survived the Criminal Just-us Cystem.... I learned there is a certain degree of hypocrisy in the groups that represent women in prison. The money and efforts that go into "services" is a mere band-aid effort in conspiracy with the criminal just-us cystem. The money and effort would be better directed at commuting the families of the incarcerated women to the prisons. The time that is spent on conducting study upon study is wasted time because statistics stay the same, the faces of the women change—but the stories are identical.

I entered Prison for Women as a young, poorly educated, Native women [sic] and ... I will soon be released with similar characteristics—but you can add another deficiency—after 7 years—I am now an ANGRY, young, poor, uneducated, Native woman!!!

Cree 1994, 47

women like Kimberly Rogers who, as we saw in Chapter 2, was charged and convicted for welfare fraud, or Indigenous women like Ms. Cree, whose histories, as we see in Box 11.1, are marked by the slow violence of colonialism (see Chapter 12). In this sense Gayle Horii (Box 11.2), a middle class white woman, is decidedly atypical.

BOX 11.2: GAYLE HORII ON WOMEN, VIOLENCE, AND INCARCERATION

I was incarcerated for seven years, for the killing of my stepmother, an act of extreme violence. I mourn this heinous deed, if I thought doing more time could undo this horrendous act or would make the world a safer place I would voluntarily return to prison. But I cannot return Anna's life and imprisonment does not lessen the violence in society.... I feel it ironic, that while incarcerated for a violent crime, I witnessed and was surrounded by death and violence inflicted both by staff and by prisoners, none of which I was able to stop ... Over my seven year imprisonment, I knew twelve women and twelve men who died while in prison or very shortly after release. Nine of these twenty-four deaths were by suicide, seven of these suicides were by women. Five of the seven were Native women....

I used to be suicidal, attempting three times to take my own life but I finally recovered through intensive therapy with a woman psychologist. I was raised in a violent home, so violent that even when I was left for dead on the blood-soaked landing of the skating rink, after being raped by a stranger when I was not yet five years old, I was afraid to tell my parents. And I was ashamed to tell anyone else. I was still too ashamed to tell anyone when at eighteen I was drugged at a party and awoke naked, face down and in pain, or at nineteen when I was date-raped by a lawyer, or at twenty-six when I was raped by a politician when I was showing real estate, or at twenty-seven when I applied for a job from a well-respected restaurateur. I masked the fear and the rage which I lived. I was schooled in violence, and when I committed a violent act, I was punished with violent means by violent people. I know that VIOLENCE results from the exploitation of POWER imbalances and the SUPPRESSION of the pain of being exploited OFTEN results in more violence.

Horii 1994, 10–12

Women, profiling, and gender scripts

Reflecting on the characteristics of criminalized women brings us back to Chapter 2 and consideration of the intersecting factors that condition women's socio-economic position and the resources at their disposal; it also alerts us to additional hidden costs of neoliberal policies and the criminalization of poverty. A case in point is the expanded definition of and efforts to prevent, deter, and sanction "welfare cheats," culminating in "increased surveillance and criminalization of welfare recipients—notably women" (Chunn and Gavigan 2014, 206). Here again we see not only the long tentacles of regulation beyond the criminal justice system (Balfour 2014a), but also social profiling and the normative framing of working and underclass people as lacking the integrity and work ethic that define the middle class. Moreover, in the high rates of Black and Indigenous mothers targeted by child welfare officials and social service workers we see racial profiling (Maynard 2017; see also Chapter 12).

Racial profiling can also play out in the actions of law enforcement personnel; there is a robust and growing body of Canadian research demonstrating that "African Canadian and Indigenous peoples, and in some cities, Middle Eastern people, are disproportionately likely to be stopped and/or searched by police than White people or people from other racialized groups" (OHRC 2017, 32). Evidence that racialized women are profiled by police notwithstanding— for example, in 2016 Edmonton police were 10 times more likely to subject Indigenous women to street stops (e.g., carding) than white women (Huncar 2017)—in the (tentative) public conversations about racial profiling it is inevitably young Black men who are foregrounded. As a result, the experiences of Black, Indigenous, and non-binary women, and their vulnerability to being framed as "expected offenders" (Dell and Kilty 2013, 52) and "profiled in gender-specific ways … as suspected drug users, drug couriers or sex workers" (OHRC 2017, 22), has largely been ignored (Maynard 2017). So while Black and other racialized women are often at the forefront of social movements that bring attention to police violence (e.g., Black Lives Matter), they have been "absented" (Walcott 2003, 35) as subjects of police misconduct and violence. As Kimberlé Crenshaw (2016) reminds us, this erasure speaks to a lack of accessible conceptual frames: "[W]hen facts do not fit with available frames, people have a difficult time incorporating new facts into their way of thinking about a problem … without frames to see how issues affect all members of a targeted group; many will fall through the cracks"—ignored by the media, policymakers, and social justice movements.

Women, police, and vulnerability

Looking at police abuse of power as gendered violence alerts us to the convergence of social processes. As we have seen throughout this text, inhabiting intersecting marginalized identities exacerbates women's risk of violence; not surprisingly, this risk is amplified in the context of the authority statutorily vested in police and can manifest in abuse of power. First, analogous to the way violent men exploit their partner's precarious migration status (see Chapter 6), the potential to be sanctioned for crimes provides a powerful threat (e.g., arrest and detention) that police are in a position to exploit (Human Rights Watch 2013; 2017). Second, profiling means poor and racialized women are more likely to come to the attention of the police—coded as "risky," they are subject to hyper-surveillance. Third, embedded tropes of Indigenous women as wanton, Black women as Jezebels, and trans women as abnormal facilitates, legitimates, and justifies violence by predators—including, as we see below, those who wear the uniform of law enforcement—at the same time as it responsibilizes victims. Finally, those same tropes delegitimate and negate the assertions of complainants that, coupled with the bureaucratic and complex structure of the police complaint process (a system that authorizes police to investigate police) as well as economic concerns, leave victims with few options. This already untenable situation is exacerbated by the fear of (and real potential for) retaliatory actions by police, which further restricts the scope of possible resistance strategies (Human Rights Watch 2013, 2017).

Hidden, denied, and/or excused, violence against marginalized women by law enforcement is a pressing problem. For example, in her research Nora Butler Burke (2018) found that migrant street-involved trans women in Montréal were subject to surveillance and punitive interventions by police and immigration authorities. Her participants reported "racist, xenophobic, and otherwise violent statements that threatened [their] safety and bodily integrity" (206). Similarly, informed by her perceived contravention of gender norms, officers from Peel Regional Police subjected Rosalyn Forrester, a pre-operative trans woman, to a "split" strip search, in which "female officers searched her top half and male officers searched her from the waist down" (Smith 2014, 151); another strip search was performed exclusively by male police (*Forrester v. Peel* 2006). Officers also recorded Ms. Forrester as "him/her" and her gender as "o" and used derogatory language throughout the interaction (Smith 2014, 166).

Police violence and acute discrimination against Indigenous women further alerts us to their intersecting nature. Human Rights Watch (2013; 2017) has documented numerous incidents of police abuse of Indigenous women and girls, including "young girls pepper-sprayed and Tasered; a 12-year-old girl attacked by a police dog; a 17-year-old punched repeatedly by an officer who had been called to help her; women strip-searched by male officers; and women injured due to excessive force used during arrest" (Human Rights Watch 2013, 7–8). They also noted "allegations of rape and sexual assault by RCMP officers, including from a woman who described how in July 2012 police officers took her outside of town, raped her, and threatened to kill her if she told anyone" (8). This is not a new phenomenon; in the late 1880s physical and sexual abuse of Indigenous women by police was a recurrent problem, and "on most of the few occasions that Aboriginal women laid charges against policemen for assault or rape, their claims were hastily dismissed as defamation or blackmail" (Carter 1993, 152).

There is a similarly troubling history of police violence against Black women. As Robyn Maynard (2017) writes, the historic framing of Black women as "immoral, wayward, and threatening" (117) renders them vulnerable to sexualized violence, over-policing, and being blamed for their victimization. At the same time the enduring Mammy trope is evident in the violence Black women experience from police when they deviate "from their designated role as subservient, and for failing to perform the submissive, content role of the Mammy" (ibid., 117). This was the conclusion of Mark Hart who, ruling on the forceful arrest of Toronto postal worker Sharon Abbott following a routine traffic stop, found evidence of "racial discrimination emanat[ing] from unconscious attitudes and belief systems ... includ[ing] that Black persons (and other groups) are expected to 'know their place' and that any Black person who talks back or refuses to comply is to be regarded as 'uppity' and needs to be dealt with harshly" (*Abbott v. Toronto Police Services Board* 2009, para. 46).

Stacy Bonds: A "travesty of justice"

The Stacy Bonds case forcefully demonstrates how racial stereotypes play out and affirms that, in the context of the white colonial state, gendered (interpersonal) police violence operates in relation to the devaluation of racialized and "othered" women. It indicates, in other words, a systemic problem—not the infamous "few bad apples." Ms. Bonds, an Ottawa-area makeup artist employed at the National Arts Centre, was observed by police in the early hours of September 6, 2008, talking to someone in a van and drinking a beer in downtown Ottawa. Shortly thereafter she was approached by police; upon request she provided her name and date of birth, the information was checked, and after additional questioning she was advised she was free to go. According to Justice Richard Lajoie who heard the case in the Ontario Court of Justice (*R. v. S. Bonds* 2010) "she walks away, but seemingly has second thoughts and wants to have more information regarding why she was stopped by the police. She is told a second time to go home. It is at that point when she is again questioning her police intervention that she is arrested" for being intoxicated in a public place—in spite of behaviour that did "not come close to public intoxication" (ibid., 3–4).

The narrative so far is already troubling. Why was Ms. Bonds temporarily detained in the first place? Did the police profile her, a 27-year-old Black woman, as a sex worker? Was she (unlawfully) arrested for being "uppity"? Was she being punished for having the audacity to question police and perhaps subtly call them out on their racist assumptions? For "not knowing her place"? For being an "angry Black woman"? As horrifying as the abuse of police power was, what Justice Lajoie calls "the most disturbing aspect of what occurred that morning" (*R. v. S. Bonds* 2010, 6) was to follow at the Ottawa police station. Surveillance video shows a protesting yet ultimately compliant Bonds being kneed in the back twice, an unidentified person putting their "hand inside [her] pants, down around her upper leg," her shirt and bra being cut off, her front torso "inspected"; she was also strip searched "in the presence of, and with the assistance of, at least three male officers" (ibid., 8–10). In short, not only was Stacy Bonds physically and sexually assaulted, but officers used "the strip search as a sexual weapon and a form of punishment to further her humiliation and degradation" (Tanovich 2011, 138). The violence was not, however, over; Ms. Bonds was then taken to a cell where she was left, for "no reason apart from vengeance and malice … for a period of three hours and 15 minutes half naked and having soiled her pants" (*R. v. S. Bonds* 2010, 11). The charges were stayed; indeed, Justice Lajoie asserted to do otherwise "would be a travesty" (ibid., 12).

It is entirely possible that what marks the Stacy Bonds case as unique is not that "law enforcement's assumption of Bonds' deviant sexuality triggered an enormous level of hostility, manifested in physical violence and her subsequent sexual and psychological humiliation" (Maynard 2017, 123), but rather that we know about it at all. The video evidence only came to light in the context of Ms. Bonds's criminal trial for assaulting a peace officer; had she, like many marginalized accused persons, pled guilty (even when they are not) to minimize the risk of a harsher sanction, avoid the costs of a trial, or simply put an end to the prolonged period of uncertainty (Campbell 2018), the case would never have reached the outraged eyes of Justice Lajoie, it would never have been reported in the media, and it certainly would never have resulted in criminal sexual assault charges (albeit not a conviction) and administrative sanctions against Sergeant Steven Desjourdy (Yogaretnam 2014). In other words, had it not been for Ms. Bonds's social and cultural capital—her (however mediated) privilege—her victimization would have remained, for all intents and purposes, invisible.

Courts and Crowns

Writing on the Stacy Bonds case, David Tanovich (2011) alerts us to an additional troubling element: Why did the Crown proceed with the charges against this young woman? After all, the Crown attorney's office knew about the video tape, must have been aware that her arrest was unlawful, recognized her minimal non-compliance as consistent with her right to resist police violence, and was aware of the sexual assault she endured and the malicious treatment to which she had been subjected. This "raises the very real possibility that the prosecution was continued in the interests of the police rather than the public … either to shield the officers from subsequent criminal and civil liability or to ensure that the officers could continue, with the blessing of the Crown and maybe the trial judge, to engage in similar conduct in the future" (ibid., 149). In other words, it speaks to a further legitimation of gendered, racial violence at the same time as it signals systemic entrenchment.

Angela Cardinal: A victim shackled and imprisoned

While Justice Lajoie put an end to the travesty of justice Stacy Bonds experienced, there is little reason to assume that the courts are not also sites of gendered violence—at least if women are marginalized, poor, and racialized. The "callous disregard" for the human rights of Angela Cardinal (Sheikh 2017)—a pseudonym for a young woman whose name is protected under a publication ban—is a yet another chilling instance of state-inflicted physical and psychological violence; that she was the Crown's witness (i.e., the victim in a criminal trial) makes the injustice all the more striking. Ms. Cardinal, an intelligent and artistic "27-year-old Indigenous woman who was homeless and living on the street" (*R. v. Blanchard*, para. 348) was subpoenaed to testify at the preliminary hearing of Lance Blanchard, a man accused and ultimately convicted of brutally physically and sexually assaulting her on June 16, 2014. Deemed a "flight risk" and "incapable of participating properly in the Court proceedings" (para. 230) by Alberta Provincial Court Judge Ray Bodnarek, she was remanded into custody under *Criminal Code* section 545(1)(b) at the end of the first day of the preliminary hearing. In fact, there was little evidence of either: she demonstrated her willingness to participate in the process and, according to Justice Eric Macklin (who adjudicated the subsequent criminal trial), while "clearly distraught, much of her testimony was given in a clear, cogent, coherent and articulate manner" (para. 348). The problem, it would appear, was that Judge Bodnarek was frustrated with her inability to recall events sequentially—notably overlooking, as we saw in Chapter 5, that life-threatening trauma often leads to episodic memory. That officers of the court perceived her as unreliable and risky, disregarding her pain and going so far as to physically confine her, powerfully illustrates the dehumanization that flows from stereotypes about "othered" women.

As a result of Judge Bodnarek's decision, Ms. Cardinal was "required to walk right past the accused [her attacker] in order to exit the courtroom …

often housed in a cell next to or near that of the accused [and] transported between the Remand Centre and the Courthouse in the same transport van" (ibid., para. 235). Moreover, throughout her testimony she was shackled and "handcuffed when not inside the courtroom" (para. 235). Ms. Cardinal, described by Justice Macklin as a "colourful character" (para. 240), explicitly called out the injustice she was experiencing. She told the court "I'm the victim and look at me. I'm in shackles. This is fantastic. This is a great system" (para. 232); when commended for her progress, she noted, "Not great progress. Look at me, I'm in shackles" (para. 233), and repeatedly, albeit apparently to no avail, reminded the court that she was the "fricking victim here" (para. 231). Indeed, it was a miscarriage of justice of tragic proportions. There will never be an opportunity to apologize to Ms. Cardinal for the violence inflicted on her by the state; on December 12, 2015, she was shot and killed in an unrelated incident (para. 2).

Gladue reports: Cultural sensitivity?

We now turn to consider another point of the criminal justice system at which Indigenous women are victimized: sentencing. Sentencing reforms introduced in 1996 (Bill C-41) and after *R. v. Gladue* in 1999 (both contextualized in the next chapter) dictate that courts are obliged to consider the background of Indigenous offenders in a Gladue report that enumerates such things as poverty; overt racism; family or community breakdown; unemployment, low income, and lack of employment opportunity; dislocation; community fragmentation; and residential school experience (Balfour 2014b).

As with other legal reforms, there is disagreement about whether Gladue principles are effective or beneficial for Indigenous offenders. Paula Maurutto and Kelly Hannah-Moffat (2016) argue that specialized Gladue courts promote awareness of the social, legal, and historic processes that contribute to the criminalization of Indigenous people and create space for alternatives to incarceration and bail. Growing rates of incarceration of Indigenous people, however, suggest Gladue reforms have had limited (positive) effect; according to the correctional investigator, between 2005 and 2015 "the number of Aboriginal women inmates almost doubled" (Sapers 2016, 43). Moreover, as Balfour (2012) points out, sentencing reforms do not alleviate the violence against which Indigenous women like Ms. Cree (Box 11.1) retaliate and which lands them in the custody of the criminal justice system in the first place (see Chapter 12). Moreover, because they are included in an offender's file, Gladue reports may affect decisions by juries, courts, parole boards, and other criminal justice officials in various and unanticipated ways (Maurutto and Hannah-Moffat 2016).

The carceral system: "Correcting" women

The violence of the state apparatus is explicitly evident in the ever-increasing numbers of women (and men) housed in Canada's correctional facilities (Balfour 2014a). In spite of a decrease in official crime rates, women's incarceration rate at the federal level rose by 35 per cent over the last decade; the trends are also evident in provincial institutions where sentences of less than two years are served (Sapers 2016). Moreover, not only are Indigenous and Black women over-represented among federally sentenced women (FSW), but for Indigenous women the disproportionality is increasingly pronounced: Making up just 4.9 per cent of the Canadian population, Indigenous women comprise 35.5 per cent of FSW (ibid.). Since 1997, when the infamous Prison for Women (P4W) closed its doors, women have been placed in one of five regional facilities or the Aboriginal Healing Lodge in Saskatchewan. Violence (both external and self-inflicted) and the repression recounted by Ms. Cree (Box 11.1) and Gayle Horii (Box 11.2) continue to be the defining features of these (albeit "prettier" than P4W) penal institutions; use of force is routine, and segregation is the accepted response to self-injury (Zinger 2017). Moreover, 46 per cent of FSW have an active prescription for psychotropic medication (Sapers 2016)—drugs that, as Jennifer Kilty (2014) notes, are "used to govern a population typically constructed as unruly, risky, and mentally unstable" (253). Furthermore, coerced compliance, occurring when women agree to take medication under threat of the loss of privileges, delayed release, and/ or segregation, constitutes an invasion on the corporal integrity of women— violence in its own right (Kilty 2012).

The gaping schism between the *Creating Choices* vision of healing spaces and the treatment of FSW in today's institutions highlights the challenges inherent in attempts to integrate "woman-centred" policies into penal institutions (Kilty 2014). As Kelly Hannah-Moffat (2010) points out, these institutions employ neoliberal "strategies of gendered governance" (193) in and through "which women are disciplined and responsibilised. Relationships, children, past victimization, mental health, self-jury, and self-esteem all become correctional targets in the pursuit of normative femininity and gender conformity" (200). The result is a perverse situation where women's experiences of gendered violence—86 per cent of FSW report experiencing physical abuse and 70 per cent have histories of sexual abuse (Sapers 2016)—are transformed into risk factors that justify repressive (and ultimately punitive) measures (Hannah-Moffat 2001). There is also a more fundamental problem: Women continue to be divided into re-formable victims of circumstance and risky women beyond redemption (ibid.). In this respect, while different criteria are now used than were applied at the Andrew Mercer Reformatory in the late 1800s, maternal discipline remains at the heart of the system. Also echoing across the decades is the response to those who reject the imposition of normative gender and class scripts; these "complex needs cases" (Sapers 2016, 20) or "unempowerable prisoners" (Hannah-Moffat 2000, 525) are subjected to harsh penal sanctions.

The Ashley Smith tragedy is a powerful illustration of correctional failure and the institutional violence experienced by women too "unruly" to be reformed into responsible female subjects; it also illustrates the costs of the correctional framing of needs and disadvantage as security risks. Upon entering the federal correctional system at the age of 18, Ms. Smith—a troubled young woman with serious mental health struggles—exhibited behaviour that was "disruptive and maladaptive"; during her time in the federal system she "was involved in approximately 150 security incidents," most involving self-harm behaviours such as head-banging and self-strangulation (Sapers 2008, 5). The institutional response was to repeatedly move her (17 transfers in under a year), to place her in administrative segregation (indeed, she spent the entire 11.5 months isolated from other prisoners), and to forcibly inject psychotropic medication, even though a psychiatric assessment was never completed (ibid.)! In this context her mental health deteriorated and her troubled behaviour escalated, triggering "even more security-focused responses" from CSC (7). Moreover, rather than taking a therapeutic approach upper management instructed front-line workers not to respond "too early"; staff who intervened in the face of evident distress were disciplined (16). On October 19, 2007, under suicide watch and therefore observed by officers at the Grand Valley Institution for Women in Kitchener, Ontario, "Ms. Smith died wearing nothing but a suicide smock, lying on the floor of her segregation cell, with a ligature tied tightly around her neck" (8). This tragic case was ruled a homicide by the coroner's inquest, which "made no findings of criminal or civil liability for individual actors"; in effect, the state was the guilty party (Kilty 2014, 242). The case also highlights systemic failure to the extent that Ashley Smith's death is the inevitable outcome of the casual dehumanization and violence that characterizes correctional facilities. It provides yet another example of how women's non-compliance with gendered and classed expectations of docility is constructed as risky and dangerous, rather than as an attempt to exert agency amidst oppressive and demoralizing conditions (ibid.). As we will see, perceived as risky and subject to dehumanizing treatment, Indigenous women and trans women face particular challenges in the carceral system.

Indigenous women as risky others

Colonial violence permeates the histories of Indigenous women incarcerated in federal prisons in Canada, of whom "52% had at least one family member attend residential school; 48% had been removed from the family home as children; 81% had experienced physical abuse and 56% sexual abuse" (CSC 2015). In prison, the violence continues. Here we see that the reading of needs as risk and the lack of cultural sensitivity in the Custody Rating Scale has particularly detrimental impacts on Indigenous women, who are more likely to be classified as "low integration potential" and "high risk and high need" (Sapers 2015, 51). In real terms this means Indigenous women "are significantly over-represented at maximum security (42%) and segregation placements (50%) but under-represented at minimum security institutions (26%)" (Sapers 2016, 62). The predictable result is delayed or denied early release (i.e., day and full parole)—according to the correctional investigator, in spite of greater partic- ipation in and completion of prison programs, "Indigenous offenders are still being released later and revoked much more often than their counterparts" (ibid., 44). In other words, Indigenous women do more and "harder" time. Moreover, CSC's extension of Gladue principles into correctional decision making notwithstanding, Indigenous women are disproportionately sanctioned for "acting out." In this context, like Ashley Smith, they resist by one of the few means at their disposal—self-injury—at a rate 17 times higher than that of their non-Indigenous counterparts (ibid.).

Trans women as deviant bodies

As we saw in the bathroom debate in Chapter 1, the inclusion of trans women in gender-segregated spaces has been characterized as a threat to women's safety. The approach to trans inmates historically embraced by CSC (impact- ing all prisoners serving sentences of two years or greater) was reversed in January 2017. However, the correctional investigator cautioned that, the policy change notwithstanding, "there does not appear to be a very deep understand- ing or appreciation for what the terms 'gender identity' and 'gender expression' actually mean ... federal corrections appears mired, if not stuck, in conven- tional attitudes and assumptions" (Zinger 2017, 17). Up until 2017, CSC policy allowed only post-operative trans women to be housed in women's prisons (CSC 2016); and indeed, with a few notable exceptions, including Ontario and British Columbia, for trans persons serving provincial sentences (less than two years) this is still the case. In short, surgery is a prerequisite for a male-to- female trans woman to be accepted as a woman in many (but no longer all) Canadian prisons; in these cases trans women who are pre-operative or who do not fit into dichotomous gender categories are held in men's facilities.

Such institutional misgendering and denial of internationally recognized rights is not only emotionally devastating (Lupick 2015), it creates a context in which trans individuals are rendered hyper-vulnerable to experiencing verbal and physical abuse from guards, and verbal, physical, and sexual violence at the hands of other prisoners (Sapers 2016). All too often the "solution" to their victimization is the de facto layering of additional punishment: hous-ing trans prisoners in segregation or protective custody—essentially solitary confinement—that deprives them of social contact and underscores their other-ness (Egale 2014; Smith 2014). For example one transgender prisoner who spent almost 10 years in the prison of their assigned birth experienced "numerous incidents where they were subjected to crude and offensive comments from CSC staff and inmates, pushed to the side by healthcare staff, refused hormone therapy treatment, refused private showers and denied recognition of a name change … desperation led the inmate to attempt suicide, self-mutilate genitalia and take pills bought from other inmates" (Zinger 2017, 16). Thus, in prisons as with other points of contact between women and the criminal justice system, we see the entrenchment of mutually reinforcing, dichotomous gender norms: Cisgender women inmates are seen through a lens of feminine vulnerability while trans women are perceived as potentially risky "others," as unintelligi-ble, or as men (Smith 2014).

Resistance: Contesting state violence

In the context of disconcertingly unequal power relations, women have contested violence by the state, its agents, and its apparatuses. Arguably the very act of being an "unruly woman" (Faith 1993) is subversive, a catalyst that renders visible the oppressive gender roles and restrictive scripts of "good girls." Moreover, that even small acts of contestation result in social sanction (e.g., the slut narrative, the bad mother trope) and sometimes evoke the full repressive power of the state affirms their regulatory nature and the extent to which they operate in the interests of maintaining the status quo. As such it is important to acknowledge women like Rosalyn Forrester (discussed above), whose Ontario Human Rights complaint against the Peel Regional Police resulted in pre-operative trans individuals having the right to choose between being strip searched by a male or female officer (Smith 2014). And the bravery of women like Viola Desmond (Figure 11.1), a pioneer of Nova Scotia's Civil Rights movement whose image now graces Canada's $10 bill; her appeal of her conviction for failing to vacate the "whites only" section of a New Glasgow movie theatre was unsuccessful but nonetheless drew atten-tion to racial segregation and mobilized the Black community (Backhouse 2001). A decade later segregation laws were abolished (ibid.). Shackled and traumatized, Angela Cardinal still found the strength to speak truth to power; similarly, when Stacy Bonds turned around and asked the police to explain why she was stopped and temporarily detained she was calling out the officers and demanding accountability. Her act of contestation was met with force and violence; that we know of her courage only because of the subsequent trial that lay bare the blatant abuse of power alerts us that there are many, many Stacy Bonds. It is therefore important to acknowledge the unobserved and uncelebrated acts of subversion by women who subtly or overtly refuse to enact the racial script of deference and/or the gender script of compliance.

Some of those acts of resistance, like Ashley Smith's self-harm, highlight the limited resources incarcerated women have at their disposal. Similarly hidden behind the closed doors of a carceral institution, Renée Acoby, an Indigenous woman initially imprisoned for crimes including drug trafficking and assault with a weapon, also paid a high price for not conforming. After her daughter was removed from her care, Ms. Acoby violently assaulted a guard, and—in an effort to escape and see her daughter—took hostages; the incident considerably extended her sentence and she is now the only woman in Canada designated a dangerous offender (L. Stone 2013).

Because violence against women, and most especially against racialized women, by state agents and institutions is so frequently "absented" (Walcott 2003, 35), putting marginalized and racialized women's lives "on the record" and inserting their experiences of state violence into the narrative can be a powerful political act. The need to "ensure that Black women's stories are integrated into demands for justice, policy responses to police violence, and media representations of victims of police brutality" (AAPF 2015) is at the heart of the #SayHerName movement launched by the African American Policy Forum. In Canada, activist and author Robyn Maynard (2017), similarly motivated to ensure the stories of Black women are not sidelined, meticulously details individual women's experiences with police—including those of Sharon Abbott and Stacy Bonds—in her book *Policing Black Lives*. When oppressed persons claim the metaphorical or real podium to tell their truths it affords a compelling counter-narrative—the two boxes in this chapter are instances of this form of resistance. While Ms. Cree's (Box 11.1) piece was originally published in the internal P4W newspaper *Tightwire*, Gayle Horii's (Box 11.2) compelling article appeared in a unique publication, *The Journal of Prisoners on Prisons*. This journal, started in 1988 under the tutelage of Professor Robert Gaucher, serves as "a vehicle for the accounts and analysis of prisoners to bring the knowledge and experience of the incarcerated to bear upon … academic arguments and concerns, and to inform public discourse about the current state of our carceral institutions" (Gaucher 2002, 7). In contrast to the appropriation of their stories by researchers claiming to "give voice" while assuming narrative authority, this journal is an example of academics using their cultural capital to extend the reach of marginalized (and all too often silenced) voices; it also challenges what counts as credible knowledge through the forms of narratives it publishes; in addition to more conventional articles

FIGURE 11.3: *Reminder*, by Jackie Traverse, 2011

and autobiographical reflections, the journal includes poetry and visual art (see Figure 11.3).

Concluding reflections

Through an intersectional lens, we have seen that the women whose experiences with state actors more closely resemble victimization than protection are overwhelmingly Indigenous, Black, trans, struggling with mental health issues, and poor—women deemed "mad" or "bad." In this respect the notion of structural violence alerts us to how the state, its agents, and apparatuses (including the law, courts, and prisons) can harm those who deviate from the norms upholding the status quo. Moreover, it appears little but rhetorical framing has changed in official perceptions of female criminality since the 1800s; in the context of neoliberalism, the ascription of risk has emerged as a powerful regulatory force that targets, discredits, and excludes from state protection women who do not conform to gender, class, and racial scripts and neoliberal behavioural expectations, while narratives of choice function to obscure structural constraints. However, in the face of repressive state power and attempts by its agents to discipline them into the role of submissive, passive, responsible, "good girls," we have also seen that deviantized women resist using the tools at their disposal—that this sometimes entails violence to self or others highlights the extent of the constraints criminalized women navigate.

The reflection about privilege with which this chapter began also directs our attention to middle class women who endeavour to help criminalized women—and how their complicity with the repressive criminal justice apparatus can contribute to the reproduction and entrenchment of structural, institutional, and symbolic violence experienced by "othered" women. At the same time, middle class reformers' role enhances their own social, economic, and cultural capital. For example, in the 1800s, training incarcerated and marginalized women to emulate middle class propriety (without the benefit of the corresponding cultural and economic capital) worked to the advantage of the matrons, affording them freedoms available to few women at the time—notably, access to professional, public work (Freedman 1984). Critiquing the tropes of female difference and fragility and the governance and carceral approaches embraced by these reformers and their contemporary counterparts, prison abolitionists Ruth Morris and Liz Elliott (1987) cheekily noted "radical feminists of the late twentieth century have stated they would prefer to end the imprisonment of women. A strong argument can be made that incarceration itself should be abolished" (156).

EXERCISE: EXAMINING REPRESENTATIONS OF GENDERED VIOLENCE

Take 15 minutes to search the Internet for images of gendered violence using common phrases such as "gendered victimization," "violence against women," "women victims," and so on.

Reflect on the sorts of images that appear.

- What kinds of violence are represented?
- Who are the victims depicted?
- How are the women represented?
- What kinds of violence are not reflected?
- What kinds of victims are not featured?

What do these representations (and absences) suggest about the recognition of violence by the state and its actors? In other words, does state violence appear?

What about other types of violence examined in this book (e.g., workplace violence, everyday intrusions)? What does the prevalence or absence of these representations tell us?

CHAPTER 12

COLONIAL VIOLENCE AGAINST INDIGENOUS WOMEN

As we have seen throughout this text, Indigenous women are particularly vulnerable to gendered interpersonal, institutional, and structural violence. For example, Indigenous women face a higher risk of sexual assault as well as intimate partner violence (IPV) in both heterosexual and LGBTQ relationships (Chapter 6), and the murder and disappearance of as many as 2,000 Indigenous women since the 1980s is a national tragedy (Settee 2016). In the previous chapter we also saw that Indigenous women are particularly vulnerable to violence by the state and its agents. Not surprisingly, Indigenous women are reluctant to call on the institutions that white middle class women may rely on—they fear violence or dismissal from the police and are mindful that they are more likely to be charged and incarcerated for defending themselves (Balfour 2012; Kuokkanen 2015). We have also seen reduced economic opportunities and significant disadvantage, including a larger gender pay gap than other groups of women—a gap that increases rather than decreases with educational attainment (Lambert and McInturff 2016, see Chapter 2). Indigenous women also experience poverty and unemployment at elevated rates (36 per cent and 13.3 per cent, respectively) (Arriagada 2016), conditions that may play some part in explaining their restricted political participation and in turn under-representation in Parliament (at only three MPs in 2017) and over-representation in the street-based sex industry.

Why is this the case? Why are Indigenous women disproportionately targeted by predators, more likely to be victimized by intimate partners, excluded by regulatory and institutional frameworks, and structurally disadvantaged? As Colleen Cardinal and Kristen Gilchrist (2014) argue, colonization is not over; having shed its more blatant tactics as military conquest and chemical weaponry (e.g., smallpox blankets), the colonial project continues today in laws, policies, and practices pivoting on myths of European racial and cultural superiority that perpetuate sexism, racism, and misogyny directed at Indigenous women. Here we once again see the utility of Nixon's (2011) concept of slow violence—colonialism is gradual, pervasive, and above all obscured. As Sarah de Leeuw (2016) notes, "slow violence gains power when it is made banal by settler-colonialists distancing ourselves from its ever-present presence and working to differentiate and striate multiple forms of violence so as to never fully address any of them" (15). In other words, to start to understand the epidemic of violence against Indigenous women we need to investigate how seemingly discrepant mechanisms co-constructing colonialism intermesh.

To this end this chapter examines some of the ways the colonial context precipitates and constitutes gendered violence against Indigenous women. We begin with a brief history of assimilationist efforts by the government, including imposed gender relations, residential schools, and the restriction of "Indian" status. The rest of the chapter examines the impacts of past and ongoing colonial (at once racist and sexist) attitudes, practices, and policies: predatory violence and the ambivalent response by the state and its agents; elevated rates of IPV; the apprehension of Indigenous children; and Indigenous women's health. The chapter closes with examples of Indigenous women's resilience and resistance, creativity and perseverance as they mobilize against the sexist, racist, slow violence of "colonialism and its handmaiden, patriarchy" (Anderson 2010, 83).

Socio-historic considerations: Colonial and legal violence

Before contact with Europeans, there was a rich diversity of cultures and nations in the territory Canada now occupies; "some Aboriginal nations were able to accumulate wealth while others were not; some were more hierarchical than others; some had matrilineal rules of descent while others were patrilineal or bilateral; and some developed sophisticated confederal structures that grouped several nations together" (RCAP 1996, 83). In this respect, it is vital that while we acknowledge the shared experience of colonization we remain mindful of the violence of pan-Indigeneity and the erasure of the unique cultures, identities, and traditions of diverse First Nations, Métis, and Inuit cultures implicit in such an approach.

The colonial erosion of women's roles and social status
Prior to colonization the roles and authority of women varied greatly, but "traditional roles were more egalitarian due to the nature of the differing relational practices between First Nations men and women prior to colonization" (Sayers and MacDonald 2001, 9). Historians agree that women were afforded respect; Kim Anderson (2010) explains that in traditional land-based

Indigenous societies "women were recognized for their unique contributions in the life-giving process.... Indigenous philosophies and practices ensured that healthy life was maintained through balance between various life forms including men and women. These principles were built into all ... political, social, and economic systems" (82). As such, the rights and status of Indigenous women stood in stark contrast to those of European women at the time, whose husbands were legally entitled to sexual relations and had the right (even the responsibility) to administer chastisement and judicious discipline (see Chapter 6).

The colonial state imposed European regulatory frameworks on First Nations, which eroded women's traditional role and excluded them from governance structures (Sayers and MacDonald 2001); for example, under the Chief and Council system (in effect until 1951), only "men could run and vote for office" (NWAC 2002, 16). In addition, it restricted women's ability to inherit property and introduced Certificates of Possession on reserves, which ensured "that only Indian men would be able to own their homes" (ibid., 14). Less explicit, but with powerful echoes today, was the construction of Indigenous women as licentious. When reports of "immorality" in the West (which included both consensual and exploitative sexual relations) came to light in the late 1880s, the myth of "wanton" Indigenous women "accustomed to being ... bought and sold as commodities" (Carter 1993, 153) was put forth by state agents; it quickly became accepted and propagated within settler society. In real terms, the colonial framing of Indigenous women as "prostitutes" and "particular threats to morality and health" (ibid., 155) legitimated restrictions on their mobility through a repressive pass system that rendered both traditional subsistence strategies, and the resources and opportunities towns afforded, inaccessible (ibid.).

Residential schools: Killing the Indian in the child

Europeans' perception of Indigenous women—and the interlocking gender, racial, and class hierarchies from which this perception emanated—was also propagated through another mechanism: the *Indian Act*, a piece of legislation whose colonial underpinnings and agenda are evident in its name. As we saw in Chapter 1, Europeans justified colonization (and its overt and slow violence) through a narrative of bringing religion and civilization to peoples they perceived to be "uncivilized" (TRC 2015a). This profound lack of respect for and recognition of the diverse cultures and traditions of First Nations continues to have ramifications today—the *Indian Act* remains the federal legislation that governs relations between Indigenous people/s and the Canadian state. Providing for the establishment of the residential school system and "Indian" status, the *Indian Act* endeavoured to facilitate the accumulation of land and resources driving the imperial project by addressing the "Indian problem" by eliminating (through assimilation) Indigenous people.

The foremost mechanism of forcible cultural assimilation was the residential school system. It was not until the Truth and Reconciliation Commission (TRC 2015a) that the federal government finally conceded to what Indigenous activists and survivors of residential schools had long been arguing: that this was an act of cultural genocide. **Cultural genocide** is the intentional targeting and destruction of the social and political structures, and cultural and religious practices, through which a group perpetuates its identity. It is achieved by seizing land, forcibly transferring populations, and restricting their movement; banning languages; forbidding spiritual practices, persecuting spiritual leaders, and destroying objects of spiritual value; and disrupting families to impede the intergenerational transmission of values and identity (TRC 2015a).

Operated by Christian missionaries, residential schools endeavoured to "civilize" Indigenous children by removing them from their parents and communities and indoctrinating them with Christian and Western values. The missionaries, and the government officials who endowed them with the administration of the schools, may not have recognized their actions as violent, but the rhetoric justifying this approach—"to kill the Indian in the child" (TRC 2015a, 130)—belies their wilful ignorance. This violence manifested not only in coercive indoctrination but also in the mistreatment of children: Residential schools were sites of poor living conditions; disease; and physical, emotional, and sexual violence. Boarding schools were exclusively run by missionaries for much of the 1800s; in the 1880s the Canadian government started to fund these church-run schools. The last institution closed in 1996 (ibid.).

We have seen, in Chapters 3, 4, and 10, how the subtler mechanisms of disciplinary power condition the ways women dress and conduct themselves in Chapters 3, 4, and 10; by contrast residential schools exemplify the explicitly coercive potential of a power that targets the soul to render the body docile so that it "may be subjected, used, transformed and improved" (Foucault 1979, 136). Indeed, as discussed in Chapter 3, Foucault described schools (like prisons) as mechanisms of disciplinary power: Students are enclosed, partitioned, and classified; supervised, hierarchized, and rewarded (and/or sanctioned). Surveillance is an essential part of such disciplinary regimes—when, as a result of continual and unverifiable surveillance, subjects become self-disciplining, the process is complete (ibid.). In addition to disciplining and frightening children into conformity through physical punishment and humiliation, residential school administrators also engaged in tactics that targeted children's souls more directly: They gave children Christian names, cut their hair, burned their clothes, and punished them for speaking their mother tongues (TRC 2015a). These tactics—constituting both institutional and structural violence—aimed to assimilate Indigenous children and remake them into "citizen labourers" of the Canadian nation-state.

Indigenous people who were forced to attend residential schools describe themselves as survivors. This term acknowledges the horrific nature of their experiences, and also their strength and resilience. Indeed, the violence experienced by the estimated 150,000 First Nations, Métis, and Inuit children who attended residential schools was systemic and profound and has resulted in numerous intergenerational effects collectively referred to as the *legacy* (TRC 2015a). These include post-traumatic stress disorder (PTSD), violence in the family, substance abuse, physical and sexual violence, and self-destructive behaviour. Most survivors feel that attending residential school extinguished their connection to their culture. This systemic denigration of Indigenous cultures is a powerful example of symbolic violence. Indeed, as a result of years of indoctrination, many survivors are secretive about or ashamed of their cultural heritage and do not speak their mother tongue in front of their children; as a result, their children are also disconnected from their culture, history, and language (see Box 12.1). The residential schools also denied generations of children an "environment of positive parenting" (TRC 2015a, 135), precipitating a lack of childrearing skills that is, in turn, used to justify the disproportionately high rates of apprehension of Indigenous children by child welfare agencies, a matter examined below.

BOX 12.1: THE IMPACTS OF RESIDENTIAL SCHOOL

I was born on Sandy Bay reserve to a 16 year old mother who lost her status because she married a big good looking Icelander. And she was happy to lose her status. She was welcomed sort of into the Icelandic community. She started as a housekeeper for my dad's aunt and nine months later I showed up. She had been to residential school. They had done a pretty good job of making her feel ashamed about who she was. She lived on the reserve, and making her feel uncomfortable about where she came from, who she was, her language—her first language was Saulteaux. So I remember that growing up as a kid, I was always sort of confused. And then my dad joined the army. We lived on military bases where my mom would say she was Spanish, dark hair, and she would say, "don't tell people where we came from. It won't help you. It is not good." I wondered, I felt very bad about that. But she was a wonderful mother. To this day she still carries that with her.

Congress of Aboriginal Peoples (CAP) 2012, 11

Central to the project of "civilizing" Indigenous children was ingraining Christian mores and values, including gender roles and relations. As with other aspects of residential schools, this endeavour pivoted on myths about Indigenous men and women: While Indigenous men were (and are) characterized as drunk, stupid, and thieving, and as exhibiting "venality of every kind," Indigenous women were (and are) additionally, as we saw above, stereotyped as oversexed and prostitutes (Green 1990, 19). In residential schools, the latter myths informed institutional practices. Not only were girls separated from boys and dressed in (highly gendered) Western clothing (see Figure 12.1), girls were framed as promiscuous for fraternizing with boys, and rather than being

FIGURE 12.1: Boys and girls at a residential school

taught about puberty or sex were shamed for their bodies (TRC 2015b). Lena McKay, a survivor of Breynat Hall, a Roman Catholic residential school in Fort Smith, Northwest Territories, described for the Truth and Reconciliation Commission what this looked like:

> [We were] not allowed to talk to the boys. We, you know, we go for meals and that, 'cause they used to meet us in the stairway, like, you know, we'd turn our heads, she'd tell us we're pants crazy.... Boy, she, one time she came to me, she just about choked me, 'cause, you know, my shirt was, one button was open.... [S]he just about choked me buttoning my shirt, because she said, "You want to show yourself to, to the men?" you know. "You're boy crazy. You're pants crazy," things like that. (TRC 2015b, 95)

This gender indoctrination and discipline even extended beyond school years: Indian Affairs and church officials often arranged marriages between older residential school students so that they would not revert back to their so-called uncivilized ways. To this end, from the 1890s to the 1930s, the state also attempted to block students from marrying non-indoctrinated peers—young women who wanted to marry young men who had not attended residential school required approval from Indian Affairs (TRC 2015a).

Gendered violence and the *Indian Act*

Whereas arranged marriages were a biological means of maintaining the effects of disciplinary power, Canada's laws pertaining to "Indian" status can be seen as state violence that has culminated in particular effects for Indigenous women (slow violence). In "the mid 1800s, Canada assumed control over defining who is 'Indian'" (CAP 2012, 11), and "Indian" status became a mandatory precondition for Indigenous people to assert their treaty and statutory rights (Kulchyski 1999). Accordingly, non-status does not mean non-Indigenous; rather, status was a colonizing and regulatory mechanism that coupled entitlement with control by the Canadian state (CAP 2012). Those who refused to participate in applying for "Indian" status, or were overlooked in the government's categorizations of various groups of people as "Indian," could not pass status on to their descendants (ibid.). When residential schools were introduced, parents resisted their children's apprehension by whatever means they could, including fleeing to the city, banding together as a community, and making legal petitions (TRC 2015a); others protected their children from residential school by enfranchising them, in other words "relinquish[ing] their Indian status in exchange for Canadian citizenship" (CAP 2012, 12)—making future generations ineligible for status (see Box 12.2).

BOX 12.2: THE EFFECTS OF INDIAN REGISTRATION POLICIES

My mother did not have a choice about enfranchisement—her father wanted to protect his children from the Residential School—in order to do this he had to enfranchise them. After 1950, the government stopped parents from enfranchising their children, however today it affects my mother's status, my status, and the status of my children.

Congress of Aboriginal Peoples 2012, 12

Early colonial laws also imposed a Christian worldview on gender relations, women's roles and rights, and the importance of marriage. From 1867, illegitimate children of "Indian" women and "non-Indian" men were not eligible for status (CAP 2012); and in 1869, a statute specifying that Indigenous women would lose their "Indian" status if they married a "non-Indian" was introduced (Hurley and Simeone 2014). This provision was subsequently included in the 1876 *Indian Act*, which additionally subjected Indigenous peoples to the Christian tradition of patrilineage, such that any woman who married an Indigenous man would inherit his band membership—in other words, status was *only* conferred through men. Another aspect of the Christian male inheritance tradition was forced on Indigenous communities in 1951, when illegitimate daughters of "Indian" men were rendered ineligible for status (CAP 2012). Discrimination against women was further compounded with the introduction of the "double-mother" rule, through which "Indians whose mother and maternal grandmother had only gained status through marriage, automatically lost status upon reaching the age of 21, if born after 1951" (ibid., 12).

Indigenous women attempted to challenge the discriminatory nature of these laws in the 1970s, but a decision by the Supreme Court of Canada (*Attorney General of Canada v. Lavell* 1974) affirmed Parliament's right to define who could, and could not, be an "Indian," reasoning—in a classic illustration of Crenshaw's (1989) characterization of courts as intersection-blind—that the rules governing marriage applied to all women equally (Hurley and Simeone 2014). The subsequent ruling on a complaint brought to the UN Human Rights Committee by Sandra Lovelace shamed and pressured the Canadian state into taking steps to rectify the status discrimination issue (Silman et al. 1987). In 1985, the Canadian government introduced the *Gender Equity in Indian Registration Act*, which restored status to women who had "married out" and those affected by the "double mother rule." It also made status available to a child with one status parent (irrespective of gender) (Hurley and Simeone 2014) and removed the provisions limiting the status of illegitimate children (CAP 2012). Problematically, however, the bill did this by introducing two levels of "Indian" status: 6(1) status, which a person can pass on to their children, and 6(2) status, which has been characterized as "half" status because "children of s. 6(2)'s will only be a status Indian if the other parent is also a status Indian" (ibid., 13). This continued to limit women's band membership and discriminated against women who had married out through the "second generation cut-off" rule (Hurley and Simeone 2014). In response, Indigenous organizations and human rights advocates characterized Bill C-31 as engendering "residual sex discrimination" (ibid., 156). Indeed, government officials predicted that in five generations, no Indigenous children would be entitled to status (ibid.). In other words, while not as overtly as residential schools, these laws would also, if relatively slowly, "kill the Indian in the child" (TRC 2015a, 130).

It would be 25 years before the federal government introduced another amendment, *Bill C-3: Gender Equity in Indian Registration Act*, in 2010. However, critics again took issue with the matter of transmission, arguing that Bill C-3 only eliminated gender discrimination for some Indigenous people, while others would continue to receive "lesser or no status because they had an Indian grandmother, instead of an Indian grandfather" (CBA 2010, 8). Moreover, Bill C-3 introduced provisions allowing non-status persons whose mother's name was removed from the registry through marriage to a non-status person to register, but bizarrely only when they parent a child, whereupon they can register themselves and their child (ibid.; *Indian Act* c. I-5, s. 6(1)(c. 1)(iv)). Here we see that the entrenchment of gender discrimination and conventional gender expectations—that women are destined to be wives and mothers—in the *Indian Act* continues to impact Indigenous women's lives (see Box 12.3). After the federal government twice received extensions to respond to a 2015 ruling by the Superior Court of Québec in *Descheneaux c. Canada* that the *Indian Act* violates section 15(1) of the *Canadian Charter of Rights and Freedoms* on the basis of sex discrimination (Kirkup 2017), on December 12, 2017, *Bill S-3: An Act to Amend the Indian Act* received royal assent. Although advocates expressed some satisfaction with the new law, the required consultations could delay access to status for women affected by the pre-1951 cut-off (APTN 2017; NWAC 2017). The Native Women's Association of Canada (NWAC 2017) contends that more needs to be done to ensure the meaningful inclusion of, and access to justice for, "women who lost their status due to sex discrimination in the *Indian Act*."

Violence against Indigenous women: An intersectional colonial legacy

While the *Indian Act* is a mechanism of violence against Indigenous peoples operating through disciplinary tactics and slow violence, another aspect of

BOX 12.3: INDIGENOUS WOMEN'S EXCLUSION

Although my grandmother raised me with traditional values, language, and teachings, I have never been included in the same traditional ceremonies as my cousins. I have worked for the band's administrative offices where some of my family lives, but I cannot live there or place my daughter in the daycare there, because I have not been eligible for membership. As I result, I moved back to the city with my child where it was easier to obtain access to services, and have been raising her without being connected to my family. Although my mother has had reserve land given to her, as it stands I presently cannot live there or inherit her property. I have no family on my father's side. Despite the fact I still do have family, I feel orphaned nonetheless because of the extra effort it takes on my part to partake in the same activities as the rest of my family. As a child I took a lot of pride in my culture and heritage. The transition to adulthood has been one of conflict, grief, loneliness, and anger.

Congress of Aboriginal Peoples 2012, 22

colonialism discussed throughout this book engenders violence: the myths and stereotypes about Indigenous women emanating from the colonial "civilizing" ideology of racial superiority and misogyny. Combined with Indigenous women's socio-economic marginalization (see Chapter 2) and the lasting impact of gender role indoctrination from residential schools, these myths exacerbate Indigenous women's risks of gendered violence at the hands of people they do not know (e.g., hate crimes, predatory violence) as well as from people they do (e.g., IPV). The statistics are striking and disturbing: Indigenous women are three times more likely to be victims of violence than their non-Indigenous counterparts; many of these woman are repeatedly victimized (Status of Women Canada 2014).

Indigenous women and predatory violence

Since the 1980s Indigenous women make up 12 per cent of recorded missing women and 16 per cent of murdered women (ibid.), despite constituting only 4.9 per cent of Canada's population (Statistics Canada 2017b). Indeed, predatory violence against Indigenous women is so pervasive that it has become the focus of awareness campaigns, activist protest, and government initiatives— collectively, these victims are referred to as missing and murdered Indigenous women (MMIW). While police (who only committed to recording if victims are Indigenous in 2014; RCMP 2017) have documented 164 missing and

1,017 murdered Indigenous women between 1980 and 2012 (RCMP 2014), Indigenous activists put the number at closer to 2,000 (Settee 2016). Moreover, as Pamela Palmater (2016) points out, "some of the provincial statistics present a much darker picture … 55 per cent of all of the women and girls that are murdered or go missing in Saskatchewan and 49 per cent in Manitoba" are Indigenous (255). As Sherene Razack (2016) notes, "Canadians live in a society where missing and murdered Indigenous women are so commonplace an occurrence that, for two years now, volunteers have organized to dredge the river that runs through the city of Winnipeg looking for the bodies of Indigenous girls and women who have disappeared" (i).

Violence against Indigenous women in urban areas plays out in a context characterized by police apathy in regard to their well-being and relatedly a lack of commitment to investigating the violence they experience, as well as racism and societal indifference that constitute Indigenous women as "valueless" and their victimization unremarkable (Amnesty International 2004). The 1971 murder of Helen Betty Osborne is emblematic of how myths about Indigenous women shape both their vulnerability to violence and the state's response. A 19-year-old Cree woman who aspired to become a teacher, Ms. Osborne was abducted, sexually assaulted, and brutally murdered by four white men in The Pas, Manitoba, where she had been attending school (Amnesty International 2004; Palmater 2016). An inquiry into police responses to violence against Indigenous women in Manitoba noted that Ms. Osborne's killers were motivated by their "assumption that Aboriginal women were promiscuous and open to enticement through alcohol or violence [and] were objects with no human value beyond sexual gratification" (Amnesty International 2004, 17). Moreover, despite police awareness that white men had been sexually assaulting women in the area, it was only 15 years later that the police investigation—which had begun by focusing on Ms. Osborne's Indigenous peers—culminated in one of the four men being convicted (ibid.).

Another case demonstrates the continuing, profound disregard for Indigenous women and also exemplifies the cascading failures of state officials who should have intervened. Tina Fontaine, described as "a happy child" from Sagkeeng First Nation who "struggled with her father's violent death" (Commisso 2014) was 15 when police found her in a vehicle with an intoxicated older man whom they arrested. In spite of having run her name through the system, which identified her as a high-risk missing person, Ms. Fontaine was released. When she was found unconscious later that night, Manitoba's Child and Family Services put her in a hotel; nine days later her body was found in Winnipeg's Red River (MacDonald 2015; Palmater 2016; Razack 2016).

As was the case for Tina Fontaine, Indigenous women and girls who are reported missing are routinely met with indifference by police, who often fail to take basic investigatory steps, sometimes assuming that the woman has simply run away (Amnesty International 2004). Indeed, there is little trust of police in Indigenous communities and reluctance to turn to law enforcement for protection (ibid.), which is certainly understandable given the history of police repression and the abuse and violence experienced by Indigenous women at the hands of agents of the state examined in the previous chapter. Relatives of MMIW also report discrimination from police during investigations, in the form of racist attitudes, inaction, and slow response (Oppal 2012). Here again we see the way stereotypes seep into the approach to victims who are Indigenous women. For example, an Ottawa officer's online comments follow-ing the suspicious death of Annie Pootoogook characterized the renowned Inuit artist as an irresponsible risk taker: "could be a suicide, accidental, she got drunk and fell in the river and drowned who knows … much of the aborigi-nal population in Canada is just satisfied being alcohol or drug abusers, living in poor conditions" (Lofaro 2016). The police officer, Chris Hrnchiar, later temporarily demoted for discreditable conduct and sent to multicultural train-ing, was admonished for misusing the authority granted him by the state and (perhaps tellingly) for inadequate self-censorship (ibid.).

It is not only police who are indifferent. Echoing the narrative by the colo-nial Canadian state, and the late 1800s media framing of Indigenous women as wanton, immoral, and prostitutes (Carter 1993), today's media coverage high-lights MMIW's (assumed or actual) involvement with substance abuse, gangs, or prostitution (Amnesty International 2004). For example, during the 2018 trial of Raymond Cormier for the murder of Tina Fontaine—for which he was ultimately acquitted (Hoye 2018)—headlines proclaiming "Tina Fontaine had drugs, alcohol in system when she was killed: toxicologist" (Stead 2018) implicitly suggested her "risky" choices made her (at least partially) responsible for the violence to which she was subjected (Balkissoon 2018). We saw similar victim blaming in the media coverage emphasizing Cindy Gladue's sex work (see Chapter 3). In general, MMIW receive less frequent and less sympathetic news coverage as compared to their non-Indigenous counterparts (Gilchrist 2010). In turn, these media portrayals inform the criminal justice process by reiterating the perceived worthlessness of Indigenous women, engendering a lack of public participation in investigations, and further apathy from police (Gilchrist 2010; Palmater 2016).

A graphic example of apathy on the part of police, the media, the state, and non-Indigenous Canadians more generally is the lack of attention afforded the estimated 40 young Indigenous women who have gone missing or been found murdered since 1969 in northern British Columbia, on the so-called Highway of Tears (Human Rights Watch 2013). It was not until Nicole Hoar, a white 25-year-old tree planter, disappeared in 2002 that the media paid attention. The police also expended considerably more resources on this case; Human Rights Watch (2013) quoted one former RCMP officer who was unequivocal: "I was up there. If they're natives, nobody gives a shit" (37). Another example is that it took years of concerted lobbying before the federal government finally capitulated to the demands of Indigenous activists and formed a commission on MMIW in 2016; at the time of writing, the commission has attracted criticism from Indigenous communities, activists, and families for being ineffective, stagnant, and overly bureaucratic (MacDonald 2017).

Intimate partner violence

Insofar as Indigenous people have been inculcated with dichotomous, Christian notions of gender, Indigenous women experience IPV for many of the same reasons as other groups of women in Western society. However, this plays out in the colonial context—and as we saw in Chapter 6, the frustration of racism may precipitate violence (Ristock 2002); the legacy of residential schools also contributes to violence in families and intimate relationships. Some Indigenous women's vulnerability to and ability to extricate themselves from IPV is further exacerbated by their ineligibility for "Indian" status via marriage or as descendants of inter-racial marriages, which renders them more reliant on their spouse for rights and supports (Amnesty International 2004). Indigenous women are also, relatively speaking, more likely to have low incomes, which can further restrict their ability to leave an abusive relationship (see Chapter 2). Moreover, a UN report has documented bias in favour of male partners in situations of IPV in community justice systems (Tauli Corpuz 2015). This is compounded when male First Nations leadership is reticent to address the problem (ibid.) and instead depoliticizes and minimizes the issue by relegating it to the private sphere (Kuokkanen 2015).

As we see in Juanita Perley's story in Box 12.4, for Indigenous women in violent relationships the combined effects of structural violence and lack of community support make reactive violence more likely. Moreover, with few resources to draw upon to resolve IPV (e.g., access to culturally sensitive shelters and social service support), Indigenous women who enact reactive or protective violence against their abusers are often charged under mandatory charging protocols—another unintended consequence of mainstream second wave feminist efforts to reform the legal approach to IPV examined in Chapter 6 (Balfour 2008, 2014a). This contributes to the disproportionate rate of incarceration of Indigenous women (see Chapter 11). In response to over-incarceration, as with status as defined by the *Indian Act*, the government has introduced reforms whose effectiveness remains questionable. One such effort, Bill C-41, amended the *Criminal Code* in 1996, thereby encoding the importance of "just" sentences that reflect both aggravating and mitigating

BOX 12.4: JUANITA PERLEY'S STORY

There was no way for the men to get work and that is probably what frustrated them most.... My husband became an alcoholic and things just went from bad to worse. I had ten children by then and I thought, where in the world will I take my children? ... Then I thought, there's the band office. Nobody lives in the band office—they only work there.... When I moved all the kids up to the band office the RCMP showed up [and] said I was going to be arrested for breaking and entering.... The Mounties contacted the chief and the chief said, "Leave them alone. We'll just move our offices into our homes until we get that family a place to stay." ... The band office tried to get my husband out of the family house. He held a certificate of possession which the chief and council tried to cancel through Indian Affairs in Ottawa but they couldn't cancel it. Indian Affairs wouldn't budge; said it was "an internal dispute" and they couldn't "interfere." ... In the meantime my husband began coming over here, still trying to beat us. Finally one day I thought, well, I can get a peace bond, so I went down to the court house and the prosecutor had a big laugh. He thought it was hilarious.... So on the way back I stopped at the hardware store and bought a box of buckshot [shotgun shells]. I thought, if that man comes back, they'll have to scrape him off the porch. At least then he'll leave us alone.

Quoted in Silman et al. 1987, 104-6

circumstances. It also incorporated elements of restorative justice, encouraging the use of minimally restrictive sanctions and specifying that alternatives to incarceration be considered for all offenders but "with particular attention to the circumstances of aboriginal offenders" (*CC* s. 718.2).

Shortly thereafter, *R. v. Gladue* (1999) precipitated further sentencing reforms. Jamie Gladue, a young Indigenous woman from British Columbia, was convicted of manslaughter in the death of her common-law husband after suffering years of abuse (Balfour 2014b). The case was appealed up to the Supreme Court of Canada (SCC), where justices agreed with her lawyers that because her Indigeneity had not been properly taken into account (as per *CC* s. 718.2(e)), neither had her life circumstances (ibid.). At the same time however, the SCC justices held that "restorative justice should not be the primary goal of sentencing in all cases involving Aboriginal offenders" (ibid., 99–100). In this respect, *R. v. Gladue* led to contradictory results. As we saw in the previous chapter, the decision set a precedent for the courts to consider

the background of Indigenous offenders (ibid.), but it also supported punitive sanctions (Balfour 2012), ultimately upholding Jamie Gladue's three-year
sentence (*R. v. Gladue* 1999).

Colonizing "care" and child welfare

The way colonialism operates "in the intimate, embodied, domestic, micro-scale
geographies of Indigenous women and children" (de Leeuw 2016, 14) is explicitly evident in the removal of Indigenous children from their homes, families, and
communities. Here we see the way policies of the colonial state first create the
problem and then mobilize the ensuing issues to justify additional violence—
structural violence begets structural violence. And while the mechanisms have
changed, the process and narratives in which the regulatory potential for social
welfare are exposed remain disturbingly consistent. It would appear the mandate
that paramount consideration be given to the best interests of the child in deter-
mining a course of action continues to be read through a racist colonial lens.

Constructing bad mothers

Analogous to residential schools, the apprehension of Indigenous children can
be seen as part of the "civilizing" project, which is in turn related to the characterization of Indigenous parents—and, reflecting Euro-Christian gender role
expectations, especially mothers—as unfit. Drawing on documents from the late
1800s, Sarah Carter (1993) demonstrates how the entrenched mother-blaming
tactic of the colonial Canadian state operated: Well aware that they were unable
to acquire either decent accommodations or the provisions to maintain their
dwellings (e.g., soap, towels), officials framed Indigenous women as "preferring tents to proper housing because tents required less work to maintain and
could be clustered in groups that allowed visiting and gossip.… Indians raised
dust with their dancing and the women's failure to clean it up spread diseases
such as tuberculosis. Administrators blamed the high infant mortality rate upon
the indifferent care of the mothers. The neglected children of these mothers
grew up 'rebellious, sullen, disobedient and unthankful'" (149).

The same process is evident today. Illustrating the ways in which
co-constructing mechanisms of violence are articulated by the colonial state
as risk factors, Jacqueline Denison and her colleagues identify a number of
interrelated indicators adhered to by child protection agents (Denison, Varcoe,
and Browne 2014). These assumptions construct Indigenous mothers as bad if
they are a single parent, or have an unreliable partner, or spent time in foster
care as a child, all of which are assumed to diminish their access to extended
family, role models of parenthood, and safe childcare. Living below the poverty

line—which is connected to the legacy of residential schools and is especially likely for Indigenous women living off reserve—also increases the likelihood of a mother being deemed inadequate, as it can restrict her access to housing that meets the standards of child protection workers. Other aspects of the legacy of residential schools, including a history of trauma, mental illness, and drug/alcohol abuse, are also seen as sources of concern (ibid.). In short, framed in the neoliberal language of risk, the outcomes of state violence are transformed into risk factors, effectively individualizing, blaming, and responsibilizing Indigenous women for the devastation wrought by colonialism. Moreover, as we see below, this is used to justify further violence against Indigenous women by the state—the removal of their children.

Children's aid or apprehension?

It has long been apparent that residential schools and child welfare agents have operated with similar aims and in cooperation with other agents of the Canadian state. In 1948, some 50 years after Indian agents began forcibly apprehending children to take them to residential schools, the Canadian Association of Social Workers officially supported the assimilationist residential school regime; in so doing they ignored the alarming rates of child abuse and deaths and instead characterized residential schools as appropriate places for child welfare placements (Blackstock 2015). Shortly thereafter, provincial social workers began to enter Indigenous homes and remove children whose parents failed to meet white middle class standards of parenting (Denison et al. 2014).

Policies facilitating the apprehension of Indigenous children became widespread in the 1960s as the era of residential schools was winding down. The "Sixties Scoop" (although the practice lasted well into the 1990s) involved thousands of children being removed from their birth families and communities to be placed, for the most part, with white families in Canada, the United States, and overseas; little attempt was made to keep families together. As Colleen Cardinal and Kristin Gilchrist (2014) note, "by 1970, one third of Indigenous children had been removed from their homes, sometimes without the knowledge or consent of their families or Nations, and with contact between relatives entirely cut off" (44). In 2017 Justice Belobaba of the Ontario Superior Court, ruling on the first of several class action suits brought by Sixties Scoop survivors against the federal government, wrote "Canada breeched the common duty of care" by failing to "take reasonable steps to prevent ... children placed in the care of non-aboriginal foster parents ... from losing their aboriginal identity" (*Brown v. Canada*, para. 88). The celebrated legal acknowledgment does not, however, capture the profound effects of the slow violence of colonialism: traumatic apprehension followed by displacement, isolation, racism, cultural assimilation, and (in a disturbing number of cases) sexual and physical abuse. Angela Ashawasegai, an Ojibwa woman and one of the plaintiffs in the above-noted lawsuit, spoke of the loss of her culture and identity, describing her youth as living "basically in survival mode" and explaining that her adoptive family "treated me like a farmhand. They abused me. I couldn't do anything right ... I was called a squaw, all these racist things" (quoted in CBC 2016c).

The practice of apprehending Indigenous children is not only a shameful relic of a colonial past. According to 2016 census data, while Indigenous "children accounted for 7.7% of all children aged 0 to 4, they accounted for more than one-half (51.2%) of all foster children in this age group" (Statistics Canada 2017c, 5). Shockingly, "there are more First Nations children in child welfare care today than at the height of residential schools" (Blackstock 2015, 97). How can we understand this? While the proportion of Indigenous children being taken "into care" for abuse is no different than for non-Indigenous children, the former are twice as likely to be removed for poverty-driven neglect (de Leeuw 2016)—part of the lasting legacy examined throughout this chapter. The impact is compounded by the fact that, as the Canadian Human Rights Tribunal (in *2016 CHRT 2*) confirmed, funding formulas for the provision of child and family services discriminate against "First Nations children and families living on reserve and in the Yukon" (para. 456). Cindy Blackstock, the executive director of the First Nations Child and Family Caring Society of Canada and a moving force behind the Human Rights Tribunal complaint, explains that a dearth of resources means the protective and preventive services social workers access to allow children to remain in their homes are not available on reserve, making it more likely that Indigenous children will be removed (Galloway 2016). As de Leeuw (2016), using Nixon's concept of slow violence, writes, the "ongoing assertion of settler colonial power, a continuum reliant on the slow, ongoing, and hidden removal of children from often lone-women-led homes and families" (20) results not only in apprehensions but also in child deaths. In short, Indigenous children who are at risk because of structural discrimination are then denied the support that would allow them to remain in their homes by discriminatory policies.

Colonial violence and women's health

The magnitude and insidiousness of colonial violence are brought into sharp relief when we consider the profound impact on health. Indeed, Karina Czyzewski (2011) argues that colonialism itself should be seen as a determinant of health for Indigenous people—one that is deeply intermeshed with other social determinants of health, including education, social resources, income, and access to healthcare. For example, Indigenous women's low educational attainment is shaped by colonial attitudes and policies characterizing them as intellectually inferior. Today, according to Statistics Canada (2017d), 30 per cent of Indigenous people between the ages of 25 and 64 have not completed high school (compared to 13 per cent of the general population), and only 10.9 per cent hold a bachelor's degree or higher (the national rate is 22.4 per cent); individuals living on reserve, "many [of whom] have to leave their communities to attend educational institutions, including high school" (8), have markedly lower rates—5.4 per cent have a bachelor's degree. Education not only impacts incomes but also, as we see below, intersects with other factors that condition the health and well-being of Indigenous women (TRC 2015a).

Furthermore, the Canadian government continues to exert control over the governance practices and resource management capacities of First Nations. The result is living conditions often characterized by severely inadequate reserve housing and, in a shocking number of communities, polluted drinking water (Caven 2013). Moreover, the drastic changes in Indigenous peoples' eating habits brought on by colonization (RCAP 1996), in concert with limited access to nutritious food, is correlated with elevated rates of type 2 diabetes in Indigenous communities; women face the additional risk of pregnancy complications from type 2 and gestational diabetes (Toth et al. 2016).

We also need to factor in the well-documented physiological impacts of chronic stress, including "weakened resistance to disease [and increased vulnerability] to many serious illnesses such as cardiovascular and immune system diseases, and adult-onset diabetes" (Mikkonen and Raphael 2010, 10). Here we can think about the stress of poverty, lack of access to adequate housing (e.g., bad or no running water, overcrowding), and food insecurity. Moreover, these factors intersect with other potential sources of stress that permeate the lives of Indigenous women (highlighted throughout this book)—discrimination based on "Indian" status (or lack thereof), racism and microaggressions, un- or under-employment, over-policing and routine police abuse of power, and surveillance by agents of the state including child welfare officers—all of which precipitate stress; collectively, they create a toxic environment.

The colonial legacy of children being apprehended that pervades Indigenous women's daily lives is not only a source of stress, it also diminishes Indigenous women's access to healthcare. The routine racism and discrimination they encounter from nurses (informed by the stereotype-laden media portrayals of Indigenous women discussed above and in Chapter 2) discourage women from visiting or staying with their children while in hospital, precipitating further judgment from healthcare professionals and reinforcing stereotypical perceptions of Indigenous women as immoral, bad, and irresponsible mothers (Denison et al. 2014). Denison and her colleagues (2014) note that although such experiences do not deter Indigenous women from seeking medical attention for their children, they are less likely to access healthcare for themselves. Indigenous women also report intensive and judgmental surveillance by child protection social workers, which can begin while they are pregnant; in order to evade this hyper-monitoring, some women relocate to different regions (ibid.).

Moreover, in addition to separating families through child apprehension, colonial beliefs and assimilationist practices have also interrupted the process of childbirth in Indigenous communities. Before colonial interference, "traditional midwives assisted with both the ceremonial and the physical aspects of birth"; among nomadic peoples, other community members were required to be knowledgeable about birth as well (NAHO 2008, 12). Midwifery in North America declined as the Western medical profession became the norm (ibid.). As a result, Indigenous women, especially in remote areas with inadequate healthcare and other infrastructure, must travel outside of their communities to access prenatal care and deliver their babies (NACM 2012a); frequently the outcome is a negative birthing experience (Yeung 2016). Relocating to give birth can lead to feelings of social and cultural isolation and depression, as well as the accruing of costs from childcare (of children left at home) or of a woman's partner accompanying her for the birth (Kolahdooz et al. 2016). When women have to travel to deliver a child, it also removes the joy and celebration of birth from their extended family and community (ibid.). Exceptionally, there are a dozen Indigenous midwifery practices in First Nations communities and cities in Ontario, Manitoba, Nunavut, Northwest Territories, and Québec (NACM 2012b). Otherwise, however, healthcare infrastructure is limited, which in turn is linked to higher infant mortality among Indigenous people—twice the national rate—and a dearth of prenatal and antenatal care (Yeung 2016).

Resistance: A long history of seeking justice

We have seen many examples of resistance throughout this book; we have also seen that women have mobilized against diverse issues that reflect the interlocking oppressions that condition their lives. Certainly Indigenous women's resistance is profoundly intersectional insofar as they insist that the issues—including gendered and racist violence and discrimination, colonization, poverty, lack of legal rights and redress (and indeed the Canadian legal system as a whole), self-determination, and resource extraction—are mutually constitutive and cannot be addressed separately.

In Chapter 1 we saw Indigenous women powerfully asserting this position in the Idle No More movement, and in this chapter we have seen that Indigenous women have effectively used the courts, both Canadian and international, to pressure the government to rectify discriminatory laws, policies, and practices. Resistance to the entangled factors confronting Indigenous women in Canada today has taken many other forms as well. Indeed, it would take volumes to fully document the myriad examples of Indigenous women's resistance, some of which are collective (e.g., creating organizations, public education campaigns, protests) while others are individual (e.g., exposing microaggressions, identity politics, education, art); and of course there are thousands of small everyday acts of contestation—the weapons of the oppressed (Scott 1990)—that go unseen and unremarked upon but "talk back" to the dominant discourse. Sometimes these moments of quiet courage become powerful symbols, instances when resistance renders power not only visible but crystal clear (Foucault 1982). This was the case when Amanda Polchies, a 28-year-old Mi'kmaq woman from Elsipogtog First Nation, New Brunswick, was faced with heavily armed RCMP officers sent to disband an Indigenous encampment trying to halt the resource extraction threatening the environment and the community's drinking water; she brandished "the only 'weapon' she had: an eagle feather. Holding it aloft, she began to pray" (Schilling 2013). The image (Figure 12.2) reverberated around the world.

Indigenous resistance to colonial power, however, dates back well before social media allowed the widespread dissemination of images, to the arrival of Europeans on the shores of what is now called Canada. That said, in yet another example of gendered symbolic power, most of the courageous acts of these women have been written out of history. We know little of, for example, the Indigenous women in the 1880s who refused to comply with the pass system (Carter 1993) or the women who, in spite of violent assimilation efforts, kept oral history alive and safeguarded traditional teachings (TRC 2015a). A few women are belatedly being recognized. Women like Nahebahwequa, an Anishinabe woman—whose name means "upright woman"—who in the 1860s protested the government's seizure of her land and that of other First Nations peoples. After failing in her efforts to petition the provincial parliament, she travelled (alone) to New York to raise awareness, ultimately taking her case to England where she (unsuccessfully) petitioned the queen (Schweyer 2017).

There have been scores of other upright women over the decades who have fought against the gendered discrimination encoded in the *Indian Act*. Women like Mary Two-Axe Earley of Caugnawage, Québec, who, in the 1950s, spoke out against the *Indian Act*'s sexist provisions (Silman et al. 1987). Women like Jeannette Lavell and Yvonne Bédard who, in 1973, brought the

FIGURE 12.2: Amanda Polchies stands her ground, 2013

same issue to the Supreme Court of Canada, which narrowly ruled "the Indian Act was exempt from the Canadian Bill of Rights" (the anti-discrimination legislation at that time) and who were vilified and "labelled 'white-washed women's libbers' who were undermining their Indian heritage" by Indigenous leaders and organizations worried the government would abolish "Indian" status altogether (ibid., 13). And the women of Tobique First Nation in New Brunswick who, after Juanita Perley occupied their band office in 1976 (see Box 12.4), organized a march from the Oka Reserve to Parliament Hill in 1979 to protest reserve housing conditions (Silman et al. 1987). Soon after-wards, another woman from Tobique, Sandra Lovelace, brought the issue to the attention of the United Nations; together with the actions of her fellow marchers, Ms. Lovelace's case precipitated the Canadian government's amend-ment of the *Indian Act* with Bill C-31 in 1985 (McIvor 2004).

Sharon McIvor is another upright woman who took up the legal battle against status discrimination in a court case that lasted from 1994 to 2009 (Hurley and Simeone 2014). Unsatisfied with the government's response (Bill C-3 in 2010), McIvor appeared before the UN Human Rights Committee in 2015 to highlight the continuing sex discrimination in the *Indian Act*, and also spoke of the murders and disappearances of Indigenous women and girls (McIvor 2015). Indigenous women's persistence on the matter continues to precipitate (albeit frustratingly incremental) changes. In addition to being heard by decision makers in the Canadian state, Sandra Lovelace (now Lovelace Nicholas) went on to join their ranks, becoming a senator in 2005.

Concluding reflections

Colonialism is an ongoing process and ideology that continues to precipitate interpersonal, institutional, symbolic, and structural violence in Indigenous women's lives. Myths constructing Indigenous women as lascivious, irresponsible, and bad mothers are reinforced in laws as well as through state institutions (and their agents)—including the police, child welfare, and healthcare—and function to disqualify First Nations, Métis, and Inuit knowledges, cultures, and experiences of victimization. These myths intersect with structural discrimination and colonial attitudes with tragic consequences that are also interconnected, such that a lack of state oversight (e.g., abuse in foster care), resources (e.g., underfunding of First Nations bands, inadequate access to healthcare), and civic and legal entitlements (e.g., police protection, "Indian" status) may lead to further marginalization, ill health, and violence—through, for example, child apprehension, interpersonal violence, and/or poor living conditions.

That said, progress, however inadequate, has come about through the resistance initiatives of Indigenous women. Moreover, the efforts of Indigenous women, including taking their claims to the United Nations and making their presence and issues known through public demonstrations, are a powerful assertion of the knowledges and experiences the colonial law has attempted to displace, disqualify, and erase. In this regard, the federal government's 2008 apology, its admission of cultural genocide, and the activities, resources, and recommendations of the Truth and Reconciliation Commission are important preliminary steps toward building a new relationship between the settler nation of Canada and First Nations, Inuit, and Métis people; it remains to be seen if, how, and when this change will manifest.

EXERCISE: KNOWING YOUR PLACE

Go to the website Native-Land.ca.

Identify the Indigenous territories, languages, and treaties of the region where you were born and where you or family members live(d). If you are not Canadian born, investigate your first place of residence in Canada.

Get into groups of 5–6 learners.

Share your findings with your groupmates.

You may also want to share your thoughts on the following:

- Did you know this before?
- How would you feel if your hometown was occupied and/or renamed?
- What will you do with this knowledge?

"NO FREE LUNCH": COSTS AND CONSEQUENCES OF GENDERED VIOLENCE IN CANADA AND GLOBALLY

In this conclusion, we begin by turning back to Susan Sontag (see the Introduction). Reflecting on how we regard the pain of others, Sontag (2003) addressed the power of images—such as the archetypal lone, white victim of interpersonal gendered violence—and how such simplifying representations can lead to a (potentially) paralyzing awareness of violence that is, at its root, uninformed. The intersectional perspective advanced in this book positions us to look beyond such imagery and unpack the multifaceted conditions of gendered violence. This conclusion summarizes and synthesizes some of the key points of the book—in particular highlighting the interplay and costs of different forms of gendered violence; the influence of law and regulatory strategies on women's lives; and what we can learn from women's resistance. Consistent with the emphasis on the interlocking nature of systems of oppression (Fellows and Razack 1998; Hill Collins 1991), we then turn our gaze outward to consider gendered violence internationally. Here the links between capitalism, neoliberalism, and patriarchy are considered in relation to the hidden violence of the global production chain and the ongoing violence of colonialism. This is not to inspire a state of "bemused awareness … that terrible things happen" (Sontag 2003, 13) internationally, but rather to highlight how, much as we have seen in Canada, our collective complicity in the reproduction of norms, practices, and discourses engenders violence—a point of departure to think about strategies to minimize, disentangle ourselves from, and change oppressive structures.

Interlocking mechanisms and forms of gendered violence

Just as law's claim to truth, and in turn its authority, "is indivisible from [its] exercise of power" (Smart 1989, 11), we have seen myriad links between myths and stereotypes about women and the disqualification of their experiences—indeed, in their justification and normalization of gendered violence, these tropes themselves constitute symbolic violence. This alerts us to the inter-relationship between different categories of overlapping and intersecting violence (interpersonal, symbolic, slow, state, and structural) that play out in diverse spaces, including institutions, workplaces, and homes. For example, the construction of women as irrational, docile, devious, and inferior in mutually reinforcing medical, social, legal, and media discourses absorbed into our habitus (symbolic violence) engenders the disciplinary and medical interventions exercised on incarcerated women when they fail to embody normative expectations of feminine conduct (state violence). Such women may have come into conflict with the law in the first place because of retaliatory actions against an abusive partner (interpersonal violence), or from involvement in criminalized activities (e.g., sex work) to earn much-needed income to counteract the impact of austerity-inspired cuts to social assistance (slow violence), or because of drug abuse resulting from residential schools (structural violence) or their legacy (slow violence). We can also consider the mutually constitutive nature of these systems. For example, as we have seen, colonization not only decimated the lives of Indigenous peoples around the world through religiously justified instrumental narratives of cultural inferiority, but also forcefully instituted dichotomous conceptions of gender. Moreover, the patriarchal social order—entrenched by colonialism—continues to inform sexual scripts and the policing of gender and racial hierarchies. We can also factor in the competitive, boundless accumulation of capital, implicated not only in the imperial project but in the expanding ability of corporations to operate without accountability to workers or the environment—a process that has accelerated in the context of neoliberalism.

At the same time, these levels of violence, working together, manifest in ways that are specific to women's social location and life circumstances. As we have repeatedly seen, women who are racialized, Indigenous, working or underclass, im/migrants, LGBTQ, or disabled are the objects of symbolic violence—the social and discursive process by which "othering," erasure, and/or discrediting become normalized—which magnifies their vulnerability to other forms of violence. For example, myths constructing Muslim women as simultaneously culturally oppressed/inferior and risky precipitate hate crimes (interpersonal violence) targeting their symbolic difference (their hijab or niqab), justify their exclusion from rights and entitlements (in principle) enjoyed by all Canadians (state violence), or limit their access to employment or advancement in the workplace through gendered, ethnocentric microaggressions, or harassment (interpersonal violence) engendered by a lack of oversight or institutional commitment (structural violence). Similarly, narratives constructing trans women and sex workers as posing risks to ("good") women, whether in school bathrooms or on neighbourhood streets (symbolic violence), engender violence by state actors, hate crimes, everyday intrusions, and predatory violence, as well as exclusion from or discrimination in conventional sectors of the labour market. Of course, women whose privilege allows them to avoid being "othered" are also subject to symbolic violence: socialized into gender roles, they decide to work in the caring professions—such as teaching—only to find that the perception of women's "caring nature" is used to undermine their professional contributions in the context of austerity-driven budget cuts that culminate in increased vulnerability to, and acts of aggression from, students (situational and slow violence).

The compounded costs of gendered violence

The interconnections between the violence women experience also result in compounded costs. As asserted in the Introduction and evident throughout this book, gendered violence ripples through society affecting not only the victim but others not directly targeted. For example, the slow violence of austerity measures engenders workplace violence for nurses, which in turn impacts patient care; simply and evidently, "there is no free lunch" (Mackenzie 2015, 34). Indeed, not only is there no free lunch, but the costs of gendered violence (in its raced and classed manifestations), while often invisible—and invisibilized—affect us all. These social, economic, and personal costs can never be calculated in their totality; some efforts have, however, been made to quantify the fiscal impact of violence conventionally considered under the "violence against women" umbrella. For example, a Department of Justice Canada study, endeavouring to assign a dollar amount to what they refer to as "spousal violence" to compare the costs to other social phenomena, conservatively calculated the direct and indirect cost to be $7.4 billion *per year* (Zhang et al. 2012).

Many costs of gendered violence are, of course, borne by victims themselves. As we have seen, microaggressions, discrimination, and harassment in the workplace have economic repercussions for women; they may be overlooked for a promotion, be fired for being "troublesome" when they attempt to get redress or relief from the violence, or may decline or quit a job and be relegated to unemployment or precarious or criminalized labour. In addition, women may be required to perform unremunerated emotional labour and care work as part of their paid occupation. Gender norms that women are expected to embody also cost time and money through ongoing aesthetic labour. We can also think about the financial implications of sexual assault. A woman loses time (and therefore hours that could be devoted to paid employment and/or study) not only in the immediate aftermath of the attack as she copes with the physical and psychological pain, but also in the months and years following. After all, if she reports the incident there will be repeated interviews with police and possibly the need to testify in court; she may also need to arrange and pay for counselling. The economic costs may well ripple through her entire life: Her inability to concentrate (a common effect of sexual assault) may preclude her getting promoted at work or prevent her from earning the grades she needs to be admitted into graduate school, impacting her lifetime earnings and even shaping her ability to enjoy her "golden years."

We can also think of the psychological costs not only of interpersonal but also of structural violence: the toll of symbolic erasure (e.g., the absence of representation, the violence of renaming residential school students) or profound misrepresentation (e.g., stereotypes). In addition, the never-ending "safety work" (Vera-Gray 2014, 237) that women engage in as they go about their lives—thinking about what streets to walk on, taking care to ensure their clothes and makeup are not "provocative," and being mindful of the potential adverse consequences of participating in online activities and communities—requires continual vigilance, emotional energy, and valuable time.

Many of these costs are exacerbated by responsibilization and victim blaming. As we have seen over and over again in this book, regardless of the nature (e.g., everyday, sexual, intimate partner), location (e.g., on the street, in the home, at work), or relationship (e.g., stranger, customer, acquaintance), women are expected to prevent violence and blamed when they are unable to do so. Indeed, the victim is not only blamed but shamed—her victimization read as evidence of, at a minimum, a lack of judgment and, at worst, a character flaw. The pervasiveness and insidiousness of victim blaming is one of the reasons women, from nurses to students to sex workers, are fearful of the repercussions that may flow from disclosure and do not report violence (precipitating yet another erasure). Of course, the ascription of blame and the responsibility vested in women (to manage risks and to look and act in such a way as to prevent violence) pivots on the assumption that gendered violence is inherent and therefore inevitable—in other words that it is *normal*.

The progress narrative, public issues, and regulatory struggles

In spite of stubborn gendered narratives of victim blaming, natural caring, and sexual passivity, women's experiences of violence, like the opportunities available to them, have changed over time. This is neither to suggest that gendered violence is simply a remnant of a bygone era—it is not—nor that all women remain second-class citizens. As the intersectional socio-historical analyses in this book have highlighted, social change has meant some forms of gendered violence have moderated while new incarnations have emerged. For example, with women's increased participation in the labour market, more women with social and cultural capital (i.e., middle class white women) began to experience sexual harassment; they subsequently fought to change it from a workplace norm to a social issue. Similarly, women reformers brought intimate partner violence (IPV) out of the parlour and into the public sphere, and we have gone from believing a man had the right (even moral imperative) to discipline his wife to recognizing IPV as a widespread social problem. Moreover, feminists have fought hard for—and won—numerous legal reforms, including the expansion of sexual assault laws, mandatory charging policies for IPV, and regulation against workplace sexual harassment. These reforms have been rightly celebrated as symbolic denunciations of gendered violence that afford those women who have the ability and desire to access regulatory mechanisms potentially useful legal tools. However, because they do not decentre the power of law (Smart 1989), these solutions fall short; as revisited throughout this book, legal solutions protect women whose privilege, behaviour, circumstances, and victimization conform to the "ideal" woman victim trope while keeping other women "othered."

Troublingly, we have seen that criminal justice solutions to gendered violence can also work to the detriment of women, and they do not adequately take women's agency and diverse identities, behaviours, and needs into account. For example, mandatory charging policies do not necessarily help women escape IPV and may run counter to their own strategies to retain financial support for their children, to maintain occupancy in their home, or to minimize the risk of fatal violence. Moreover, women are deemed bad choice makers if they do not immediately, continuously, and cooperatively work with criminal justice personnel (Johnson and McConnell 2014). This discounting of women's ability to exercise (however constrained) agency speaks to a long history of protectionist rhetoric used by both male lawmakers and middle and upper class women activists to "help" risky and vulnerable women conform to normative expectations of femininity. Examples from the nineteenth and early twentieth centuries include middle class women working in concert with state authorities to rehabilitate "unruly women" by incarcerating and instructing them in middle class womanhood; imposing protective measures on women factory workers in the name of sexual morality rather than (and at the cost of) worker rights; and mobilizing narratives of white slavery, venereal disease, and moral risk to criminalize women supporting themselves through the provision of sexual services. Just as these women's

concern for the maintenance of white middle class feminine sexual propriety blinded them to their race and class privilege (and the fragility of the
sisterhood they espoused), today's neoliberal regulatory strategies ignore the
structural inequalities impacting women's lives and, indeed, render unfea-
sible the "responsible choices" women are urged to make. In other words,
the failure of legal solutions lies in their inability to address the interlocking
systems that precipitate and condition both gendered violence and the resistance strategies at a woman's disposal.

Resistance and alternative approaches: Rejecting norms and fighting back

The prominent place of legal reforms in feminist activism, while speaking to the class and racial privilege of mainstream second wave, governance,
and carceral feminists, also underscores our cultural preclusion to punish.
Indeed, our relish for revenge, whether in celebrating women stabbing leering
"mashers" with hat pins in the early 1900s (Abbott 2014) or women like Jane
Hurshman, who shot her sadistically abusive husband Billy Stafford nearly
a century later (Vallée 1986), is telling. However, there is ample evidence
that, at a societal level, violence does not decrease gendered violence; and
it does not, and cannot, change the relations of power in which gendered
violence unfolds. One alternative is restorative justice. A powerful example
is the process initiated by the family of Helen Betty Osborne, the young
Indigenous woman for whose murder, as we saw in Chapter 12, only one of
the four white men responsible was convicted. After this individual, Dwayne
Johnson, was released on parole, Osborne's family included him in a traditional healing circle—they were committed to ensuring he understood
the significance of his crime and its impact (Amnesty International 2004).
That the mere notion of having a dialogue with the killer of a loved one is
unthinkable for many of us demonstrates that Indigenous approaches to justice
radically depart from the punitive, adversarial, colonial model that appears
normal to many Canadians. This still-marginal victim-centred approach
shifts the focus from the offender and the need to exact retribution and
instead creates a space for the acknowledgment of harm, the assumption of
responsibility by the perpetrator, and restitution (Van Wormer 2009). While
some women may welcome "strategies that are solution-based rather than
problem-based processes, give voice to marginalized people, and focus on
healing and reconciliation" (ibid., 107), restorative justice does not, of course,
address the deeply entrenched causes of gendered violence any more than
do conventional approaches.

Sometimes women's resistance to gendered violence does speak to the conditions of its emergence. In this respect challenges to middle class feminisms have fruitfully precipitated more inclusive movements and structural analyses. We have seen attention drawn to intersectional experiences: from unions and activists highlighting gendered violence at diverse workplaces, including call centres, the sex industry, and middle class homes; to Black Lives Matter and Idle No More calling attention to state violence against racialized and Indigenous women, and the related symbolic violence of invisibilization and devaluing stereotypes; to women rejecting the beauty imperative that positions them as inherently flawed by protesting pageants and celebrating their "too large" bodies and natural hair; to women asserting their importance in the economy and the family by removing their labour power in national strikes. In calling attention to gendered violence, women have consciously sought to claim and reclaim space—in activist blogs challenging normative beauty tropes; on campuses through creative and collective protests against sexual violence; on the street in Slut Walks, Take Back the Night, and women's marches—powerfully rejecting the gendered expectations that women make themselves small, restrict their movements, and be quiet and reserved. At the same time we have seen that resistance is inevitably partial, conditioned by the interplay of personal identity, agency, contexts, social structures, and access to resources that also shapes women's perception of the issues.

Always fraught and sometimes violent, other instances of resistance have highlighted the constraints women face on a daily basis and the courage it takes to resist in such contexts. We have seen women—disproportionately, Indigenous, racialized, and/or poor women with little reason to trust the police, inadequate financial and social resources to leave, and slim odds of avoiding incarceration—literally fight back against their abusive partners, sometimes fatally. Similarly, some women in prison turn to violence, either against themselves or others, as the only means of resistance available. These constraints in turn illustrate the importance of allyship and intersectional, culturally appropriate, needs-based, respectful support directed by those whose lives are impacted. We have also seen that women's resistance can be partial in another way—in rejecting some norms while not challenging others. The foremost example is women's engagement with beauty practices; indeed, beauty and fashion can simultaneously be sites of conformity and resistance, for example queer femmes, who embrace a normatively feminine aesthetic while rejecting its accompanying (hetero)sexuality, and Black women entrepreneurs who started salons that at once capitalized on the beauty imperative and provided space and financial backing for Civil Rights organizing (Craig 2006). Thinking about the interplay of the beauty imperative with capitalism and neoliberalism in our contemporary, globalized world also highlights the need to reflect on the relationship between women's social location, experiences of violence, and situated resistance globally.

Widening the scope: Reflections on gendered violence globally

We have seen that Canadian and migrant women workers' precarity and lack of access to labour rights results in workplace environments conducive to microaggressions, sexual harassment, and situational and predatory violence. We have also seen how the violence experienced by these differentially situated groups is facilitated by structural and slow violence, including austerity measures and the weakening of organized labour under neoliberalism, operating in tandem with the invisibilization, minimization, and undervaluing of women's paid and unpaid labour. Of course these workers' experiences are also shaped by globalization, which encompasses national and international labour markets, trade relations, production chains, and distribution of wealth—processes that they, and we, are not merely caught up in as workers but also participate in as consumers. Taking a holistic view of the interlocking systems that engender violence, we now turn to reflect briefly on how mutually supporting discourses and practices constructing gender, class, and racial norms and expectations in Canada perpetuate gendered violence in other parts of the world. To this end we examine three seemingly disparate examples—the garment industry, mineral extraction, and international development—that are connected through capitalism, colonialism, neoliberalism, and patriarchy. These snapshots of internationally interlocking systems of oppression are a point of entry to thinking about our implication in gendered violence more broadly. In this context, the maxim "there is no free lunch" takes on an additional layer of meaning, reminding us that there are *always* costs. Our ability to purchase cheap clothes and participate in "fast fashion," to signify our emotional commitment with a diamond ring, to have the latest electronic gadget to take ever more selfies, and to support (and feel good about ourselves for doing so) international development projects that aspire to "uplift" women takes a costly toll not only on the environment but also in terms of gendered violence. It is women working and living halfway around the world who pay the price.

Hidden violence and resistance behind the tools of femininity

As we saw in Chapter 10, women's gender performances and practices, entwined with consumption, are deeply tied to capitalism. While our engagement with gender, race, and class as they intersect to construct the Western beauty ideal may be self-evident—reflecting, for example, the normative expectation that a woman through her clothing, hairstyle, and accessories must appear fashionable, appropriate, and not *slutty*—the products we consume for our performances also reproduce gender, race, and class hierarchies among workers down the global production line: the women in Southeast Asia who produce clothing for export to Western countries including Canada, and the women in Africa who work in the mining zones from which the materials for electronics and jewellery originate.

For example, Canada is among the largest importers of apparel manufactured in Cambodia, where companies employ a casual (rather than permanent) labour force to maximize control over workers, avoid paying benefits, and circumvent labour rights (Human Rights Watch 2015). Analogously to their counterparts in the Global North—the retail clerks selling these products whose working conditions we touched on in Chapter 2 (see Poster, Crain, and Cherry 2016)—the vast majority of garment workers are young women routinely subjected to labour abuses, including "forced overtime ... lack of rest breaks, denial of sick leave ... union-busting strategies ... pregnancy-based discrimination, sexual harassment, and denial of maternity benefits" (Human Rights Watch 2015, 7). In the Global South, however, this mistreatment is facilitated by additional structural conditions, including reticence by impoverished governments to enforce labour standards against multinational corporations for fear they will relocate elsewhere. Moreover, we see the same gendered practices and scripts: Women, hired based on stereotypical perceptions of their docility, are employed in the lowest and most poorly paid positions (e.g., seamstresses as opposed to supervisors) (Evans 2017). In turn, male union leaders may perceive women's concerns (e.g., the issue of termination upon pregnancy) as secondary (ibid.). As a result women, routinely sexually harassed and touched by both managers and male colleagues, have little recourse. As a Cambodian garment worker told Human Rights Watch (2015), "There is one male worker who harasses me a lot. Each day it's something different. One day he says 'Oh your breasts look larger than usual today.' On another day, he says, 'You look beautiful in this dress—you should wear this more often so I can watch you.' There are others who purposely brush past us or pinch our buttocks while walking. Sometimes I feel like complaining. I don't like it at all. But who do I complain to?" (9).

Just like women workers in the 1800s who, as we saw in Chapter 7, were judged by women reformers to be at-risk and morally risky, women workers in the Global South whose assertiveness transgresses feminine gender norms of passivity hazard being characterized as morally questionable (Evans 2017). However, in the context of gender scripts and a lack of cultural capital that facilitates their exploitation—and at the same time constrains their resistance—women garment workers in Southeast Asia perform everyday acts of resistance (Scott 1990), including joking about their superiors and purposely slowing output. Sometimes resistance is unambiguous. For example, Cambodian women organized an event showcasing their working conditions in a fashion show that was "juxtaposed and interspersed with dramatic recreations of recent killings" in the industry (Evans 2017, 7). Women also collectively campaigned for more inclusive union leadership; as a result, 30 per cent of leadership positions in the Vietnam General Confederation of Labour must now be held by women (ibid.). Thus, in spite of constraints, women's experiences are not limited to victimization. As with the image of the lone victim of violence in this book's Introduction, it is important to expand the frame to take contextual factors, agency, and resistance into account.

Another site that is more complex than dominant narratives suggest, and likewise enmeshed with capitalism, colonialism, and gender, is mining and its relationship to conflict. The Democratic Republic of Congo in particular is a country known for its mineral riches (used in cellphones and jewellery) and its civil conflicts (Laudati 2013; Rustad, Østby, and Nordås 2016). At the same time, Western countries' "focus on rape as a weapon of war has combined with the international attention [on] 'conflict minerals' [to produce] a global discourse that closely associates mining and sexual violence" (Bashwira et al. 2014, 109). The issue is, not surprisingly, more complicated. While on the one hand women living close to artisanal and small mining operations are more likely to be sexually victimized—especially if armed actors are present—on the other hand artisanal mining presents important economic opportunities for women, including work in mineral processing, jobs as cooks or cleaners, and/or opportunities as entrepreneurs selling food and supplies (Rustad et al. 2016). However, regulatory and humanitarian solutions to violence in conflict-ridden and/or resource extraction areas focus on the former while ignoring the latter. As a result, protectionist solutions are promoted that involve women curtailing their movement and use of public space, or simply removing themselves from mining areas altogether—a "solution" that fails to take into account the economic opportunities mining offers, and with it women's agency and ability to make decisions based on their own risk–benefit calculations (Bashwira et al. 2014). Moreover, similar to the protectionist labour legislation problematized in Chapter 7, not only do artisanal mining regulations restrict pregnant women from working in gold processing (without providing them with alternative means of income), but officials apply the regulation over-broadly, excluding pregnant and breastfeeding women from all mining activities (ibid.). Women who work as managers/intermediaries between artisanal miners and buyers are also marginalized by regulations positioning them as superfluous to the business process and a threat to the transparency and traceability increasingly demanded by the international community (ibid.). Ironically, then, Western consumers' demands for conflict-free gemstones, fuelled by the desire to minimize sexual violence, may result in policies and practices that exacerbate the poverty of women in the countries from which these resources are derived. This in turn, as we have seen throughout this book, may decrease their options and increase their vulnerability to gendered violence.

In addition to shaping regulation that leaves them economically marginalized, the assumption that Congolese women are exclusively victimized by conflict mineral extraction invisibilizes their resistance and survival strategies. Women, including sexual assault victims who have been rejected by their family, take advantage of the distraction of violent unrest to steal food and other necessities, and women working as mineral intermediaries have formed a collective to defend their interests (Bashwira et al. 2014). Here we see that, like mandatory charging policies for IPV (Chapter 6), regulatory and humanitarian responses pivoting on characterizations of women as exclusively victims ignore the complex interplay of context and agency and ultimately fail to alleviate the conditions engendering violence. In short, when we consider women in the Global South we are again confronted with the problematic framing of the woman victim of violence, alone and without context. To return to Sontag (2003), excluding the broader context not only simplifies, it allows us to feel sympathetic without considering culture, history, politics; it allows us to overlook our complicity.

Conflating charity and colonization

The mutual constitution of neoliberalism, capitalism, patriarchy, and colonialism and their relationship to gendered violence (examined in this book as they unfold in Canada) come into even sharper focus when we consider two interrelated forms of international economic development: structural adjustment programs and microcredit. Here a rather different (but decidedly neoliberal) image of poor, racialized, rural women taking control of their lives through entrepreneurial spirit emerges. A closer look complicates the picture, highlighting how neoliberal rhetoric obscures structural inequality, this time on an international scale. It also troubles the narrative—reverberating with colonial rhetoric of "civilizing savages"—of "bringing" equality to the "underdeveloped."

Guided by the ethos of neoliberalism, structural adjustment involves relaxing government regulation on the market and production of goods, which, as we have already seen in Canada and Cambodia, creates the conditions for exploitation and violence against women workers (Sparr 1994); it also entails privatization and a corresponding decrease in public-sector jobs, which together further reduce the rate and quality of women's employment (Detraz and Peksen 2016). Many impoverished nations do not enter into structural adjustment voluntarily but rather as a condition of financing by international institutions. The two major orchestrators of structural adjustment, the World Bank and the International Monetary Fund (IMF), operate in countries colonized by Western nations (Cabezas, Reese, and Waller 2008)—in this respect, economic "development" can be considered as both a capitalist extension of colonialism and a neoliberal project. Indeed, feminist scholars have long argued that, rather than promoting economic stability, structural adjustment reflects (and entrenches) the profoundly unequal relationship between rich countries and the Global South (Cabezas et al. 2008; Detraz and Peksen 2016; Sparr 1994).

A trenchant example of how the international shift to neoliberalism in the 1980s continues to negatively impact women's economic position and rights in the Global South is microcredit. Bangladesh, a country often presented as an object of pity in Western news and home of the emblematic and influential microcredit agency Grameen Bank, illustrates the gendered implications of applying a neoliberal solution to socio-economic problems engendered by neoliberalism. Lauded as a progressive model of development by colonialist institutions such as the IMF and World Bank, microcredit programs advance a framing of "poor women as potential entrepreneurs who needed small injections of cash to be able to sell chickens, eggs, puffed rice, and so on in the rural economy" (Karim 2016, 204). Such programs appeal to "donors' desire to create non-Western societies that conform to Western capitalist norms, as well as local nationalist desires to become equal with the West" (ibid., 203). As microcredit gained popularity, Grameen Bank and other similar non-governmental organizations in Bangladesh started to cover their costs through these programs, which were not as benevolent as their rhetoric suggests; as Laura Karim (2016) points out, microfinancing loans are often granted on the condition that borrowers purchase the products (e.g., hybrid seeds) of multinational agribusinesses. In conceptualizing women as entrepreneurs, the programs also fail to take gender dynamics into account. For example, in Bangladesh, rural women often comply with their husband's expectation that they hand over loans, making women more vulnerable to both their husbands and the microfinance institutions that demand timely payments whether or not the loan generates any income for its recipient (ibid.). In this context—with the support of Nijera Kori, an organization that aims to enhance their collective capacity to address gender and class oppression by, among other means, improving women's legal and rights literacy—some Bangladeshi women reject microcredit and mobilize as rural labourers and small farmers (Paprocki 2016).

In short, structural adjustment and microcredit in many ways exemplify the complexities and interlocking oppressions of capitalism, colonialism, neoliberalism, and class, race, and gender hierarchies, as well as how both the institutions and narratives are supported by those in the West. This, along with the situation of women workers in the garment and mining industries, draws our attention to the relationship between symbolic power and structural violence—the misrepresentation or invisibilization of the dynamic and ongoing interplay of agency and structure—and how reconstituting the roles and organization of a society in the image of a more dominant and powerful one is inevitably and inherently violent.

Final reflections

The brief glimpses of women's experiences of violence in the Global South presented above resonate with a key theme of the previous chapters: the mutual constitution of systems and forms of gendered violence. Consistent with the goal of this book—nuancing both the issue of gendered violence and the regulatory discourses and practices mobilized to address it—these international examples are yet another reason not to reproduce the "cross-class female chivalry" (Thomas 2005, 207) of previous generations. Of course, complicating dominant narratives of women's victimization presents no easy solutions. How do we to disentangle ourselves from the engines creating the conditions of gendered violence both in Canada and around the world: myths, stereotypes, and normative expectations; regulation; media; capitalism; colonialism; neoliberalism; and globalization? And how do we do so responsibly, challenging the exploitation and violence engendered through our workplace practices and policies, consumption patterns, and international financial and trade agreements while also respecting women's agency, social and personal aspirations, and need for gainful employment? Moreover, how do we make sense of our own social location, the privileges and oppressions it engenders, and the inevitable partiality of our resistance? Extending beyond the frame of the conventional imagery and narrative of the lone victimized woman has provided a point of entry to recognize the contexts in which gendered violence plays out and interrogate the manifestations of gendered violence, resistance strategies, and the implications of regulatory responses for women in different social, economic, institutional, and geographical locations. Appreciating that gendered violence emerges in the context of inequality, and understanding the ways symbolic, interpersonal, state, structural, and slow violence interlock is, of course, merely the first step.

EXERCISE: IDEAL WORLD—PART 2

Envision a world where there is no gendered violence.

Write down what your ideal world would look like and how this might be achieved.

Compare this vision with the list you did for the exercise in the introductory chapter.

- Has your perspective changed?
- If so, how? If not, why do you think this is the case?
- Are you more or less optimistic about realizing a society without gendered violence?

Share your insights and reflections with other learners.

GLOSSARY

anti-essentialist position A perspective that does not frame a group (in the context of this book, women) as a uniform, coherent, and cohesive collective but rather acknowledges differences within the population (e.g., intersectionality).

carceral feminism A feminist perspective that envisions the criminal justice system (e.g., more robust and punitive laws; greater use of incarceration) as a mechanism to address gendered violence.

cultural capital The symbolic markers of class location, which can be embodied (e.g., taste, social competencies, mannerisms), material (e.g., markers of wealth such as clothes, property, home), or institutionalized (e.g., credentials or qualifications) (Bourdieu 1986).

cultural genocide The intentional targeting and destruction of the social and political structures and the cultural and religious practices through which a group affirms and perpetuates its identity. It is achieved by, for example, seizing land, forcibly transferring populations, and restricting their movement; banning languages; forbidding spiritual practices, persecuting spiritual leaders, and destroying objects of spiritual value; and disrupting families to impede the intergenerational transmission of values and identity (TRC 2015a).

cyber-misogyny A term coined to capture the diverse manifestations of gendered abuse, violence, and harassment directed toward women and girls on the Internet, including not only name calling and derogatory terms but also cyberstalking, cyberbullying, and extortion (West Coast Leaf 2014).

deviantization The social process by which a behaviour comes to be understood as deviant (e.g., media campaigns on drunk driving) or by which an individual comes to be perceived as deviant (e.g., through the response of social actors, agents of the state such as police, or state institutions such as the courts).

disciplinary power A form of power through which the productive value of the body is harnessed by transforming the mind and spirit. It manifests through training, hierarchical classification, surveillance, and examination, eventually fostering self-discipline or self-regulation of the subject's behaviour (Foucault 1979).

discourses Ways of describing ideas and issues (e.g., acceptable female sexuality and the ideal victim) that assign meaning to social practices. Circulated through the media, the education system, the government, and other political, social, and economic apparatuses, discourses become dominant "truths" or knowledges (Foucault 1980).

gaslighting A form of psychological abuse. Victimizers use manipulative tactics to foster self doubt and undermine their victim's confidence in their own opinions, perceptions, and memories.

governance feminism A strain of feminism that embraces regulatory solutions and whose adherents work alongside, or in, state apparatuses to effect change through legal and institutional mechanisms (Halley 2006).

interlocking systems of oppression Broad systems of social and/or economic organization, including, for example, capitalism, imperialism/colonialism, racism/racial hierarchies, sexism/gender hierarchies, which are interreliant and mutually constituting (Fellows and Razack 1998; Hill Collins 1991).

intersectionality Multiple aspects of identity shaping people's experiences; facets include but are not limited to gender, race, class, sexual orientation, dis/ability, age, citizenship status, ethnicity, and religion. These attributes are mutually constituted in and through hierarchical social structures (Hill Collins 2015; Crenshaw 1989).

invisible labour The work we do not see and/or do not consider. It includes work that is unpaid or underpaid (e.g., internships, promotional work); symbolically invisibilized (e.g., confused with gendered care work or with leisure); and physically and geographically obscured (e.g., through global outsourcing) (Poster et al. 2016).

LGBTQ An acronym commonly used to refer to lesbian, gay, bisexual, trans (including transgender, transsexual, and non-binary), and queer identities. In this text this term is intended to be inclusive of identities and experiences that cannot be defined as normatively heterosexual and/or cisgender.

mainstream second wave feminism The strain of feminism that dominated from the 1960s into the 1990s. This strain of feminism fought for increased state and regulatory tools to combat violence against women.

microaggressions Everyday indignities that can be verbal, behavioural, or environmental—and may or may not be intentional—that express discrimination, stereotypical assumptions, hostility, disrespect, or indifference toward racialized people, women, and members of other marginalized groups (Basford, Offermann, and Behrend 2014; Sue et al. 2007).

migrant A legal status assigned to individuals who are temporary workers in the country; migrants are excluded from many of the rights and protections to which Canadian citizens, landed immigrants, and refugees are entitled (e.g., healthcare, social services, and some labour protections) (CCR 2016a).

misogynoir A composite of misogyny and anti-Black racism. The term speaks to Black women's unique experiences of racism and systemic discrimination (Maynard 2017).

moral regulation A social and regulatory process that operates through the encouragement of normative forms of expression and the marginalization and prohibition of non-compliant behaviours, which are in turn framed as wrong and harmful (Corrigan 1981). In the neoliberal context, moral regulation is often expressed through narratives of risk (Hunt 1997).

neoliberalism An ideology that embraces the principle that individualized, market-based competition is the superior mode of organization and that has influenced social and economic policies to favour free markets, free trade, and private property rights (Harvey 2007; Mudge 2008). In its emphasis on personal autonomy, competition, and self-sufficiency, neoliberalism invisibilizes social and economic disadvantages engendered by social structures (Gingrich 2008).

patriarchy A mode of social organization premised on male authority, lineage, property rights, and political leadership; it is reflected, reproduced, and entrenched through discourses and ideologies holding men to be superior to women.

predatory violence Acts by individuals intent on harm; in this book it is used to describe violence perpetrated by an individual without a legitimate relationship to the workplace (Lowman 2000).

privilege A quality that emanates from identity characteristics favoured in the dominant social order (e.g., whiteness) that function as assets granting their holder unearned benefits (McIntosh 1989).

racial profiling A form of discrimination emanating from race-based stereotypes, wherein individuals are singled out, subjected to greater scrutiny, or otherwise treated differently on the basis of their (perceived) race, religion, colour, ethnicity, region, or ancestry (OHRC 2017).

resistance The tactics and strategies used to subvert, contest, or counter oppressive power relations, social structures, or dominant discourses. Resistance exists in a mutually constitutive relationship with power (Foucault 1980).

responsibilization The shifting of risk management and accountability onto individuals and away from social structures, institutions, and the state. This allows for individuals to be blamed for their own misfortune.

safety work The often unseen and unacknowledged work women do to prevent, avoid, and manage harassment on the street, online, in the workplace, and in other private, community, or public spaces (Vera-Gray 2014; 2016b).

scripts Normative expectations that provide guidelines for people's interactions in particular social contexts. Scripts inform both the performance and the perception of social roles, making them important for both parties in a social interaction (Longmore 1998).

sexual scripts Normative forces that, together with gendered scripts, govern how sexual interactions play out (Simon and Gagnon 1986).

situational violence Violence that is not premeditated but rather erupts in the context of an interaction or exchange. In this text it is applied to aggression directed at a worker by a client, consumer, or patient (Leblanc and Barling 2004).

slow violence The eventual outcomes of decisions made by and in the interests of state or non-governmental agents that may not appear violent but precipitate harms (Nixon 2011). For example, neoliberal austerity measures set in motion the slow violence of healthcare and welfare cutbacks, resulting in increases in ill health among low-income Canadians.

social determinants of health The social, institutional, and interpersonal factors and resources that affect and facilitate health and well-being or, if they are lacking, ill health. Examples of social determinants of health include income, employment, education, housing, child development, healthcare, and social support networks (Montesanti and Thurston 2015).

social profiling Discrimination on the basis of visible signs of poverty or marginality, which pivots on class-based stereotypes and stigmatic assumptions (CDPDJ 2009).

stigma A negatively perceived attribute that discredits and taints its bearer. Stigma is not analogous to a stereotype, but rather that element of an individual's identity (e.g., disability, race, gender) that marks them as different and "less than" (Goffman 1963).

structural discrimination Occurs when laws, policies, and practices pivoting on normative assumptions implicitly serve to disadvantage some groups (albeit not with the explicit goal of doing so) and in turn work to the advantage of more privileged populations (Link and Phelan 2001).

structural stigma When a population is, based on stereotypes or discriminatory assumptions, perceived to be risky or at-risk; this perception justifies regulation, surveillance, and intervention to manage individuals belonging to the (risky) group (Hannem 2012).

structural violence The violence resulting from and facilitated through social structures and institutions that create and entrench inequality, systematically undermining the ability of individuals to realize their potential (Galtung 1969).

symbolic violence A product of symbolic power. Symbolic power is the ability to create distinctions and ascribe value and, thereby, affirm the categorizations and hierarchical assessment that permeate the social realm (e.g., taste, culture, credentials). For example, the state, the church, the media, and the law exercise power over the symbolic—the power to define. Symbolic violence occurs when these distinctions—and the associated hierarchical assessment—are naturalized, perceived as common sense, and accepted, even when we know better (Bourdieu 1990, 1998).

WORKS CITED

AAPF (African American Policy Forum). 2015. "#SayHerName." http://
www.aapf.org/sayhername/.

Abbott, Karen. 2014. "'The Hatpin Peril': Terrorized Men Who Couldn't
Handle the 20th-Century Woman." *Smithsonian Magazine*, April 24.
https://www.smithsonianmag.com/history/hatpin-peril-terrorized-
men-who-couldnt-handle-20th-century-woman-180951219/?no-ist.

Abraham, Margaret, and Evangelia Tastsoglou. 2016. "Addressing Domestic
Violence in Canada and the United States: The Uneasy Co-habitation
of Women and the State." *Violence Against Women* 64 (4): 568–85.

Abu-Ras, Wahiba M., and Zulema E. Suarez. 2009. "Muslim Men and
Women's Perception of Discrimination, Hate Crimes, and PTSD
Symptoms Post 9/11." *Traumatology* 15 (3): 48–63. https://doi.
org/10.1177/1534765609342281.

Adams, Adrienne, Chris Sullivan, Deborah Bybee, and Megan Greeson.
2008. "Development of the Scale of Economic Abuse." *Violence Against
Women* 14 (5): 563–88. https://doi.org/10.1177/1077801208315529.

Addo, Frankly. 2017. "University Is Still a White Middle-Class
Affair—It's Not Just Cambridge." *The Guardian*, February 14.
https://www.theguardian.com/commentisfree/2017/feb/14/
university-white-middle-class-cambridge-diverse-education.

Aggarwal, Ujju, Edwin Mayorga, and Donna Nevel. 2012. "Slow Violence
and Neoliberal Education Reform: Reflections on a School Closure."
Peace and Conflict 18 (2): 156–64. https://doi.org/10.1037/a0028099.

AHRC (Alberta Human Rights Commission). 2012. "Sexual Harassment
Information Sheet." https://www.albertahumanrights.ab.ca/
Documents/SexualHarass.pdf.

Alberta Education. 2016. "Guidelines for Best Practices: Creating Learning
Environments that Respect Diverse Sexual and Gender Identities and

Expressions." https://education.alberta.ca/media/1626737/91383-attachment-1-guidelines-final.pdf.

Allard, Sharon. 1991. "Rethinking Battered Woman Syndrome: A Black Feminist Perspective." *UCLA Women's Law Journal* 1: 191–207.

Alvarez, Alex, and Ronet Bachman. 2016. *Violence: The Enduring Problem*. Los Angeles, CA: Sage.

Ameeriar, Lalaie. 2012. "The Gendered Suspect: Women at the Canada–U.S. Border after September 11." *Journal of Asian American Studies* 15 (2): 171–95. https://doi.org/10.1353/jaas.2012.0014.

Amnesty International. 2004. "Canada—Stolen Sisters: A Human Rights Response to Discrimination and Violence against Indigenous Women in Canada." https://www.amnesty.ca/sites/amnesty/files/Stolen%20Sisters%202004%20Summary%20Report_0.pdf.

Anderson, Hanah, and Matt Daniels. 2016. "A Polygraph Joint: Film Dialogue from 2,000 Screenplays, Broken Down by Gender and Age." *Polygraph*. http://polygraph.cool/films/.

Anderson, Kim. 2010. "Affirmations of an Indigenous Feminist." In *Indigenous Women, and Feminism: Politics, Activism, Culture*, edited by Cheryl Zuzack, Sharu Huhndorg, Jeanne Perreault, and Jean Barman, 81–91. Vancouver: University of British Columbia Press.

Anderson, Solanna, Jessica Xi Liu, Vivian Liu, Jill Chattier, Andrea Krüsi, Sarah Allan, Lisa Maher, and Kate Shannon. 2015. "Violence Prevention and Municipal Licensing of Indoor Sex Work Venues in the Greater Vancouver Area: Narratives of Migrant Sex Workers, Managers and Business Owners." *Culture, Health & Sexuality* 17 (7): 825–41. https://doi.org/10.1080/13691058.2015.1008046.

Aniston, Jennifer. 2016. "For the Record." *The Huffington Post*, July 12. https://www.huffingtonpost.com/entry/for-the-record_us_57855586e4b03fc3ee4e626f.

APTN News. 2017. "Bill Passes to End Discrimination in the *Indian Act*." December 6. http://aptnnews.ca/2017/12/06/bill-end-discrimination-indian-act-passes-vote-senate/.

Armstrong, Elizabeth A., Laura Hamilton, Elizabeth M. Armstrong, and Lotus Seeley. 2014. "'Good Girls': Gender, Social Class, and Slut Discourse on Campus." *Social Psychology Quarterly* 77 (2): 100–22. https://doi.org/10.1177/0190272514521220.

Armstrong, Lynzi. 2016. "'Who's the Slut, Who's the Whore?' Street Harassment in the Workplace among Female Sex Workers in New Zealand." *Feminist Criminology* 11 (3): 285–303. https://doi.org/10.1177/1557085115588553.

Armstrong, Pat, Hugh Armstrong, Albert Banerjee, Tamara Daly, and Marta Szebehely. 2011. "Structural Violence in Long-Term Residential Care." *Women's Health & Urban Life* 10 (1): 111–29.

Arriagada, Paula. 2016. *First Nations, Metis and Inuit Women*. Ottawa, ON: Statistics Canada. http://www.statcan.gc.ca/pub/89-503-x/2015001/article/14313-eng.htm.

ASPS (American Society of Plastic Surgeons). 2016. "New Statistics Reflect the Changing Face of Plastic Surgery." News release, February 25. https://www.plasticsurgery.org/news/press-releases/new-statistics-reflect-the-changing-face-of-plastic-surgery.

AVP (Anti-Violence Project). 2003. "Building Safer Communities for Lesbian, Gay, Transgender, Bisexual and HIV-Affected New Yorkers." New York City Gay & Lesbian Anti-Violence Project. http://www.ncavp.org/backup/document_files/DVWheel.pdf.

AWCBC (Association of Workers Compensations Boards of Canada). n.d. "Fatality Statistics." http://awcbc.org/?page_id=14.

Axelrod, Paul. 1990. "Student Life in Canadian Universities: The Lessons of History." *Canadian Journal of Higher Education* 20 (3): 17–28.

Backhouse, Constance. 1985. "Nineteenth-Century Canadian Prostitution Law: Reflection of a Discriminatory Society." *Histoire Sociale* 18 (36): 387–423.

———. 1991. *Petticoats & Prejudice: Women and Law in Nineteenth Century Canada*. Toronto, ON: Women's Press.

———. 2001. "The Historical Construction of Racial Identity and Implications for Reconciliation." Paper presented at the Department of Canadian Heritage for the Ethnocultural, Racial, Religious, and Linguistic Diversity and Identity Seminar, Halifax, Nova Scotia, November 1–2.

Backhouse, Constance, Donald McRae, and Nitya Lyer. 2015. *Report of the Task Force on Misogyny, Sexism, and Homophobia in Dalhousie University Faculty of Dentistry*. Halifax: Dalhousie University.

Bailey, Jane, and Valerie Steeves. 2013. "Will the Real Digital Girl Please Stand Up?" In *New Visualities, New Technologies: The New Ecstasy of Communication*, edited by Hille Koskela and J. Macgregor Wise, 41–66. New York: Ashgate Publishing.

Bains, Marc. 2015. "Why Doesn't Serena Williams Have More Sponsorship Deals?" *The Atlantic*, August 31. https://www.theatlantic.com/entertainment/archive/2015/08/serena-williams-sponsorship-nike-us-open/402985/.

Bakan, Abigail B., and Daiva Stasiulis. 1997. "Foreign Domestic Worker Policy and the Social Boundaries of Modern Citizenship." In *Not One of the Family: Foreign Domestic Workers in Canada*, edited by Abigail Bakan and Daiva Stasiulis, 29–52. Toronto, ON: University of Toronto Press. https://doi.org/10.3138/9781442677944-004.

Baker, Douglas D., David E. Terpstra, and Kinley Larntz. 1990. "The Influence of Individual Characteristics and Severity of Harassing Behavior on Reactions to Sexual Harassment." *Sex Roles* 22 (5–6): 305–25. https://doi.org/10.1007/BF00288336.

Baker, Katie. 2016. "Here Is the Powerful Letter the Stanford Victim Read Aloud to Her Attacker." *BuzzFeed News*, June 3. https://www.buzzfeed.com/katiejmbaker/heres-the-powerful-letter-the-stanford-victim-read-to-her-ra?utm_term=.tloRE70QJ#.fdWjYbZ67.

Balfour, Gillian. 2008. "Falling between the Cracks of Retributive and Restorative Justice: The Victimization and Punishment of Aboriginal Women." *Feminist Criminology* 3 (2): 101–20. https://doi.org/10.1177/1557085108317551.

———. 2012. "Do Law Reforms Matter? Exploring the Victimization–Criminalization Continuum in the Sentencing of Aboriginal Women in Canada." *International Review of Victimology* 19 (1): 85–102.

———. 2014a. "Regulating Women: Introduction." In *Criminalizing Women: Gender and (In)Justice in Neo-Liberal Times*, 2nd ed., edited by Gillian Balfour and Elizabeth Comack, 146–76. Winnipeg, MB: Fernwood.

———. 2014b. "Sentencing Aboriginal Women to Prison." In *Within the Confines: Women and the Law in Canada*, edited by Jennifer Kilty, 93–116. Toronto, ON: Women's Press.

Balkissoon, Denise. 2018. "Even after Death, Canada Denies Tina Fontaine Dignity." *The Globe and Mail*, February 28. https://www.theglobeandmail.com/opinion/even-after-death-canada-denies-tina-fontaine-dignity/article37821254/.

Bandele, Monifa, Zahra Billoo, Gaylynn Burroughs, Melanie L. Campbell, Sung Yeon Choimorrow, Alida Garcia, Alicia Garza, Carol Jenkins, Avis Jones-DeWeever, Carol Joyner, Janet Mock, Jessica Neuwirth, Terry O'Neill, Carmen Perez, Jody Rabhan, Kelley Robinson, Kristin Rowe-Finkbeiner, Linda Sarsour, Heidi L. Sieck, Emily Tisch Sussman, Jennifer Tucker, and Winnie Wong. 2017. Guiding Vision and Definition of Principles. The Women's March on Washington. https://static1.squarespace.com/static/584086c7be6594762f5ec56e/t/587ffb20579fb355 4668c111/1484782369253/WMW+Guiding+Vision+%26+Definition+of+Principles.pdf.

Banerjee, Albert, Tamara Daly, Hugh Armstrong, Pat Armstrong, Stirling Lafrance, and Marta Szebehely. 2008. *"Out of Control": Violence against Personal Support Workers in Long-Term Care.* Toronto, ON: York University and Carleton University. https://www.longwoods.com/articles/images/ Violence_LTC_022408_Final.pdf.

Banet-Weiser, Sarah. 2017. "'I'm Beautiful the Way I Am': Empowerment, Beauty, and Aesthetic Labour." In *Aesthetic Labour: Rethinking Beauty Politics in Neoliberalism*, edited by Ana Sofia Elias, Rosalind Gill, and Christina Scharff, 265–82. London, UK: Palgrave Macmillan. https://doi.org/10.1057/978-1-137-47765-1_15.

Banner, Lois. 1983. *American Beauty*. Chicago, IL: University of Chicago Press.

Barry, Kathleen. 1979. *Female Sexual Slavery*. Upper Saddle River, NJ: Prentice-Hall.

Bartholomew, Kathleen. 2006. *Ending Nurse-to-Nurse Violence: Why Nurses Eat Their Young*. Marblehead, MA: HCPro.

Bartky, Sandra Lee. 1997. "Foucault, Femininity, and the Modernization of Patriarchal Power." In *Feminist Social Thought: A Reader*, edited by Diana T. Meyers, 93–111. New York: Routledge.

Barton, Adriana. 2014. "And the Top 10 Most Dangerous Jobs Are …" *The Globe and Mail*, January 15. https://www.theglobeandmail.com/ life/the-hot-button/and-the-top-10-most-dangerous-jobs-are/ article16352517/.

Bartow, Anne. 2012. "Sexual Assault Prevention Tips Guaranteed to Work." *Silent Thoughts* (blog), December 21. https:// wordingmythoughts.wordpress.com/2012/12/21/ sexual-assault-prevention-tips-guaranteed-to-work/.

Basford, Tessa E., Lynn R. Offermann, and Tara S. Behrend. 2014. "Do You See What I See? Perceptions of Gender Microaggressions in the Workplace." *Psychology of Women Quarterly* 38 (3): 340–9. https://doi.org/10.1177/0361684313511420.

Bashwira, Marie-Rose, Jeroen Cuvelier, Dorothea Hilhorst, and Gemma van der Haar. 2014. "Not Only a Man's World: Women's Involvement in Artisanal Mining in Eastern DRC." *Resources Policy* 40: 109–16. https:// doi.org/10.1016/j.resourpol.2013.11.002.

Bauer, Greta R., and Ayden I. Scheim. 2015. *Transgender People in Ontario, Canada: Statistics to Inform Human Rights Policy*. Trans PULSE Project. http://transpulseproject.ca/research/statistics-from-trans-pulse-to-inform-human-rights-policy/.

BCNU (BC Nurses' Union). 2017a. "BCNU Violence Hotline." https:// www.bcnu.org/a-safe-workplace/health-and-safety/bcnu-violence-hotline.

———. 2017b. "Violence. Not Part of the Job." https://www.bcnu.org/ news-and-events/campaigns-and-initiatives/current-campaigns/violence.

Bechdel, Alison. 1985. "The Rule." http://bechdeltestfest.com/about/.

Becker, Howard. 1973. *Outsiders: Studies in the Sociology of Deviance.* New York: The Free Press.

Belak, Brenda, and Darci Bennett. 2016. *Evaluating Canada's Sex Work Laws: The Case for Repeal.* Vancouver, BC: Pivot Legal Society.

Benedet, Janine, Scott Anderson, Shauna Butterwick, Natalie Clark, Sarah Hunt, and Lucia Lorenzi. 2016. *Sexual Assault at the University of British Columbia: Prevention, Response, and Accountability.* Vancouver, BC: University of British Columbia. http://fnis2017.sites.olt.ubc.ca/files/2016/09/USAP-Report-20-June-Submitted.pdf.

Benoit, Cecilia, and Leah Shumka. 2015. "Sex Work in Canada." Centre for Addictions Research, May 7. http://www.understandingsexwork.ca/sites/default/files/uploads/2015%2005%2007%20Benoit%20%26%20Shumka%20Sex%20Work%20in%20Canada_1.pdf.

Benoit, Cecilia, Leah Shumka, Rachel Phillips, Mary Clare Kennedy, and Lynne Belle-Isle. 2015. "Issue Brief: Sexual Violence against Women in Canada." Brief commissioned by the Federal-Provincial-Territorial Senior Officials for the Status of Women, December. http://www.swc-cfc.gc.ca/svawc-vcsfc/issue-brief-en.pdf.

Benoit, Cecilia, Michaela Smith, Mikael Jansson, Samantha Magnus, Nadia Ouellet, Chris Atchison, Lauren Casey, Rachel Phillips, Bill Reimer, Dan Reist, et al. 2016. "Lack of Confidence in Police Creates a 'Blue Ceiling' for Sex Workers' Safety." *Canadian Public Policy* 42 (4): 456–68. https://doi.org/10.3138/cpp.2016-006.

Benston, Margaret. 1969. "The Political Economy of Women's Liberation." *Monthly Review* 21 (4): 31–44. https://doi.org/10.14452/MR-021-04-1969-08_2.

Beres, Melanie A. 2014. "Rethinking the Concept of Consent for Anti-Sexual Violence Activism and Education." *Feminism & Psychology* 24 (3): 373–89. https://doi.org/10.1177/0959353514539652.

Berger, John. 1972. *Ways of Seeing.* London, UK: British Broadcasting Corporation and Penguin Books.

Bernier, Liz. 2014. "Culture of Enforcement." *Canadian HR Reporter,* December 1. www.hrreporter.com.

Bernstein, Elizabeth. 2010. "Militarized Humanitarianism Meets Carceral Feminism: The Politics of Sex, Rights, and Freedom in Contemporary Antitrafficking Campaigns." *Signs* 36 (1): 45–71. https://doi.org/10.1086/652918.

Bhuyan, Rupaleem, Bethany Osborne, Sajedeh Zahraei, and Sarah Tarshis. 2014. *Unprotected, Unrecognized: Canadian Immigration Policy and Violence against Women, 2008–2013.* Toronto, ON: Migrant Mothers Project.

Bird, Elizabeth. 2002. "The Academic Arm of the Women's Liberation Movement: Women's Studies 1969–1999 in North America and the United Kingdom." *Women's Studies International Forum* 25 (1): 139–49. https://doi.org/10.1016/S0277-5395(02)00217-0.

Bittle, Steven. 2012. *Still Dying for a Living: Corporate Crime Liability after the Westray Mine Disaster.* Vancouver, BC: University of British Columbia Press.

Black Lives Matter. n.d. "A HerStory of the #BlackLivesMatter Movement." https://blacklivesmatter.com/about/herstory/.

Blackstock, Cindy. 2015. "Should Governments Be above the Law? The Canadian Human Rights Tribunal on First Nations Child Welfare." *Children Australia* 40 (2): 95–103. https://doi.org/10.1017/cha.2015.6.

Block, Sheila, and Grace-Edward Galabuzi. 2011. *Canada's Colour Coded Labour Market: The Gap for Racialized Workers.* Ottawa, ON: Canadian Centre for Policy Alternatives.

BlogTO. 2017. "Pride Toronto Says Yes to Black Lives Matter Demands." January 18. https://www.blogto.com/city/2017/01/pride-toronto-says-yes-black-lives-matter-demands/.

Boateng, Godfred O. 2015. "Exploring the Career Pathways, Professional Integration and Lived Experiences of Regulated Nurses in Ontario, Canada." PhD diss., McMaster University.

Boateng, Godfred O., and Tracey L. Adams. 2016. "'Drop Dead … I Need Your Job': An Exploratory Study of Intra-Professional Conflict amongst Nurses in Two Ontario Cities." *Social Science & Medicine* 155: 35–42. https://doi.org/10.1016/j.socscimed.2016.02.045.

Bonazzo, John. 2016. "Leslie Jones Called Out Racist 'Ghostbusters' Trolls on Twitter." *Observer*, July 18. http://observer.com/2016/07/leslie-jones-called-out-racist-ghostbusters-fans-on-twitter/.

Borel, Kathryn. 2016. "Statement from Kathryn Borel on Jian Ghomeshi." *The Globe and Mail*, May 11. https://www.theglobeandmail.com/news/national/statement-from-kathryn-borel-on-jian-ghomeshi/article29974726/.

Bourdieu, Pierre. 1984. *Distinction: A Social Critique of the Judgement of Taste.* London, UK: Routledge.

———. 1986. "The Forms of Capital." In *Handbook of Theory and Research for the Sociology of Education*, edited by J. Richardson, 241–58. New York: Greenwood.

———. 1990. *The Logic of Practice.* Cambridge, MA: Polity Press.

———. 1998. *Masculine Domination.* Stanford, CA: Stanford University Press.

———. 2007. *Sketch for a Self-Analysis.* Translated by R. Nice. Chicago, IL: University of Chicago Press.

Boutilier, Alex. 2017. "Liberal MP Swamped by Hate Mail, Threats over Anti-Islamophobia Motion in Commons." *Toronto Star*, February 16. https://www.thestar.com/news/canada/2017/02/16/liberal-mp-swamped-by-hate-mail-threats-over-anti-islamophobia-motion-in-commons.html.

Bowland, Adelyn. 1994. "Sexual Assault Trials and the Protection of 'Bad Girls': The Battle between the Courts and Parliament." In *Confronting Sexual Assault: A Decade of Legal and Social Change*, edited by Julian Roberts and Renate Mohr, 241–67. Toronto, ON: University of Toronto Press.

Boyle, Kaitlin M. 2015. "Social Psychological Processes That Facilitate Sexual Assault within the Fraternity Party Subculture." *Sociology Compass* 9 (5): 386–99. https://doi.org/10.1111/soc4.12261.

Brennan, Shannon, and Andrea Taylor-Butts. 2008. *Sexual Assault in Canada, 2004 and 2007*. Ottawa, ON: Statistics Canada. http://www.statcan.gc.ca/pub/85f0033m/85f0033m2008019-eng.pdf.

Brewer, Kirstie. 2015. "The Day Iceland's Women Went on Strike." *BBC News*, October 23. http://www.bbc.com/news/magazine-34602822.

Brock, Deborah. 2003. "Moving beyond Deviance: Power, Regulation and Governmentality." In *Making Normal: Social Regulation in Canada*, edited by Deborah Brock, 9–31. Toronto, ON: Nelson Thompson Learning.

Brock, Deborah, Kara Gillies, Chantelle Oliver, and Mook Sutdhibhasilp. 2000. "Migrant Sex Work: A Roundtable Analysis." *Canadian Women's Studies* 20 (2): 84–91.

Broll, Ryan, and Laura Huey. 2015. "'Just Being Mean to Somebody Isn't a Police Matter': Police Perspectives on Policing Cyberbullying." *Journal of School Violence* 14 (2): 155–76. https://doi.org/10.1080/15388220.2013.879367.

Bronskill, Jim. 2016. "RCMP Earmarks $100M in Compensation for Sexual Harassment against Female Mounties." *Global News*, October 6. https://globalnews.ca/news/2986688/rcmp-to-settle-in-class-action-harassment-claims-from-former-mounties/.

Brooks, Kim. 2002. "Finding Answers: The Kimberly Rogers Inquest." *Jurisfemme Publications* 21 (3). http://nawl.ca/en/jurisfemme/entry/finding-answers-the-kimberly-rogers-inquest.

Brophy, James, Margaret Keith, and Michael Hurley. 2017. "Assaulted and Unheard: Violence against Healthcare Staff." *New Solutions* 27 (4): 1–26.

Brown, Lorne. 1992. "The RCMP and Its Ancestors." In *Re-thinking the Administration of Justice*, edited by Dawn Currie and Brian MacLean, 185–213. Halifax, NS: Fernwood.

Brown, Taylor, and Jody Herman. 2015. *Intimate Partner Violence and Sexual Abuse among LGBT People: A Review of Existing Research.* Los Angeles, CA: The William Institute.

Brown, Trevor. 2000. *Charging and Prosecution Policies in Cases of Spousal Assault: A Synthesis of Research, Academic, and Judicial Responses.* Ottawa, ON: Department of Justice.

Browne, Tamara Kayali. 2015. "Is Premenstrual Dysphoric Disorder Really a Disorder?" *Journal of Bioethical Inquiry* 12 (2): 313–30. https://doi.org/10.1007/s11673-014-9567-7.

Brownmiller, Susan. 1975. *Against Our Will: Men, Women and Rape.* New York: Simon & Schuster.

Bruckert, Chris, and Stacey Hannem. 2013. "'Rethinking the Prostitution Debates: Transcending Structural Stigma in Systemic Responses to Sex Work." *Canadian Journal of Law and Society* 28 (10): 43–63.

Bruckert, Chris, and Colette Parent. 2004. *Organized Crime and Human Trafficking in Canada: Tracing Perceptions and Discourses.* Ottawa, ON: Royal Canadian Mounted Police.

Buckley, Kelly. 2010 "'Keeping It Real': Young Working Class Femininities and Celebrity Culture." PhD diss., Cardiff University School of Social Sciences.

Budd, John W. 2016. "The Eye Sees What the Mind Knows: The Conceptual Foundations of Invisible Work." In *Invisible Labor: Hidden Work in the Contemporary World*, edited by Marion G. Crain, Winifred R. Poster, and Miriam A. Cherry, 28–46. Oakland, CA: University of California Press.

Burawoy, Michael. 2008. "Durable Domination: Gramsci Meets Bourdieu." Lecture presented at the Haven Centre, University of Wisconsin, Madison, March 19.

Burczycka, Marta. 2016. *Family Violence in Canada: A Statistical Profile, 2014.* Ottawa, ON: Canadian Centre for Justice Statistics. http://www.statcan.gc.ca/pub/85-002-x/2016001/article/14303-eng.pdf.

Butler, Bethonie. 2014. "The Story Behind That '10 Hours of Walking in NYC' Viral Street Harassment Video." *Washington Post*, October 29. https://www.washingtonpost.com/blogs/she-the-people/wp/2014/10/29/the-story-behind-that-10-hours-of-walking-in-nyc-viral-street-harassment-video/?utm_term=.84607db587d7.

Butler, Judith. 1990. *Gender Trouble: Feminism and the Subversion of Identity.* New York: Routledge.

———. 1999. "Performativity's Social Magic." In *Bourdieu: A Critical Reader*, edited by Richard Schusterman, 113–28. Oxford, UK: Blackwell.

Butler Burke, Nora. 2018. "Double Punishment: Immigration Penalty and Migrant Trans Women Who Sell Sex." In *Red Light Labour: Sex Work*

Regulation, Agency and Resistance, edited by Elya Durisin, Emily van der Meulen, and Chris Bruckert, 203-12. Vancouver, BC: University of British Colombia Press.

Butterfly (Asian and Migrant Sex Workers Network). n.d. *Butterfly Voices: Collecting Stories of Migrant Sex Workers around the World*. Toronto, ON: Butterfly.

———. 2015. "Stop the Harm from Anti-Trafficking Policies & Campaigns: Support Sex Workers' Rights, Justice, and Dignity." https://www. butterflysw.org/harm-of-anti-trafficking-campaign-.

———. 2016. *Journey of the Butterflies*. Toronto, ON: Butterfly.

Cabezas, Amalia L., Ellen Reese, and Marguerite Waller, eds. 2008. *The Wages of Empire: Neoliberal Policies, Repression, and Women's Poverty*. Boulder, CO: Paradigm.

Cabrera, Nolan León. 2014. "Exposing Whiteness in Higher Education: White Male College Students Minimizing Racism, Claiming Victimization, and Recreating White Supremacy." *Race, Ethnicity and Education* 17 (1): 30–55. https://doi.org/10.1080/13613324.2012.725040.

Cader, Fathima, and Brittany-Andrew Amofah. 2016. "Why Do Discussions about Carding Ignore the Experiences of Women and Trans People?" *NOW*, November 28. https://nowtoronto.com/news/ carding-racial-profiling-women-trans-people/.

Calliste, Agnes. 1989. "Canada's Immigration Policy and Domestics from the Caribbean: The Second Domestic Scheme." In *Race, Class, Gender: Bonds and Barriers*, edited by Jesse Vorst, 133–65. Winnipeg: The Society for Socialist Studies.

———. 1993. "Women of Exceptional Merit: Immigration of Caribbean Nurses to Canada." *Canadian Journal of Women and the Law* 6 (1): 85–102.

Campbell, Kathryn. 2018. *Miscarriages of Justice in Canada: Causes, Responses, Remedies*. Toronto, ON: University of Toronto Press.

Canadian Nurses Association. 2014. "Joint Position Statement: Workplace Violence and Bullying." http://cna-aiic.ca/~/media/cna/page-content/ pdf-en/workplace-violence-and-bullying_joint-position-statement.pdf.

Canby, Vincent. 1980. "'Nine to Five,' Office Comedy." *The New York Times*, December 19. http://www.nytimes.com/movie/review?res=950DEEDE 1538F93AA25751C1A966948260.

CAP (Congress of Aboriginal Peoples). 2012. *Final Report: Exploratory Process on Indian Registration, Band Membership and Citizenship*. Ottawa, ON: Congress of Aboriginal Peoples.

Capers, Bennett. 2012. "Real Women, Real Rape." *UCLA Law Review* 60 (4): 826–82.

Carbone, Gina. 2015. "Carrie Fisher Blasts Superficial Fans: 'Youth and Beauty Are Not Accomplishments'." *Moviefone*, December 30. https://www.moviefone.com/2015/12/30/carrie-fisher-blasts-superficial-fans-youth-and-beauty-are-not-accomplishments/.

Cardinal, Colleen, and Kristen Gilchrist. 2014. "Resisting Colonial Violence(s) Together: Stories of Loss, Renewal, and Friendship from Algonquin Territory." In *Within the Confines: Women and the Law in Canada*, edited by Jennifer M. Kilty, 35–51. Toronto, ON: Women's Press.

Cartar, Lydia, Melanie Hicks, and Steve Slane. 1996. "Women's Reactions to Hypothetical Male Sexual Touch as a Function of Initiator Attractiveness and Level of Coercion." *Sex Roles* 35 (11–12): 737–50. https://doi.org/10.1007/BF01544089.

Carter, Sarah. 1993. "Categories and Terrains of Exclusion: Constructing the 'Indian Woman' in the Early Settlement Era in Western Canada." *Great Plains Quarterly* 13: 147–61.

CASWLR and Pivot. 2016. "Joint Submission for Canada's Review before the UN Committee on the Elimination of All Forms of Discrimination against Women, 65th Session." http://tbinternet.ohchr.org/Treaties/CEDAW/Shared%20Documents/CAN/INT_CEDAW_NGO_CAN_25385_E.pdf.

Catalyst. 2017. "Women CEOs of the S&P 500." June 14. http://www.catalyst.org/knowledge/women-ceos-sp-500.

Caven, Febna. 2013. "Being Idle No More: The Women behind the Movement." *Cultural Survival Quarterly Magazine* 37 (1): 6–7. https://www.culturalsurvival.org/publications/cultural-survival-quarterly/being-idle-no-more-women-behind-movement.

CBA (Canadian Bar Association). 2010. *Bill C-3: Gender Equity in Indian Registration Act*. Ottawa, ON: CBA, National Aboriginal Law Section.

CBC. 1998. "Montreal Massacre: Legacy of Pain" (video). *Fifth Estate*, December 1. http://www.cbc.ca/fifth/episodes/40-years-of-the-fifth-estate/montreal-massacre-a-legacy-of-pain.

———. 2014. "Lauren Wiggins, Moncton Teen, Takes Stand against 'Unjust' School Dress Code." *CBC News*, May 4. http://www.cbc.ca/news/canada/new-brunswick/lauren-wiggins-moncton-teen-takes-stand-against-unjust-school-dress-code-1.3071203.

———. 2016a. "Coquitlam Mayor Richard Stewart Wore Same Suit for 15 Months and Nobody Noticed." *CBC News*, February 23. http://www.cbc.ca/news/canada/british-columbia/coquitlam-richard-stewart-suit-1.3459469.

———. 2016b. "Sexting: Schools Stepping up to Help Kids" (video). *The National*, October 5. https://www.youtube.com/watch?v= lZ6UrObr274.

———. 2016c. "Sixties Scoop Survivors Recall Painful Memories in Ontario." *CBC News*, August 23. http://www.cbc.ca/news/canada/ toronto/sixties-scoop-supporters-1.3732037.

CCCP (Canadian Centre for Child Protection). 2014. "Keeping Teens Safe from Online Sexual Exploitation." https://www.cybertip.ca/pdfs/ C3P_SaferInternetDay_KeepingTeensSafe_en.pdf.

———. 2017. "A Resource Guide for Families: Addressing Self/Peer Exploitation." https://www.cybertip.ca/pdfs/SPEX_FamilyGuide_ Web_single_en.pdf.

CCOHS (Canadian Centre for Occupational Health and Safety). 2012. "Violence in the Workplace." http://www.ccohs.ca/oshanswers/ psychosocial/violence.html.

———. 2016. "Violence against Health Care Workers. It's Not 'Part of the Job'." *Health and Safety Report* 13 (9). http://www.ccohs.ca/newsletters/ hsreport/issues/2015/09/ezine.html.

———. 2017. "Bullying in the Workplace." Government of Canada. https:// www.ccohs.ca/oshanswers/psychosocial/bullying.html.

CCR (Canadian Council for Refugees). 2016a. "Migrant Workers: Precarious and Unsupported—A Canada-Wide Study on Access to Services for Migrant Workers." http://ccrweb.ca/sites/ccrweb.ca/files/ migrant-workers-2016.pdf.

———. 2016b. "Temporary Foreign Worker Program: A Submission by the Canadian Council for Refugees to the Standing Committee on Human Resources, Skills and Social Development and the Status of Persons with Disabilities." http://ccrweb.ca/sites/ccrweb.ca/files/tfwp-review- submission_1.pdf.

CDPDJ (Commission des droits de la personne et des droits de la jeunesse). 2009. "The Judiciarization of the Homeless in Montréal: A Case of Social Profiling—Executive Summary of the Opinion of the Commission." http://www.cdpdj.qc.ca/Publications/Homeless_ Summary.pdf.

CFLR (Canadian Foundation for Labour Rights). 2016. Restrictive Labour Laws in Canada: Summary of Legislation Restricting Collective Bargaining and Trade Union Rights in Canada, 1982–2016. https:// labourrights.ca/issues/restrictive-labour-laws-canada.

CGSP (Centre for Global Social Policy). 2017. "Canada Quietly Introduced New Rules for Migrant Caregivers in November 2014." Gender, Migration, & the Work of Care. http://cgsp.ca/story/

canada-quietly-introduced-new-rules-for-migrant-caregivers-in-november-2014/.

Chambers, Lori. 2007. "Unprincipled Exclusions: Feminist Theory, Transgender Jurisprudence, and Kimberly Nixon." *Canadian Journal of Women and the Law* 19 (2): 305–34.

Chan, Wendy, and Dorothy Chunn. 2014. *Racialization, Crime, and Criminal Justice in Canada.* Toronto, ON: University of Toronto Press.

Chapman, Ben. 2017. "International Women's Day 2017: Iceland Becomes First Country in the World to Make Firms Prove Equal Pay." *Independent*, March 8. http://www.independent.co.uk/news/business/news/iceland-equal-pay-international-womens-day-2017-world-first-country-a7618986.html?cmpid=facebook-post.

Chatelain, Marcia, and Kaavya Asoka. 2015. "Women and Black Lives Matter." *Dissent* 62 (3): 54–61. https://doi.org/10.1353/dss.2015.0059.

Chechak, Derek, and Rick Csiernik. 2014. "Canadian Perspectives on Conceptualizing and Responding to Workplace Violence." *Journal of Workplace Behavioral Health* 29 (1): 55–72. https://doi.org/10.1080/15555240.2014.866474.

Chiasson, Ali. 2017. "Toronto Woman's Facebook Photos from Women's March Flooded with Sexist Comments." *CBC News*, January 17. http://www.cbc.ca/news/canada/toronto/facebook-toronto-women-march-women-s-march-sexist-1.3956339.

Cho, Sumi, Kimberlé Williams Crenshaw, and Leslie McCall. 2013. "Toward a Field of Intersectionality Studies: Theory, Applications, and Praxis." *Signs* 38 (4): 785–810. https://doi.org/10.1086/669608.

Chunn, Dorothy, and Shelley Gavigan. 2014. "From Welfare Fraud to Welfare as Fraud: The Criminalization of Poverty." In *Criminalizing Women: Gender and (In)Justice in Neoliberal Times*, 2nd ed., edited by Gillian Balfour and Elizabeth Comack, 197–218. Winnipeg, MB: Fernwood.

Clamen, Jenn, and Kara Gillies. 2018. "Will the Real Supporters of Workers' Rights Please Stand Up? Union Engagement with Sex Work in Canada." In *Red Light Labour: Sex Work Regulation, Agency and Resistance*, edited by Elya Durisin, Emily van der Meulen, and Chris Bruckert, 305–16. Vancouver, BC: University of British Colombia Press.

Clark, Lynda. 2014. "Women in Niqab Speak: A Study of the Niqab in Canada." Canadian Council of Muslim Women. http://ccmw.com/wp-content/uploads/2013/10/WEB_EN_WiNiqab_FINAL.pdf.

CLC (Canadian Labour Congress). 2011. Model Program—or Mistake? http://ccrweb.ca/files/clc_model-program-or-mistake-2011.pdf.

———. 2015. "Ending Violence against Women." http://canadianlabour.ca/issues-research/ending-violence-against-women.

Cleary, Michelle, Glenn E. Hunt, and Jan Horsfall. 2010. "Identifying and Addressing Bullying in Nursing." *Issues in Mental Health Nursing* 31 (5): 331–5. https://doi.org/10.3109/01612840903308531.

Clement, Wallace. 1988. *The Challenge of Class*. Ottawa, ON: University of Carleton Press.

CMWRC (Coalition for Migrant Worker Rights Canada). 2017. "Our Movement." http://migrantrights.ca/en/our-movement/.

CNA (Canadian Nurses Association). 2015. "Registered Nurses Profile (including Nurse Practitioners), Canada, 2015." https://www.cna-aiic.ca/en/on-the-issues/better-value/health-human-resources/nursing-statistics/canada.

CNN. 2013. "CNN Grieves That Guilty Verdict Ruined 'Promising' Lives of Steubenville Rapists" (video). *YouTube*, March 17. https://www.youtube.com/watch?v=MvUdyNko8L.

Cohen, Albert. 1955. *Delinquent Boys: The Culture of the Gang*. New York: Free Press.

Cohen, Lawrence E., and Marcus Felson. 1979. "Social Change and Crime Rate Trends: A Routine Activity Approach." *American Sociological Review* 44 (4): 588–608. https://doi.org/10.2307/2094589.

Colaguori, Claudio. 2010. "Symbolic Violence and the Violation of Human Rights: Continuing the Sociological Critique of Domination." *International Journal of Criminology & Sociological Theory* 3 (2): 388–400.

Cole, Susan. 1982. "Home Sweet Home." In *Still Ain't Satisfied: Canadian Feminism Today*, edited by Maureen Fitzgerald, Connie Guberman, and Margie Wolfe, 55–67. Toronto, ON: Women's Press.

Collinson, David L., and Jeff Hearn. 1996. "Breaking the Silence: On Men, Masculinities and Managements." In *Men as Managers, Managers as Men*, edited by David Collinson and Jeff Hearn, 1–24. London, UK: Sage. https://doi.org/10.4135/9781446280102.n1.

Comack, Elizabeth. 2012. *Racialized Policing: Aboriginal People's Encounters with Police*. Winnipeg, MB: Fernwood.

———. 2014a. "The Feminist Engagement with Criminology." In *Criminalizing Women: Gender and (In)Justice in Neoliberal Times*, 2nd ed., edited by Gillian Balfour and Elizabeth Comack, 12–46. Winnipeg, MB: Fernwood.

———. 2014b. "Making Connections: Introduction." In *Criminalizing Women: Gender and (In)Justice in Neoliberal Times*, 2nd ed., edited by Gillian Balfour and Elizabeth Comack, 48–72. Winnipeg, MB: Fernwood.

Comack, Elizabeth, and Gillian Balfour. 2004. *The Power to Criminalize: Violence, Inequality and the Law*. Halifax, NS: Fernwood.

Commisso, Christina. 2014. "Tina Fontaine: Murdered Aboriginal Teen Struggled with Father's Violent Death." *CTV News*, August 20. https://www.ctvnews.ca/canada/tina-fontaine-murdered-aboriginal-teen-struggled-with-father-s-violent-death-1.1967508.

Connell, Catherine. 2013. "Fashionable Resistance: Queer 'Fa(t)shion' Blogging as Counterdiscourse." *Women's Studies Quarterly* 41 (1): 209–24. https://doi.org/10.1353/wsq.2013.0049.

Connell, Raewyn. 2008. "Masculinity Construction and Sports in Boys' Education: A Framework for Thinking about the Issue." *Sport Education and Society* 13 (2): 131–45. https://doi.org/10.1080/13573320801957053.

Conroy, Shana, and Adam Cotter. 2017. *Self-Reported Sexual Assault in Canada, 2014*. Ottawa, ON: Statistics Canada.

Cooper, Vicki, and David Whyte. 2017. "Introduction: The Violence of Austerity". In *The Violence of Austerity*, edited by Vicki Cooper and David Whyte, 1–32. London, UK: Pluto Press. https://doi.org/10.2307/j.ctt1pv8988.4.

Corrado, Raymond R., Irwin M. Cohen, and Jesse L. Cale. 2013. "Aboriginal Resource Access in Response to Criminal Victimization in an Urban Context." In *Aboriginal Policy Research Series Volume 2: Setting the Agenda for Change*. Toronto, ON: Thompson Educational Publishing. https://ir.lib.uwo.ca/cgi/viewcontent.cgi?article=1308&context=aprci.

Corrigan, Philip. 1981. "On Moral Regulation: Some Preliminary Remarks." *Sociological Review* 29 (2): 313–37. https://doi.org/10.1111/j.1467-954X.1981.tb00176.x.

Cortina, L.M., and E.A. Leskinen. 2013. "Workplace Harassment Based on Sex: A Risk Factor for Women's Mental Health Problems." In *Violence against Women and Mental Health*, edited by Claudia García-Moreno and Anita Riecher-Rössler, 139–47. Basel, Switzerland: Karger. https://doi.org/10.1159/000342028.

Cox, Arisa. 2014. "I Stood Firm on My Hair, and Won Self-Respect." *Toronto Star*, August 5. https://www.thestar.com/life/2014/08/05/i_stood_firm_on_my_hair_and_won_selfrespect.html.

Craig, Elaine. 2014. "The Ethical Obligations of Defence Counsel in Sexual Assault Cases." *Osgoode Law Journal* 51 (2): 427–67.

———. 2016. "The Inhospitable Court." *University of Toronto Law Journal* 66 (2): 197–243. https://doi.org/10.3138/UTLJ.3398.

Craig, Maxine. 2006. "Race, Beauty, and the Tangled Knot of Guilty Pleasure." *Feminist Theory* 7 (2): 159–77. https://doi.org/10.1177/1464700106064414.

Crawford, Alison. 2017. "Justice Robin Camp Resigns after Judicial Council Recommends Removal." *CBC News*, March 9. http://www.cbc.ca/news/politics/justice-robin-camp-judicial-council-1.4017233.

Crawley, Mike. 2017. "Premier Kathleen Wynne Bombarded on Social Media by Homophobic, Sexist Abuse." *CBC News*, January 25. http://www.cbc.ca/news/canada/toronto/kathleen-wynne-twitter-abuse-1.3949657.

Cree, Ms. 1994. "Entrenched Social Catastrophe." *Journal of Prisoners on Prisons* 5 (2): 45–7.

Crenshaw, Kimberlé. 1989. "Demarginalizing the Intersection of Race and Sex: A Black Feminist Critique of Antidiscrimination Doctrine, Feminist Theory and Antiracist Politics." *University of Chicago Legal Forum* 1989: 139–67.

———. 1991. "Mapping the Margins: Intersectionality, Identity Politics, and Violence against Women of Color." *Stanford Law Review* 43 (6): 1241–99. https://doi.org/10.2307/1229039.

———. 2016. "The Urgency of Intersectionality." Recorded October 2016 at *TEDWomen*. TED video, 18:35. https://www.ted.com/talks/kimberle_crenshaw_the_urgency_of_intersectionality#t-270935.

Creswell, Julie. 2017. "Millennials' Lust for Makeup Is the Lipstick on Retail's Pig." *The New York Times*, November 22. https://www.nytimes.com/2017/11/22/business/millennials-cosmetics-boom.html?smid=nytcore-ipad-share&smprod=nytcore-ipad;%20https://www.nytimes.com/2017/05/11/fashion/sephora-beauty-retail-technology.html?_r=0.

CRIAW (Canadian Research Institute for the Advancement of Women). 2007. "Women's Experiences of Social Programs for People with Low Incomes." CRIAW FACTsheet. http://www.criaw-icref.ca/sites/criaw/files/Womens_experiences_of_social_programs_for_people_with_low_incomes_e.pdf.

Crocker, Diane, and Valery Kalemba. 1999. "The Incidence and Impact of Women's Experiences of Sexual Harassment in Canadian Workplaces." *Canadian Review of Sociology* 36 (4): 541–58. https://doi.org/10.1111/j.1755-618X.1999.tb00963.x.

CSC (Correctional Service Canada). 1990. *Creating Choices: Report on the Task Force on Federally Sentenced Women*. Ottawa, ON: Correctional Service of Canada.

———. 2015. "Social Histories of Aboriginal Women Offenders." Correctional Service of Canada. http://www.csc-scc.gc.ca/research/005008-err14-7-eng.shtml.

———. 2016. "Gender Dysphoria." http://www.csc-scc.gc.ca/politiques-et-lois/800-5-gl-eng.shtml.

CUPE (Canadian Union of Public Employees). 2014. "1973–1982: CUPE Becomes a Seasoned Political Force." May 7. https://cupe.ca/1973-1982-cupe-becomes-seasoned-political-force.

———. 2015. "CUPE Equality History Digital Timeline." October 20. https://cupe.ca/cupe-equality-history-digital-timeline.

———. 2016. "Nurse Fired for Speaking Up about Patient Violence to Make First Public Statement Wednesday in North Bay." February 22. https://cupe.ca/nurse-fired-speaking-about-patient-violence-make-first-public-statement-wednesday-north-bay.

Currie, Dawn. 1990. "Battered Women and the State." *Journal of Human Justice* 1 (2): 77–96.

CWF (Canadian Women's Foundation). 2014. "Fact Sheet: Moving Out of Violence." http://www.canadianwomen.org/sites/canadianwomen.org/files//FactSheet-VAWandDV_19_08_2016_formatted.pdf.

———. 2016. "Fact Sheet: Sexual Assault and Harassment." http://www.canadianwomen.org/sites/canadianwomen.org/files/Fact%20sheet_SexualAssaultHarassmentFormatted_18_08_2016.pdf.

———. 2017a. "Fact Sheet: The Gender Wage Gap in Canada." http://www.canadianwomen.org/wp-content/uploads/2017/09/Facts-About-Gender-Wage-Gap.pdf.

———. 2017b. "Fact Sheet: Women in Poverty." http://www.canadianwomen.org/wp-content/uploads/2017/09/Facts-About-Women-and-Poverty.pdf.

Czyzewski, Karina. 2011. "Colonialism as a Broader Social Determinant of Health." *International Indigenous Policy Journal* 2 (1). https://doi.org/10.18584/iipj.2011.2.1.5.

Dabla-Norris, Era, Kalpana Kochhar, Nujin Suphaphiphat, Frantisek Ricka, and Evridiki Tsounta. 2015. "Causes and Consequences of Income Inequality: A Global Perspective." International Monetary Fund (IMF), June 15. https://www.imf.org/en/Publications/Staff-Discussion-Notes/Issues/2016/12/31/Causes-and-Consequences-of-Income-Inequality-A-Global-Perspective-42986.

Dalal, M. 2014. "Labiaplasty Defended by Plastic Surgeons." *CBC News*, April 3. http://www.cbc.ca/news/health/labiaplasty-defended-by-plastic-surgeons-1.2594658.

Daly, Tamara, Albert Banerjee, Pat Armstrong, Hugh Armstrong, and Marta Szebehely. 2011. "Lifting the 'Violence Veil': Examining Working Conditions in Long-Term Care Facilities Using Iterative Mixed

Methods." *Canadian Journal on Aging* 30 (2): 271–84. https://doi.
org/10.1017/S071498081100016X.

d'Arge, Dahlia. 2013. "The Enemy Within: Sexual Assault and Rape in the
US Armed Forces." *Lewis Honors College Capstone Collection*, Paper 10.
University of Kentucky. https://uknowledge.uky.edu/honprog/10.

Davidson, Travis William. 2015. "A Review of Transgender Health in
Canada." *University of Ottawa Journal of Medicine* 5 (2): 40–5. https://doi.
org/10.18192/uojm.v5i2.1280.

Davis, Angela. 1983. *Women, Race, and Class*. New York: Vintage.

———. 1994. "Politics, Fashion, and Nostalgia." *Critical Inquiry* 21 (1): 37–
45. https://doi.org/10.1086/448739.

DAWN (Disabled Women's Network of Canada). 2014. "Factsheet:
Women with Disabilities and Violence." http://www.dawncanada.
net/?attachment_id=995.

de Beauvoir, Simone. (1949) 1997. *The Second Sex*, translated by H.M.
Parshley. London, UK: Vintage Books.

de Leeuw, Sarah. 2016. "Tender Grounds: Intimate Visceral Violence and
British Columbia's Colonial Geographies." *Political Geography* 52: 14–23.
https://doi.org/10.1016/j.polgeo.2015.11.010.

De Luca, Robyn. 2014. "The Good News about PMS" (video). *TED Talks*.
https://www.ted.com/talks/robyn_stein_deluca_the_good_news_
about_pms/transcript?language=en.

Dearden, Lizzie. 2016. "Burkini Ban: Why Is France Arresting Muslim
Women for Wearing Full-Body Swimwear and Why Are People so
Angry?" *Independent*, August 24. http://www.independent.co.uk/news/
world/europe/burkini-ban-why-is-france-arresting-muslim-women-
for-wearing-full-body-swimwear-and-why-are-people-a7207971.html.

December17.org. 2017. International Day to End Violence against Sex
Workers. http://www.december17.org/.

Dell, Colleen, and Jennifer Kilty. 2013. "The Creation of the *Expected*
Aboriginal Woman Drug Offender in Canada: Exploring Relations
between Victimization, Punishment, and Cultural Identity." *International
Review of Victimology* 19 (1): 51–68. https://doi.org/10.1177/
0269758012447215.

Denison, Jacqueline, Colleen Varcoe, and Annette J. Browne. 2014.
"Aboriginal Women's Experiences of Accessing Health Care When State
Apprehension of Children Is Being Threatened." *Journal of Advanced
Nursing* 70 (5): 1105–16. https://doi.org/10.1111/jan.12271.

Department of Justice. 2017. "Cyberbullying and the Non-consensual
Distribution of Intimate Images." http://www.justice.gc.ca/eng/rp-pr/
other-autre/cndii-cdncii/p3.html.

Deschamps, Marie. 2015. *External Review into Sexual Misconduct and Sexual Harassment in the Canadian Armed Forces.* Ottawa, ON: National Defense and the Canadian Armed Forces. http://www.forces.gc.ca/en/caf-community-support-services/external-review-sexual-mh-2015/summary.page.

Detraz, Nicole, and Dursun Peksen. 2016. "The Effect of IMF Programs on Women's Economic and Political Rights." *International Interactions* 42 (1): 81–105. https://doi.org/10.1080/03050629.2015.1056343.

DiManno, Rosie. 2015. "A Final Indignity for Cindy Gladue." *Toronto Star,* April 2. https://www.thestar.com/news/gta/2015/04/02/a-final-indignity-for-cindy-gladue-dimanno.html.

Dobash, Russell, R. Emerson Dobash, and Sue Gutterridge. 1986. *The Imprisonment of Women.* Oxford, UK: Basil Blackwell.

Doolittle, Robyn. 2017. "Why Police Dismiss 1 in 5 Sexual Assault Claims as Baseless." *The Globe and Mail*, February 3. https://www.theglobeandmail.com/news/investigations/unfounded-sexual-assault-canada-main/article33891309/.

D'Souze, Jason, and Ash Kelly. 2017. "Vancouver Woman Says Hijab Invites Racial Abuse, Harassment." *CBC News*, May 28. http://www.cbc.ca/news/canada/british-columbia/vancouver-woman-says-hijab-invites-racial-abuse-harassment-1.4134789.

Dubinsky, Karen. 1993. *Improper Advances: Rape and Heterosexual Conflict in Ontario, 1880–1929.* Chicago, IL: University of Chicago Press.

DuBois, Ellen. 1979. "The Nineteenth Century Women Suffrage Movement and the Analysis of Women's Oppression." In *Capitalist Patriarchy and the Case for Socialist Feminism*, edited by Zillah Eisenstein, 137–50. New York: Monthly Review Press.

DuBois, Teresa. 2012. "Police Investigation of Sexual Assault Complaints: How Far Have We Come Since Jane Doe?" In *Sexual Assault in Canada: Law, Legal Practice and Women's Activism*, edited by Elizabeth A. Sheehy, 191–210. Ottawa, ON: University of Ottawa Press.

Durisin, Elya, and Robert Heynen. 2016. "Producing the 'Trafficked Woman': Canadian Newspaper Reporting on Eastern European Exotic Dancers during the 1990s." *Atlantis* 37.2 (1): 8–24.

Edwards, Cheryl. 2010. "Workplace Violence & Harassment in Canada: Ontario's OHS Provisions in Perspective." Paper presented at the Canadian Bar Association 2010 National Administrative Law, Labour & Employment Law and Privacy & Access Law Conference, Ottawa, Ontario.

Edwards, Susan. 1987. "'Provoking Her Own Demise': From Common Assault to Homicide." In *Women, Violence and Social Control*, edited by Jalna Hanmer and Mary Maynard, 152–68. Atlantic Highlands, NJ:

Humanities Press International. https://doi.org/10.1007/978-1-349-18592-4_11.

Egale. 2014. "Gender Segregation of Trans People in Canadian Correctional Facilities." Press release, July 3. https://egale.ca/trans-correctional-placements/.

Eggertson, Laura. 2011. "Targeted." *Canadian Nurse*. https://canadian-nurse.com/articles/issues/2011/june-2011/targeted.

Ehrenreich, Barbara, and Deirdre English. 1973. *Witches, Midwives & Nurses: A History of Women Healers*. Old Westbury, NY: Feminist Press.

Elias, Ana Sofia, Rosalind Gill, and Christina Scharff. 2017. "Aesthetic Labour: Beauty Politics in Neoliberalism." In *Aesthetic Labour: Rethinking Beauty Politics in Neoliberalism*, edited by Ana Sofia Elias, Rosalind Gill, and Christina Scharff, 3–49. London, UK: Palgrave Macmillan. https://doi.org/10.1057/978-1-137-47765-1_1.

Elgin, Peter, and Stephen Hester. 2003. *The Montreal Massacre: A Story of Membership Categorization Analysis*. Waterloo, ON: Wilfrid Laurier Press.

Elkin, William. 1982. "Rethinking 'Bill 82': A Critical Examination of Mandatory Special Education Legislation in Ontario." *Ottawa Law Review* 14: 314–39.

Elmi, Arij. 2017. "I'm Not an Alarmist—But as a Muslim Woman I Am Genuinely Alarmed." *CBC*, February 1. http://www.cbc.ca/2017/i-m-not-an-alarmist-but-as-a-muslim-woman-i-am-genuinely-alarmed-1.3961385.

Emejulu, Akwugo, and Leah Bassel. 2017. "Women of Colour's Anti-Austerity Activism." In *The Violence of Austerity*, edited by Vicki Cooper and David Whyte, 117–22. London, UK: Pluto Press. https://doi.org/10.2307/j.ctt1pv8988.15.

Engeln, Renee. 2017. *Beauty Sick: How the Cultural Obsession with Appearance Hurts Girls and Women*. New York: HarperCollins.

Erickson, Karla. 2010. "Talk, Touch and Intolerance: Sexual Harassment in an Overtly Sexualized Work Culture." In *Gender and Sexuality in the Workplace*, edited by Christine L. Williams and Kirsten Delinger, 179–202. Bingley, UK: Emerald Publishing Group. https://doi.org/10.1108/S0277-2833(2010)0000020011.

ETFO (Elementary Teachers Federation of Ontario). 2017. "Submission to the Standing Committee on Finance and Economic Affairs 2017 Pre-budget Hearings." January 25.

Evans, Alice. 2017. "Patriarchal Unions = Weaker Unions? Industrial Relations in the Asian Garment Industry." *Third World Quarterly* 38 (7): 1619–38. https://doi.org/10.1080/01436597.2017.1294981.

EVAW (End Violence Against Women). 2016. "I Just Want to Be Free" (video). *YouTube*, March 7. https://www.youtube.com/watch?v=lJ-qpvibpdU.

Everitt, Joanna. 2010. "Women in Politics: Why Is It an Issue?" *CBC News*, September 6. http://www.cbc.ca/news/canada/new-brunswick/women-in-politics-why-is-it-an-issue-1.885060.

Facey, Marcia. 2010. "'Maintaining Talk' among Taxi Drivers: Accomplishing Health-Protective Behaviour in Precarious Workplaces." *Health & Place* 16 (6): 1259–67. https://doi.org/10.1016/j.healthplace.2010.08.014.

Fact Finding Team. 2013. "Fact Finding Report: Commerce Undergraduate Society (CUS) FROSH CHANTS". University of British Columbia. https://president.ubc.ca/files/2013/09/Fact-Finding-Report-copy.pdf.

Fagen, Ruth. 1986. "Sewing Solidarity: The Eaton's Strike of 1912." *Canadian Woman Studies* 7 (3): 96–8.

Fairbairn, Jordan, and Dillon Black. 2015. "Cyberviolence against Women & Girls." Ottawa Coalition to End Violence Against Women. http://www.octevaw-cocvff.ca/sites/default/files/CyberViolenceReport_OCTEVAW.pdf.

Fairchild, Kimberly. 2010. "Context Effects on Women's Perceptions of Stranger Harassment." *Sexuality & Culture* 14 (3): 191–216. https://doi.org/10.1007/s12119-010-9070-1.

Faith, Karlene. 1993. *Unruly Women: The Politics of Confinement and Resistance*. Vancouver, BC: Press Gang Publishers.

Farley, Liz. 2017. "I Coined the Term 'Sexual Harassment.' Corporations Stole It." *The New York Times*, October 18. https://www.nytimes.com/2017/10/18/opinion/sexual-harassment-corporations-steal.html.

Favaro, Laura. 2017. "'Just Be Confident Girls!': Confidence Chic as Neoliberal Governmentality." In *Aesthetic Labour: Rethinking Beauty Politics in Neoliberalism*, edited by Ana Sofia Elias, Rosalind Gill, and Christina Scharff, 283–99. London, UK: Palgrave Macmillan. https://doi.org/10.1057/978-1-137-47765-1_16.

Fellows, Mary Louise, and Sherene Razack. 1998. "The Race to Innocence: Confronting Hierarchical Relations among Women." *Journal of Gender, Race & Justice* 1: 335–52.

Feng, Benny. 2015. "#WhoWillYouHelp PSA" (video). *YouTube*, March 7. https://www.youtube.com/watch?v=__IwV2T2S1c.

Fessenden, Marissa. 2015. "American Women in the 1900s Called Street Harassers 'Mashers' and Stabbed Them with Hatpins." *Smithsonian Magazine*, October 2. https://www.smithsonianmag.com/smart-news/women-1900s-called-street-harassers-mashers-and-stabbed-them-hatpins-180956816/.

Fields, Jill. 2001. "'Fighting the Corsetless Evil': Shaping Corsets and Culture, 1900–1930." In *Beauty and Business: Commerce, Gender, and Culture in Modern America*, edited by Philip Scranton, 109–40. New York: Routledge.

Fine, Cordelia. 2017. *Testosterone Rex: Myths of Sex, Science and Society*. New York: W. W. Norton & Company.

Fine, Sean. 2015. "Muslim Convert Attacked While Wearing Niqab in Toronto." *The Globe and Mail*, October 4. https://www.theglobe andmail.com/news/national/muslim-convert-attacked-while-wearing-niqab-in-toronto/article26646425/.

Fingard, Judith. 1993. "The Prevention of Cruelty, Marriage Breakdown and the Rights of Wives in Nova Scotia, 1880–1900." *Journal of the History of the Atlantic Region* 23 (2): 84–101.

Finnie, Ross, Kaveh Afshar, Eda Bozkurt, Masashi Miyairi, and Dejan Pavlic. 2016. *Barista or Better? New Evidence on the Earnings of Post-Secondary Education Graduates: A Tax Linkage Approach*. Ottawa, ON: Education Policy Research Initiative.

Fitzgerald, Maureen, Connie Guberman, and Margie Wolfe. 1982. *Still Ain't Satisfied! Canadian Feminism Today*. Toronto, ON: Women's Press.

Flecker, K. 2016. "New Country, New Job—New Risks." *Monitor Magazine* 22 (5): 27–9.

Florence, Sarah. 2016. "I'm Fat, and I'm Tired of People Who Won't Admit It." *xojane*, September 30. https://www.xojane.com/healthy/im-fat-and-i-admit-it.

Fomina, Angelina. 2016. "Pink Tax Is Real: Women Pay 43% More for Personal Care Products in Canada." *ParceHub*, March 30. https://www.parsehub.com/blog/pink-tax-is-real-women-pay-43-more-for-personal-care-products-in-canada/.

Forestell, Nancy. 2016. "Early Women's Movement(s) in Canada." In *Canadian History: Post-Confederation*, edited by John Belshaw, 145–48. Vancouver: BC Open Textbooks Project.

Forrester, Monica. 2016. "Canada Should Be 'Most Concerned about the Most Marginalized Sex Workers.'" *Ricochet*, September 19. https://ricochet.media/en/1406/our-country-should-be-most-concerned-about-the-most-marginalized-sex-workers.

Foster, Lorne, Les Jacobs, and Bobby Siu. 2016. *Race Data and Traffic Stops in Ottawa, 2013–2015: A Report on Ottawa and the Police Districts*. Ottawa, ON: Ottawa Police Service Board and Ottawa Police Service. https://www.ottawapolice.ca/en/about-us/resources/.TSRDCP_York_Research_Report.pdf.

Foucault, Michel. 1972. *The Archaeology of Knowledge*. Translated by A.M. Sheridan Smith. New York: Pantheon Books.

———. 1978. *The History of Sexuality*, vol. 1. New York: Random House.

———. 1979. *Discipline and Punish.* Translated by Alan Sheridan. London, UK: Allen Lane.

———. 1980. *Power/Knowledge: Selected Interviews & Other Writings 1972–1977.* Edited by Colin Gordon. Translated by Colin Gordon, Leo Marshall, John Mepham, and Kate Soper. New York: Pantheon.

———. 1982. "The Subject and the Power." *Critical Inquiry* 8 (4): 775–95.

———. 1983. "Afterword." In *Michel Foucault: Beyond Structuralism and Hermeneutics*, 2nd ed., by Hubert L. Dreyfus and Paul Rabinow, 208–26. Chicago, IL: The University of Chicago Press.

———. 1991. "Governmentality." In *The Foucault Effect: Studies in Governmentality*, edited by Graham Burchell, C. Gordon, and P. Miller. London, UK: Harvester.

Fournier, Pascale. 2002. "The Ghettoisation of Difference in Canada: Rape by Culture and the Danger of a Cultural Defence in Criminal Law Trials." *Manitoba Law Journal* 29 (1): 81–119.

FPTWG (Federal-Provincial-Territorial Working Group). 2002. *Final Report of the Ad Hoc Federal-Provincial-Territorial Working Group Reviewing Spousal Abuse Policies and Legislation.* Ottawa, ON: Department of Justice.

Frances, Raelene, Linda Kealey, and Joan Sangster. 1996. "Women and Wage Labour in Australia and Canada, 1880–1980." *Labour*: 54–89.

Francis, Angelyn. 2015. "#BeenRapedNeverReported: 1 Year Later, What's Changed? Co-Creators Reflect Back." *Huffington Post*, November 1. http://www.huffingtonpost.ca/2015/11/01/been-raped-never-reported-one-year-later_n_8444162.html.

Franklin, Cortney A. 2016. "Sorority Affiliation and Sexual Assault Victimization: Assessing Vulnerability Using Path Analysis." *Violence Against Women* 22 (8): 895–922. https://doi.org/10.1177/1077801215614971.

Freedman, Estelle. 1984. *Their Sisters' Keepers: Women's Prison Reform in America, 1830–1930.* Ann Arbour, MI: University of Michigan Press.

———. 2013. *Redefining Rape: Sexual Violence in the Era of Suffrage and Segregation.* Cambridge, MA: Harvard University Press.

Friday, Joe. 2017. *Findings of the Office of the Public Sector Integrity Commissioner in the Matter of an Investigation into a Disclosure of Wrongdoing (Case Report).* Ottawa, ON: Public Health Agency of Canada.

Friedman, Gerald. 2014. "Workers without Employers: Shadow Corporations and the Rise of the Gig Economy." *Review of Keynesian Economics* 2 (2): 171–88. https://doi.org/10.4337/roke.2014.02.03.

Friedman, Uri. 2016. "Why Thousands of Women in Iceland Left Work Two Hours Early This Week." *The Atlantic*, October 27.

https://www.theatlantic.com/international/archive/2016/10/iceland-women-gender-pay-gap/505460/.

Galabuzi, Grace-Edward. 2005. "The Racialization of Poverty in Canada: Implications for Section 15 Charter protection." Paper presented at the National Anti-Racism Council of Canada National Conference, Ottawa, Ontario, November 10–13.

Galerand, Elsa, Martin Gallié, and Jeanne Ollivier-Gobeil. 2015. *Domestic Labour and Exploitation: The Case of the Live-in Caregiver Program in Canada (LCP)*. Montreal, QC: PINAY and the UQAM Service to Communities.

Galloway, Gloria. 2016. "Ottawa Discriminated against Aboriginal Children by Underfunding Services, Tribunal to Rule." *The Globe and Mail*, January 25. https://www.theglobeandmail.com/news/politics/ottawa-discriminated-against-aboriginal-children-by-underfunding-services-tribunal-to-rule/article28389918/.

Galtung, Johan. 1969. "Violence, Peace, and Peace Research." *Journal of Peace Research* 6 (3): 167–91. https://doi.org/10.1177/002234336900600301.

Garau, Annie. 2017. "'Sex Strike' May Happen in Kenya to Make Men Vote." *All That Is Interesting*, January 29. http://all-that-is-interesting.com/kenya-sex-strike.

Garcia, Venessa, and Patrick McManimon. 2011. *Gendered Justice: Intimate Partner Violence and the Criminal Justice System*. Plymouth, UK: Rowen & Littlefield.

Garland, David. 2001. *The Culture of Control: Crime and Social Order in Contemporary Society*. Chicago, IL: University of Chicago Press.

Gaucher, Robert. 2002. *Writing as Resistance: The Journal of Prisoners on Prisons Anthology*. Ottawa, ON: University of Ottawa Press.

Gavigan, Shelley. 1989/1990. "Petit Treason in Eighteen Century England: Women's Inequity before the Law." *Canadian Journal of Women and the Law* 3 (2): 335–74.

George Hull Centre for Children and Families. 2011. "Family Group Conferencing/Family Group Decision Making Coordinator Manual for Ontario." http://www.georgehullcentre.on.ca/usercontent/resources/FGC-Manual-Eng.pdf.

Gerber, Paula. 2016. "Countries That Still Criminalize Homosexuality." https://antigaylaws.org/.

Gibson, Owen, and Pete Pattison. 2014. "Death Toll among Qatar's 2022 World Cup Workers Revealed." *The Guardian*, December 23. https://www.theguardian.com/world/2014/dec/23/qatar-nepal-workers-world-cup-2022-death-toll-doha.

Giese, Rachel. 2016. "Canadian Politics Are Sexist. What Are Men Going to Do about It?" *Maclean's*, December 16. http://www.macleans.ca/news/canada/canadian-politics-are-sexist-what-are-men-going-to-do-about-it/.

Gilchrist, Kristen. 2010. "'Newsworthy' Victims? Exploring Differences in Canadian Local Press Coverage of Missing/Murdered Aboriginal and White Women." *Feminist Media Studies* 10 (4): 373–90. https://doi.org/10.1080/14680777.2010.514110.

Gill, Rosalind. 2008. "Empowerment/Sexism: Figuring Female Sexual Agency in Contemporary Advertising." *Feminism & Psychology* 18 (1): 35–60. https://doi.org/10.1177/0959353507084950.

Gill, Rosalind, and Ana Sofia Elias. 2014. "'Awaken Your Incredible': Love Your Body Discourses and Postfeminist Contradictions." *International Journal of Media and Cultural Politics* 10 (2): 179–88. https://doi.org/10.1386/macp.10.2.179_1.

Gillespie, Gordon, Paula Grubb, Katheryn Brown, Maura Boesch, and Deborah Ulrich. 2017. "'Nurses Eat Their Young': A Novel Bullying Educational Program for Student Nurses." *Journal of Nursing Education and Practice* 7 (7): 11–21. https://doi.org/10.5430/jnep.v7n7P11.

Gillies, Kara, and Chris Bruckert. 2018. "Pimps, Partners, and Procurers: Criminalizing Street-Based Sex Workers' Relationships with Partners and Third Parties." In *Red Light Labour: Sex Work Regulation, Agency and Resistance*, edited by Elya Durisin, Emily van der Meulen, and Chris Bruckert, 82–93. Vancouver, BC: University of British Colombia Press.

Gillis, Roy, and Shaidl Diamond. 2012. "Dynamic of Partner Abuse in Sexual and Gender Minority Communities." In *Cruel but Not Unusual: Violence in Canadian Families*, 2nd ed., edited by Romona Alaggia and Cathy Vine, 231–4. Waterloo, ON: Wilfrid Laurier University Press.

Gillis, Wendy. 2013. "Rehtaeh Parsons: A Family's Tragedy and a Town's Shame." *Toronto Star*, April 12. https://www.thestar.com/news/canada/2013/04/12/rehtaeh_parsons_a_familys_tragedy_and_a_towns_shame.html.

Gingrich, Luann Good. 2008. "Social Exclusion and Double Jeopardy: The Management of Lone Mothers in the Market-State Field." *Social Policy and Administration* 42 (4): 379–95. https://doi.org/10.1111/j.1467-9515.2008.00610.x.

Godenzi, Alberto, Martin D. Schwartz, and Walter S. DeKeseredy. 2001. "Toward a Gendered Social Bond/Male Peer Support Theory of University Woman Abuse." *Critical Criminology* 10 (1): 1–16. https://doi.org/10.1023/A:1013105118592.

Goffman, Erving. 1963. *Stigma: Notes on the Management of Spoiled Identity.* Englewood Cliffs, NJ: Prentice Hall.

Gonzales, Christina. 2015. "The Nanny Diaries: Toronto's Filipino Caregivers Talk about Low Wages, Long Days and Immigration Delays." *Toronto Life*, August 27. https://torontolife.com/city/toronto-filipino-caregiver-nanny-diaries/.

Goodley, Dan. 2013. "Dis/entangling Critical Disability Studies." *Disability & Society* 28 (5): 631–44. https://doi.org/10.1080/09687599.2012.717884.

Goodmark, Leigh. 2008. "When Is a Battered Woman Not a Battered Woman? When She Fights Back." *Yale Journal of Law and Feminism* 20 (1): 75–129.

Gordon, Linda. 1988. *Heroes of Their Own Lives.* New York: Penguin.

Gordon, Rachel, Robert Crosnoe, and Xne Wang. 2014. *Physical Attractiveness and the Accumulation of Social and Human Capital in Adolescence and Young Adulthood: Assets and Distractions.* Hoboken, NJ: Wiley.

Goudreau, Jenna. 2011. "The Hidden Dangers of Cosmetic Surgery." *Forbes*, June 16. https://www.forbes.com/sites/jennagoudreau/2011/06/16/hidden-dangers-of-cosmetic-surgery/#5dfe67797b2b.

Government of Canada. 2015. "Public Service Employee Survey Results by Question for Public Service." http://www.tbs-sct.gc.ca/pses-saff/2014/results-resultats/bq-pq/00/org-eng.aspx#s7.

———. 2017a. "Extend or Change Your Live-In Caregiver Program Work Permit." https://www.canada.ca/en/immigration-refugees-citizenship/services/work-canada/permit/caregiver-program/extend-change-permit.html.

———. 2017b. *Harassment and Sexual Violence in the Workplace Public Consultations.* Ottawa, ON: Employment and Social Development Canada.

Green, Rayna. 1990. "The Pocahontas Perplex: The Image of Indian Women in American Culture." In *Unequal Sisters: A Multi-Cultural Reader in US Women's History*, edited by Ellen Carol Dubois and Vicki L. Ruiz, 15–21. New York: Routledge.

Green, Tristin K. 2005. "Work Culture and Discrimination." *California Law Review* 93 (3): 623–84.

Greenberg, Janelle. 1984. "The Victim in Historical Perspective: Some Aspects of the English Experience." *Journal of Social Issues* 40 (1): 77–101. https://doi.org/10.1111/j.1540-4560.1984.tb01083.x.

Grinberg, Emanuella. 2014. "Meredith Vieira Explains #WhyIStayed." *CCN*, September 17. http://www.cnn.com/2014/09/09/living/rice-video-why-i-stayed/index.html.

Gross, Liza. 2010. "Invisible in the Media." *UN Chronicle* XLVII (1): 27–32.

Halifax Regional Police. n.d. "Preventing human trafficking." https://www.halifax.ca/fire-police/police/programs-services/preventing-human-trafficking.

Hallett, Tim. 2007. "Between Deference and Distinction: Interaction Ritual through Symbolic Power in an Educational Institution." *Social Psychology Quarterly* 70 (2): 148–71. https://doi.org/10.1177/019027250707000205.

Halley, Janet. 2006. *Split Decisions: How and Why to Take a Break from Feminism.* Princeton, NJ: Princeton University Press.

Ham, Julie. 2011. *What's the Cost of a Rumour? A Guide to Sorting Out the Myths and Facts about Sporting Events and Trafficking.* Bangkok, Thailand: Global Alliance Against Trafficking in Women.

Hamermesh, Daniel S. 2011. *Beauty Pays: Why Attractive People Are More Successful.* Princeton, NJ: Princeton University Press.

Hamilton, Jamie Lee, and Becki Ross. 2016. "Why Some Objections to Sex Workers Memorial Smack of Moralism and Sex Shame." *Daily Xtra,* October 14. https://www.dailyxtra.com/vancouver/news-and-ideas/opinion/objections-sex-workers-memorial-smack-moralism-and-sex-shame-208319.

Hango, Darcy. 2016. *Cyberbullying and Cyberstalking among Internet Users Aged 15 to 29 in Canada.* Ottawa, ON: Statistics Canada.

Hannah-Moffat, Kelly. 2000. "Prisons That Empower: Neo-Liberal Governances in Canadian Women's Prisons." *British Journal of Criminology* 40 (3): 510–31. https://doi.org/10.1093/bjc/40.3.510.

———. 2001. *Punishment in Disguise: Penal Governance and Federal Imprisonment of Women in Canada.* Toronto, ON: University of Toronto Press.

———. 2010. "Sacrosanct or Flaws: Risk, Accountability and Gender-Responsive Penal Politics." *Current Issues in Criminal Justice* 22 (2): 193–215.

Hannem, Stacey. 2012. "Theorizing Stigma and the Politics of Resistance." In *Stigma Revisited: Implications of the Mark*, edited by Stacey Hannem and Chris Bruckert, 10–29. Ottawa, ON: University of Ottawa Press.

———. 2016. "Let's Talk about Sex Work: Report of the REAL Working Group for Brantford, Brant, Haldimand, and Norfolk, Assessing the Needs of Sex Workers in Our Community." REAL: Resources, Education, Advocacy for Local Sex Work. https://www.researchgate.net/publication/304580013_Let%27s_Talk_About_Sex_Work_Report_of_the_REAL_Working_Group_for_Brantford_Brant_Haldimand_and_Norfolk_Assessing_the_Needs_of_Sex_Workers_in_Our_Community.

Hannem, Stacey, and Chris Bruckert. 2014. "Legal Moralism, Feminist Rhetoric, and the Criminalization of Consensual Sex in Canada." In *Within the Confines: Women and Law in Canada*, edited by Jennifer Kilty, 318–43. Toronto, ON: Women's Press.

Haque, Umair. 2016. "The Reason Twitter's Losing Active Users." *Harvard Business Review*, February 12. https://hbr.org/2016/02/the-reason-twitters-losing-active-users.

Harper, Stephen. 2006. "Text of Harper's Speech." *The Globe and Mail*, June 22. https://www.theglobeandmail.com/news/national/text-of-harpers-speech/article20414337/.

Harper, Stephen. 2015. "Harper: Why Would Canadians Embrace Practice from Anti-Women Culture?" *Global News*, March 10. https://globalnews.ca/video/1874586/harper-why-would-canadians-embrace-practice-from-anti-women-culture.

Harris, Fredrick C. 2015. "The Next Civil Rights Movement?" *Dissent* 62 (3): 34–40. https://doi.org/10.1353/dss.2015.0051.

Harris, Mike. (1995) 2010. "Common Sense Revolution" (video). *YouTube*, December 5. https://www.youtube.com/watch?v=MLPU8zB_N7g.

———. (1997) 2010. "Ontario Teachers Strike Attack Ad" (video). *YouTube*, December 5. https://www.youtube.com/watch?v=dbZBmg9gSXY.

Harris, Sophia. 2017a. "Canadian Woman Threatened with Being 'Dropped in an Acid Bath' for Boycotting Trump Products." *CBC News*, April 11. http://www.cbc.ca/news/business/trump-boycott-twitter-baycott-ivanka-1.4061114.

———. 2017b. "'Kill Her and Be Done with It': MP Behind Anti-Islamophobia Motion Reads Out Hate Mail." *CBC News*, February 16. http://www.cbc.ca/news/politics/threats-hate-islamophobia-khalid-1.3986563.

Harvey, David. 2007. *A Brief History of Neoliberalism*. New York: Oxford University Press.

Helmer, Aedan. 2017. "Timeline: Everything We Know in the Abdirahman Abdi Case." *Ottawa Sun*, March 6. http://ottawasun.com/2017/03/06/timeline-everything-we-know-in-the-abdirahman-abdi-case.

Hepworth, Julie, and Christine Griffin. 1990. "The 'Discovery' of Anorexia Nervosa: Discourses of the Late 19th Century." *Text-Interdisciplinary Journal for the Study of Discourse* 10 (4): 321–38. https://doi.org/10.1515/text.1.1990.10.4.321.

Hill, Jemele. 2014. "Janay Rice, in Her Own Words." *ESPN*, November 28. http://www.espn.com/nfl/story/_/id/11913473/janay-rice-gives-own-account-night-atlantic-city.

Hill Collins, Patricia. 1991. *Black Feminist Thought: Knowledge, Consciousness, and the Politics of Empowerment.* New York: Routledge.

——. 2015. "Intersectionality's Definitional Dilemmas." *Annual Review of Sociology* 41 (1): 1–20. https://doi.org/10.1146/annurev-soc-073014-112142.

Hodson, Randy, Vincent Roscigno, and Steven Lopez. 2006. "Chaos and the Abuse of Power: Workplace Bullying in Organizational and Interactional Context." *Work and Occupations* 33 (4): 382–416. https://doi.org/10.1177/0730888406292885.

Hollaback! n.d. "About." https://ottawa.ihollaback.org/about/.

hooks, bell. 2000. *Feminism Is for Everybody: Passionate Politics.* London, UK: Pluto Press.

Horii, Gayle. 1994. "Disarm the Infamous Thing." *Journal of Prisoners on Prisons* 5 (2): 10–22.

Horodyski, Mary. 1986. "Women and the Winnipeg General Strike of 1919." *Manitoba History* 11 (Spring): 28–37.

Houle, Patricia, Martin Turcotte, and Michael Wendt. 2017. *Changes in Parents' Participation in Domestic Tasks and Care for Children from 1986 to 2015.* Ottawa, ON: Statistics Canada. http://www.statcan.gc.ca/pub/89-652-x/89-652-x2017001-eng.pdf.

Hoye, Bryce. 2018. "Crown Won't Appeal Raymond Cormier's Acquittal in Death of Tina Fontaine." *CBC News,* March 13. http://www.cbc.ca/news/canada/manitoba/raymond-cormier-tina-fontaine-no-appeal-1.4574899.

Hsiung, Ping-Chung, and Katherine Nichol. 2010. "Policies on and Experiences of Foreign Domestic Workers in Canada." *Sociology Compass* 4 (9): 766–78. https://doi.org/10.1111/j.1751-9020.2010.00320.x.

Hudon, Tamara. 2016. *Visible Minority Women.* Ottawa, ON: Statistics Canada.

Hudson, Deborah. 2015. *Workplace Bullying and Harassment: Costly Conduct.* Kingston, ON: Industrial Relations Centre (IRC), Queen's University.

Huff, Darrell. 1954. *How to Lie with Statistics.* London, UK: Victor Gollancz.

Hughes, Everett Cherrington. 1945. "Dilemmas and Contradictions of Status." *American Journal of Sociology* 50 (5): 353–9. https://doi.org/10.1086/219652.

Hugill, David. 2010. *Missing Women, Missing News: Covering Crisis in Vancouver's Downtown Eastside.* Halifax, NS: Fernwood Publishing.

Human Rights Watch. 2013. *Those That Take Us Away: Abusive Policing and Failure in the Protection of Indigenous Women in Northern British Columbia, Canada.* New York: Human Rights Watch.

———. 2015. "'Work Faster or Get Out': Labor Rights Abuses in Cambodia's Garment Industry." https://www.hrw.org/sites/default/files/reports/cambodia0315_brochure_web.pdf.

———. 2017. "Submission to the Government of Canada on Police Abuse of Indigenous Women in Saskatchewan and Failures to Protect Indigenous Women from Violence." https://www.hrw.org/news/2017/06/19/submission-government-canada-police-abuse-indigenous-women-saskatchewan-and-failures.

Huncar, Andrea. 2017. "Indigenous Women Nearly 10 Times More Likely to Be Street Checked by Edmonton Police, New Data Shows." *CBC News*, June 27. http://www.cbc.ca/beta/news/canada/edmonton/street-checks-edmonton-police-aboriginal-black-carding-1.4178843.

Hunt, Alan. 1997. "Moral Regulation and Making-up the New Person: Putting Gramsci to Work." *Theoretical Criminology* 1 (3): 275–301. https://doi.org/10.1177/1362480697001003001.

Hunt, Sarah. 2013. "Decolonizing Sex Work: Developing an Intersectional Indigenous Approach." In *Selling Sex: Experience, Advocacy, and Research on Sex Work in Canada*, edited by Emily van der Meulen, Elya Durisin, and Victoria Love, 82–100. Vancouver, BC: University of British Columbia Press.

Hurley, Mary C., and Tonina Simeone. 2014. "Bill C-3: Gender Equity in Indian Registration Act." *Aboriginal Policy Studies* 3 (3): 153–72.

Hutchins, Hope, and Maria Sinha. 2013. "Impact of Violence against Women." In *Measuring Violence against Women: Statistical Trends*, edited by Maria Sinha, 77–93. Ottawa, ON: Statistics Canada. http://www.statcan.gc.ca/pub/85-002-x/2013001/article/11766-eng.pdf.

Hutchinson, Marie. 2013. "Bullying as Workgroup Manipulation: A Model for Understanding Patterns of Victimization and Contagion within the Workgroup." *Journal of Nursing Management* 21 (3): 563–71. https://doi.org/10.1111/j.1365-2834.2012.01390.x.

Ibrahim, Awad. 2011. "Will They Ever Speak with Authority? Race, Post-Coloniality and the Symbolic Violence of Language." *Educational Philosophy and Theory* 43 (6): 619–35. https://doi.org/10.1111/j.1469-5812.2010.00644.x.

Ibrahim, Dyna. 2016. "Police-Reported Intimate Partner Violence." In *Family Violence in Canada: A Statistical Profile, 2014*. Ottawa, ON: Canadian Centre for Justice Statistics. http://www.statcan.gc.ca/pub/85-002-x/2016001/article/14303-eng.pdf.

Ibrahim, Mariam. 2015. "'I Thought I Would Be Killed': Alberta MLA Delivers Gripping Legislature Speech on Domestic Violence." *National Post*, November 17. http://nationalpost.com/news/

canada/i-thought-i-would-be-killed-alberta-mla-delivers-gripping-legislature-speech-on-domestic-violence/.

Idle No More. n.d. "Calls for Change." http://www.idlenomore.ca/calls_for_change.

ILO (International Labour Organization). n.d. "Ratifications of C189: Countries That Have Not Ratified This Convention." http://www.ilo.org/dyn/normlex/en/f?p=NORMLEXPUB:11310:0:NO:1131 0:P11310_INSTRUMENT_ID:2551460:NO.

———. 2011. "C189—Domestic Workers Convention, 2011 (No. 189)." http://www.ilo.org/dyn/normlex/en/f?p=NORMLEXPUB:12100:0:: NO::P12100_ILO_CODE:C189.

IPU (Inter-Parliamentary Union). 2016. *Sexism, Harassment and Violence against Women Parliamentarians.* https://www.ipu.org/pdf/publications/issuesbrief-e.pdf.

IRCC (Immigration, Refugees and Citizenship Canada). 2016. "Temporary Foreign Workers: Intended Destination and Program." Temporary Residents: Work Permit Holders—Ad Hoc IRCC. http://open.canada.ca/data/en/dataset/67fd1fae-4950-4018-a491-62e60cbd6974?wbdisable=true.

Izadi, Elahe. 2016. "Street Harassment of Women Just Became a Hate Crime in This Country." *The Washington Post*, July 14. https://www.washingtonpost.com/news/worldviews/wp/2016/07/14/harassing-women-on-the-street-just-became-a-hate-crime-in-this-county/?utm_term=.1e0af3b4ec9c.

Jean, Michaëlle. 2012. "Message of the Rt. Hon. Michaëlle Jean on the Occasion of Frobruary." Michaëlle Jean Foundation. http://www.fmjf.ca/en/message-de-la-tres-honorable-michaelle-jean-loccasion-de-frovrier/.

Jeffrey, Leslie Ann. 2005. "Canada and Migrant Sex Work: Challenging the 'Foreign' in Foreign Policy." *Canadian Foreign Policy* 12 (1): 33–48. https://doi.org/10.1080/11926422.2005.9673387.

Jenkins, Nash. 2016. "*Ghostbusters* Star Leslie Jones Attacked by Racist Trolls on Twitter." *Time*, July 19. http://time.com/4412232/leslie-jones-ghostbusters-tweets/.

Johnsen, Rosemary. 2017. "On the Origins of 'Gaslighting.'" *Los Angeles Review of Books*, March 9. https://lareviewofbooks.org/article/on-the-origins-of-gaslighting/.

Johnson, Holly. 1987. "Getting the Facts Straight: A Statistical Overview." In *Too Few to Count*, edited by Ellen Adelburg and Claudia Currie, 23–46. Vancouver, BC: Press Gang.

———. 2012. "Limits of a Criminal Justice Response: Trends in Police and Court Processing of Sexual Assault." In *Sexual Assault in Canada: Law,*

Legal Practice and Activism, edited by Elizabeth Sheehy, 613–34. Ottawa, ON: University of Ottawa Press.

———. 2017. "Why Doesn't She Just Report It? Apprehensions and Contradictions for Women Who Report Sexual Violence to the Police." *Canadian Journal of Women and the Law* 29 (1): 36–59. https://doi.org/10.3138/cjwl.29.1.36.

Johnson, Holly, and Ashley McConnell. 2014. "Agency and Choice: Gendered Constructions of Victim Worthiness in Domestic Violence Court." In *Within the Confines: Women and Law in Canada*, edited by Jennifer M. Kilty, 118–43. Toronto, ON: Women's Press.

Johnson, Holly, and Myrna Dawson. 2011. *Violence against Women in Canada: Research and Policy Perspectives*. Toronto, ON: Oxford University Press.

Johnson, Val Marie. 2007. "'The Rest Can Go to the Devil': Macy's Workers Negotiate Gender, Sex and Class in the Progressive Era." *Journal of Women's History* 19 (1): 32–57. https://doi.org/10.1353/jowh.2007.0017.

Jozkowski, Kristen N., Zoë D. Peterson, Stephanie A. Sanders, Barbara Dennis, and Michael Reece. 2014. "Gender Differences in Heterosexual College Students' Conceptualizations and Indicators of Sexual Consent: Implications for Contemporary Sexual Assault Prevention Education." *Journal of Sex Research* 51 (8): 904–16. https://doi.org/10.1080/00224499.2013.792326.

Kadi, Joanna. 1996. *Thinking Class: Sketches from a Cultural Worker*. Boston, MA: South End Press.

Karaian, Lara. 2012. "Lolita Speaks: 'Sexting,' Teenage Girls and the Law." *Crime, Media, Culture* 8 (1): 57–73. https://doi.org/10.1177/1741659011429868.

Karim, Laura. 2016. "The 'Scandal' of Grameen: The Nobel Prize, the Bank, and the State in Bangladesh." In *Seduced and Betrayed: Exposing the Contemporary Microfinance Phenomenon*, edited by Milford Bateman and Kate Maclean, 203–18. Albuquerque: University of New Mexico Press.

Karim, Yadgar. 2017. "Ottawa Street-Based Sex Workers and the Criminal Justice System: Interactions under the New Legal Regime." MA thesis, University of Ottawa.

Kelly, Joan, and Michael Johnson. 2008. "Differentiation among Types of Intimate Partner Violence: Research Update and Implications for Interventions." *Family Court Review* 46 (3): 476–99. https://doi.org/10.1111/j.1744-1617.2008.00215.x.

Kelly, Liz. 1987. "The Continuum of Sexual Violence." In *Women, Violence and Social Control*, edited by Mary Manard and Jalna

Hanmer, 46–60. London, UK: Palgrave Macmillan. https://doi. org/10.1007/978-1-349-18592-4_4.

Keogh, Jeanie. 2013. "Time to Slay the Perfect Mother Myth." *Herizons*. http://www.herizons.ca/node/545.

Khan, Janaya. 2016. "Black Lives Matter Toronto Co-founder Responds to Pride Action Criticism." *NOW Magazine*, July 6. https://nowtoronto. com/news/exclusive-black-lives-matter-pride-action-criticism/.

Kilbourne, Jean. 2010. *Killing Us Softly 4: Advertising's Image of Women* (film). Northampton, MA: Media Education Foundation.

Kilty, Jennifer M. 2012. "'It's Like They Don't Want You to Get Better': Psy Control of Women in the Carceral Context." *Feminism & Psychology* 22 (2): 162–82. https://doi.org/10.1177/0959353512439188.

———. 2014. "Examining the 'Psy-Carceral Complex' in the Death of Ashley Smith." In *Criminalizing Women: Gender and (In)Justice in Neoliberal Times*, 2nd ed., edited by Gillian Balfour and Elizabeth Comack, 236–54. Winnipeg, MB: Fernwood.

Kilty, Jennifer M., and Sylvie Frigon. 2016. *The Enigma of a Violent Woman*. New York: Routledge.

Kimmel, Michael. 2002. "'Gender Symmetry' in Domestic Violence: A Substantive and Methodological Research Review." *Violence Against Women* 8 (11): 1332–63. https://doi.org/10.1177/107780102237407.

Kipnis, Laura. 2006. *The Female Thing: Dirt, Sex, Envy, Vulnerability*. London, UK: Serpent's Tail.

Kirkpatrick, Clifford, and Eugene Kanin. 1957. "Male Sex Aggression on a University Campus." *American Sociological Review* 22 (1): 52–8. https:// doi.org/10.2307/2088765.

Kirkup, Kristy. 2017. "Federal Government Changes Course on Ending Sex Discrimination in Indian Act." *CBC News*, November 7. http:// www.cbc.ca/news/politics/indian-act-legislation-change-course-1.4392291.

Kittilson, Miki Caul, and Kim Fridkin. 2008. "Gender Candidate Portrayals and Election Campaigns: A Comparative Perspective." *Politics & Gender* 4 (3): 371–92. https://doi.org/10.1017/S1743923X08000330.

Koch, Sabine C., Stefan Konigorski, and Monika Sieverding. 2014. "Sexist Behavior Undermines Women's Performance in a Job Application Situation." *Sex Roles* 70 (3–4): 79–87. https://doi.org/10.1007/s11199-014-0342-3.

Kolahdooz, Fariba, Katherine Launier, Forouz Nader, Kyoung June Yi, Philip Baker, Tara-Leigh McHugh, Helen Vallianatos, and Sangita Sharma. 2016. "Canadian Indigenous Women's Perspectives of Maternal

Health and Health Care Services: A Systematic Review." *Diversity and Equality in Health and Care* 13 (5): 334–48.

Kpelitse, Koffi-Ahoto, Rose Anne Devlin, and Sisira Sarma. 2014. "The Effect of Income on Obesity among Canadian Adults." Working Paper No: 2014–C02. Toronto, ON: Canadian Centre for Health Economics.

Krais, Beate. 1993. "Gender and Symbolic Violence: Female Oppression in the Light of Pierre Bourdieu's Theory of Social Practice." In *Bourdieu: Critical Perspectives*, edited by Craig Calhoun, Edward LiPuma, and Moishe Postone, 156–77. Chicago, IL: University of Chicago Press.

Kramer, Kirsten. 2014. "Unwanted Motherhood and the Canadian Law of Infanticide." In *Within the Confines: Women and Law in Canada*, edited by Jennifer M. Kilty, 318–46. Toronto, ON: Women's Press.

Krüsi, A., K. Pacey, L. Bird, C. Taylor, J. Chettier, S. Allan, D. Bennett, J.S. Montaner, T. Kerr, and K. Shannon. 2014. "Criminalization of Clients: Reproducing Vulnerabilities for Violence and Poor Health among Street-Based Sex Workers in Canada—A Qualitative Study." *BMJ Open* 4 (6): 1154–9. https://doi.org/10.1136/bmjopen-2014-005191.

Kulchyski, Peter. 1999. "Aboriginal Peoples and Hegemony in Canada." In *Debates on Social Inequality: Class, Gender, and Ethnicity in Canada*, edited by M. Reza Nakhaie, 297–306. Toronto, ON: Harcourt Brace & Company.

Kuokkanen, Rauna. 2015. "Gendered Violence and Politics in Indigenous Communities: The Cases of Aboriginal People in Canada and the Sami in Scandinavia." *International Feminist Journal of Politics* 17 (2): 271–88. https://doi.org/10.1080/14616742.2014.901816.

Lam, Elene. 2014. "Brief to the Senate Standing Committee on Legal and Constitutional Affairs Regarding Bill C-36 (Protection of Communities and Exploited Persons Act)." Butterfly. https://sencanada.ca/content/sen/committee/412/lcjc/briefs/c-36/c-36_brief_butterfly_e.pdf.

Lam, Elene, and Chanelle Gallant. 2018. "Migrant Sex Worker Justice: Building Alliances across Movements." In *Red Light Labour: Sex Work Regulation, Agency and Resistance*, edited by Elya Durisin, Emily van der Meulen, and Chris Bruckert, 293–304. Vancouver, BC: University of British Colombia Press.

Lambert, Brittany, and Kate McInturff. 2016. "Making Women Count: The Unequal Economics of Women's Work." Canadian Centre for Policy Alternatives/Oxfam. https://www.policyalternatives.ca/sites/default/files/uploads/publications/National%20Office/2016/03/Making_Women_Count2016.pdf.

Landsberg, Adina, Kate Shannon, Andrea Krüsi, Kora DeBeck, M.-J. Milloy, Ekaterina Nosova, Thomas Kerr, and Kanna Hayashi. 2017.

"Criminalizing Sex Work Clients and Rushed Negotiations among Sex Workers Who Use Drugs in a Canadian Setting." *Journal of Urban Health* 94 (4): 563–71. https://doi.org/10.1007/s11524-017-0155-0.

Langton, Marianne. 1982. "Is Your Job Hazardous to Your Health?" In *Still Ain't Satisfied! Canadian Feminism Today*, edited by Maureen Fitzgerald, Connie Guberman, and Margie Wolfe, 181–94. Toronto, ON: Women's Press.

LaPrairie, Carol. 1987. "Native Women and Crime in Canada: A Theoretical Model." In *Too Few to Count*, edited by Ellen Adelburg and Claudia Currie, 103–12. Vancouver, BC: Press Gang.

Laros, Samantha. 2014. "The Impact of Obesity on Employment Participation and Earnings among Working-Age Women in Canada: Evidence from the NPHS Longitudinal Data." MA thesis, University of Western Ontario.

Laudati, Ann. 2013. "Beyond Minerals: Broadening 'Economies of Violence' in Eastern Democratic Republic of Congo." *Review of African Political Economy* 40 (135): 32–50. https://doi.org/10.1080/03056244.2012.760446.

Lauzen, Martha M. 2017. *It's a Man's (Celluloid) World: Portrayals of Female Characters in the Top 100 Films of 2016*. San Diego: Center for the Study of Women in Television & Film. http://womenintvfilm.sdsu.edu/wp-content/uploads/2017/02/2016-Its-a-Mans-Celluloid-World-Report.pdf.

———. 2018. *The Celluloid Ceiling: Behind-the-Scenes Employment of Women on the Top 100, 250, and 500 Films of 2016*. San Diego: Center for the Study of Women in Television & Film. https://womenintvfilm.sdsu.edu/wp-content/uploads/2018/01/2017_Celluloid_Ceiling_Report.pdf.

LaViolette, Nicole. 2014. "Sexual Orientation, Gender Identity and the Refugee Determination Process in Canada." *Journal of Research in Gender Studies* 4 (2): 68–123.

Law, Tuulia. 2016. "Managing the 'Party': Third Parties and the Organization of Labour in Ontario Strip Clubs." PhD diss., University of Ottawa.

Lazar, Michelle. 2017. "'Seriously Girly Fun!': Recontextualising Aesthetic Labour as Fun and Play in Cosmetics Advertising." In *Aesthetic Labour: Rethinking Beauty Politics in Neoliberalism*, edited by Ana Sofia Elias, Rosalind Gill, and Christina Scharff, 51–66. London, UK: Palgrave Macmillan. https://doi.org/10.1057/978-1-137-47765-1_2.

Leblanc, Daniel, and Ian Bailey. 2018. "Brenda Lucki Vows 'No Stone Unturned' on Bullying, Sexism as She Takes the Helm of RCMP." *The Globe and Mail*, March 9. https://www.theglobeandmail.com/

news/national/brenda-lucki-taking-helm-of-rcmp-as-force-struggles-with-bullying-sexism/article38259775.

Leblanc, Mireille, and Julian Barling. 2004. "Understanding the Many Faces of Workplace Violence." In *Counterproductive Work Behavior: Investigations of Actors and Targets*, edited by Suzy Fox and Paul Spector, 41–63. Washington, DC: APA Publishing.

Lee, Youn Ju, Kunsook Bernstein, Mihyoung Lee, and Kathleen Nokes. 2014. "Bullying in the Nursing Workplace: Applying Evidence Using a Conceptual Framework." *Nursing Economics* 32 (5): 255–67.

Leong, Yee Mun Jessica, and Joanna Crossman. 2016. "Tough Love or Bullying? New Nurse Transitional Experiences." *Journal of Clinical Nursing* 25 (9–10): 1356–66. https://doi.org/10.1111/jocn.13225.

Lewis, Dio, Elizabeth Cady Stanton, and James Read Chadwick. 1882. "The Health of American Women." *North American Review* 135 (313): 503–24.

Link, Bruce, and Jo Phelan. 2001. "Conceptualizing Stigma." *Annual Review of Sociology* 27 (1): 363–85. https://doi.org/10.1146/annurev.soc.27.1.363.

Livingston, Beth. 2015. "Cornell International Survey on Street Harassment." *Hollaback!* https://www.ihollaback.org/cornell-international-survey-on-street-harassment/#ca.

Lockman, Darcy. 2017. "Where Do Kids Learn to Undervalue Women? From Their Parents." *Washington Post*, November 10. https://www.washingtonpost.com/outlook/where-do-kids-learn-to-undervalue-women-from-their-parents/2017/11/10/724518b2-c439-11e7-afe9-4f60b5a6c4a0_story.html?utm_term=.be8d208c8ee0.

Lofaro, Joe. 2016. "Ottawa Officer Demoted for Three Months for 'Racist' Facebook Post about Dead Inuk Artist." *Ottawa Citizen*, December 7. http://ottawacitizen.com/news/local-news/ottawa-officer-demoted-for-three-months-for-racist-facebook-post-about-dead-inuk-artist.

Longmore, Monica A. 1998. "Symbolic Interactionism and the Study of Sexuality." *Journal of Sex Research* 35 (1): 44–57. https://doi.org/10.1080/00224499809551916.

Los, Maria. 1994. "The Struggle to Redefine Rape in the Early 1980s." In *Confronting Sexual Assault: A Decade of Legal and Social Change*, edited by Julian Roberts and Renate Mohr, 20–56. Toronto, ON: University of Toronto Press.

Lowman, John. 2000. "Violence and the Outlaw Status of (Street) Prostitution." *Violence Against Women* 6 (9): 987–1011. https://doi.org/10.1177/10778010022182245.

———. 2014. "Tripping Point: Brief to the Standing Committee on Justice and Human Rights on the *Protection of Communities and Exploited Persons*

Act." http://184.70.147.70/lowman_prostitution/HTML/SCJHR/ Tripping_Point_Lowman_Brief_to_the_SCJHR_on_Bill_C36.pdf.

Lu, Vanessa. 2016. "Call Centre Workers Speak Out about Abuse by Public." *Toronto Star*, December 7. https://www.thestar.com/ business/2016/12/07/call-centre-workers-speak-out-about-abuse-by-public.html.

Lu, Yuqian, and Feng Hou. 2017. *Transition from Temporary Foreign Workers to Permanent Residents, 1990–2014*. Ottawa, ON: Statistics Canada. http:// www.statcan.gc.ca/pub/11f0019m/11f0019m2017389-eng.htm.

Lucero, Gabrielle. 2015. "Military Sexual Assault: Reporting and Rape Culture." *Stanford Journal of Public Policy* 6 (1): 1–32.

Lupick, Travis. 2015. "Living Nightmare for Transgender Inmate at All-Male Prison." *Toronto Star*, December 13. https://www.thestar.com/news/ canada/2015/12/13/living-nightmare-for-transgender-inmate-at-all-male-prison.html.

Lutgen-Sandvik, Pamela, and Sarah J. Tracy. 2012. "Answering Five Key Questions about Workplace Bullying: How Communication Scholarship Provides Thought Leadership for Transforming Abuse at Work." *Management Communication Quarterly* 26 (1): 3–47. https://doi. org/10.1177/0893318911414400.

Lyons, Dan. 2017. "Jerks and the Start-Ups They Ruin." *The New York Times*, April 1. https://mobile.nytimes.com/2017/04/01/opinion/sunday/jerks-and-the-start-ups-they-ruin.html.

MacDonald, Nancy. 2015. "Welcome to Winnipeg: Where Canada's Racism Problem Is at Its Worst." *Maclean's*, January 22. http://www.macleans.ca/ news/canada/welcome-to-winnipeg-where-canadas-racism-problem-is-at-its-worst/.

MacDonald, Neil. 2017. "Commission on Missing, Murdered Indigenous Women Has Become a Fortress of Bureaucratic Incompetence." *CBC News*, May 20. http://www.cbc.ca/news/opinion/ mmiwg-inquiry-1.4124403.

Mackenzie, Hugh. 2015. "The Long Shadow." *On Policy: The Canadian Centre for Policy Alternatives Ontario*, 12–15. https://www. policyalternatives.ca/sites/default/files/uploads/publications/ Ontario%20Office/2015/06/Ontario%20Policy%20magazine%20-%20 Summer%202015-%20final.pdf.

———. 2017. *Shortchanging Ontario Students: An Overview and Assessment of Education Funding in Ontario*. Toronto, ON: Elementary Teachers' Foundation of Ontario.

MacKinnon, Catharine A. 1982. "Feminism, Marxism, Method, and the State: An Agenda for Theory." *Signs* 7 (3): 515–44. https://doi.org/10.1086/493898.

———. 1987. *Feminism Unmodified: Discourses on Life and Law*. Cambridge, MA: Harvard University Press.

MacKinnon, Mark, and Keith Lacey. 2001. "Bleak House." *The Globe and Mail*, August 18. http://www.vcn.bc.ca/august10/politics/1019_kimrogers.html.

Macklin, Audrey. 2003. "Dancing across Borders: 'Exotic Dancers,' Trafficking and Canadian Immigration Policy." *International Migration Review* 37 (2): 464–500. https://doi.org/10.1111/j.1747-7379.2003.tb00145.x.

MacLellan, Duncan. 2009. "Neoliberalism and Ontario Teachers' Unions: A 'Not-So' Common Sense Revolution." *Socialist Studies: The Journal of the Society for Socialist Studies* 5 (1): 51–74.

MacLeod, Linda. 1980. *Wife Battering in Canada: The Vicious Circle*. Hull, QC: Advisory Council on the Status of Women.

Mahony, Tina Hotton, Joanna Jacob, and Heather Hobson. 2017. *Women and the Criminal Justice System*. Ottawa, ON: Statistics Canada.

Maine, D'Arcy. 2014. "A Timeline of the NFL's and Ravens' Reactions to Ray Rice Incident." *ESPN*, September 10. http://www.espn.com/espnw/news-commentary/article/11489146/a-timeline-nfl-ravens-reactions-ray-rice-incident.

Majury, Diana. 1994. "Seaboyer and Gayme: A Study of Inequity." In *Confronting Sexual Assault: A Decade of Legal and Social Change*, edited by Julian Roberts and Renate Mohr, 268–92. Toronto, ON: University of Toronto Press.

Marcellin, Roxanne L., Greta R. Bauer, and Ayden I. Scheim. 2013. "Intersecting Impacts of Transphobia and Racism on HIV Risk among Trans Persons of Colour in Ontario, Canada." *Ethnicity and Inequalities in Health and Social Care* 6 (4): 97–107. https://doi.org/10.1108/EIHSC-09-2013-0017.

Maroney, Heather Jon. 1987. "Feminism at Work." In *Feminism and Political Economy: Women's Work, Women's Struggles*, edited by Heather Jon Maroney and Meg Luxton, 85–108. Agincourt, ON: Methuen Publishers.

Maroney, Heather Jon, and Meg Luxton. 1997. "Gender at Work: Canadian Feminist Economy since 1988." In *Understanding Canada: Building the New Canadian Political Economy*, edited by Wallace Clement, 85–117. Montréal, QC: McGill-Queen's University Press.

Martin, Del. 1976. *Battered Wives*. New York: Simon & Schuster Inc.

———. 1978. "Battered Women: Society's Problem." In *The Victimization of Women*, edited by Jan Chapman and Margaret Gates, 111–41. Beverly Hills, CA: Sage.

Martin, Kevin. 2016. "'He Made Me Hate Myself' Victim Says of Justice
    Robin Camp." *The Calgary Sun*, September 6. http://calgarysun.
    com/2016/09/06/he-made-me-hate-myself-victim-says-of-justice-
    robin-camp-in-rape-comments-controversy.

Marx, Karl. (1859) 1974. *Capital*, vol. 1. New York: International.

Matas, Robert. 2012. "Don't Be 'That Guy' Ad Campaign Cuts
    Vancouver Sex Assaults by 10 Per cent in 2011." *The Globe and Mail*,
    January 21. https://www.theglobeandmail.com/news/british-
    columbia/dont-be-that-guy-ad-campaign-cuts-vancouver-sex-
    assaults-by-10-per-cent-in-2011/article1359241/.

Maurutto, Paula, and Kelly Hannah-Moffat. 2016. "Aboriginal Knowledges
    in Specialized Courts: Emerging Practices in Gladue Courts." *Canadian
    Journal of Law and Society* 31 (3): 451–71. https://doi.org/10.1017/
    cls.2016.35.

Maxwell, Ashley. 2017. *Adult Criminal Court Statistics in Canada, 2014/2015*.
    Ottawa, ON: Statistics Canada. http://www.statcan.gc.ca/pub/85-
    002-x/2017001/article/14699-eng.pdf.

Maynard, Robyn. 2015. "Fighting Wrongs with Wrongs? How Canadian
    Anti-Trafficking Crusades Have Failed Sex Workers, Migrants, and
    Indigenous Communities." *Atlantis: Critical Studies in Gender, Culture &
    Social Justice* 37 (2): 40–56.

————. 2017. *Policing Black Lives: State Violence in Canada from Slavery to the
    Present*. Winnipeg, MB: Fernwood.

McDonald, Paula. 2012. "Workplace Sexual Harassment 30 Years On: A
    Review of the Literature." *International Journal of Management Reviews* 14
    (1): 1–17. https://doi.org/10.1111/j.1468-2370.2011.00300.x.

McInnes, Sadie. 2017. "Violence against Trans People in Canada:
    A Primer." Canadian Centre for Policy Alternatives Manitoba
    Office, February 14. https://policyfix.ca/2017/01/30/
    violence-against-trans-people-in-canada-a-primer/.

McIntosh, Heather. 2013. "Women and Politics in the Media." *Global Media
    Journal Canadian Edition* 6 (2): 99–104.

McIntosh, Peggy. 1989. *White Privilege: Unpacking the Invisible
    Knapsack. National SEED Project on Inclusive Curriculum*. Wellesley,
    MA: National SEED Project. https://nationalseedproject.org/
    white-privilege-unpacking-the-invisible-knapsack.

McIvor, Sharon. 2004. "Aboriginal Women Unmasked: Using Equality
    Litigation to Advance Women's Rights." *Canadian Journal of Women and
    the Law* 16: 106–36.

————. 2015. "Sharon McIvor Delivers FIFIA Statement in the UN
    Human Rights Committee, July 6, 2016." FIFIA-AFAI Canada. http://

fafia-afai.org/en/sharon-mcivor-delivers-fafia-statement-in-the-un-human-rights-committee-july-6-2015/.

McLaughlin, Eliotte. 2014. "Janay Rice: Ray Rice Was 'Terrified' after Hitting Me." *CNN*, December 1. http://www.cnn.com/2014/12/01/us/ray-rice-wife-janay-today-show.

McLean, Lorna. 2002. "'Deserving' Wives and 'Drunken' Husbands: Wife Beating, Marital Conduct, and the Law in Ontario, 1850–1910." *Social History* 35 (69): 59–81.

McLean, Siân A., Susan J. Paxton, Eleanor H. Wertheim, and Jennifer Masters. 2015. "Photoshopping the Selfie: Self Photo Editing and Photo Investment Are Associated with Body Dissatisfaction in Adolescent Girls." *International Journal of Eating Disorders* 48 (8): 1132–40. https://doi.org/10.1002/eat.22449.

McRobbie, Angela. 2004. "Notes on 'What Not to Wear' and Post-Feminist Symbolic Violence." *Sociological Review* 52 (2): 99–109. https://doi.org/10.1111/j.1467-954X.2005.00526.x.

Meister, Alyson, Amanda Sinclair, and Karen A. Jehn. 2017. "Identities under Scrutiny: How Women Leaders Navigate Feeling Misidentified at Work." *Leadership Quarterly* 28 (5): 672–90. https://doi.org/10.1016/j.leaqua.2017.01.009.

Messner, Michael A. 1992. *Power at Play: Sports and the Problem of Masculinity*. Boston, MA: Beacon Press.

Meyer, Doug. 2012. "An Intersectional Analysis of Lesbian, Gay, Bisexual, and Transgender (LGBT) People's Evaluations of Anti-Queer Violence." *Gender & Society* 26 (6): 849–73. https://doi.org/10.1177/0891243212461299.

Mikkonen, Juha, and Dennis Raphael. 2010. *Social Determinants of Health: The Canadian Facts*. Toronto, ON: York University School of Health Policy and Management.

Millar, Hayli, and Tamara O'Doherty. 2015. *The Palermo Protocol & Canada: The Evolution and Human Rights Impacts of Anti-Trafficking Laws in Canada (2002–2015)*. Vancouver, BC: SWAN. https://www.ufv.ca/media/assets/criminology/Palermo-Project-Key-Findings-Report-15-October-2015-with-copyright-2.pdf.

Millbank, Jenni. 2003. "Gender, Sex and Visibility in Refugee Claims on the Basis of Sexual Orientation." *Georgetown Immigration Law Journal* 18: 71–110.

Mitchell, Margaret. (1982) 2017. "NDP Margaret Mitchell Gets Heckled over Domestic Abuse Speech by Male MPs" (video). *YouTube*, March 9. https://www.youtube.com/watch?v=BPhu6gNeRV4.

Mohanty, Chandra Talpade. 2003. *Feminism without Borders: Decolonizing Theory, Practicing Solidarity*. Durham, NC: Duke University Press. https://doi.org/10.1215/9780822384649.

Montesanti, Stephanie Rose, and Wilfreda E. Thurston. 2015. "Mapping the Role of Structural and Interpersonal Violence in the Lives of Women: Implications for Public Health Interventions and Policy." *BMC Women's Health* 15 (1): 100. https://doi.org/10.1186/s12905-015-0256-4.

Monture, Patricia. 1990. "The Voices of Aboriginal People." In *Creating Choices: Report Written by the Task Force for Federally Sentenced Women*. Ottawa, ON: Correctional Service of Canada.

Moreau, Bernice. 1997. "Black Nova Scotian Women's Experience of Educational Violence in the Early 1900s: A Case of Colour Contusion." *Dalhousie Review* 77 (2): 179–206.

Morgan, Robin. 1968. "Miss America Goes Down." *Rat*, September 20–October 3. https://library.duke.edu/digitalcollections/wlmpc_maddc04031/.

Morris, Marika. 2016. *Women's Leadership Matters: The Impact of Women's Leadership in the Canadian Federal Public Service*. Ottawa, ON: Centre for Women in Politics and Public Leadership, Carleton University.

Morris, Ruth, and Liz Elliot. 1987. "Behind Closed Doors." In *Too Few to Count*, edited by Ellen Adelburg and Claudia Currie, 145–62. Vancouver, BC: Press Gang.

Morton, Peggy. 1971. "A Woman's Work Is Never Done." In *From Feminism to Liberation*, edited by E.H. Altbach, 211–27. Cambridge, MA: Schenkman.

Moylan, Lois Biggin, Meritta B. Cullinan, and Jeanne E. Kimpel. 2014. "Differences in Male and Female Nurses' Responses to Physical Assault by Psychiatric Patients: A Supplemental Finding of a Mixed-Methods Study." *Journal of Psychosocial Nursing and Mental Health Services* 52 (12): 36–42. https://doi.org/10.3928/02793695-20140903-01.

Moyser, Melissa. 2017. "Women and Paid Work." Ottawa, ON: Statistics Canada. http://www.statcan.gc.ca/pub/89-503-x/2015001/article/14694-eng.pdf.

Mudge, S.L. 2008. "What Is Neo-Liberalism?" *Socio-economic Review* 6 (4): 703–31. https://doi.org/10.1093/ser/mwn016.

Mulvey, Laura. 2015. "Introduction: 1970s Feminist Film Theory and the Obsolescent Object." In *Feminisms: Diversity, Difference and Multiplicity in Contemporary Film Cultures*, edited by Laura Mulvey and Anne Backman Rogers, 17–26. Amsterdam: Amsterdam University Press.

Munn, Melissa. 2012. "The Mark of Criminality." In *Stigma Revisited: Implications of the Mark*, edited by Stacey Hannem and Chris Bruckert, 147–69. Ottawa, ON: University of Ottawa Press.

Murphy, Emily. 1922. *The Black Candle.* Toronto, ON: Thomas Allen.

Murphy, Mary. 2016. "NYC Couple Complains American Airlines Thought Boyfriend Was Sex Trafficker." *PIX New York*, January 7. http://pix11.com/2016/01/07/nyc-woman-complains-american-airlines-thought-boyfriend-was-sex-trafficker/.

Murtha, Tara. 2015. "'9 to 5' Turns 35, and It's Still Radical Today." *Rolling Stone*, December 18. https://www.rollingstone.com/politics/news/9-to-5-turns-35-and-its-still-radical-today-20151218.

NACM (National Aboriginal Council of Midwives). 2012a. "Aboriginal Midwifery in Canada." http://aboriginalmidwives.ca/aboriginal-midwifery-in-canada.

———. 2012b. "Aboriginal Midwifery Practices in Canada." http://aboriginalmidwives.ca/aboriginal-midwifery/practices-in-Canada.

NAHO (National Aboriginal Health Organization). 2008. *Celebrating Birth—Aboriginal Midwifery in Canada*. Ottawa, ON: National Aboriginal Health Organization.

Nasser, Shanifa. 2016. "The Quiet Pain of Prejudice That Black Women Feel Looking for Work in Toronto." *CBC News*, November 5. http://www.cbc.ca/news/canada/toronto/the-quiet-pain-of-prejudice-that-black-women-feel-looking-for-work-in-toronto-1.3838195.

National Center for PTSD. 2016. "Understanding PTSD and PTSD Treatment." https://www.ptsd.va.gov/public/understanding_ptsd/booklet.pdf.

Nelson, Charmaine. 2017. "The Canadian Narrative about Slavery Is Wrong." *The Walrus*, July 21. https://thewalrus.ca/the-canadian-narrative-about-slavery-is-wrong/.

Nero, Dominick. 2017. "Why Do Action Heroines Do This?" *Fandor*, January 5. https://www.fandor.com/posts/why-do-action-heroines-do-this.

Ng, Eddy, Rana Haq, and Diane-Gabrielle Tremblay. 2014. "A Review of Two Decades of Employment Equity in Canada: Progress and Propositions." In *International Handbook on Diversity Management at Work: Country Perspectives on Diversity and Equal Treatment*, 2nd ed., edited by A. Klarsfeld, L. Booysen, G. Combs, E. Ng, I. Roper, and A. Tatli, 46–67. Cheltenham, UK: Edward Elgar. https://doi.org/10.4337/9780857939319.00008.

Nicolle, Leanne. 2017. "How I Brought a Powerful Sexual Harasser Down." *The Globe and Mail*, October 14. https://beta.theglobeandmail.

com/opinion/how-i-brought-a-powerful-sexual-harasser-down/
article36593410/.

Nixon, Rob. 2011. *Slow Violence and the Environmentalism of the Poor.*
Cambridge, MA: Harvard University Press. https://doi.org/10.4159/
harvard.9780674061194.

Nova Scotia. 2012. "Human Resources Management Manual 500."
Treasury Board Office. https://novascotia.ca/treasuryboard/manuals/
PDF/500/50409.pdf.

NSHRC (Nova Scotia Human Rights Commission). n.d. "Sexual
Harassment: Legal Position." Halifax, NS: NSHRC.

NWAC (Native Women's Association of Canada). 2002. *Violations to
Indigenous Human Rights.* Ottawa, ON: Native Women's Association.
———. 2017. "NWAC Responds to Latest Version of Bill S-3."
November 9. https://www.nwac.ca/2017/11/nwac-responds-
latest-version-bill-s-3/.

Oakes, Summer. 2013. "The Skinny of Fashion's Body-Image Issue."
Huffington Post, July 31. https://www.huffingtonpost.com/summer-
rayne-oakes/the-skinny-of-fashions-body-image-issue_b_3308004.
html.

O'Connell Davidson, Julia. 2006. "Will the Real Sex Slave Please Stand
Up?" *Feminist Review* 83 (1): 4–22. https://doi.org/10.1057/palgrave.
fr.9400278.

O'Doherty, Tamara. 2015. "Victimization in the Canadian Off-Street Sex
Industry," PhD diss., Simon Fraser University.

O'Doherty, Tamara, Hayli Millar, Alison Clancey, and Kimberly
Mackenzie. 2018. "Misrepresentations, Inadequate Evidence, and
Impediments to Justice: Human Rights Impacts of Canada's Anti-
Trafficking Efforts." In *Red Light Labour: Sex Work Regulation, Agency
and Resistance*, edited by Elya Durisin, Emily van der Meulen,
and Chris Bruckert, 104–20. Vancouver, BC: University of British
Columbia Press.

OECD (Organisation for Economic Co-operation and Development).
2016. "Social Expenditure Update." http://www.oecd.org/els/soc/
OECD2016-Social-Expenditure-Update.pdf.

OFL (Ontario Federation of Labour). 2002. "The Privatization of Ontario's
Education System: 1995–2001—OFL 'Education Is a Right' Task Force
Report on Publicly-Funded Education in Ontario." http://ofl.ca/
wp-content/uploads/2002.01.01-Report-EducationPrivatization.pdf.
———. 2016. "Closing the Gap: A Workers' Agenda for Pay Equity"
Ontario Submission to the Ontario Gender Wage Gap Strategy. http://
ofl.ca/wp-content/uploads/2016.01.15-SUB-GenderWageGap.pdf.

OHRC (Ontario Human Rights Commission). 2016. "Sexualized and Gender-Specific Dress Codes: FAQs." http://www.ohrc. on.ca/en/ohrc-policy-position-gender-specific-dress-codes/ dress-code-faqs#_ftnref7

———. 2017. *Under Suspicion: Research and Consultation Report on Racial Profiling in Ontario.* Toronto, ON: Ontario Human Rights Commission.

Olds, David, Harriot Kitzman, Robert Cole, Jo-Ann Robinson, Kimberley Sidora, Dennis Luckey, Charles Henderson Jr., Carol Hanks, Jessica Bondy, and John Holmberg. 2004. "Effects of Nurse Home-Visiting on Maternal Life Course and Child Development: Age 6 Follow-Up Results of a Randomized Trial." *Pediatrics* 114 (6): 1550–9. https://doi. org/10.1542/peds.2004-0962.

O'Meara, Jennifer. 2016. "What 'The Bechdel Test' Doesn't Tell Us: Examining Women's Verbal and Vocal (Dis)Empowerment in Cinema." *Feminist Media Studies* 16 (6): 1120–3. https://doi.org/10.1080/14680777. 2016.1234239.

O'Neill, B. 2015. "Unpacking Gender's Role in Political Representation in Canada: The Story of Women's Political Representation in Canada." *Canadian Parliamentary Review* 38 (2): 22–30.

Oppal, Wally T. 2012. *Forsaken: The Report of the Missing Women Commission of Inquiry, Executive Summary.* Victoria, BC: Government of British Columbia.

Orbach. Susie. 2017. "The Making of the Body." In *Aesthetic Labour: Rethinking Beauty Politics in Neoliberalism*, edited by Ana Elias, Rosalind Gill, and Christina Scharff, vii–x. London, UK: Palgrave Macmillan.

Ortega, Sertio. 2012. "Guess the Airline—March 2012 Answer." *Air Odyssey.net*, April 1. https://airodyssey.net/2012/04/01/ guess-the-airline-march-2012-answer/.

Oxfam. 2016. "Shortchanged: Make Work Paid, Equal & Valued for Women." https://www.oxfam.ca/sites/default/files/file_attachments/ shortchanged_briefing_note.pdf.

———. 2017. *Tourism's Dirty Secret: The Exploitation of Hotel Housekeepers.* https://www.oxfam.ca/sites/default/files/file_attachments/tourisms_ dirty_secret_-_oxfam_canada_report_-_oct_17_2017.pdf.

Palmater, Pamela. 2016. "Shining Light on the Dark Places: Addressing Police Racism and Sexualized Violence against Indigenous Women and Girls in the National Inquiry." *Canadian Journal of Women and the Law* 28 (2): 253–84. https://doi.org/10.3138/cjwl.28.2.253.

Paprocki, Kasia. 2016. "Moral and Other Economies: Nijera Kori and Its Alternatives to Microcredit." In *Seduced and Betrayed: Exposing the*

Contemporary Microfinance Phenomenon, edited by Milford Bateman and Kate Maclean, 265–78. Albuquerque: University of New Mexico Press.

Paris, Evelyn. 2014. "Capitalism and Our Idea of Beauty." *The AdorGalore Blog*, April 1. https://ardorgalore.wordpress.com/2014/04/01/capitalism-and-our-idea-of-beauty/.

Pasha-Robinson, Lucy. 2017. "Kenyan Women Urged to Withhold Sex Until Their Husbands Register to Vote." *Independent*, January 17. http://www.independent.co.uk/news/world/africa/kenyan-women-withhold-sex-husbands-register-vote-kenya-mp-mishi-mboko-elections-a7532376.html.

Paulson, Bob. 2016. "'We Failed You. We Hurt You': Text of Apology from RCMP Commissioner Bob Paulson." *CBC News*, October 6. https://www.ctvnews.ca/canada/we-failed-you-we-hurt-you-text-of-apology-from-rcmp-commissioner-bob-paulson-1.3104743.

Payton, Laura. 2017. "Liberal MP Iqra Khalid Reads Threats She's Received over Motion 103." *CTV News*, February 16. http://www.ctvnews.ca/politics/liberal-mp-iqra-khalid-reads-threats-she-s-received-over-motion-103-1.3288801.

Pedersen, Diana. 1986. "'Keeping Our Good Girls Good': The YMCA and the 'Girl Problem,' 1870–1930." *Canadian Women's Studies* 7 (4): 20–4.

Pennell, Joan, and Gale Burford. 2000. "Family Group Decision Making: Protecting Children and Women." *Child Welfare* 79: 131–58.

Pennisi, Sarah, and Stephanie Baker Collins. 2016. "Workfare under Ontario Works: Making Sense of Jobless Work." *Social Policy and Administration*. https://doi.org/10.1111/spol.12271.

Perry, Barbara. 2014. "Gendered Islamophobia: Hate Crime against Muslim Women." *Social Identities* 20 (1): 74–89. https://doi.org/10.1080/13504630.2013.864467.

Perry, Imani. 2007. "Let Me Holler at You: African-American Culture, Postmodern Feminism, and Revisiting the Law of Sexual Harassment." *Georgetown Journal of Gender and the Law* VIII: 111–27.

Perreault, Samuel. 2015. *Criminal Victimization in Canada, 2014*. Ottawa, ON: Canadian Centre for Justice Statistics, Statistics Canada.

Pilon, Marilyn. 1999. *Canada's Legal Age of Consent to Sexual Activity*, revised in 2001. Ottawa, ON: Library of Parliament, Law and Government Division.

Poland, Bailey. 2016. *Haters: Harassment, Abuse, and Violence Online*. Lincoln: University of Nebraska Press. https://doi.org/10.2307/j.ctt1fq9wdp.

Popkin, Susan, Tama Leventhal, and Gretchen Weismann. 2010. "Girls in the 'Hood: How Safety Affects the Life Chances of Low Income Girls." *Urban Affairs Review* 45 (6): 715–44. https://doi.org/10.1177/1078087410361572.

Poster, Winifred R., Marion G. Crain, and Miriam A. Cherry. 2016.
    "Introduction: Conceptualizing Invisible Labor." In *Invisible Labor:
    Hidden Work in the Contemporary World*, edited by Marion G. Crain,
    Winifred R. Poster, Miriam A. Cherry, 3–27. Oakland, CA: University of
    California Press.

PRC (Pew Research Centre). 2015. "Raising Kids and Running a
    Household: How Working Parents Share the Load." http://www.
    pewsocialtrends.org/2015/11/04/raising-kids-and-running-a-household-
    how-working-parents-share-the-load/.

Premji, Stephanie, Yogendra Shakya, Megan Spasevski, Jessica Merolli,
    Sehr Athar, and Precarious Employment Core Research Group. 2014.
    "Precarious Work Experiences of Racialized Immigrant Women in
    Toronto: A Community-Based Study." *Just Labour: A Canadian Journal of
    Work and Society* 22 (Autumn): 122–43.

Public Health Ontario. 2014. *Healthy Babies Healthy Children Process
    Implementation Evaluation: Executive Summary*. Toronto, ON: Queen's
    Printer for Ontario.

Purdy, Chris. 2015. "Domestic Violence Laws Change across Canada
    Following Horrific Year." *Huffington Post Alberta*, December 18. http://
    www.huffingtonpost.ca/2015/12/18/a-most-violent-year-changes-for-
    domestic-abuse-victims-follow-killings_n_8836194.html.

Purkayastha, Bandana. 2009. "Many Views on Peace." In *Advances in Military
    Sociology: Essays in Honor of Charles C. Moskos*, edited by Giuseppe
    Caforio, 43–57. Bingley, UK: Emerald Publishing Group. https://doi.
    org/10.1108/S1572-8323(2009)000012A008.

Raine, Kim. 2004. *Overweight and Obesity in Canada: A Population Health
    Perspective*. Ottawa, ON: Canadian Institute for Health Information.

Randall, Melanie. 2010. "Sexual Assault Law, Credibility, and 'Ideal Victims':
    Consent, Resistance, and Victim Blaming." *Canadian Journal of Women
    and the Law* 22 (2): 397–433. https://doi.org/10.3138/cjwl.22.2.397.

———. 2013. "Restorative Justice and Gendered Violence? From Vaguely
    Hostile Skeptic to Cautious Convert: Why Feminists Should Critically
    Engage with Restorative Approaches to Law." *Dalhousie Law Journal*
    36 (2): 461–99.

Rayburn, Corey. 2006. "To Match a Sex Thief: The Burden of Performance
    in Rape and Sexual Assault Trials." *Columbia Journal of Gender and Law*
    15 (2): 437–84.

Razack, Sherene. 2008. *Casting Out: The Eviction of Muslims from Western Law
    & Politics*. Toronto, ON: University of Toronto Press.

———. 2016. "Sexualized Violence and Colonialism: Reflections on the Inquiry
    into Missing and Murdered Indigenous Women." *Canadian Journal of Women
    and the Law* 28 (2): i–iv. https://doi.org/10.3138/cjwl.28.2.i.

RCAP (Royal Commission on Aboriginal Peoples). 1996. "Report of the Royal Commission on Aboriginal Peoples, Volume 1: Looking Forward, Looking Back." http://data2.archives.ca/e/e448/e011188230-01.pdf.

RCMP (Royal Canadian Mounted Police). 2014. *Missing and Murdered Aboriginal Women: A National Operational Overview.* Ottawa, ON: RCMP.
———. 2017. "RCMP Statement on Human Rights Watch Report." *RCMP News,* June 19. http://www.rcmp.gc.ca/en/news/2017/rcmp-statement-human-rights-watch-report.

Reaume, Geoffrey. 2014. "Understanding Critical Disability Studies." *Canadian Medical Association Journal* 186 (16): 1248–9. https://doi.org/10.1503/cmaj.141236.

Reger, Jo. 2014. "Micro-Cohorts, Feminist Discourse, and the Emergence of the Toronto Slut Walk." *Feminist Formations* 26 (1): 49–69. https://doi.org/10.1353/ff.2014.0005.

Rempel, Michelle. 2016. "Confront Your Sexism." *National Post,* April 18. http://nationalpost.com/opinion/michelle-rempel-confront-your-sexism.

Rice, Waubgeshig. 2017. "Public Service Harassment Investigations Only 'Scratch the Surface,' Say Experts." *CBC News,* February 27. http://www.cbc.ca/beta/news/canada/ottawa/public-service-workplace-bullying-1.3998012.

Richardson, Kay, Kerry Parry, and John Corner. 2013. *Political Culture and Media Genre: Beyond the News.* New York: Palgrave Macmillan. https://doi.org/10.1057/9781137291271.

Ringdal, Nils Johan. 2004. *Love for Sale: A World History of Prostitution.* New York: Grove/Atlantic.

Ristock, Janice Lynn. 2002. *No More Secrets: Violence in Lesbian Relationships.* New York: Routledge.

Rob Bliss Creative. 2014. "10 Hours of Walking in NYC as a Woman" (video). *YouTube,* October 28. https://www.youtube.com/watch?v=b1XGPvbWn0A.

Roscigno, Vincent J., Randy Hodson, and Steven H. Lopez. 2009. "Workplace Incivilities: The Role of Interest Conflicts, Social Closure and Organizational Chaos." *Work, Employment and Society* 23 (4): 747–73. https://doi.org/10.1177/0950017009344875.

Rose, Joseph. 2002. "The Assault on School Teacher Bargaining in Ontario." *Relations Industrielles* 57 (1): 100–26. https://doi.org/10.7202/006712ar.

Rose, Nikolas. 1996. "Death of the Social: Re-figuring the Territory of Government." *Economy and Society* 25 (3): 327–56. https://doi.org/10.1080/03085149600000018.
———. 1999. *Powers of Freedom: Reframing Political Thought.* Cambridge, MA: Cambridge University Press.

Rose, Nikolas, and Peter Miller. 1992. "Political Power beyond the State: Problematics of Government." *British Journal of Sociology* 43 (2): 173–205. https://doi.org/10.2307/591464.

Rosenberg, Harriet. 1987. "Motherwork, Stress and Depression. The Costs of Privatized Social Reproduction." In *Feminism and Political Economy: Women's Work, Women's Struggles*, edited by H. J. Maroney and M. Luxton, 181–96. Toronto, ON: Methuen.

Ross, Becki. 2010. "Sex and (Evacuation from) the City: The Moral and Legal Regulation of Sex Workers in Vancouver's West End, 1975–1985." *Sexualities* 13 (2): 197–218. https://doi.org/10.1177/1363460709359232.

Ross, Selena. 2015. "'Motivated by Hate': Muslim Girls Told Not to Walk Alone at Night in Toronto." *The Globe and Mail*, November 17. https://www.theglobeandmail.com/news/toronto/assault-of-toronto-woman-being-treated-as-a-hate-crime/article27291302/.

Rotenberg, Cristine. 2016. *Prostitution Offences in Canada: Statistical Trends*. Ottawa, ON: Canadian Centre for Justice Statistics.

———. 2017. *From Arrest to Conviction: Court Outcomes of Police-Reported Sexual Assaults in Canada, 2009 to 2014*. Ottawa, ON: Canadian Centre for Justice Statistics.

Rubin, Janice, and Parisa Nikfarjam. 2015. *CBC Workplace Investigation Regarding Jian Ghomeshi*. Rubin Thomlinson LLP. http://www.cbc.radio-canada.ca/_files/cbcrc/documents/press/report-april-2015-en.pdf.

Rush, Curtis. 2011. "Cop Apologizes for 'Sluts' Remark at Law School." *Toronto Star*, February 18. https://www.thestar.com/news/gta/2011/02/18/cop_apologizes_for_sluts_remark_at_law_school.html.

Rustad, Siri Aas, Gudrun Østby, and Ragnhild Nordås. 2016. "Artisanal Mining, Conflict, and Sexual Violence in Eastern DRC." *Extractive Industries and Society* 3 (2): 475–84. https://doi.org/10.1016/j.exis.2016.01.010.

Sachgau, Oliver. 2015. "Speech Therapy Can Prevent a Lifetime of Struggles, So Why Are Kids Waiting so Long for It?" *The Globe and Mail*, June 5. https://www.theglobeandmail.com/life/health-and-fitness/health/free-speech/article26141731/.

Salas, Ximena Ramos. 2015. "The Ineffectiveness and Unintended Consequences of the Public Health War on Obesity." *Canadian Journal of Public Health* 106 (2): 79–81.

Sanday, Peggy Reeves. 1981. "The Socio-Cultural Context of Rape: A Cross-Cultural Study." *Journal of Social Issues* 37 (4): 5–27. https://doi.org/10.1111/j.1540-4560.1981.tb01068.x.

———. 1996. "Rape-Prone versus Rape-Free Campus Cultures." *Violence Against Women* 2 (2): 191–208. https://doi.org/10.1177/1077801296002 002006. https://web.sas.upenn.edu/psanday/articles/selected-articles/ rape-prone-versus-rape-free-campus-cultures/.

———. 2007. *Fraternity Gang Rape: Sex, Brotherhood, and Privilege on Campus.* 2nd ed. New York: New York University Press.

Sapers, Howard. 2008. *A Preventable Death.* Ottawa, ON: Office of the Correctional Investigator. http://www.oci-bec.gc.ca/cnt/rpt/oth-aut/ oth-aut20080620-eng.aspx?texthighlight=a+preventable+death.

———. 2015. "Annual Report of the Office of the Correctional Investigator, 2014–2015." Office of the Correctional Investigator. http:// www.oci-bec.gc.ca/cnt/rpt/pdf/annrpt/annrpt20142015-eng.pdf.

———. 2016. "Annual Report of the Office of the Correctional Investigator 2015–2016." Office of the Correctional Investigator. http:// www.oci-bec.gc.ca/cnt/rpt/pdf/annrpt/annrpt20152016-eng.pdf.

SAVE (Sexual Assault Voices of Edmonton). n.d. "We Dream of a World Free of Sexual Violence." http://www.savedmonton.com/.

Sayers, Judith F., and Kelly A. MacDonald. 2001. "A Strong and Meaningful Role for First Nations Women in Governance." In *First Nations Women, Governance and the Indian Act: A Collection of Policy Research Reports*, edited by Judith Sayers, Kelly A. MacDonald, Jo-Anne Fiske, Melonie Newell, Evelyn George, and Wendy Cornet, 1–54. Ottawa, ON: Status of Women.

Schilling, Vincent. 2013. "Woman with Eagle Feather: The Photo 'Heard' Round the World." *Indian Country Today*, November 21. https://indiancountrymedianetwork.com/news/first-nations/ woman-with-eagle-feather-the-photo-heard-round-the-world/.

Schmidt, Daniella A. 2013. "Bathroom Bias: Making the Case for Trans Rights under Disability Law." *Michigan Journal of Gender & Law* 20 (1): 155–86.

Schmidt, Samantha. 2017. "A Politician Cracked That Women Belong in the Kitchen. A 'furious' Woman Just Took His Job." *The Washington Post*, November 9. https://www.washingtonpost.com/news/morning-mix/ wp/2017/11/09/a-politician-cracked-that-women-belong-in-the- kitchen-a-furious-woman-just-took-his-job/?utm_term=.fe69e3e7af64.

Schwartz, Martin D., and Walter DeKeseredy. 1997. *Sexual Assault on the College Campus: The Role of Male Peer Support.* Thousand Oaks, CA: Sage Publications.

Schweyer, Jenny. 2017. "An 'Upright Woman'—First Nations Social Justice Pioneer." *Light Magazine*, March 3. http://lightmagazine.ca/2017/03/ an-upright-woman-first-nations-social-justice-pioneer/.

Scott, James. 1990. *Domination and the Arts of Resistance: Hidden Transcripts.* New Haven, CT: Yale University Press.

Scott, Katerina, D.B. Lim, Tim Kelly, Mark Holmes, Barbara MacQuarrie, Nadine Wathen, and Jennifer MacGregor. 2017. *Domestic Violence at the Workplace: Investigating the Impact of Domestic Violence Perpetration on Workers and Workplaces.* Toronto, ON: University of Toronto.

Segal, Murray. 2015. "Independent Review of the Police and Prosecution Response to the Rehtaeh Parsons Case." Submitted to the Honourable Diana Whalen, Minster of Justice and Attorney General, and the Honourable Joanne Bernard, Minister for the Status of Women, October 8, 2015. https://novascotia.ca/segalreport/Parsons-Independent-Review.pdf.

Segrave, Kerry. 1994. *The Sexual Harassment of Women in the Workplace, 1600 to 1993.* Jefferson, NC: McFarland & Company.

———. 2014. *Beware the Masher: Sexual Harassment in American Public Places, 1880–1930.* Jefferson, NC: McFarland & Company.

Seltzer, Leon. 2015. "Trauma and the Freeze Response: Good, Bad, or Both?" *Psychology Today*, July 8. https://www.psychologytoday.com/blog/evolution-the-self/201507/trauma-and-the-freeze-response-good-bad-or-both.

Senate of Canada. 2017. "Proceedings of the Standing Senate Committee on Legal and Constitutional Affairs." Issue No. 28, 42nd Parliament, 1st Session, May 10, 2017. https://sencanada.ca/en/Content/Sen/Committee/421/LCJC/28ev-53308-e.

Serano, Julia. 2013. *Excluded: Making Feminist and Queer Movements More Inclusive.* Berkeley, CA: Seal Press.

Settee, Priscilla. 2016. "Indigenous Women Charting Local and Global Pathways Forward." *English Journal* 106 (1): 45–50.

Sharma, Nandita. 2002. "Immigrant and Migrant Workers in Canada: Labour Movements, Racism and the Expansion of Globalization." *Canadian Woman Studies* 21 (4): 18–25.

Sharma, Raghubar. 2012. *Poverty in Canada.* Toronto, ON: Oxford University Press.

Shaw, Margaret. 1989. *Survey of Federally Sentenced Women.* Ottawa, ON: Correctional Service of Canada.

Sheehy, Elizabeth A., and Daphne Gilbert. 2015. "Responding to Sexual Assault on Campus: What Can Canadian Universities Learn from US Law and Policy?" Working Paper No. 2015–26. University of Ottawa Faculty of Law. https://papers.ssrn.com/sol3/papers.cfm?abstract_id=2641844.

Sheikh, Muneeza. 2017. "Take It from a Human Rights Lawyer: The System Screwed Up in Seeking Justice for 'Angela Cardinal'." *CBC News*, June 7. http://www.cbc.ca/news/opinion/angela-cardinal-justice-1.4148357.

Sherlock, Tracy. 2013. "UBC Investigation into Rape Chant Reveals Allegations of Other Disturbing Incidents, Sexualized Activities." *Vancouver Sun*, September 18. http://www.vancouversun.com/investigati on+into+rape+chant+reveals+allegations+other+disturbing+incidents+ sexualized+activities/8927539/story.html.

Siegel, Reva. 1996. "'The Rule of Love': Wife Beating as Prerogative and Privacy." *Yale University Journal* 105 (8): 2117–207. https://doi. org/10.2307/797286.

Silliker, Amanda. 2017. "Unknown Caller." *Canadian Occupational Safety*, February 28. http://digital.carswellmedia.com/i/781149-feb-march-2017/0.

Silman, Janet, Lily Harris, Ida Paul, Eva Saulis, Mavis Goeres, Joyce Sappier, Juanita Perley, Bet-te Paul, Shirley Bear, Glenna Perley, Caroline Ennis, et al. 1987. *Enough Is Enough: Aboriginal Women Speak Out.* Toronto, ON: Women's Press.

Silva, Kumarini, and Kaitlynn Mendes. 2015. "Introduction: (In)visible and (Ir)relevant: Setting a Context." In *Feminist Erasures: Challenging Backlash Culture*, edited by Kumarini Silva and Kaitlynn Mendes, 1–15. New York: Palgrave Macmillan. https://doi. org/10.1057/9781137454928_1.

Simon, George. 2014. "Gaslighting Revisited: A Closer Look at This Manipulation Tactic." *Counselling Resource*, March 25. https://counsellingresource.com/features/2014/03/25/ gaslighting-revisited-a-closer-look-at-this-manipulation-tactic/.

Simon, William, and John H. Gagnon. 1986. "Sexual Scripts: Permanence and Change." *Archives of Sexual Behavior* 15 (2): 97–120. https://doi. org/10.1007/BF01542219.

Simons, Meredith. 2017. "Don't Like What a Woman Is Saying? Call Her Ugly." *The Washington Post*, January 26. https://www.washingtonpost. com/posteverything/wp/2017/01/26/dont-like-what-a-woman-is- saying-call-her-ugly/?utm_term=.b4cbb291a149.

Sims, David. 2016. "The Ongoing Outcry against the *Ghostbusters* Remake." *The Atlantic*, May 18. https://www.theatlantic.com/entertainment/ archive/2016/05/the-sexist-outcry-against-the-ghostbusters-remake- gets-louder/483270/.

Singh, Simran. 2016. "'It Was Deeply Frightening': Federal Strategy Will Aim to Fight Cyber Violence against Women." *CBC News*, July 13. http:// www.cbc.ca/news/canada/gender-violence-women-1.3668361.

Sinha, Marie. 2013. *Measuring Violence against Women: Statistical Trends*. Ottawa, ON: Canadian Centre for Justice Statistics. http://www.statcan.gc.ca/pub/85-002-x/2013001/article/11766-eng.pdf.

Skeggs, Beverly. 1997. *Formation of Class and Gender: Becoming Respectable*. London, UK: Sage.

Skourtes, Stephanie. 2016. "Invisible, Undervalued and Excluded: Practicing Working-Class Girlhood in Affective Space." *Journal of Youth Studies* 19 (3): 389–402. https://doi.org/10.1080/13676261.2015.1076158.

Slane, Andrea. 2013. "Sexting and the Law in Canada." *Canadian Journal of Human Sexuality* 22 (3): 117–22. https://doi.org/10.3138/cjhs.22.3.C01.

Smart, Carol. 1984. *The Ties That Bind: Law, Marriage and the Reproduction of Patriarchal Relations*. London, UK: Routledge & Kegan Paul.

———. 1989. *Feminism and the Power of Law*. London, UK: Routledge.

———. 1990. "Law's Power, the Sexed Body, and Feminist Discourse." *Journal of Law and Society* 17 (2): 194–210. https://doi.org/10.2307/1410085.

Smith, Alexis N., Marla B. Watkins, Michael J. Burke, Michael S. Christian, Caitlin E. Smith, Alison Hall, and Shalei Simms. 2013. "Gendered Influence: A Gender Role Perspective on the Use and Effectiveness of Influence Tactics." *Journal of Management* 39 (5): 1156–83. https://doi.org/10.1177/0149206313478183.

Smith, Allison. 2014. "Stories of os: Transgender Women, Monstrous Bodies, and the Canadian Prison System." *Dalhousie Journal of Legal Studies* 23: 149–71.

Smith, Dorothy. 1987. *The Everyday World as Problematic*. Boston, MA: Northeastern University Press.

Smith, Joanna. 2017. "Liberal Definition of Middle Class Canadians 'Not Useful,' Says Economist." *CBC News*, September 22. http://www.cbc.ca/news/politics/liberal-middle-class-economy-definition-1.4302113.

Snider, Laureen. 1999. "Towards Safer Societies: Punishment, Masculinities and Violence against Women." *British Journal of Criminology* 38 (1): 1–39.

Snider, Laureen. 2014. "Making Change in Neoliberal Times." In *Criminalizing Women: Gender and (In)Justice in Neoliberal Times*, 2nd ed., edited by Gillian Balfour and Elizabeth Comack, 268–89. Winnipeg, MB: Fernwood.

Snider, Laureen. 2015. *About Canada: Corporate Crime*. Halifax, NS: Fernwood.

Sontag, Susan. 2003. *Regarding the Pain of Others*. New York: Farrar, Straus and Giroux.

Sparr, Pamela. 1994. *Mortgaging Women's Lives: Feminist Critiques of Structural Adjustment*. Atlantic Highlands, NJ: Zed Books.

Spector, Malcolm, and John I. Kitsuse. 1977. *Constructing Social Problems*. Menlo Park, CA: Cummings.

St. Amand, Amy. 2010. "'We, the Invisible': Women of the Civil Rights Movement in Canada." *Journal of Undergraduate Studies at Trent* 3 (1): 28–37.

St. John, Allen. 2017. "Tennis's Battle of the Sexes: Who's the Greatest Athlete of All Time, Roger Federer or Serena Williams?" *Forbes*, January 31. https://www.forbes.com/sites/allenstjohn/2017/01/31/tenniss-battle-of-the-sexes-whos-better-roger-federer-or-serena-williams/2/.

St. Pierre, Melissa, and Betty Barrett. 2015. *Intimate Partner Violence in LGBTQ Communities*. Toronto, ON: Rainbow Health Ontario. https://www.rainbowhealthontario.ca/wp-content/uploads/2016/07/RHO_FactSheet_LGBTQIntimatePartnerViolence_E.pdf.

Standing Committee on the Status of Women. 2014. "A Study on Sexual Harassment in the Federal Workplace." http://publications.gc.ca/collections/collection_2014/parl/xc71-1/XC71-1-1-412-2-eng.pdf.

Stasiulis, Daiva, and Abigail Bakan. 2003. *Negotiating Citizenship: Migrant Women in Canada and the Global System*. New York: Palgrave MacMillan. https://doi.org/10.1057/9780230286924.

Statistica. 2016. "Retail Store Sales of Cosmetics and Fragrances in Canada from 2010 to 2015 (in billion Canadian dollars)." *The Statistics Portal*. https://www.statista.com/statistics/435227/retail-store-sales-of-cosmetics-and-fragrances-in-canada/.

Statistics Canada. 2014. "High-Income Trends among Canadian Taxfilers, 1982 to 2012." *The Daily*. http://www.statcan.gc.ca/daily-quotidien/141118/dq141118b-eng.htm.

———. 2015a. *Bill C-46: Records Applications Post-Mills: A Caselaw Review*. Department of Justice. http://www.justice.gc.ca/eng/rp-pr/csj-sjc/ccs-ajc/rr06_vic2/rr06_vic2.pdf.

———. 2015b. "Portrait of Families and Living Arrangements in Canada." Families, Households, and Marital Status, 2011 [Catalogue no. 98–312–XWE2011001]. http://www12.statcan.gc.ca/census-recensement/2011/as-sa/98-312-x/98-312-x2011001-eng.cfm.

———. 2016a. "Payroll Employment, Earnings and Hours, January 2016." *The Daily*. http://www.statcan.gc.ca/daily-quotidien/160331/dq160331b-eng.htm.

———. 2016b. "Retail Store Sales by Selected Commodity." CANSIM table 080–0022. http://www.statcan.gc.ca/tables-tableaux/sum-som/l01/cst01/trad52-eng.htm.

———. 2016c. "Sexual Misconduct in the Canadian Armed Forces, 2016". *The Daily*. http://www.statcan.gc.ca/daily-quotidien/161128/dq161128a-eng.pdf.

———. 2017a. "2016 Census." Data Tables. http://www12.statcan.
gc.ca/census-recensement/2016/dp-pd/dt-td/Rp-eng.cfm?TABID
=2&LANG=E&APATH=3&DETAIL=0&DIM=0&FL=A&FRE
E=0&GC=0&GK=0&GRP=1&PID=110561&PRID=10&PTYP
E=109445&S=0&SHOWALL=0&SUB=0&Temporal=2017&TH
EME=120&VID=0&VNAMEE=&VNAMEF=.

———. 2017b. "Aboriginal Peoples in Canada: Key Results from the 2016
Census." *The Daily*. http://www.statcan.gc.ca/daily-quotidien/171025/
dq171025a-eng.htm.

———. 2017c. "Diverse Family Characteristics of Aboriginal Children
Aged 0 to 4." *The Daily*. http://www12.statcan.gc.ca/census-
recensement/2016/as-sa/98-200-x/2016020/98-200-x2016020-eng.pdf.

———. 2017d. "Education in Canada: Key Results from the 2016 Census."
The Daily. http://www.statcan.gc.ca/daily-quotidien/171129/dq171129a-
eng.pdf.

———. 2017e. "Labour in Canada: Key Results from the 2016 Census." *The
Daily*. http://www.statcan.gc.ca/daily-quotidien/171129/dq171129b-
eng.pdf.

———. 2017f. "Police-Reported Hate Crimes, 2015." *The Daily*. http://
www.statcan.gc.ca/daily-quotidien/170613/dq170613b-eng.htm.

———. 2017g. "Proportion of People Aged 25 to 54 Employed in the Top
20 Occupations for Women in 2015, Canada, 1987 and 2015." Women
and Paid Work [Catalogue no. 89–503-X]. http://www.statcan.gc.ca/
pub/89-503-x/2015001/article/14694/tbl/tbl07-eng.htm.

———. 2017h. "The Surge of Women in the Workforce." *The Daily*. http://
www.statcan.gc.ca/pub/11-630-x/11-630-x2015009-eng.htm.

Status of Women Canada. 2014. "Action Plan to Address Family Violence
and Violent Crimes against Aboriginal Women and Girls." Government
of Canada. http://ywcacanada.ca/data/research_docs/00000309.pdf.

Stead, Sylive. 2018. "Remembering the Victims." *The Globe and Mail*,
February 1. https://www.theglobeandmail.com/news/national/
remembering-the-victims/article37819083/.

Stephens, Dionne P., and Layli D. Phillips. 2003. "Freaks, Gold Diggers,
Divas, and Dykes: The Sociohistorical Development of Adolescent
African American Women's Sexual Scripts." *Sexuality & Culture* 7 (1):
3–49. https://doi.org/10.1007/BF03159848.

Stevens, Andrew. 2016. *Call Centers and the Global Division of Labor: A Political
Economy of Post-Industrial Employment and Union Organizing*. New York:
Routledge.

Stockman, Farah. 2017. "Women's March on Washington Opens
Contentious Dialogues about Race." *The New York Times*, January 9.

https://www.nytimes.com/2017/01/09/us/womens-march-on-washington-opens-contentious-dialogues-about-race.html.

Stone, Laura. 2013. "Women Behind Bars: Canada's Only Female Dangerous Offender." *Calgary Herald*, February 5. http://www.calgaryherald.com/Women+Behind+Bars+Canada+only+female+dangerous+offender/5547732/story.html.

Stone, Zara. 2013. "South Korean High Schoolers Get Plastic Surgery for Graduation." *The Atlantic Daily*, June 27. https://www.theatlantic.com/international/archive/2013/06/south-korean-high-schoolers-get-plastic-surgery-for-graduation/277255/.

Stop Street Harassment. 2017. "Harassment Stories." http://www.stopstreetharassment.org/blog/stories/.

Stratcom. 2018. "EFTO All-Member Workplace Survey Results." ETFO. http://www.etfo.ca/AboutETFO/MediaRoom/MediaReleases/Shared%20Documents/ViolenceSurvey.pdf.

Strauss, Kendra, and Siobhán McGrath. 2017. "Temporary Migration, Precarious Employment and Unfree Labour Relations: Exploring the 'Continuum of Exploitation' in Canada's Temporary Foreign Worker Program." *Geoforum* 78: 199–208. https://doi.org/10.1016/j.geoforum.2016.01.008.

Stumpf, Juliet. 2006. "The Crimmigration Crisis: Immigrants, Crime, and Sovereign Power." *American University Law Review* 56 (2): 367–419.

Sue, Derald Wing, Christina M. Capodilupo, Gina C. Torino, Jennifer M. Bucceri, Aisha Holder, Kevin L. Nadal, and Marta Esquilin. 2007. "Racial Microaggressions in Everyday Life: Implications for Clinical Practice." *American Psychologist* 62 (4): 271–86. https://doi.org/10.1037/0003-066X.62.4.271.

Suthibhasilp, Noulmook, Lillian Petroff, and Dora Nipp. 2000. *Trafficking in Women Including Thai Migrant Sex Workers in Canada*. Ottawa, ON: Status of Women Canada.

Szekely, Reka. 2017. "Evacuations and Kevlar: Parents Raise the Alarm about Violence in Durham Schools." *Durham Region*, April 20. https://www.durhamregion.com/news-story/7250240-evacuations-and-kevlar-parents-raise-the-alarm-about-violence-in-durham-schools/.

Tam, Adrienne. 2016. "Jennifer Aniston Is Absolutely Right … Well, Almost." *The Daily Telegraph*, May 14. https://www.dailytelegraph.com.au/rendezview/jennifer-aniston-is-absolutely-right-well-almost/news-story/9726d716bded2b4540c48cf230c89e86.

Tanovich, David. 2011. "Bonds: Gendered and Racialized Violence, Strip Searches, Sexual Assault and Abuse of Prosecutorial Power." *Criminal Reports* 79: 132–50.

Tanovich, David, and Elaine Craig. 2016. "Whacking the Complainant: A Real and Current Systemic Problem." *The Globe and Mail*, February 10. https://www.theglobeandmail.com/opinion/whacking-the-complainant-is-a-real-and-current-systemic-problem/article28695366/.

Task Force on Respect and Equality. 2015. "Report of the Task Force on Respect and Equality: Ending Sexual Violence at the University of Ottawa." University of Ottawa. https://www.uottawa.ca/president/sites/www.uottawa.ca.president/files/report-of-the-task-force-on-respect-and-equality.pdf.

Tauli Corpuz, Victoria. 2015. "Report of the Special Rapporteur on the Rights of Indigenous Peoples." Presented to the UN Human Rights Council, 30th session, August 6. http://www.ohchr.org/EN/Issues/IPeoples/SRIndigenousPeoples/Pages/SRIPeoplesIndex.aspx.

Taylor, Erica. 2013. "Little Known Black History Fact: Black Is Beautiful" (audio file). *The Tom Joyner Morning Show*. https://blackamericaweb.com/2013/11/26/little-known-black-history-fact-black-is-beautiful/.

Thomas, Sue. 2005. "Crying 'the Horror' of Prostitution: Elizabeth Robins's 'Where Are You Going To?' and the Moral Crusade of the Women's Social and Political Union." *Women a Cultural Review* 16 (2): 203–21. https://doi.org/10.1080/09574040500156412.

Thompson, Deborah. 1993. "'The Woman in the Street:' Reclaiming the Public Space from Sexual Harassment." *Yale Journal of Law and Feminism* 6 (2): 313–48.

Thompson, Nicole. 2016. "Federal Live-in Caregiver Program Being Criticized for Exploiting Workers." *Global News*, September 12. https://globalnews.ca/news/2934036/federal-live-in-caregiver-program-being-criticized-for-exploiting-workers/.

Todd, Amanda. 2012. "My Story: Struggling, Bullying, Suicide, Self Harm" (video). *YouTube*, September 7. https://www.youtube.com/watch?v=vOHXGNx-E7E.

Tolley, Erin. 2015. "Visible Minority and Indigenous Members of Parliament." *The Samara Blog*, November 26. http://www.samaracanada.com/samarablog/blog-post/samara-main-blog/2015/11/26/visible-minority-and-indigenous-members-of-parliament.

Toth, Ellen L., Kristin-Lee Keith, Randy Littlechild, Joy Myskiw, Kari Meneen, Kelli Buckreus, and Richard T. Oster. 2016. "High Frequency of Pre-Existing Type 2 Diabetes in a Series of Pregnant Women Referred for 'Gestational Diabetes' in a Large Canadian Indigenous

Community." *Canadian Journal of Diabetes* 40 (6): 487–9. https://doi. org/10.1016/j.jcjd.2016.04.012.

Toupin, Louise. 2013. "Clandestine Migrations by Women and the Risk of Trafficking." In *Sex Work: Rethinking the Job, Respecting the Workers*, edited by Colette Parent, Chris Bruckert, Patrice Corriveau, Nengeh Mensah, and Louise Toupin, 111–32. Vancouver, BC: University of British Columbia Press.

TRC (Truth and Reconciliation Commission of Canada). 2015a. *Honouring the Truth, Reconciling for the Future: Summary of the Final Report of the Truth and Reconciliation Commission of Canada*, vol. 1. Toronto, ON: Lorimer Publishers.

———. 2015b. "The Survivors Speak: A Report of the Truth and Reconciliation Commission of Canada." http://www.trc.ca/websites/trcinstitution/ File/2015/Findings/Survivors_Speak_2015_05_30_web_0.pdf.

Tutty, Leslie. 1998. *Shelters for Abused Women in Canada: A Celebration of the Past, Challenges for the Future*. Ottawa, ON: Health Canada. http://www. academia.edu/1590855/Shelters_for_abused_women_in_Canada_A_ celebration_of_the_past_challenges_for_the_future.

UN Human Rights Committee. 2015. Concluding Observations on the Sixth Periodic Report of Canada. CCPR/C/CAN/CO/6. http:// docstore.ohchr.org/SelfServices/FilesHandler.ashx?enc=6QkG1d%2fPP RiCAqhKb7yhskswUHe1nBHTSwwEsgdxQHJBoKwgsS0jmHCTV% 2fFsa7OKzz9yna94OOqLeAavwpMzCD50TanJ2C2rbU%2f0kxdos%2b XCyn4OFm3xDYg3CouE4uXS.

UN Women. 2012. *Facts and Figures: Leadership and Political Participation*. Geneva: United Nations. http://www.unwomen.org/en/what-we-do/ leadership-and-political-participation/facts-and-figures.

Ussher, Jane. 2012. "The Myth of Premenstrual Moodiness." *The Conversation*, December 11. https://theconversation.com/the-myth-of- premenstrual-moodiness-10289.

USW (United Steelworkers). 2016. "Call Centre Workers Launch Campaign to Stop 'Dehumanizing' Abuse." December 7. https://www.usw.ca/ news/media-centre/articles/2016/call-centre-workers-launch- campaign-to-stop-dehumanizing-abuse.

———. n.d. "It Happens Constantly. I Am so Numb to It Now That Sometimes I Don't Even Notice How Terrible Customers Are to Me." Hang Up on Abuse. http://www.hanguponabuse.ca/so_numb.

Vallée, Brian. 1986. *Life with Billy*. Toronto, ON: Seal Books.

Vallée, Brian, and Hana Gartner. 2007. *Life with Billy/Life after Billy*. (DVD). Toronto, ON: CBC Learning.

Valverde, Mariana. 1985. *Sex, Power, and Pleasure*. Toronto, ON: Canadian Scholars' Press.

———. 1989. "The Love of Finery: Fashion and the Fallen Woman in Nineteenth-Century Social Discourse." *Victorian Studies* 32 (2): 168–88.

Van Natta, Don, and Kevin Van Valkenburg. 2014. "Rice Case: Purposeful Misdirection by Team, Scant Investigation by NFL." *ESPN*, September 19. http://www.espn.com/espn/otl/story/_/id/11551518/how-ray-rice-scandal-unfolded-baltimore-ravens-roger-goodell-nfl.

Van Wormer, Katherine. 2009. "Restorative Justice as Social Justice for Victims of Gendered Violence: A Standpoint Feminist Perspective." *Social Work* 54 (2): 107–16. https://doi.org/10.1093/sw/54.2.107.

Vance, Carol S. 1992. "More Danger, More Pleasure: A Decade after the Barnard Sexuality Conference." In *Pleasure and Danger: Exploring Female Sexuality*, edited by Carol S. Vance, xvi–xxxix. London, UK: Pandora Press.

Vandereycken, Walter. 1993. "The Sociocultural Roots of the Fight against Fatness: Implications for Eating Disorders and Obesity." *Eating Disorders* 1 (1): 7–16. https://doi.org/10.1080/10640269308248262.

Vera-Gray, Fiona. 2014. "The Great Problems Are in the Street: A Phenomenology of Men's Stranger Intrusions on Women in Public Space." PhD diss., London Metropolitan University.

———. 2016a. "Have You Ever Wondered How Much Energy You Put into Avoid Being Assaulted? It May Shock You." *The Conversation*, September 21. https://theconversation.com/have-you-ever-wondered-how-much-energy-you-put-in-to-avoid-being-assaulted-it-may-shock-you-65372.

———. 2016b. "The Hidden Work of Being a Woman in Public." *The f word*, April 29. https://www.thefword.org.uk/2016/04/dolls-eye-theatre-blog/.

———. 2016c. "Men's Intrusion: Rethinking Street Harassment." *50–50 Democracy*, November 30. https://www.opendemocracy.net/5050/fiona-vera-gray/men-s-intrusion-rethinking-street-harassment.

Vosko, Leah F., and Lisa F. Clark. 2009. "Canada: Gendered Precariousness and Social Reproduction." In *Gender and the Contours of Precarious Employment*, edited by Leah F. Vosko, Martha MacDonald, and Iain Campbell, 26–42. New York: Routledge.

Walcott, Rinaldo. 2003. *Black Like Who?* Toronto, ON: Insomniac Press.

Walia, Harsha. 2010. "Transient Servitude: Migrant Labour in Canada and the Apartheid of Citizenship." *Race & Class* 52 (1): 71–84. https://doi.org/10.1177/0306396810371766.

Walker, Lenore. 1979. *The Battered Woman*. New York: Harper & Row.

———. 2000. *The Battered Woman's Syndrome*. New York: Springer Publishing.

Walkowitz, Judith R. 1992. *City of Dreadful Delight: Narratives of Sexual Danger in Late-Victorian London*. Chicago, IL: University of Chicago Press. https://doi.org/10.7208/chicago/9780226081014.001.0001.

Waller, Willard. 1937. "The Rating and Dating Complex." *American Sociological Review* 2 (5): 727–34. https://doi.org/10.2307/2083825.

Wathen, Nadine, Jennifer MacGregor, and Barb MacQuarrie, with the Canadian Labour Congress. 2014. Can Work Be Safe, When Home Isn't? Initial Findings of a Pan-Canadian Survey on Domestic Violence and the Workplace. Centre for Research & Education on Violence Against Women and Children. http://canadianlabour.ca/sites/default/files/media/dvwork_survey_report_2014_enr.pdf.

WCDWA (West Coast Domestic Workers' Association). 2015. "About Us." http://www.wcdwa.ca/.

Webb, Cary. 2015. "Why I'm Over the Size Acceptance Movement." *xojane*, January 4. https://www.xojane.com/issues/why-im-over-the-size-acceptance-movement-or-hey-sa-what-have-you-done-for-me-lately.

Weedon, Chris. 1987. *Feminist Practice and Poststructuralist Theory*. Cambridge, MA: Blackwell.

WEF (World Economic Forum). 2016. "Rankings: The Global Gender Gap Report 2016." http://reports.weforum.org/global-gender-gap-report-2016/rankings/.

Weininger, Elliot. 2005. "Pierre Bourdieu on Social Class and Symbolic Violence." In *Approaches to Class Analysis*, edited by Eric Olin Wright, 82–118. Cambridge, UK: Cambridge University Press.

Weitzer, Ronald. 2012. "Sex Trafficking and the Sex Industry: The Need for Evidence-Based Theory and Legislation." *Journal of Criminal Law & Criminology* 101 (4): 1337–69.

Welch, Paige. 2016. "Miss America 1968: When Civil Rights and Feminist Activists Converged on Atlantic City." *The Conversation*, September 9. http://theconversation.com/miss-america-1968-when-civil-rights-and-feminist-activists-converged-on-atlantic-city-64850.

Welsh, Sandy, Jacquie Carr, Barbara MacQuarrie, and Audrey Huntley. 2006. "'I'm Not Thinking of It as Sexual Harassment': Understanding Harassment across Race and Citizenship." *Gender & Society* 20 (1): 87–107. https://doi.org/10.1177/0891243205282785.

West, Candace, and Don H. Zimmerman. 1987. "Doing Gender." *Gender & Society* 1 (2): 125–51. https://doi.org/10.1177/0891243287001002002.

West Coast Leaf. 2014. *CyberMisogyny: Using and Strengthening Canadian Legal Responses to Gendered Hate and Harassment Online*. Vancouver, BC: West Coast Leaf. http://www.westcoastleaf.org/wp-content/uploads/2014/10/2014-REPORT-CyberMisogyny.pdf.

———. n.d. "*R. v. O'Connor* [1995]." http://www.westcoastleaf.org/
    our-work/r-v-oconnor-1995/.

Westcott, Mark, Marian Baird, and Rae Cooper. 2006. "Reworking Work:
    Dependency and Choice in the Employment Relationship." *Labour &*
    Industry 17 (1): 5–17. https://doi.org/10.1080/10301763.2006.10669336.

Whitehead, Stephen M. 2002. *Men and Masculinities: Key Themes and New*
    Directions. Cambridge, UK: Polity Press.

Williams, Kent. 1992. "Using Battered Woman Syndrome Evidence with
    a Self-Defense Strategy in Minnesota." *Law & Inequality: A Journal of*
    Theory and Practice 10 (1): 107–36.

Wilson, Catherine, Kevin Douglas, and David Lyon. 2011. "Violence against
    Teachers: Prevalence and Consequences." *Journal of Interpersonal Violence*
    26 (12): 2353–71. https://doi.org/10.1177/0886260510383027.

Winterdyk, John. 2005. *Canadian Criminology*. 2nd ed. Toronto, ON: Prentice
    Hall.

Wolf, Naomi. 1991. *The Beauty Myth: How Images of Beauty Are Used against*
    Women. New York: Morrow.

Woo, Andrea. 2016. "Six RCMP Officers Who Spoke Out about
    Sexual Harassment." *The Globe and Mail*, October 6. https://www.
    theglobeandmail.com/news/national/six-rcmp-officers-
    who-spoke-out-about-sexual-harassment/article32287259/.

Woolley, Alice, Jennifer Koshan, Elaine Craig, and Joclyn Dowie. 2015.
    "Formal Complaint to the Canadian Judicial Council." http://
    s3.documentcloud.org/documents/2510250/cjc-complaint-r-camp.pdf.

WorkSafeBC. 2015. "Statistics: 2015 Annual Report and 2016–2018 Service
    Plan." https://www.worksafebc.com/en/resources/about-us/annual-
    report-statistics/2015-annual-report/statistics-2015?lang=en&origin=
    s&returnurl=https%3A%2F%2Fwww.worksafebc.com%2Fen%2Fsear
    ch%23q%3D2015%2520statistics%26sort%3Drelevancy%26f%3Alangu
    age-facet%3D%5BEnglish%5D.

Yeung, Sharon. 2016. "Conceptualizing Cultural Safety: Definitions and
    Applications of Safety in Health Care for Indigenous Mothers in
    Canada." *Journal for Social Thought* 1 (1): 1–13.

Yogaretnam, Shaamini. 2014. "Ottawa Sgt. Steven Desjourdy Guilty of
    Discreditable Conduct for Leaving Prisoner Topless." *Ottawa Citizen*,
    April 9. http://ottawacitizen.com/news/local-news/ottawa-sgt-steven-
    desjourdy-guilty-of-discreditable-conduct-for-leaving-prisoner-topless.

Younghusband, Lynda. 2010. "How Safe Are Our Teachers?" *Education*
    Canada 49: 48–50.

Zanetti, Aheda. 2016. "I Created the Burkini to Give Women Freedom, Not
    to Take It Away." *The Guardian*, August 24. https://www.theguardian.

com/commentisfree/2016/aug/24/i-created-the-burkini-to-give-women-freedom-not-to-take-it-away.

Zhang, Ting, Josh Hoddenbagn, Susan McDonald, and Katie Scrim. 2012. *An Estimation of the Economic Impact of Spousal Violence in Canada, 2009.* Ottawa, ON: Department of Justice.

Zinger, Ivan. 2017. "Annual Report of the Correctional Investigator, 2016–2017." Office of the Correctional Investigator. http://www.oci-bec. gc.ca/cnt/rpt/pdf/annrpt/annrpt20162017-eng.pdf.

Zöllner, Alexander M., Jacquelynn M. Pok, Emily J. McWalter, Garry E. Gold, and Ellen Kuhl. 2015. "On High Heels and Short Muscles: A Multiscale Model for Sarcomere Loss in the Gastrocnemius Muscle." *Journal of Theoretical Biology* 365: 301–10. https://doi.org/10.1016/ j.jtbi.2014.10.036.

Cases cited

2016 CHRT 2. January 26, 2016, File No.: T1340/7008

2016 ONWSIAT 250 or *2016 ONWSIAT 1813*

Abbott v. Toronto Police Services Board, 2009 HRTO 1909

Attorney General of Canada v. Lavell, [1974] SCR 1349

Barreau du Québec (syndic adjoint) c. Laflamme [2015] QCCDBQ 065

Brown v. Canada (Attorney General), 2017 ONSD 251

Canada v. Bedford, 2012 ONCA 186

Crouch v. Snell, 2015 NSSC 340

Descheneaux c. Canada (Procureur Général), 2015 QCCS 3555

Forrester v. Peel (Regional Municipality) Police Services Board et al. 2006 HRTO 13

Janzen v. Platy Enterprises [1989] 1 SCR 1252

R. v. Barton, 2017 ABCA 216

R. v. Blanchard, 2016 ABQB 706

R. v. Gladue [1999] 1 SCR 688

R. v. Lavallee [1990] 1 SCR 852

R. v. Mills [1999] 3 SCR 668, 180 DLR (4th) 1 [Mills]

R. v. Ryan [2013] SCC 3

R. v. S. Bonds, Ontario Court of Justice. Oral decision by Justice Lajoie on October 27, 2010. Ottawa, ON: #998–09–13642

R. v. Seaboyer; R. v. Gayme [1991] 2 SCR 577

R. v. Wagar 2015 ABCA 327

Robichaud v. Canada (Treasury Board) [1987] 2 SCR 84

Vancouver Rape Relief Society v. Nixon et al. (2003) BCSC 1936

Vancouver Rape Relief Society v. Nixon (2005) BCCA 601

Workplace Safety and Insurance Appeals Tribunal. Decision NO. 177/16. *2016 ONWSIAT 250*

Legislation cited

Alberta Human Rights Act, RSA 2000, Chapter A-25.5

Alberta Occupational Health and Safety Code, 2009

An Act to Foster Adherence to State Religious Neutrality and, in Particular, to Provide a Framework for Religious Accommodation Requests in Certain Bodies. October 18, 2017, National Assembly of Québec, 41st legislature, 1st session

An Act Respecting Labour Standards, CQLR c N-1.1

Anti-terrorism Act, 2015 (S.C. 2015, c. 20)

Bill C-10: An Act to Enact the Justice for Victims of Terrorisms Act and to Amend the State Immunity Act, the Criminal Code, the Controlled Drugs and Substances Act, the Correction and Conditional Release Act, the Youth Criminal Justice Act, the Immigration and Refugee Protection Act and Other Acts. 2011

Bill C-16: An Act to Amend the Canadian Human Rights Act and the Criminal Code, 2016

Bill C-31: An Act to Amend the Indian Act 1985

Bill C-41: An Act to Amend the Criminal Code (Sentencing) and Other Acts in Consequence Thereof, 1995, 35th Parliament, 1st Session

Bill C-45: Amendments to the Income Tax Act and Related Regulations, 2012

Bill S-3: An Act to Amend the Indian Act in Response to the Superior Court of Québec Decision in Descheneaux c. Canada (Procureur général), 2017

Canada Labour Code R.S.C., 1985, c. L-2

Canada Occupational Health and Safety Regulations (SOR/86–304)

Canadian Charter of Rights and Freedoms. Part I of the Constitution Act, 1982, Being Schedule B to the Canada Act 1982 (UK), 1982

Canadian Human Rights Act (R.S.C., 1985, c. H-6)

Criminal Code (R.S.C., 1985, c. C-46)

Cyber-Safety Act, SNS 2013, c 2

Divorce Act, S.C. 1968–69, c. 24

Domestic Workers Convention, 2011 *(No. 189) Convention Concerning Decent Work for Domestic Workers.* International Labour Organization

Education Amendment Act, 1980, SO 1980, c 61

Education Quality Improvement Act, SO 1997, c 31

Employment Equity Act (S.C. 1995, c. 44)

Employment Standards Code Amendment Act (Leave for Victims of Domestic Violence, Leave for Serious Injury or Illness and Extension of Compassionate Care Leave), Government of Manitoba

Firearms Act (S.C. 1995, c. 39)

Gender Equity in Indian Registration Act (S.C. 2010, c. 18)

Immigration and Refugee Protection Act (S.C. 2001, c. 27), s. 117

Indian Act (R.S.C., 1985, c. I-5)

Nova Scotia Human Rights Act, RSNS 1989, Ch 214

Occupational Health and Safety Act, R.S.O. 1990, c. O.1

Occupational Health and Safety Regulation, BC Reg 296/97

Ontario Factories Act, 1884, S.O. 1884, c. 39

Protection of Communities and Exploited Persons Act (S.C. 2014, c. 25)

Protecting Canadians from Online Crime Act. 2014, c. 31

Québec Act Respecting Labour Standards, 2002, s. 81.18

Zero Tolerance for Barbaric Cultural Practices Act (S.C. 2015, c. 29)

CREDITS

Page 3. Figure I.1: Niday Picture Library/Alamy Stock Photo. **Page 22.** Figure 1.1: CN301,S205/Fonds Cour supérieure. District judiciaire de Québec. Greffes de notaires/Greffe de Jean-Antoine Panet (1772–1786)/Vente d'un esclave par le Sieur George Hipps á l'honorable Hector Théophile Cramahé/14 novembre 1778. **Page 52.** Box 2.3: Reproduced by permission of The Globe and Mail Inc. **Page 61.** Figure 2.2: Image provided by the Reykjavík Museum of Photography. **Page 79.** Box 3.2: Material republished with express permission of National Post, a division of Postmedia Network Inc. **Page 95.** Box 4.1: © CBC Licensing. **Page 107.** Figure 4.2: AP Photo/Josh Reynolds. **Page 119.** Figure 5.1: Courtesy of Holly Johnson. **Page 127.** Figure 5.2: Sexual Assault Voices of Edmonton. **Page 147.** Figure 6.2: Used by permission of Seal Books, a division of Penguin Random House Canada Limited. **Page 154.** Figure 7.1: 9 to 5 © 1980 Twentieth Century Fox. All rights reserved. **Page 156.** Figure 7.2: Getty/Photoshot. **Page 166.** Box 7.1: © CBC Licensing. **Page 182.** Box. 8.1: Courtesy Monica Forrester. **Page 185.** Box 8.2: Courtesy United Steelworkers. **Page 187.** Figure 8.1: BC Nurses' Union. **Page 192.** Figure 8.2: Rick Madonik. **Page 196.** Figure 8.3: Image courtesy of Ine Beljaars. **Page 201.** Box 9.1: Reproduced with permission from Christina Gonzales. **Page 214.** Box 9.2: Courtesy of Elene Lam, Butterfly. **Page 226.** Figure 10.1: AP Photo. **Page 229.** Figure 10.2: © Ahiida Pty Ltd. **Page 243.** Figure 10.3: SPUTNIK/Alamy Stock Photo. **Page 249.** Figure 11.1: Viola Desmond hand-coloured portrait, 16-80-30220, ca. 1945. Wanda and Joe Robson Collection, Sydney, NS. Beaton Institute, Cape Breton University. **Page 250.** Figure 11.2: Image from Government of Ontario, Inspector of Prisons and Public Charities, Annual Report of the Inspector of Prisons and Public Charities: Upon the Common Gaols, Prisons and Reformatories of the Province of Ontario; Being for the Year ending 30th September 1902 (Toronto: Printed by C.B. Robinson, 1902). Courtesy of The Thomas Fisher Rare Book Library,

University of Toronto. **Page 253.** Box 11.1: Courtesy of *Journal of Prisoners on Prisons.* **Page 254.** Box 11.2: Courtesy of *Journal of Prisoners on Prisons.* **Page 266.** Figure 11.3: Courtesy of *Journal of Prisoners on Prisons*/Jackie Traverse. **Page 274.** Figure 12.1: Mission Community Archives. **Page 289.** Figure 12.2: Photo of Amanda Polchies kneeling and holding an eagle feather aloft before a wall of police officers on October 17, 2013, when heavily armed RCMP tactical units raided a Mi'kmaq-led anti-fracking camp in Rexton, NB. © Ossie Michelin for APTN.

INDEX